EATING
IN
ITALY

EATING
IN
ITALY

A Traveler's
Guide to the Gastronomic
Pleasures
of Northern Italy

FAITH HELLER WILLINGER

Photographs by
FAITH ECHTERMEYER

HEARST BOOKS
New York

Book design by Richard Oriolo

Library of Congress Cataloging-in-Publication Data
Willinger, Faith Heller.
Eating in Italy.

Includes index.
1. Gastronomy. 2. Dinners and dining—Italy,
Northern. 3. Wine and wine making—Italy, Northern.
I. Title.
TX641.W55 1989   641'.0945'1   88-34714
ISBN 0-688-06883-9

Printed in the United States of America
First Edition
1 2 3 4 5 6 7 8 9 10

Italia, ti voglio bene assai

FOR MAX, MASSIMO, AND DAD

Grazie
and thank you

This book took many years to write.
I began to amass the information without a specific plan, just because
I wanted to know everything about Italian regional *cucina*. The inspiration
to round up my accumulated knowledge, and to learn more, straight
from the source, came from Annie.

Thanks to Ann, who became an instant believer,
and Laurie, a quick convert. It frequently worried me to work
with such positive editors, who found no fault with my obsessions.

Thanks also to Kathie, who copy-edited
with the delicacy of a pastry chef.

Thanks to Faith, who read computer
printouts and photographed with style and tastebuds.

Thanks to Richard, who understood
Italy from an out-of-body chocolate experience.

And finally, thank you and *grazie*
to the people who fed me food, wine, information and
encouragement, who took the time to explain, who directed
me down some fine roads. To
Angelo, Annie, Ann, Ampelio, Annalisa, Adriana, Alvaro, Antonio, Andrea, Alfredo,
Aurelia, Arturo, Aimo, Afra, Alan, Beatrice, Barbara, Bruno, Bruce, Burt, Bert, Bertha, Betta,
C., Carmen, Carol, Cristina, Cesare, Clara, Claudia, Carlo, Claudio,
Dina, Dania, Duccio, Enzo, Ezio, Elda, Enrico, Edoardo, Enza, Emiliana, Ettore, Eugenio, Elisabetta,
Elio, Faith, Fiametta, Fabrizio, Franca, Franco, Fausto, Francesca, Francesco,
Girolamo, Gualtiero, Gianna, Giuliana, Gianfranco, Gianpaolo, Giovanni,
Giannola, Giacomo, Giorgio, Giuliano, Gioacchino, Gloria, Herb, Henry B., Judy,
Julia, Joan, Ken, Kyle, Lisa, Laura, Laurie, Livio, Lucio, Lydie, Lucia, Luigi,
Lou, Mario, Massimo, Maurizio, Maggie, Marco, Marvin, Marie, Marcella, Marion,
Nuccio, Nerio, Neil, Nadia, Osvaldo, Piermario, Pierangelo, Paolo, Primo,
Patrizia, Philip, Paola, Rinaldo, Realmo, Roberto, Rose, Rosy, Roccaldo,
Rory, Romano, Stefano, Sally, Silvano, Scott, Sabine, Sauro, Sergio, Sandro,
Schultzy, Silvana, Suzanne, Tonino, Torquato, Tobia, Ugo,
Umberto, Vanna, Vasco, Victor, Vittorio, Vittorio Fiore,
Walter, Wayne, Wendy, and especially
the Wags!

CONTENTS

INTRODUCTION

Being an American in Italy has its advantages for me. My attachment to the traditional foods of the various regions of the country doesn't go back to my infancy, isn't tied emotionally to my family history. Rather, it has been formed with the help of Italians who do have these ties, whose palates have helped me develop a sense of the flavors of each province. Traveling in the eleven regions of the north that are covered in this book, I began to grasp the nature of the foods and wines of each area, unencumbered by the roots that in some cases bind Italians to their own regional traditions to the exclusion of all others—and in others stir a rebellion against anything local.

I learned that Italian regional cooking, *la cucina tradizionale*, is defined by geography, climate, and conquest. Natural boundaries—the mountains, lakes, rivers, and seas—divide the land into a patchwork of microsystems where soil and climate determine the main ingredients. The olive tree thrives in the meager rocky soil of Toscana, and olive oil is dominant in kitchens there. The fertile plains of the Po Valley provide pasture for the livestock that produce the meat and cheese for the recipes of Lombardia and Emilia-Romagna. The tasty vegetables that grow in the rich alluvial soil of Venezia's lagoon, and the fish from her waters, are the basis of that region's specialties.

Italy's northern mountain ranges block off the Nordic cold, and the lakes and seas temper the winter weather. New York and Napoli may be on the same latitude, but lemon trees grow in Napoli. So are Boston and Firenze, but the sight of a snowflake brings traffic to a halt around the Duomo. Palm trees and olives unexpectedly flourish in the foothills of the Alps.

As for conquest—every populace bent on conquest, or escape from conquest, seems to have passed through the Italian peninsula. Some never left, and were assimilated into this Mediterranean melting pot.

Diet soda, Campari, and Chianti in a Tuscan wine bar

Farro, a barleylike grain found today in parts of Friuli, Umbria, and parts of Toscana, fed the Roman legions. And some pastries served in Veneto, Friuli, and Lombardia are remnants of Austrian domination of the eighteenth century. But while eddying political powers engaged the city-states in a game of musical boundaries, life in the countryside was relatively un-

Hanging out is the national pastime,
even in the rain.

imaginable grain, meat and fish smokers, candy makers, tableware artisans.

I fell in love with Italy as an adult. In an unfamiliar language, I had to learn how to carry out simple everyday tasks. Shopping for groceries, ordering a coffee or a meal or a glass of wine, reciting my choice of three flavors for a *gelato*—all took practice. I had to learn about the regions of the country, each with its own unique dishes and wines. I studied with my son, Max, read his Italian schoolbooks, and learned about the geography of rivers, mountains, and seas, the names of the winds, and about the waves of influence that make up each region's history. I learned the language, traveled, asked questions, and listened (one of the few calorie-free aspects of studying Italian cookery!).

The answers, which have been acquired over fifteen years of living in Italy, are all here in this guide. The first part of the book explains basic, everyday Italian gastronomic behavior, and includes introductions to the country's special foods, the tools for making and serving them, and the cooking experience itself. The second part deals with the eleven regions that make up northern Italy (the southern border of Toscana, Umbria, and Le Marche represents a Mason-Dixon line for me, dividing the more formal restaurant and winemaking traditions of the north from the south, with its simpler, more Mediterranean approach to food and wine). Each chapter reveals the character of a different region (a unit similar to one of our states), starting with a brief geographical and historical introduction. "The Menu" explains local foods in the order they appear on a menu: appetizers, soups, main courses, cheese, fruit, dessert. "The Wine List" describes some of the best local selections. In "Regional Specialties" you'll read about local products for the kitchen or table, many of them unavailable outside the area. The creators of these products are masters at their work, passionate monomaniacs who are interested in excellence and are excited about what they're doing, which makes their products such a pleasure to use.

Under the "Guide" for each region, you'll find an alphabetical listing, by location, of the sources of this distinctive regional *cucina* and special food-related products: restaurants, markets, specialty food shops,

affected. The church defined the boundaries of the village, and many never ventured beyond the sound of its bell, or perhaps beyond the provincial capital. (*Campanilismo*, from "campanile," means an almost claustrophobic localism—the negative aspect of this provincialism.)

With the advent of the bicycle, then the Fiat 500, and now highways, television, and jet travel, this localism appears to be fading fast. But there are still gastronomic traditionalists, tenaciously clinging to the past, reinterpreting and adapting it to suit the present. My contact with these exceptional devotees has been an amazing experience for the palate, eye, and intellect. It was a joy to track down both native and "born again" winemakers, restaurant owners, cooks, bread bakers, *grappa* distillers, coffee roasters, vinegar makers, pastry chefs, farmers, cheesemakers, pasta rollers, butchers, truffle hunters, rice growers, millers of every bars, housewares stores, bakeries, wine shops, ice cream stores, cheesemakers. I've mentioned some hotels and inns convenient for touring, because people always ask me where to stay. This is not a hotel guide, though. For a complete list with prices, head for the local E.P.T. office (Ente Provinciale di Turismo), often in the center of town.

All geographical names are in Italian (Firenze, not Florence; Torino, not Turin) because that's the way they appear on the best maps. (Check the index if you're not certain.) Because of the fluctuating exchange rate, prices are broadly categorized: Restaurants are listed as inexpensive (under 20,000 lire per person), moderate (25,000 to 50,000), and expensive (over 60,000). Hotel prices are inexpensive (around 50,000 lire for a double), moderate (around 80,000 lire), expensive (around 120,000), and luxury (over 175,000). Due to ever-fluctuating exchange rates, prices are given in lire. Banks give the best rate of exchange. At the time this book went to press, one American dollar was worth about 1,250 lire. The Italian government has been threatening for years to knock three zeroes off the present monetary system, an effort at simplification known as the "heavy lira." Its acceptance is probably far in the future, although Italians are full of surprises.

Special tips are scattered throughout: a vocabulary list of *gelato* flavors, a key to opening and closing hours, types of pasta, wine terminology.

At the back of the book you'll find a food glossary and an index—and a few blank pages for notes, because, after all, this is only an introduction, a starting point for your own discovery of regional Italian foods, and in the process, Italy and the Italians at their best.

EATING IN ITALY

■

THE RESTAURANT

Before I start to tell you when and how and what to eat, and where, it's only fair to let you know what I look for in a restaurant. The first requirement, more important than anything else, is good food that relates to the area. It pleases me to find regional specialties on the menu, but even if the food isn't traditional, it should be made with the best, freshest seasonal produce. I like food to look like food. I am not impressed with braided, curled, tied, or sculpted arrangements on my plate—I dislike the idea that someone has been playing with my meal. Some Italians, uninterested in dining out on the same food they eat at home, appreciate this "new wave" cooking more than I do.

Fine wine makes any meal better, and I love to drink interesting regionals, usually the best complement for the local *cucina*. Although I may opt for the locally produced house wine in an inexpensive country *trattoria*, I won't accept a poor selection in an expensive restaurant. I enjoy efficient service but will accept a lot less if there's good food to be found. I don't like to be hurried through a meal. I love a family restaurant with tradition and roots, especially one with three generations in the kitchen.

Although I have eaten some wonderful meals in large and medium-size cities, in Italy the best food is generally found in rural areas, in towns without much of a cultural or artistic patrimony. Just getting to them may be a lesson in local geography. The Touring Club Italiano's *Atlante Stradale d'Italia*—three large green soft-covered atlases for Northern, Central, and Southern Italy—are essential for getting around in the countryside. They are easy to read, with no folding and unfolding required, and are equipped with an index, indispensable for locating some of the obscure villages mentioned in this book.

"Why are you here in the middle of nowhere?" I frequently asked restaurant owners after an extraordinary meal in a village that none of my Italian friends had ever heard of.

"Because this is where I'm from" was invariably the answer. It's not only a question of roots, however, but of raw materials, of friends and neighbors who produce the best wines, cheeses, and prosciutto, of knowing who has the early-ripening cherries, or the sweetest butter or tastiest olive oil. Many of these restaurant owners have worked in the big cities; some have studied in France; most have traveled extensively in Italy to see what their colleagues are up to. But invariably the most profound influence comes from the local gastronomic heritage, from their own memories of mouth-filling flavors and regional tastes, always sharper and more intense in their native habitat than when transported elsewhere.

A trip to the village market is the ideal way to find out what's local and what's in season. Look at "The Menu" in this book for the region in which you'll be eating, and check the menu posted outside most restaurants for signs of traditional cooking. While you're examining the menu, look at the diners if you can: They should be mostly Italian (local customers won't come back if the food isn't good). Tourist centers tend to have the worst restaurants, since patrons are unlikely to return; they take advantage of a captive audience with food that is better left undescribed. It may be difficult to get a good meal in Venezia or Firenze, but it will probably be impossible in Siena, San Gimignano, or Assisi, where most visitors spend only a few hours and therefore don't concentrate on the food. An empty restaurant at mealtime is a poor sign, naturally—except during soccer championships, when most of the country is glued to the TV set in the local bar. Skip all restaurants with a German tourist bus parked in front. Beware of restaurants with waiters in costume, and don't place too much importance on decor; at times I welcome a sincerely ugly restaurant. As a general rule, avoid restaurants near train stations or major tourist attractions, which cater to the unwary and the rushed. I tend to distrust a restaurant that displays a menu translated into four languages.

THE MENU

Navigating an Italian menu takes practice. A typical meal consists of four courses, although some can become marathons of eight or more tastes.

*Gastronomic traditions
are handed down from
generation to generation.*

The *primo*, or first course, is pasta, either sauced or in broth, rice or risotto, or soup.

The *secondo* is usually fish, meat, or poultry, although *frittate* (pan-fried flans), mushrooms, and substantial vegetable dishes may also be listed. Meat and fish are frequently priced by weight: 100 grams (*un'etto*, or 100 gg) is about 4 ounces.

Italians like their fish cooked simply, so the fresh tastes of the sea stand out, unhidden by sauce and undamaged by overhandling. Fish may be brought to the table in its entirety, complete with head, tail, and fins, to be examined for freshness. Grilled, boiled, or baked fish may be served whole, presenting a project that do-it-yourself surgeons will relish. Italian waiters make a wonderful drama of deboning fish with a fork, a spoon, and a flourish, dividing it up into individual portions and leaving behind an intact skeleton of head, bones, and tail.

Next is a *contorno*, a side dish of vegetables at room temperature (and often overcooked) or a green salad dressed at the table with olive oil and vinegar.

Most Italians end their meal with fruit, considered a palate refresher. Unwashed fruit is served with a bowl of water for a rinse, and is then peeled—with the exception of cherries, grapes, plums, and apricots. Ripe peaches are one of the great joys of the summer in Italy. Some Italians have perfected the art of peeling fruit to the point that they can carve without picking the fruit up in their hands, a treat to watch. Fresh fruit salad, called *macedonia*, is made daily in many restaurants.

A more elaborate repast will begin with an *antipasto* (appetizer), usually based on local *salumi* (a general term for cured meats like prosciutto and salami), often served with fresh figs or cantaloupe in season. Some restaurants display a platter-filled table (frequently self-service; watch other diners for a clue), others wheel a cart to your table, displaying assorted marinated vegetables, olives, fish, and salads, listed as *antipasto misto*. Its price is indicated by the letters "p.v.," which stands for *presso da vedere*, "price to be seen," determined by what and how much you eat; or "s.q.," *secondo quantità*, "according to the quantity." Your menu will also list cheeses and fruits with the same indication.

Dessert is looked upon as a special treat, not an everyday finish to the meal. *Torte* (cakes), *crostate* (open-faced fruit tarts), and *gelato* (ice cream) are found on most menus, as is *tiramisù*, a rich mascarpone dessert originally from Veneto, which seems to be a favorite everywhere. Fancy restaurants serve *piccola pasticceria*, little pastries or cookies, after dessert.

Many restaurants offer a tasting menu *(menu degustazione)*, a series of samples of their regional or sea-

WHEN YOU'RE ORDERING

I'd like to eat something traditional.
Vorrei mangiare qualcosa di tradizionale.
Voh-RAY mahn-JAR-ay kwal-COH-za dee tra-DITS-yah-NAH-lay

I'd like to eat something light.
Vorrei mangiare qualcosa di leggero.
Voh-RAY mahn-JAR-ay kwal-COH-za dee lay-JAIR-oh

I'd like to eat a half portion of . . .
Vorrei mangiare mezza porzione di . . .
Voh-RAY mahn-JAR-ay METS-zah portz-YOH-nay dee . . .

We'd like to split a portion of . . .
Vorremo dividere una porzione in due di . . .
Voh-RAY-mo dee-vee-DAY-ray OON-ah ports-YOHN-ay een DOO-ay dee . . .

I'd like to eat fish.
Vorrei mangiare pesce.
Voh-RAY mahn-JAR-ay PEH-shay

I'd like to eat meat.
Vorrei mangiare carne.
Voh-RAY mahn-JAR-ay CAR-nay

Can you cook without salt?
Puo cucinare senza sale?
Pwoh koo-chee-NAH-ray SEN-zah SAH-lay?

I am a vegetarian.
Sono un vegetariano [una vegetariana].
SOH-noh oon veh-jeh-tah-ree-AH-noh [OON-ah veh-jeh-tah-ree-AH-nah]

---

sonal best, often matched with appropriate wines.

The Italian menu is flexible enough to satisfy carnivore and vegetarian alike. If you want to keep it light, order the *antipasto* and skip the main course, or skip the *antipasto* and *primo,* concentrating on meat and vegetables, choosing the regional dishes that seem the most interesting. But ordering pasta and a salad is poor form—three courses is the minimum for a meal in Italy.

Time has eroded the clear distinction in style and price between and *osteria* or *locanda,* a *trattoria,* and a *ristorante.* Often an *osteria* will serve more elegant and expensive food than a *ristorante.*

RESERVATIONS, SERVICE, AND TIPPING

Reserving a table in a restaurant is a sign of respect, and Italians are pleased by the commitment. Reservations for dinner in small restaurants may be hard to come by, especially during trade fairs. But it is usually not necessary to make a reservation for lunch, except in the most formal restaurants. Do call to cancel one if you can't keep it. Someone at your restaurant will probably understand English; in any event, Italians are great communicators and will try to figure out what you want even if they don't understand what you are saying. Many country restaurants don't take credit cards, so be prepared to pay in lire. (If you can supply the exchange rate from a newspaper or bank, you may be able to pay in dollars or traveler's checks.)

The tip should be left in cash. How much depends on the quality of the service, the type of restaurant, and the size of the cover and service charges. Most restaurants charge a fixed cover charge for occupying a set table, listed on the menu as *coperto.* This varies with the type of restaurant—linens, crystal, silver, and flowers on the table will mean a higher *coperto.* The *servizio* is a percentage for service, automatically added to the total cost of your meal. The higher the cover and service charges, the lower your tip should be. If the *servizio* is more than 15 percent, the tip should be reduced to a gesture—one small bill per person. There is no excuse for poor or surly service, which should never be rewarded with a tip.

WHEN TO *E*AT

There is no shortage of occasions for eating in Italy, both during and between meals, and there is no shortage of vocabulary for any of these occasions!

You can have breakfast (*la colazione* or *la prima colazione*) at your hotel or in a bar-caffè. Hotels and *pensione* usually offer a continental breakfast: a choice of coffee, tea, hot chocolate, or *caffè latte* (small pitchers of American-style coffee and milk), plus fresh rolls, rusks, butter, preserves, and maybe fresh croissants.

Breakfast in a bar-caffè—usually served between 7:00 and 10:30—is a far better choice: The coffee will be richer, the pastry fresher, and the scene worth watching. However, if you sit at a table, prices may increase anywhere from 50 to 300 percent. Most Italians stand at the counter for their breakfast. The procedure may seem confusing at first: You look over the pastries, then go to the cashier (*cassa*), state your order, and pay for it. You'll get a receipt, which you give to the barman or place on the counter as you restate your order. Weight down your receipt with a 50- or 100-lire coin, the correct tip for all this confusion. The coffee choices in a bar-caffè may seem endless, but the classic breakfast drink is a *cappuccino*.

Around 10 a.m., light breakfasters may be ready to "put something under their teeth," as the Italian expression goes. Order a *panino* (sandwich), *toast* (a grilled ham and cheese on America-style bread), a *pasta* (pastry), or a quick shot of caffeine—all of which are always available at the bar-caffè for between-meal hunger.

Lunch (*pranzo* or *colazione*) starts at 12:30 or 1:00 and lasts from thirty minutes to three hours. Time,

cost, calories, and hunger may be factors in what you decide to do for this meal on any given day. A stand-up snack or self-serve lunch is a possible alternative to a restaurant meal. Sandwiches with a wide variety of fillings are available in a *paninoteca,* a bar specializing in sandwiches, either made to order or ready-made (the latter found under a napkin in a self-service display case of pastry and rolls). Grocery stores will split a roll and sell enough *salumi* to fill it. Most bread bakeries sell freshly made flatbreads, called *focaccia* or *schiacciata,* and pizza, sold by the slice or weight. (Avoid pizza shops displaying gaudily garnished pizza; they're exclusively for tourists and the pizza is indigestible.)

If you're staying in a city or town for a few days, one way to make your visit especially pleasant is to become a "local." Choose a small, simple neighborhood restaurant that looks interesting, and eat lunch there every day. The second day, your waiter will be pleased to see you, and on the third you'll receive a generous welcome. A relaxed lunch can begin with an aperitif accompanied by salty snacks, and end with a long lingering *caffè* in the sunshine—one of the great joys of mealtime in Italy.

Dinner (*cena* or *pranzo*) is served from 7:30 on, although most Italians dine around 8:30. The before-dinner *aperitivo* can be taken in a bar. On the coast in the summer, where life is less formal, dinner often starts after 9:30. Italians dress casually, yet with great elegance, when they dine out. Restaurants require neither jacket nor tie—but no athletic attire, please.

THE *B*AR-CAFFÈ

Many restaurant meals are prefaced with a drink and postscripted with a coffee at a bar-caffè, one of the best places to observe the natives and partake of their rituals. An Italian bar isn't only for the consumption

of alcoholic drinks: you can also get breakfast, make a phone call, take a coffee break, grab a snack or gelato, check out the poster of what's playing at the movies, flip through the local newspaper, or listen to

THE BAR-CAFFÉ MENU

CAFFETTERIA

■

Caffè or *espresso* ▪ Italian espresso coffee, served in a demitasse cup

Caffè freddo ▪ iced coffee, usually served highly sugared

Caffè d'orzo ▪ an ersatz coffee, made from barley *(orzo)*

Camomilla ▪ camomile tea—a relaxing, diuretic infusion

Cappuccino ▪ literally, "the little hood" or "the little monk."

Espresso topped with foamy steamed milk the color of Capuchin monks' robes. Often called *cappuccio* in some areas.

Cioccolata calda ▪ at its best, a cup of hot, thick, almost black bitter hot chocolate. *Con panna:* topped with unsweetened whipped cream.

Latte ▪ milk. Served hot *(caldo)*, steamed, in a glass; or if you insist, cold *(freddo)*.

Thè or tè ▪ tea: usually a little pot of hot water with a tea bag. Served *al latte* (with milk) or *al limone* (with a slice of lemon)

Tè freddo ▪ iced tea, usually served highly sugared

Tisana ▪ an herbal infusion (tea)

APERITIVI

■

Aperol ▪ Orange-colored and -flavored, usually served in a glass with a sugar-coated rim

Biancosarti ▪ yellow, all natural, vague flavor

Campari ▪ this famous cherry-red aperitif is made from herbs, bitter orange peel, and soaked quinine bark, among other ingredients, and is said to be stimulating and habit-forming

Campari bitter ▪ 25 percent alcohol, is served plain, with a twist of lemon, or on the rocks. *Campari soda,* 10 percent alcohol, is a Campari-flavor carbonated beverage

Carpano ▪ brownish red bitters

Cinzano ▪ a famous brand of vermouth, this is a fortified wine flavored with herbs and roots. The *rosso* (red) and *bianco* (white) are sweet; the *secco* is white and dry.

Cynar ▪ dark brown, distilled from artichokes. Also used as a digestive.

Martini ▪ a famous brand of vermouth, a fortified wine flavored with herbs and roots. The *rosso* (red) and *bianco* (white) are sweet, the *secco* is also called dry.

Milano-Torino ▪ a cocktail of Campari and Carpano

Negroni ▪ a cocktail of Campari and gin

Punt e Mes ▪ brown bitters

Riccadonna ▪ a brand of vermouth, a fortified wine flavored with herbs and roots

BIBITE

■

Acqua minerale ▪ mineral water. Either *gassata* (fizzy) or *naturale* (still).

Aranciata ▪ orange carbonated beverage

Aranciata amara ▪ bitter orange carbonated beverage

Birra ▪ beer, which may be *nazionale* (from Italy) or *estera* (imported). *Alla spina* means draft, or on tap.

Crodino ▪ nonalcoholic fizzy bitters, in a cute little bottle

Spremuta ▪ freshly squeezed juice: *di arancia* (orange), *di pompelmo* (grapefruit), or *di tarocchi* (blood oranges)

Succo di frutta ▪ fruit juice, usually pear, peach, or apricot, bottled in single portions

Gazosa ▪ sweetened mineral water, sometimes with a slight lemon flavor

San Pellegrino Bitter ▪ also nonalcoholic fizzy bitters, in a cute little bottle

Roadside barbecues are often a community affair.

a soccer match. Most of these activities are done standing up, since sitting down, inside or out, means higher prices with a surcharge for table service. Bear in mind that Italians think cold beverages are bad for the digestion. If yours isn't cold enough for you, ask for *ghiaccio* (ice)— *con molto ghiaccio* if you'd like more than two or three cubes.

If there's a big navy or black and white "T" (for *tabacchi*) displayed outside, you can also buy cigarettes, three different kinds of matches, salt, stamps, and bus tickets at the bar-caffè.

THE *P*ICNIC

Italians love to eat outdoors. However, their idea of a picnic isn't a light meal on a blanket—it's closer to a five-course Sunday lunch, complete with collapsible chairs and table, tablecloth, refrigerated beverages, and an umbrella for shade. Making a modest version of this is simple, however, thanks to grocery stores and specialty shops (*alimentari, salumeria,* or *gastronomia*) that will sell enough cold cuts for a sandwich, a wedge of cheese, a handful of olives or artichoke hearts, and a chilled bottle of wine or mineral water.

Most grocery shops also have take-out containers of prepared foods and salads, which can be ordered by the portion *(porzione)* or by weight (*un'etto* is 100 grams, around 4 ounces). You can buy basic picnic equipment at one of the lower-priced department stores—UPIM, Standa, Coin, Rinascente—or in a housewares store.

Choose inexpensive equipment that will last through your trip or more expensive ware that can serve as a memento when you return home—local pottery, designer flatware, brightly colored plastic picnic sets, elegant Richard Ginori china. Whatever you choose, don't forget the *cavatappi* (corkscrew)! Wine always tastes better from a glass, with or without a stem, and inexpensive *osteria* glasses (short and squat, without a stem) are almost unbreakable, and easy to tuck into a lunch basket.

A do-it-yourself meal may also be the ticket to train and plane travel. Italian train and airline food at its very best is mediocre; you'll do much better with a picnic—and this is true if you're traveling the *autostrade* as well (the food in the Autogrill restaurants along the Italian highways seems to have been inspired by airline food).

PICNIC SUPPLIES

.

cavatappi corkscrew

apribottiglia bottle opener

posate flatware

forchetta fork

coltello knife

cucchiaio spoon

bicchieri glasses

tovaglioli di carta paper napkins

piatto plate

sale e pepe salt and pepper

TRAVEL FOOD

.

Eating in the dining car of a train conjures up images of the *Orient Express*, of the Grand Tour, of a time when people traveled with trunks. Times have changed. The self-service car serves some of the most unattractive, indigestable food in all of Italy. Dining-car offerings are prepared on the train and are usually overcooked; the wine bottles have aluminum screw tops. Occasionally the Italian State Railway chooses to honor (or promote) the cooking and wines of a particular region, and the results are a bit more interesting—the level rises to mediocre. The best bet is to provide your own self-catered lunch or dinner.

The same holds true for airline food. I don't know why the food in planes is so horrible. The names they give the dishes on airline menus are entertaining enough, but the reality is as close to cuisine as Musak is to music. Especially offensive is the attempt to serve pasta, usually overcooked beyond belief. Airline meals are precooked or browned and then baked—not microwaved—on board, to finish the cooking. As anyone who has ever reheated a meal knows, there is no excuse for the food baked in flight. The salad, although not particularly exciting, is the only item consistently worth eating. The added space in business class is a pleasure but the food and wines aren't much of an improvement, although I do appreciate eating on a real dish and drinking out of glass, not plastic. Eating in first class is a big improvement, but the simple things are the best, like TWA's roast lamb or Alitalia's tin of Petrossian beluga caviar. On flights departing from Italy, TWA serves a snack called the "Italian Harvest" in first class: *prosciutto,* salami, assorted cheeses, and Villa Banfi's lovely red Brunello di Montalcino. I'd like to hope that this excellent effort will spread to business and economy classes. The wine selection, even in first class, and even on Alitalia, isn't very good, and I suggest that you bring your own, which is permissible on all international flights.

My favorite food to bring along on a flight to Italy is Chinese take-out. If I can't get that, I like delicatessen or anything I might miss eating in Italy. Coming from Italy I purchase *l'ultima,* the last picnic of the trip, in the best *alimentari* or *gastronomia* the day before departure. Peck or Il Salumaio in Milan, and Fior Fiore or Volpi in Rome are my favorite shops for airline picnics.

LOGISTICS

GETTING AROUND

Theoretically it is possible to reach most of the villages mentioned in this book via the Italian State Railway (*Ferrovie dello Stato*) and/or local intercity bus companies. The trip could, however, take a few days. Public transportation may work well locally (Firenze to Pisa or Siena or Lucca), but it becomes complicated when crossing regional frontiers. Those willing to tackle the railway should purchase the paperback schedule for all of northern Italy's trains, sold at newsstands. Watch out for seemingly insignificant symbols (which are explained in the complex key) that denote special holiday trains. Service to the hinterlands is slow, tourists are rare, and the trains stop at every station, but this can be fun if time is of no concern. Cross-referencing to the Touring Club Italiano's road atlas (see page 40) would probably be helpful.

The Italian government has clearly chosen to strengthen the highway system rather than the railroads, and although the *autostrada* isn't the most beautiful way to see the countryside, it is the fastest way of getting around most of Italy. The toll roads with the worst reputation (clogged with traffic or slowed by geography or weather) are the Padana Valley; the plains of the river Po, which gets blanketed by a fierce fog in the winter; the Bologna–Firenze, which crosses the Apennine Mountains and is under constant construction; and the road that hugs the Ligurian coast, plowing through mountains and hovering over the city of Genova on stilts.

WEATHER

From a gastronomic point of view, the best season for a visit to Italy is winter. The weather is cold, crisp, with snow in the mountains and in some northern cities. Seasonal dishes become richer, more complex, and respond to Italy's wonderful regional red wines.

Spring begins in March in most of northern Italy, but it is occasionally completely rained out. Baby lamb, the season's first tender green vegetables, field greens, and ripe strawberries and cherries add a fresh, light touch to the *cucina*.

Italians summers are hot, and un-air-conditioned for the most part. Most Italians take the month of August to cool off and head for the seaside or the mountains, which will be crowded and expensive. Summer herbs, tomatoes, eggplants, sweet peppers, melons, and peaches compensate for the excessive heat, and white wine seems to evaporate from the bottle.

The Italian autumn feels like summer with naturally air-conditioned nights. The *vendemmia*, the harvest of wine grapes, is the season's greatest event. Ripe figs, grapes, peaches, and the last memories of summer tomatoes and peppers grace the table in the sweetest of the Italian seasons. Olives are pressed in the late fall, producing pungent, fresh extra virgin olive oil.

The only constant for Italian winter is its unpredictability. Sometimes spring never comes and summer emerges directly after a long, wet, chilling winter. Snow can appear as far south as Roma, causing total chaos in cities unused to the complications of slippery cobblestone. Winter can also include spells of weather that seem like a close imitation of spring.

"CHIUSO"

Chiuso (closed), often accompanied by a vacillating up-raised index finger, a "no-no" gesture, is probably the most disappointing word in the Italian language. Due to a different cultural timetable, holidays of dubious nature, local customs, the dreaded strike, and the even more dreaded restoration, the place you felt was going to be the highlight of your trip may be shut.

All restaurants and bars have a regular *giorno di chiusura*, one or two days a week when they are closed. Fish restaurants are almost always closed on Mondays, since Sunday is the fisherman's day off and many fish markets are closed on Mondays.

Banks, stores, offices, and many restaurants close for *feste nazionali*, the national holidays on January 1, New Year's Day; April 25, commemorating the liberation of Italy in 1945; and May 1, Labor Day. They also close for *feste religiose* (religious holidays): *Pasqua* and *Pasquetta*, Easter Sunday and "little Easter" Monday; All Saints' Day on November 1; Immaculate Con-

OPEN ... CLOSED

The long midday break is still the rule in Italy, although it is becoming less so in the large cities. In general, business hours are as follows:

Restaurants: Open at 12:30 for lunch, at 7:30 for dinner
Fish restaurants are usually closed on Monday.

Banks: Open Monday–Friday 8:30–1:30, 2:45–3:45

Shops: Open Monday–Saturday 9:00–12:30 or 1:00, 3:30–7:30
Usually closed Monday morning; Saturday afternoon in the summer.
Food shops are closed Sunday, one afternoon a week, and Saturday afternoon in the summer.

Markets: Monday–Saturday 8:30–1:30
(Great bargains on unsold produce can be found after 1:00.)

HOLIDAYS

Banks, stores, offices, and many restaurants are closed on these national holdiays:

January 1–New Year's Day	August 15–Assumption Day
April 25–Liberation Day	November 1–All Saints' Day
Easter Sunday	December 8–Immaculate Conception
Easter Monday	December 25–Christmas
May 1–Labor Day	December 26–Saint Stephen's Day

ception on December 8; *Natale,* Christmas; and *Santo Stefano,* December 26. The entire country closes tighter than a clam on *ferragosto,* August 15. Many Italians lengthen a one-day holiday into a minor vacation by combining it with the nearest weekend.

Every village in Italy has a home-town patron saint's day, a holiday that many consider sacred, even if the banks aren't always closed.

Banks are open Monday through Friday from 8:30 a.m. to 1:30 p.m. and from 2:45 to 3:45 p.m., or from 3:00 to 4:00 p.m.

Shops are normally open Monday through Saturday, 9:30 a.m. to 1:30 p.m. and from 3:30 to 7:30 p.m.,

closed Monday mornings year-round and Saturday afternoons in the summer. Bakery, fruit and vegetable, and other food shops are closed on Sunday, and each town has one afternoon a week when food stores close, although in the summer they may also shut down on Saturday afternoon.

Markets are open Monday through Saturday mornings from around 8:30 a.m. until 1:30 p.m. After 1:00, when the vendors are dismantling their stands, great bargains can be found on unsold produce.

Chiuso per ferie ("closed for vacation") shuts down many restaurants for an entire month, at times in July, but more often in August—when it may be almost impossible to find a good restaurant open, except on the coast or in major summer resort areas where they close during the winter off-season.

Unless you read the Italian newspapers, watch the TV, or listen to the radio, you'll probably be unaware of an upcoming *sciopero* (strike). At times a form of national protest, or a union display of strength to help in contract bargaining, or a sign of solidarity among workers, most strikes don't last more than four or five hours, but this can be enough to foil your plans for a trip to the museum, the post office, or the bank. Transportation strikes will delay the arrival of planes, trains, and ferries. City transportation, buses, and cabs will be unavailable, and every native with a car will try to squeeze his vehicle into a town designed for the horse and carriage. It always rains, of course, during a transportation strike.

Chiuso per restauro ("closed for restoration") means that you'll arrive only to find an intricate web of netting or bamboo mats draped from a Tinkertoy scaffolding totally obscuring whatever it is you've come to see. Buy the postcard and wait for your next trip, forgiving the Italians, because their attention to restoration is the reason why so much is still there for you to see.

Special foods and beverages

Italy presents the serious eater with a wealth of unusual foods and beverages that can be very different from products of the same name at home. Many of these specialties are easy to find, once you know what you're looking for, and are well worth seeking out. (See the Glossary for a more complete listing.)

ARRIVING HOME

Many of my friends—and I—have, over the years, devised ingenious schemes to lead U.S. Customs astray. So it was with great surprise that I learned, from the United States Department of Agriculture, that most Italian foods can be brought into the U.S. if you declare them. You can even bring back some fruits and vegetables. They'll be inspected and returned to you if found pest-free. Truffles and mushrooms can be brought in if they're completely free of soil. Dried foods like beans, rice, grains and flours, and all baked goods are okay. Cheese must be fully cured; fresh cheese like mozzarella, toma, and ricotta are not allowed. Roast coffee, (not green), either whole or ground, is fine, as are all canned or jarred products.

The big surprise is that seeds are on the list of approved products; the only exceptions are corn, cotton, cucumber, lentil, melon, pearl millet, potato, pumpkin, rice, squash, and wheat seeds. No meat products, either fresh or cured, can be brought into the United States.

One word of caution: The Beagle Brigade, an eager squad of canine sniffers, is on guard at international airports, just waiting for a whiff of forbidden prosciutto or truffle dirt. Watch out!

WINE

Italy was called Enotria, or "land of the vine," by the ancient Greeks, and over four million acres of vineyards dominate the Italian landscape today. The grape varieties and winemaking styles vary with the geography, climate, and customs of the individual areas. Many fine wines are easiest to find in their native regions, and are best tasted with the local *cucina*. But they don't remain in the provinces forever, as wine stewards, restaurant owners, and importers attend tastings and scour the countryside for lesser-known quality wines.

Italian wine consciousness ranges from the "red or white?" mentality to cork-sniffing wine stewards swirling long-stemmed crystal goblets the size of a football. The only point of agreement is that wine is the best complement to Italian food. Traditionally, most Italians order red wines in the winter with its hearty cold-weather dishes, and white wines with the lighter foods of summer. Residents of some areas that produce mostly red wine tend to drink it all year round, and white-wine–producing areas may be equally loyal. The house wine, called *vino della casa* or *vino sfuso*, is sold in quarter-, half-, and one-liter carafes, and may not be a bad choice in countryside restaurants that produce their own wine, but in a city the house wine will most likely turn out to be mediocre at best. In simple restaurants one wine will ably accompany a meal, but in more wine-oriented establishments, two or more wines may be served, and a tasting menu may feature a different glass of wine with each course. Fine wines are one of Italy's great bargains, and discovering and drinking them in Italy is just part of the experience, since many can be found in the U.S., inspiring gastronomic memories of meals past.

Bottled Italian wines can be divided into two main groupings. Wines labeled with the letters DOC, which stand for *Denominazione di Origine Controllata,* or DOCG, *Denominazione di Origine Controllata e Garantita,* are controlled (and guaranteed with the "G") by laws determining geographic origin, grape variety, character or taste, yield, and aging requirements. These laws have, in most cases, contributed to an improvement in the general quality of wine, but there are gaping loopholes: permissible grape yields per acre are often too high for quality production; rigid traditionalism dominates the choice of grape varieties; and wine or concentrates from outside the DOC growing zone may be used to "correct" a wine, not exactly a "controlled" origin.

The law also gives individualist Italians something to rebel against, a chance to make an unique statement about what a wine should be. The wines in this second grouping are sold as unclassified table wine, *vino da tavola,* and may range from banal to divine. Winemakers striving for excellence may want to grow nontraditional grapes, and thus be excluded from the DOC classifications. Their *vino da tavola* represents a personal commitment not dictated by law. But much table wine is inferior and to be avoided.

The regional wine lists in this book represent a limited selection, an orientation toward drinking-quality Italian wines. For a complete listing of all regional wines and vintage information, see Burton Anderson's *Pocket Guide to Italian Wines.*

MINERAL WATER

Over 150 companies in Italy bottle *acqua minerale* as it gushes forth from more than 250 springs. Subject to frequent bacteriological analyses to ensure purity,

WINE TERMS
·

abboccato slightly sweet

amabile semi-sweet

annata vintage year

asciutto dry

barrique 225-liter oak barrel, used for aging

bianco white

brut dry sparkling wine

dolce sweet

enoteca wine store

frizzante effervescent, slightly bubbly

metodo classico or **metodo champenois** the classic Champagne method of making bottle-fermented sparkling wines

passito wine, usually sweet, made from semi-dried grapes

produttore producer

riserva reserve, a special selection DOC or DOCG wine with longer aging requirements

rosato rosé

rosso red

secco dry

spumante sparkling

vendemmia harvest, vintage year

mineral water must be bottled as is, as it comes from its source, as *acqua minerale naturale* (natural mineral water) or with the addition of CO_2, as *acqua minerale gassata* (sparkling mineral water). Fizzy *gassata* is preferred by most Italians and is considered a better thirst quencher. The phrase *addizionata di gas acido carbonico* will appear somewhere in the jumble of information printed on the label—including analysis results, bottling date, and a list of minerals that looks like a big chunk of the periodic table, followed by decimals with as many zeroes as an Italian banknote.

The water with the lowest mineral salt content, from 0 to 0.2 grams per liter, is defined as *acqua*

*Aperitifs taste
especially wonderful
by moonlight.*

oligominerale on the label, although the term *minerale* (used to indicate water that contains over a gram of salt per liter) may get lost in the fine print. *Acqua minerale* must, by law, have therapeutic or sanitary properties, which are also stated on the bottle's busy label: aids digestion; beneficial for kidney stones, liver function, gout, and correlated unhealthy conditions; is a diuretic; or recommended in the diet of suckling babies. An instant spa in your glass!

The most popular brands of low-salt waters are Fiuggi, Levissima, Lora Recoaro, and Panna, my personal favorite. Among the higher-salt-content waters, I like San Pellegrino, with its slight bicarbonate taste and aggressive effervescence. Ferrarelle, known for being neither fizzy nor still, is widely distributed. Local brands of water can also be tasty. Your waiter will ask if you'd like your water *gassata* or *naturale* when he brings your menu or when you order.

Most Italians drink *acqua minerale* because it tastes good and is supposed to be good for you, but there is nothing wrong with the tap water, *acqua del rubinetto,* except that it may have a slightly chemical flavor. Tap water in Roma is excellent. The sign *Acqua Non Potabile,* usually seen on fountains, means the water isn't fit for drinking, although if you see Italians filling up plastic containers it means that the water hasn't undergone chemical analysis, but is considered okay to drink by the locals.

THE APERITIF

The *aperitivo* is an appetite-stimulating beverage, sipped during a ritual loiter preceding meals. Italy has many unusual aperitif liquors that are laced with essences of herbs and bark and are supposed to prepare your digestive tract for the upcoming assault of a meal. An aperitif can be consumed in a bar, restaurant, or even self-catered in your hotel room, although it's at its best in an outdoor *caffè.* Few restaurants have a full bar or make cocktails, although they may serve a glass of spumante or a mixture of fruit juice and spumante as an *aperitivo.* Bars will probably have an *aperitivo della casa,* a house cocktail, usually made with white wine, bitters of some kind, and a mystery ingredient, and they may also offer white wine by the glass, in addition to the usual aperitifs (see the list on page 20). Nonalcoholic carbonated bitters *(analcolico)* are also served. Most Italians don't drink cocktails before a meal, and they tend to savor Scotch whiskey, aged rum, or grappa after a meal, not before.

BREAD

It's hard to realize, when faced with the numerous regional breads available in Italy today, that before World War II white bread was eaten only by the wealthy and the sick. Most rural Italians lit their wood-burning ovens once a week to make bread with flour that was frequently mixed with inexpensive grains,

Freshly baked bread cools in a wicker basket and perfumes the room.

BREAD

•

pane bianco   white bread

pane nero or **pane integrale**   whole-wheat bread

pane francese   French bread

pane con le olive   bread flavored with olive paste

pane ai cinque cereali   five-grain bread (rice, rye, oat, wheat, and barley flours)

pane di mais   cornmeal bread, sometimes made with walnuts

pane di noci   walnut bread

carta da musica   "sheets of music": unleavened wafer-thin, large flat disk of traditional Sardinian cracker bread

ciabatta   "slipper": low flatbread

panini   rolls

rosette   "little roses": hollow, all-crust rolls

grissini   breadsticks

pane casereccio or **pane casalingo**   home-style coarse-textured bread

focaccia, schiacciata, or **pizza bianca**   freshly baked pizza crust, plain or with sliced potatoes, onions, or eggplant, depending on the season and the bakery, brushed with olive oil and sold by weight, per slice

producing a darker, coarser, less palatable loaf. In the city bread bakeries and ovens catered to both classes, selling white bread and rolls, and darker, more economical *pane nero.* (City dwellers would bring a Sunday chicken or roast, or a dish of lasagna, to their neighborhood *forno* (bread oven) to be cooked in the still-hot ovens after the baking was done, since most homes had no oven.)

White bread was a sign of wealth, something to be aspired to, and with the postwar economic prosperity Italy was swept up in a wave of tasteless, anemic, industrially produced breadsticks and crackers. Even tan soft-crusted presliced packaged white bread appeared. But some traditional breadmakers, working with flour, water, starter, and salt, and clad year-round in shorts, rubber sandals, undershirt, and a heavy dust-

ing of flour, kept baking. And in the past ten years a new interest in bread and grains has created a marketplace for shops selling all kinds of bread, traditional and innovative, local and from other regions. But the basic *pane* that graces most tables is white, with a crust that can range from crisp and flaky, to a heavy country crunch, to a disappointing stale, soggy has-been. *Pane nero* or *pane integrale* (whole-wheat bread) is common. The *ciabatta,* a crusty flat "slipper" of a loaf, has become popular throughout Italy. Each region sticks staunchly to its traditional breads, from the saltless Tuscan *filone* to the golden crusted *biove* of Piemonte to the phallic *banane* of Lombardia. And

> "Three lackeys in green, gold and powder entered, each holding a great silver dish containing a towering mound of macaroni. . . . The appearance of those monumental dishes of macaroni was worthy of the quivers of admiration they evoked. The burnished gold of the crusts, the fragrance of sugar and cinnamon they exuded, were but preludes to the delights released from the interior when the knife broke the crust; first came a mist laden with aromas, then chicken livers, hard-boiled eggs, sliced ham, chicken, and truffles in masses of piping-hot, glistening macaroni, to which the meat juice gave an exquisite hue of suede."
>
> —Giuseppe di Lampedusa, *The Leopard*

every region seems to love the hollow, crispy *rosette,* popular throughout the country.

PASTA

It's hard to imagine a world without pasta—freshly rolled, leathery, egg-yolk-orange, or dry, toothsome, wheaty, hugging its sauce. Who invented it? Pasta, like the wheel, was a product of necessity, an inexpensive solution to hunger using readily available ingredients: water and wheat. Many historical references to pasta exist: fourth-century Etruscan frescoes and implements; the Roman cookbook of Apicio, *De re coquinaria,* with a chapter devoted to pasta; Abu Abdallàh Muhammad ibn Muhammad ibn Idris's travel guide, written in 1154, with its mention of food made from flour in the form of strings, in the Palermo area of Sicily; and the inventory of Ugolino Scarpa, a meticulous Genovese accountant, dated February 2, 1279, which includes a "case filled with macaroni," bequeathed by Ponzio Bastone to his heirs. All this before Marco Polo came back from China! But no matter where it came from, it is in Italy that pasta has become an art form, a local gastronomic expression that magically changes form with the variables of climate, creativity, and myriad seasonal sauces. The result may be down-to-earth food to feed the hungry or subtly spiced creations to tantalize the jaded palate.

Pasta can be made with flour of wheat, wheat bran, whole wheat, buckwheat, cornmeal, emmer, or chestnut. It may contain whole eggs, egg yolks (duck eggs are reputed to be best), or water. There are three basic categories of pasta: dry, which is industrially produced by extrusion through bronze or Teflon dies and dried; fresh, which is hand- or machine-rolled; and stuffed, which ideally is handmade and filled. The names, shapes, flours, and fillings may change from village to village. In general, the smaller and lighter the pasta, the lighter the sauce should be. Stuffed pasta should be sauced as simply as possible or served in broth, so the subtle flavors of the filling can be tasted.

Long strands of pasta, whole and uncut, are twirled around the tines of a fork (without the assistance of a soup spoon). If you're not up to fork-twirling, ask for the easier-to-manage *pasta corta* (short lengths of pasta): *penne* ("quills"), *fusilli* ("spirals"), or *rigatoni* ("big stripes").

RISOTTO

Italians use many varieties of rice, in four main size categories. *Originario* is the shortest grain, followed by *semifino, fino,* and *superfino,* the largest (longer than ¼ inch). Vialone Nano, Arborio, Carnaroli, and Baldo are all perfect for *risotto*—with enough starch to enrich and thicken the cooking liquid and enough hardness to remain firm.

Risotto can be one of the world's finest dishes. The rice is barely toasted in butter over low heat, and then broth is added, a bit at a time during a slow cooking process, until almost all liquid is absorbed. Grated parmesan and butter are mixed in before serving. Seasonal vegetables, fish, seafood, meat, herbs, or spices may be added to flavor the risotto during cooking. Frequent stirring with a wooden fork is necessary throughout the cooking process, to prevent sticking and to keep the grains of rice separate. Although some chefs parboil the rice and finish cooking it when it's ordered, the very best risotto is prepared to order. Many restaurants insist on cooking at least two portions (they say one portion doesn't come out well, but I suspect that the logistics of dozens of single-portion pots of risotto demanding constant stirring may be the determining factor), but they may make an exception if they're not too busy. *Risotto* shouldn't be a mass of rice stuck together in a blob. Cooked to perfection

Sensory shopping in Firenze's San Lorenzo market

with first-rate rice, it should be creamy, not quite liquid and not quite solid—individual short, rounded grains cooked *al dente* and generously coated with a translucent sauce. The mixture should slowly slip across a tilted plate or soup dish. This consistency is known as *all' onda,* wavy.

EXTRA VIRGIN OLIVE OIL

Extra virgin olive oil is the first-pressing, lowest-acidity, and best of the oils. (Any oil with the word "virgin" is obtained without chemical solvents.) Like all olive oils, it is cholesterol-free. At its best it is produced from hand-picked olives that are quickly transported to the olive mill, where they are washed, picked over, and crushed with millstones. The resulting pulp is smeared on woven straw disks which are piled up on a spindle like a stack of records, and then pressed. The liquid that runs off is separated, by centrifuge or by removing the floating oil, and the vegetable water discarded. The resulting olive oil is always green, although some producers filter theirs to create a more transparent product. Extra virgin olive oil is at its most flavorful in the early winter, when it is freshly pressed—dense and murky green, with a peppery bite. Olive oil doesn't go bad if stored in a cool dark place (a producer I know stores all his in grottos; mine seems to do okay in a closet), but the flavor will slowly deteriorate, and the oil should be consumed within eighteen months. Umbrian, Ligurian, and most

of all Tuscan extra virgin olive oils are popular in Italy, but lesser-known oils from other regions, notably Le Marche, Veneto, Romagna, and Lombardia, can frequently be of high quality. The best extra virgin olive oil will have the words *prodotto e imbottigliato,* meaning it is produced and bottled by the same company, printed on the label; or *selezionato,* meaning it was chosen and milled under the guidance of an olive oil expert. Otherwise the olives may have been grown in areas outside the production zone.

Acidity increases with diminishing levels of virginity: *extra vergine*—less than 1%; *sopraffino vergine, fine vergine,* and *vergine*—not more than 4%. All other olive oils are made from high-acidity oil, chemically corrected, deodorized, and stripped of color. Beware.

THE TRUFFLE

According to folklore, truffles are the result of lightning striking a tree or the ground. In actuality, truffles are a fungus that grows four to eight inches below ground in parasitical symbiosis with the roots of oak, poplar, chestnut, hazelnut, willow, and walnut trees. Supposedly, the harder the wood of the tree, the better and the more intense the perfume and flavor of the truffles.

There are two types of truffles. Black truffles, *Tuber melanosporum,* are found from December through May throughout Italy. They are usually served cooked. *Tuber magnatum,* white truffles, are found from late Sep-

THE MARKET

The local outdoor markets, a cornucopia of seasonal plenty available six days a week from early morning to 1:30 p.m., provide the fresh raw ingredients that are the backbone of all quality Italian cooking. A ten-minute stroll through a market provides a timeless experience—a panorama of fruit and vegetables, the hustle of commerce, an unguarded view of the Italians engrossed in their daily shopping ritual, and an idea of what's in season. *Primizia,* the produce anticipating the season, tiny and expensive, is preciously displayed, out-of-town vegetables and fruit are neatly packed in wooden crates, and freshly picked local bounty is piled up in mounds. The selection may range from hand-picked mountain blueberries to South American exotics cradled in Styrofoam. The color and flavor of the market change with the seasons—wild mushrooms with moist dirt clinging to their stems, asparagus tied together with a supple twig, baskets of field greens, vegetables with tops and roots that have just recently been in touch with the earth. In other market sections the poultry has feathers and claws, the wild boar's head leaves no doubt about the identity of nearby slabs of maroon-colored, black-bristle-covered meat. Whole fish are lined up on crushed ice on slanting marble counters. Nothing is prepackaged or processed. This is primal shopping, guided by the senses.

Although they may appear similar (eight lettuce specialists?), each stall has its faithful customers, and vendors are quick with greetings, recipes, advice, and a piece of fruit for a toddler.

Some stands sell a wide range of produce; others focus on one strictly local seasonal item—a mountain of fragrant strawberries piled on fern fronds, or potatoes dusty with earth, or shiny red and yellow peppers, or long-stemmed green and purple artichokes.

The larger markets usually have butchers, fishmongers, bread, cheese, and cold-cut vendors, as well as housewares stands that sell a wide range of reasonably priced items—cheese graters, pasta strainers, plastic containers and bowls, espresso makers, and every possible replacement part for the various sizes of the classic *caffettiera,* the Model T of Italian coffee pots.

Smaller towns have a weekly market day, when a major piazza is crowded with wide umbrellas shading stands of inexpensive shoes, clothing, army surplus, wicker furniture, plants, linens, and sewing supplies in addition to the food.

Medium-size cities have a central market, permanently or semi-permanently installed, usually selling vegetables, fruit, and flowers and surrounded by complementary grocery stores, bakeries, and fish and butcher shops.

The big cities usually depend on small neighborhood markets, tucked into small piazzas or at various intersections, disappearing without a trace in the afternoon.

The market experience is a vital Italian tradition, a physical involvement with fresh food and people intent on purchasing the seasonal best. It's an important key to understanding the *cucina regionale.*

tember through January in northern and central Italy. The best white truffles are from Piemonte and are eaten raw, sliced paper-thin. (Most Piemontese feel that black truffles are little more than garnish, not at all in the same league as the white variety.)

Aphrodisiacs? Scientists claim the distinctive truffle perfume resembles the smell of pigs in rut. Porcine exploitation may be the perverse truffle-hunting technique favored by the French, but the Italians, rather than trying to control sex-crazed pigs, use dogs to

The unforgettable fffft-fffft-fffft
sound of the truffle crossing the blade of the
slicer is music to the food lover's ears.

hunt their truffles. Selectively bred and fed an occasional taste of truffle, these hounds are worth quite a bit, since truffles can be sold for 3,000,000 lire per kilo and a skilled hunter can dig up to two kilos in an evening. It is said that the best *trifulaû*, or truffle hunter, can detect the presence of truffles by beating the ground with a special stick, feeling the vibrations and listening to the sound of the thud. The best truffle locations are a closely guarded secret, handed down in the family, known only to *trifulaû*, dog, and stick.

A perfect truffle should be compact and comparatively smooth. Excess convolutions hold dirt and increase the weight. Tiny holes in the surface indicate the presence of worms. Smaller truffles are supposed to be more intensely flavored than the big ones. The fresher the better.

FRUIT

During one of his first trips to Italy, my brother ordered an orange for dessert. He deftly peeled the fruit, only to find a bloody red, pulpy mass of stuff, looking nothing like any orange he'd ever seen, which he proceeded to cut up, toy with, and finally abandon. He'd been given a *tarocco*, a blood orange.

Some varieties of fruit that you'll find in Italy's markets will be new to you, a special treat, but even the familiar fruits will bear a nose-prickling perfume unlike many in this country. Most fruit in Italy has never seen the inside of a refrigerator and is often sold with its leaves attached, a proof of freshness. In the Italian fruit calendar, spring comes in with *fragoline*, tiny wild strawberries that taste like delicate, perfumed flowers; the loquat *(nespolo)*, a small tart orange fruit that looks like a bruised apricot; and cherries *(ciliege)*, pale and sour or deep purple-black. Summer brings in golden, lightly fuzzed, blushing *albicocche*, apricots; *susine* and *prugne*, purple and red plums; and best of all, the tiny greenish blue *claudia* plum. Peaches *(pesche)* surely never tasted sweeter or juicier than on a hot summer day. Ripe, musky, orange-colored *melone* (named cantaloupe after the papal estate of Cantalupo, the first grower of this luscious fruit in Europe) is paired with *prosciutto*, a strange but successful combination. Fresh figs *(fichi)*, green- or purple-skinned, filled with seed and sweet, fragrant pulp, are served with *prosciutto* or *salame*. Late summer sees the ripening of grapes *(uva)*, either green *(bianca)* or purple *(nera)*, served in a bowl of water. Prickly pears *(fichi d'India)* come from the south—thorn-covered, with a sweet, musky flavor. Fall, with its cooler weather, is the time of the pomegranate *(melograno)*, the deep orange, tart, mushy persimmon *(cachi)*, and the fruit of the Mediterranean strawberry tree, *Arbutus andrachne, corbezzolo*. And a sure sign that winter has arrived is the smoky scent of chestnuts *(castagne)* roasting in the street-vendors' brasiers.

VEGETABLES

Vegetarians and vegetable lovers, rejoice! Italians eat many vegetables that you've probably never seen, even if they do tend to overcook them a bit. Most are highly seasonal, usually perishable, and at times regional (Tuscan black cabbage is unknown by the

Sun-ripened tomatoes are one of the joys of the Italian summer.

turn them into crunchy bites. Summer is the reign of the tomato *(pomodoro,* literally "golden apple," because tomatoes from the New World were yellow). Tomatoes are often served green in salads, a good treatment when they are tart and crisp. But the ripe red plum tomato, the *san marzano,* tastes of summer sun and achieves glory as the perfect sauce for pasta. Glossy dark purple or lilac and white eggplant *(melanzane)* and ripe yellow or red bell peppers *(peperoni)* are important summer flavors. Wild mushrooms have a brief but intense season in the fall, and sometimes in the spring when the weather is right. Imperial agaric mushrooms *(ovoli)* are eaten raw in salads; *porcini* are eaten raw or cooked; morels *(spugnoli)* and chanterelles *(galletti* or *finferle)* are eaten cooked and are at their best with fresh pasta. Italy's most important winter vegetables are beans and grains, the protein of the poor. Lentils *(lenticchie),* barley *(orzo),* ground cornmeal *(polenta),* rice *(riso),* beans *(fagioli),* and emmer *(farro),* an ancient Roman grain with a wheaty taste, are winter favorites. Three main varieties of red *radicchio* appear on the winter table, both raw and cooked; *treviso,* with its elongated white-ribbed red leaves, often cooked with about three inches of its root; *castelfranco,* with pale green and red marbleized leaves; and *verona,* a small purple lettuce-like head. Anise-flavored fennel *(finocchio)* is eaten raw or cooked.

HERBS AND SPICES

Pungent green herbs are a note that echoes throughout regional Italian cooking. They are sold fresh at vegetable markets and produce stores, in any quantity desired, from a few leaves to a massive bunch. Fruit tree leaves may also be used like herbs in the preparation of preserves or fruit desserts. Bay leaves *(alloro* or *lauro)* are usually not sold at the market, but the plant is used as a hedge all over Italy. I pick my bay leaves in Firenze's Boboli Gardens. Basil *(basilico),* the perfect companion to the tomato, is delicate when green and tender, and the small-leafed Ligurian type is strong enough to stand up to garlic and aged pecorino cheese in the classic pesto. The Ligurians, great herb lovers, also liven up many dishes with marjoram *(maggiorana),* and stuff pasta, or flavor its dough, with borage *(boragine).* Trendy tarragon *(dragoncello)* is traditional only in the Siena area. Fennel *(finocchio sel-*

nearby Ligurians, who have kept their wonderful white and purple asparagus a secret from everyone). Spring is the greatest of the Italian vegetable seasons. Artichokes *(carciofi)* can be conical, with purple thorn-tipped leaves, or green-leafed cones on long stems, stacked in sheaves, both served either raw or cooked. *Agretti,* a word I've never been able to find translated, looks like an antlered relative of the chive family and has a pleasant sour taste with no hint of onion. Wild field greens with tongue-twisting names, too young and tender to be bitter, are dressed with extra virgin olive oil. Asparagus can be spaghetti slim and dark green, or the size of cigars, either white fading to a purplish tip or the more common green, and can be eaten with your fingers. Baby zucchini end in a bright yellow flower, a sure sign of freshness, and cases of zucchini flowers are destined for deep-fryers that will *vatico)* grows wild throughout much of Italy; its green leafy fronds, which resemble dill, are used in the spring, and its seeds, sometimes still attached to the pistils of the flower, gently spice winter dishes. Gnarled, bushy evergreens spiked with deep green needles and tipped with lilac flowers in the spring, rosemary *(rosmarino,* or *ramerino* in Toscana) is a major Italian flavor. Sage *(salvia),* with large gray-green, slightly fuzzy leaves, is another important herb available all year round. But the most popular of herbs is parsley *(prezzemolo).* The bright green, flat, three-sectioned leaves are minced, and impart a distinct flavor to the dishes where they appear, unlike their wimpy curly relative, which is unknown in Italy.

Spices have been a symbol of wealth ever since Italian navigators expanded the world's horizons and returned with pungent seeds and barks—expensive exotic imports used in minute quantities to perfume or disguise the flavor of food. But pepper is the only spice commonly used throughout all of Italy. Each region's attitude toward spices is different, based on availability and cultural influences. Wealthy Emilia; Austria-influenced Lombardia; and Veneto, whose capital, Venice, was home of the Rialto market, a stock exchange for the republic's spice trade—all take their spices more seriously than do the more herbally oriented Toscana, Umbria, Le Marche, and Liguria. Spices are also known as *droghe* (drugs) and are often sold in *drogherie* (drugstores).

MEAT AND GAME

The Mediterranean diet, a regime forced by poverty on much of Italy, calls for lots of pasta, grains, and fresh vegetables, and limited amounts of animal fats, dairy products, and meat. Italians don't eat large portions of meat. After an antipasto of thinly sliced *salumi* or a portion of pasta has taken the edge off your hunger, you probably won't want to eat a big chunk of meat either. Traditionally, beef or veal rarely found its way to the average Italian's daily table, and even courtyard animals (chickens, rabbits) were considered food for festivites. Fresh pork was eaten when the yearly pig was slaughtered, but most of it was destined to be preserved as sausage *(salsiccie),* salame, and *prosciutto.* Spring is the season for lamb *(agnello),* a tiny newborn animal with chops the size of a quarter. Game is known as *cacciagione* and is hunted in the

cooler winter months, after the fall harvest. Some markets sell a variety of small feathered birds that can include lark, woodcock, partridge, and thrush. Plumed pheasant, wild rabbit with its fur still on, and hairy, black-bristled wild boar are also found in the fall game season. Courtyard animals, known as *animali da cortile,* are available all year round and include chicken *(pollo),* squab or pigeon *(piccione),* quail *(quaglia),* and guinea hen *(faraona).* Chicken may be sold with its head, feet, and feathers, and filled with unborn eggs in the spring. Eggs *(uova)* are graded by freshness; best of all are the *uova da bere,* eggs fresh enough to be sucked raw from the shell. Rabbit *(coniglio),* if you can overlook cultural prejudices, is quite a tasty bite. A butcher displaying a large poster of a horse isn't an equestrian fan, but sells horsemeat *(cavallo),* darker and a bit sweeter than beef and said to give strength to the ill. Tripe *(trippa),* looking like a faded beige Latex bathing cap, is an Italian favorite.

FISH AND SEAFOOD

Most Italian seafood, if it is local and fresh, will probably be unfamiliar to you. Italians eat a wide variety of fresh- and saltwater fish from the surrounding seas (only five regions of the country have no coast) and inland lakes and rivers. Stiff, yellowed, cardboardish, seemingly inedible dried salt cod *(baccalà),* sold dry or, on Fridays, reconstituted, is imported from Nordic countries. But most other seafood is Italian, from tiny larval anchovies, known as *bianchetti* or *gianchetti* or *schiuma di mare* and not much bigger than worms, to imposing swordfish *(pescespada),* complete with sword. Most of the quality fish and seafood caught in Italian waters are directed to the major market in Milano, although fresh fish can be found throughout Italy, especially by the sea. Eel *(anguilla),* is sold live and squirming, and has a nervous system that just won't quit. Newborn elvers *(cee* or *cie)* are found only in the spring. Squid *(calamaro)* is sold, black with its ink, in Styrofoam cases. Flying squid *(totano)* is twice the size of the *calimaro.* Octopus, with its mottled gray skin and lots of suction cups, is called *polipo* or *polpo.* The *moscardino* is a smaller curled version of the octopus. Cuttlefish *(seppie)* are often sold black with their ink, and contain an internal bone, the cuttlebone, known to pet bird owners. The fish that Alan Davidson's *Mediterranean Seafood* calls "smooth hound" is the Italian's more delicate; the deeper, rockier Tirreno and Ligure seas, with their tastier, more flavorful fish.

PIZZA AND FLATBREADS

Simple rustic flattened breads of flour and water, baked in the ashes or on the stone floor of the hearth, must be almost as old as man. *Pizza,* or *focaccia,* is the original take-out food, an inexpensive edible plate awaiting the artistry that embroiders the wheat-and-water crust with local tastes of *prosciutto,* herbs, greens, tomatoes, or cheese. The *torta al testo, focaccia, schiacciata,* and *piadina* are all traditional flatbreads from different regions. Pizza achieves glory in Napoli (is it the water? or the sea air? or the humidity?), a gastronomic siren whose fresh, straightforward song will never be as sweet when heard elsewhere.

The best pizza is made to order. It should be deftly rolled out into a perfect circle, sauced, and slipped on a long-handled paddle into a wood-burning brick oven, its dome-shaped ceiling redistributing the dry heat produced by burning embers, its porous brick walls absorbing the moisture given off by the cooking pizza. The T-shirted *pizzaiolo* performing these acts is an exhibitionist, his marble work station a stage in front of the brick oven backdrop. He may feign indifference to your interest in his crisp, precise movements, but his performance improves with admiring spectators.

Most popular of all *pizze* is the *margherita,* made with tomatoes, mozzarella, and basil—the red, white, and green of the Italian flag—named after Queen Margherita, who had this unusual street food brought to her during a visit to Naples in 1889. The *napoletana* is a purist's pizza of tomatoes, garlic, and oregano. The *marinara* adds garlic and anchovy filets to the classic uncooked tomato base. The *capricciosa,* or "capricious," pizza's contents depend on the caprice of the chef, but will probably include artichoke hearts, mushrooms, olives, ham, and hot dog slices. The "four seasons" of the *quattro stagioni* are usually quadrants of artichoke hearts, mushrooms, olives, and ham. The *calzone* is a folded half-moon pizza with filling inside and tomato sauce baked on top. Most pizzerie have a house pizza, named after either the restaurant or an explosive device, which will usually contain everything the *pizzaiolo* can fit on the crust, including a fried egg or sliced hot dogs *(wurstel),* and will be the

palombo, a tasty medium-size sharky-looking fish. Clams come in a variety of sizes and colors, from the tiny purple and grayish-yellow wedge shells, called either *arsella* or *tellina,* to the tube-shaped razor shell *cannolicchio,* or the warty venus *(tartufo di mare),* a ridged clam with a tightly pleated shell. The best clams to grace a strand of pasta are the *vongola verace,* the "true" carpet-shell clam, grayish yellow and medium size, and the brownish date-shell clam *(dattero di mare),* looking very date-like. Scallops, called *capesante,* are often cooked in their shells. As usual, Italians on each coast feel that their own fish and seafood is the best—the sandy, shallow Adriatico, whose fish is said to be

GELATO

·

albicocca apricot

amarena sour cherry

ananas pineapple

arancia orange

bacio chocolate with hazelnut pieces

banana banana

caffè coffee

castagna chestnut

ciliegia cherry

cioccolato chocolate

cocco coconut

cocomero or *anguria* watermelon

crema egg-yolk custard

datteri dates

diaspora or *caco* persimmon

fico fig

fragola strawberry

fragoline wild strawberries

frutti di bosco wild berries

gianduia milk-chocolate hazelnut cream

lampone raspberry

limone lemon

macedonia fruit salad

malaga raisin

mandarino tangerine

mela apple

melone cantaloupe

menta mint

mirtillo blueberry

more blackberry

nespola medlar, loquat

nocciola hazelnut

noce walnut

panna whipped cream

pera pear

pesca peach

pescanoce nectarine

pistacchio pistachio

pompelmo grapefruit

ribes black or red currant

riso rice pudding

stracciatella chocolate chip

stracciatella di menta or *after eight* mint chocolate chip

tarocchi blood orange

tartufo chocolate chip truffle (usually a lumpy-looking hunk of bittersweet-chocolate-studded dark chocolate *gelato* with a candied-cherry center)

tiramisù trifle-like

torroncino nougat

uva grape

vaniglia vanilla

viscole or *marasche* black sour cherries

zuppa inglese trifle

most expensive item on the menu. Some creative chefs are experimenting with a wide range of ingredients, and you may find gorgonzola cheese, eggplant, red radicchio lettuce, artichokes, ripe bell peppers, zucchini, or even fruit toppings offered.

Brightly colored precooked vegetable-and-cheese-topped rectangles in the windows of snack bars in tourist areas or around train stations may resemble, or even be identified as, pizza. Don't believe it. This is food for the unwary, or for those with superior digestive systems.

Cooling off in the summer with friends and gelato

GELATO

Anyone who has ever dug a short plastic spoon into a squat paper cup of Italian *gelato* knows that ice cream and *gelato* are not the same thing. Ice cream—iced rich cream—turns most flavors into pastels. *Gelato,* a combination of whole milk, eggs, sugar, and natural flavoring—or fresh fruit and sugar in the fruit flavors—is a less firmly frozen, softer, more intensely flavored and colored creation, essential to the Italian summer. Arabs brought what came to be known as *sorbetto* to Sicily; but *gelato* is said to have been first created by Bernardo Buontalenti for the court of Franceso dé Medici in 1565. In a recent region-wide competition, Tuscan *gelato* artisans came up with a

delicately perfumed, egg-yolk-rich, almost orange-colored velvety flavor called Buontalenti, homage to a Renaissance artist.

Although *gelato* is available all year, the sunny spring and summer months are the season when it becomes a driving force in the Italian culture, an excuse for an expedition into the cooler night air, a chance to hang out, something to meet over, a preface or postscript to the evening's activities, Italian air-conditioning. Many *gelato* shops (*gelaterie*) stay open until 1 a.m. or even later in the summer.

The best *gelaterie* will display a sign, *Produzione Propria, Nostra Produzione,* or *Produzione Artigianale*—all indicating that their *gelato* is homemade. The best fruit *gelato* is made from crushed fresh ripe seasonal fruit. Although freezing should diminish flavors, somehow *gelato* winds up tasting more intense than the fruit from which it has been made. The best milk-based *gelato* is flavored with all natural ingredients and has a silky consistency. They will all melt faster than ice cream does. Colors should seem natural, not too intense. If the pistachio is bright green, it's been artificially colored and probably artificially flavored. Fruit flavors should reflect seasonal fruits. *Gelato* sitting in plastic bins is industrially produced; homemade *gelato* is always stored in stainless steel bins, which can be sterilized and reused.

Semifreddo, literally "half cold," is made from the same base as *gelato* but has whipped cream folded in. It vaguely resembles a mousse, which is what the chocolate flavor is called.

Sorbetto (fruit sorbet) has become popular in many Italian restaurants and is often served halfway through the meal, to separate the fish and meat courses and act as a palate cleanser, but instead it anesthetizes the mouth in time for the arrival of the red wine. I feel that the *sorbetto* belongs at the end of the meal, not in the middle.

Granita, slushy grainy water ices, usually come in lemon or coffee flavors and are normally found in bars.

Gelato is purchased with the same receipt system as *caffè* in a bar. If you want a paper cup (*coppa*), check out the sizes, usually displayed prominently with prices printed on the sides. If you want a cone (*cono*), there will probably be a choice of sizes as well. March up to the cashier and ask for either a *coppa* or a *cono,* state the price (size) that you want, and pay. Take your receipt to the counter after having worked out your selections (more than four per serving is considered poor form) and restate your order with your choice of flavors. If you have ordered chocolate, you may be asked if you'd like some *panna,* unsweetened whipped cream.

COFFEE

A perfect cup of thick rich *espresso* or a foamy brown and white *cappuccino* may be worth the trip to Italy. The flavors are intense, harmonious, and stimulating. Italians drink *caffè,* espresso coffee, all day long in its various forms. *Cappuccino* is consumed at breakfast or instead of a meal, and it's considered poor form—a social gaffe akin to finishing a fine meal with a milkshake—to order *cappuccino* after a meal. Go native and ask for a *caffè macchiato,* espresso coffee "stained" with a little milk. Coffee will always be at its best in a busy bar because the coffee beans are freshly ground as needed, in a machine that shrieks like a buzzsaw, invariably whenever you try to use the public phone. The constantly maintained steam pressure of a frequently used coffee machine is a crucial factor in the production of rich brown *caffè.* Sugar is served in individual packages, from a collective self-service sugar bowl with long-handled spoons, or from a shaker that, with luck, spits out a portion of sugar at a time. Italians seem to be capable of dissolving large quantities of sugar in a tiny demitasse cup.

Caffè, the basic unit of the bar, is made in a machine that forces steam through freshly roasted and ground coffee beans, and served in a small demitasse cup. Properly made from quality coffee beans, *caffè* will be topped with a burnished golden foam, known as *crema.* There are numerous varieties of the *caffè,* which can be served stronger (*ristretto,* made with less water), weaker (*lungo,* made with more water), "corrected" with a shot of brandy or liquor (*corretto*), or "stained" with a bit of steamed milk *(macchiato).* Cappuccino, called *cappuccio* in some parts of Italy, is made of espresso and foamy steamed milk, and is the color of the Capuchin monks' robes. The stronger, darker *marocchino* is made with less milk; the lighter *caffè latte,* made with more milk, is served in a bigger cup. Decaffeinated coffee is usually called *Hag,* the brand name of Italy's most popular decaf. All variations of *caffè* can be made with *Hag.*

Italian coffee can easily be brought back from your trip. Andrea Trinci, master coffee roaster of Tricaffè (see page 212), recommends having the coffee ground, since most home grinders don't get an even grind, and vacuum-sealed in small 250-gram packages, if possible. Once opened, keep coffee in an airtight container.

After discovering the glories of an Italian *caffè,* you may want to buy an *espresso* maker. The *macchinetta da caffè,* simple, inexpensive, and easy to use, is available at all housewares stores, along with spare parts for every possible eventuality. (The most famous model, a classic, is the Bialetti Moka, but lots of less expensive copies are available.) From a pure modern design standpoint, Alessi's coffee makers by Aldo Rossi and Richard Sapper, and Girmi's linear electric *caffè concerto* (make sure you get the 110-volt USA model), are probably the most attractive choices. The Rolls-Royce of coffee makers, La Pavoni, works with pressurized steam, has a wand for steaming *cappuccino* milk, and sports wonderful, classic chrome lines, but may be hard to find in the 110-volt model. And for those who can't be without a *caffè,* the individual-size demitasse-cup-shaped coffee thermos may be just what you're looking for, and can be found at most well-equipped housewares stores.

DIGESTIVE LIQUORS

Digestivi (digestive liquors, also known as *amari*) are mostly alcohol infusions or distillates made from herbs, barks, and roots. They are consumed at the end of a meal, after coffee is served, to aid and stimulate digestion, a process of great interest to Italians. Many unwritten laws that govern eating habits (regulating food and beverage temperature, use of spices, cooking methods, and after-meal activities) are dictated by an obsession with the functions of the liver, the body's filter, an organ not to be taken lightly. Americans are thought to be concerned only with the stomach, a rather simplistic approach to digestion. Fernet Branca, made from a blend of herbs, roots, and alcohol, is the most famous *digestivo*—and the bitterest, a punishment for overworked taste buds, an acquired taste and said to be slightly habit-forming. Fernet is available in reg-

Nonino's grappa and fruit distillates are elegantly packaged.

QUALITY GRAPPA PRODUCERS
·

Trentino–Alto Adige
Poli
Zeni
Pojer & Sandri

Friuli
Nonino
Jermann
Distilleria Aquileia
   di Comar

Veneto
Nardini
Maculan

Piemonte
Romano Levi
Angelo Gaja
Ceretto
Castello di Neive

Emilia-Romagna
Castelluccio

Toscana
Cappezzana
Altesino
Tenuta Caparzo
Castello di Ama
Monte Vertine
Felsina

Umbria
Lungarotti

ular and mint flavors, the latter an unsuccessful attempt at palatability. Another popular after-dinner drink is Sambuca, an anise-flavored liqueur, served *con le mosche* (with coffee bean "flies" floating in the glass). Homemade infusions of herbs, spices, or fruit in alcohol are occasionally found in country restaurants. Spirits—such as cognac, *grappa,* or whiskey (served without ice)—are considered a more sophisticated conclusion to a meal.

GRAPPA

Grappa is distilled from pomace, the grape skins and pits left over after the winemaking process. It has long been a traditional drink and source of warmth in Italy's colder northern regions. Aggressive, alcoholic, and raw, like whiskey in the cowboy movies, *grappa* was tossed down in shots, a peasant painkiller for the physical and spiritual aches of poverty, a breakfast rinse for the coffee cup. Children were given a shot of *grappa* before heading out in the cold for school.

Giannola Nonino's distillery in Friuli has been making *grappa* for almost a century, but fifteen years ago she started producing *grappa monovitigno,* each distilled in modern custom-made copper stills from a single grape variety, using fresh pomace from fine wineries. The bottles are wonderful to look at. A simple chemistry-lab look, with a silver-topped stopper and a label hanging from a colored string, doesn't interrupt the clean lines of the clear *grappa* in its glass globe. This *grappa* is perfumed, 50 percent alcohol, intense, and the price is elevated. Nonino also makes *ùe,* a distilled grape must that is more delicate than *grappa,* made from seven varieties of grapes. The *ùe* made from *picolit,* a Friulano dessert wine grape, is sold in a hand-blown bottle made by Venini of Murano. The latest Nonino produce is *le frute,* distilled from local mountain strawberries, raspberries, blackberries, pears, and apricots.

Other makers, following the lead of Giannola Nonino, have vastly improved the quality of their *grappa.* Elegant packaging has contributed to the new image for this former rustic "schnapps," which is now considered a sophisticated choice to conclude a fine meal.

Romano Levi is a poetic Hobbit-like spirit who assures me that he completes Piemonte's life cycle and will therefore live forever. He gets his grape pomace from Angelo Gaja and other outstanding wine producers and then distills it over direct fire in his Rube Goldberg copper maze, pressing the distilled grape skins into bricks, drying them to use as fuel to feed the fire of the still. The ashes are then given back to the wine producer from whence the seeds and skins came, to fertilize the vineyard soil. The labels of Levi's potent *grappa*—up to 60 percent alcohol—are handwritten in black and red ink on torn paper, and the names are graceful poetry: "Dear Maria, I have to talk to you," "A dream I have dreamed," and "Grappa of the wild women who scale the hills."

COMPLETING THE PICTURE

The food experience in Italy does not stop at table, but extends to the kitchens, back roads, festivals, newsstands, bookstores, and housewares shops.

READING MATERIAL

I love to read, to learn something about the region I'm in, and I always have a *Blue Guide* with me when I travel; it lists monuments and museums and also usually includes the address of the E.P.T, the local tourist office, which provides travelers with free maps, information about local events, and a list with prices, of all hotels in the province. (Someone there will speak English.) I also always travel with Burton Anderson's *Pocket Guide to Italian Wines,* a slim, informative book, indispensable for anyone who wants to know more about Italian wines. The Touring Club Italiano's *Atlante Stradale d'Italia*—three large green soft-covered map books, easy to read, extremely detailed, and equipped with an index—are essential for anyone traveling by car with the intention of abandoning the main highway, and can be purchased in most bookstores in Italy. For big-city shopping I refer to *Made in Italy* by Annie Brody and Patricia Schultz, an introduction to the shopping experience in Roma, Firenze, Milano, and Venezia. And for a feel of the provinces I love to read Italo Calvino's *Fairy Tales,* fables from all regions of Italy. It provides a link to the rich regional folk tradition—a wealth of kings, queens, knights, trolls, trap doors, dragons, thieves, witches, and spells embroidered on the everyday fabric of life in the provinces.

COOKING SCHOOLS

Learning to cook at one of Italy's many schools can be an interesting experience, as varied as the regional *cucina,* with classes taught by a housewife in her home kitchen, by a titled hostess teaching from the kitchen of a country estate, or by the elegant hotels of Venezia. Most courses are created for the American home cook who has some culinary skills and would like to participate in a gastronomic vacation. A selection of schools is listed here by city.

BOLOGNA

Giuliano Hazan
Hazan Classics
P.O. Box 285
Circleville, NY 10919
Tel. (914) 692-7104

Marcella Hazan's son Giuliano directs a cooking school in Bologna. The curriculum covers all aspects of Italian cookery, with an emphasis on technique and pasta making. The staff includes cooking and baking professionals. Basic courses last eleven days, and consist of eighteen sessions and a field trip to a *parmigiano-reggiano* dairy in Parma. A second cycle for professionals or perfectionists extends the course by ten days and covers advanced pasta, polenta, pickling, sausage making, a formal banquet, and a diploma project where students plan, shop, prepare, and serve a menu of their own choice. Lessons are taught by professionals.

FIRENZE

Giuliano Bugialli
53 Wooster St.
New York, NY 10013
Tel. (212) 334-6430

Via dei Pilastri 52
Firenze
Tel. 055/242128

Culinary star Giuliano Bugialli hosts a one-week total immersion in Florentine gastronomy, with demonstrations, lessons, historical lectures, slides, market visits, and dinners in his favorite restaurants. Many of the recipes covered in class are complicated and contain hard-to-find ingredients, but they are generally faithful to the local tastes and traditions. No food processors allowed! Giuliano's most dramatic moment is the pasta demonstration, where he cranks yards of fresh egg pasta from his machine, flipping festoons in the air, a feat that would leave a less dexterous demonstrator wrapped up like a mummy. The wines served are not up to the rest of the experience.

Giovanna Folonari
Via Maggio 39
Firenze 50125
Tel. 055/86648

Giovanna Folonari Ruffino hosts and directs the "Tuscan Experience," nine days of cooking with professional chefs from some of Toscana's best restaurants. Lessons are held at one of the Ruffino villas, but this course also leaves ample time for non-kitchen activities like exploring shops and museums, visiting neighboring estates, and tasting wines produced by the Ruffino winery. Accomodations are in a four-star hotel in Firenze. Giovanna's hospitality and elegance

make this glimpse of the lifestyles of the Tuscan aristocracy an unforgettable experience.

GAIOLE IN CHIANTI

The Villa Table
Badia a Coltibuono
Gaiole in Chianti
Tel. 0577/806208

2561 Washington St.
San Francisco, CA 94115
Tel. (415) 346-0890

Badia a Coltibuono, an eleventh-century abbey, villa, and winery, is the setting for "The Villa Table," where up to twelve houseguests share Lorenza de' Medici's heritage and style for a week of cooking lessons. Lorenza, who has published many cookbooks in Italy and has given demonstrations in Europe and America, is a gifted teacher, and her uncomplicated fresh Italian cooking, based on produce from the Coltibuono estate, is tasty and practical. Participants cook with Lorenza in the morning, tour the Tuscan countryside in the afternoon, dine in the evening in important private villas and castles, and taste the Coltibuono wines, extra virgin olive oil, vinegar, and honey. Guests experience the Tuscan lifestyle, lolling in the frescoed fifteenth-century drawing room, reading from the extensive library, strolling through the Renaissance gardens or the estate's woods, enjoying the swimming pool or sauna.

TODI

The Cooking School of Umbria
Casella Postale 17
Todi
Tel. 075/887370

The newly opened Cooking School of Umbria is taught by father and son Donaldo and Dino Soviero in a fully equipped restored farmhouse (22-burner kitchen, wine room, library). It immodestly calls itself "The True Cooking of Italy" in a slick brochure that offers a series of cooking programs in addition to a hot air balloon picnic, a private, dinner-by-reservation-only restaurant, and a gold-lettered diploma tied with a gold ribbon for all participants. Master Chef Donaldo

Soviero bottles a line of pasta sauces with his picture on the label.

TORGIANO

Le Tre Vaselle
Via Garibaldi 48
Torgiano
Tel. 075/982447

Le Tre Vaselle, a five-star Relais & Chateaux hotel, offers cooking classes taught by the chef of their restaurant, one of the best in Umbria. A bilingual guide will translate as well as escort participants through the Umbrian countryside to unknown hill towns, a chocolate factory, or special restaurants. A visit to the Wine Museum, the best of its kind in Italy, and a wine tasting of Lungarotti wines highlight the sessions, custom-tailored to the schedule of the group. Contact Romano Sartore for information.

UDINE

Gianna Modotti
Via Palmanova 133
Udine
Tel. 0432/602766

Gianna Modotti, who teaches at the Cipriani school in Venezia, also gives lessons from her kitchen in Udine, featuring the cooking of her native Friuli, one of Italy's most interesting and unknown regional *cucine*. Gianna and her stylish daughter-in-law Anna teach practical, everyday traditional cooking and entertaining. A true sense of hospitality and warmth makes these lessons a treat. Gianna teaches in Italian, but services of a translator are available. Courses can be specially scheduled with advance notice.

VENEZIA

Hotel Gritti Palace
Campo Santa Maria del Giglio 2467
Venezia
Tel. 041/794611

The Hotel Gritti Palace has been holding cooking courses every summer since 1974. Massimo Alberini, an Italian journalist, directs the courses, and American cooking teacher and writer Julie Dannenbaum coordinates and teaches one of the four courses. Many of Italy's best cooks and restaurant owners have taught at the Gritti. The 1987 season featured demonstrations by the chef of the Peck restaurant of Milano; regional cooking of Romagna by Gianfranco Bolonesi of the highly rated restaurant La Frasca; a cooking course by chef Alfredo Marzi of the cruise ship "Love Boat"; and fast-and-fresh-cooking by Julie Dannenbaum. All participants lunch on dishes prepared during the lesson, accompanied by two wines chosen by the Gritti's wine steward. An American translator is on hand to explain and interpret. Each course consists of five lessons, and you can choose to take some or all of them, to suit your schedule.

Hotel Cipriani
Isola della Giudecca 10
Venezia
Tel. 041/50744

The Cipriani Hotel program offers four four-day cooking courses—two on fish cooking with Marcella Hazan, one with a guest chef (in 1987 Christian Bodiguel, executive chef of the *Orient Express* deluxe train), and one with Gianna Modotti, who chooses an interesting theme each year (cooking with herbs and field greens, a carefully researched course on foods of ancient Roma, a dietetic Italian *cucina* coordinated by a cardiologist). Lessons are in the native language of the teacher, but services of a translator are available.

Hazan Classics
P.O. Box 285
Circleville, NY 10919
Tel. (914) 692-7104

Marcella Hazan, who deserves to be knighted for her contribution to greater understanding of Italian cooking, teaches a few courses out of her rooftop kitchen in Venezia, limited to six lucky students per session. All the wisdom that went into Marcella's best-selling books will be yours for a week of personal, loosely structured, hands-on lessons from one of the best cooking teachers in Italy. Since demand exceeds available space, reservations are accepted two years in advance, but this course is well worth the wait. Marcella's kitchen, in a sixteenth-century palace, is a work of art and a tribute to Italian craftsmanship.

Fulvia Sesani
Castello 6140
Venezia
Tel. 041/29823

Fulvia Sesani, a kind of Venetian Martha Stewart, teaches food for entertaining out of her patrician palace. The oval dining room, the table settings of heirlooms, the comfortable terrace overlooking a canal, are impressive. Fulvia's high-tech home kitchen is equipped with everything, a collection that she's amassed in her world travels.

HOUSEWARES

If you enjoy cooking or eating Italian, you're probably interested in the special tools used to prepare or serve regional food. Most are sold in tempting shops known as *casalinghi,* "domestic goods" emporiums: combination houseware-hardware stores with stocks of soap, wax, paint, mothballs, plastics, cooking utensils, storage containers, glassware, picnic equipment, and more—a vast array of wares for the house displayed in an almost overwhelming wall of floor-to-ceiling open shelves in an invariably tiny shop with barely enough room to turn around in. They always seem to have everything, sometimes even a choice of different models of a wide selection of household items, some unique to Italy. Housewares sections in department stores seem to have a less extensive selection but better prices at times, with self-service displays that simplify shopping, and they accept credit cards. In the neighborhood shops you'll have to ask for or point to what you want, and pay in cash. Most outdoor markets have at least one housewares stand, with a limited but interesting selection of necessities, reasonably priced.

The section devoted to coffee and its accessories in a *casalinghi* or department store will be large. The classic coffee maker, *la macchinetta,* is a three-part traditional home espresso pot, and comes in sizes from 1 to 22 espresso cups. All parts are replaceable, from the *filtro* (filter,) *manico* (handle), *contenitore per il caffè* (the part that holds the coffee), to the *guarnizione* (rubber gasket that holds the filter in place). An un-

Larger-than-life housewares
from a shop in Milan

usual accessory sold for the *macchinetta* is called *il rompigetto;* a shower-cap-like device, it fits inside the top section, where the coffee bubbles out, to prevent spattering. The Neapolitan-style coffee maker, *la napoletana,* makes drip espresso coffee (water is boiled in the bottom section, the pot is turned over, and the water filters through coffee) and is the choice of some purists. It is sold in sizes from 1 to 20 espresso cups, although the larger sizes are hard to find.

Parmigiano fans may be on the lookout for the special knife, *coltello per parmigiano,* with its short teardrop-shaped blade—not for cutting or slicing but for breaking off a chunk of the cheese. The *gratella* or *griglia* is a rectangular cast-iron pan with a ridged surface for stovetop grilling of vegetables, meat, poultry, and fish; a personal favorite, this is a tool I wouldn't like to be without. The most practical cheese grater, *grattugia,* will have a section to collect the grated cheese. The rolling pin *(mattarello)* with zero, one, or two handles, depending on use and local custom, has no moving parts. The long-handled pins are for pasta making, the short ones for shaping pizza dough. Some cooks wonder how they ever lived without the *mezzaluna,* a crescent-shaped double-handled rocking knife, used by practically every Italian housewife. Chestnuts can be roasted over a stovetop burner in the *padella per castagne* (chestnut-roasting pan), which looks like a long-handled frying pan with holes in the bottom. The *piastra di terracotta refrattaria* (terracotta pizza stone) simulates an Italian brick pizza oven in your own home oven. Most shops have a large selection of sifters *(setaccio),* with circular bentwood frames, metal mesh screens, and no moving parts. The screen comes in different gauges, including a silk screen for sifting ultra-fine flour. Probably my favorite Italian utensil is the *tostapane,* a cordless Italian toaster. It consists of a hole-punctured stainless steel square topped with a wire grid screen, and a U-shaped metal handle (no moving parts). It's used for toasting bread of any thickness over a gas flame, an essential tool in the preparation of *fettunta,* Tuscan garlic bread, always on the menu in my kitchen.

THE NEWSSTAND

A daily visit to the neighborhood *edicola* (newsstand) is a must for most Italians, who are avid readers of periodicals on a vast range of subjects. Food and wine magazines abound, each with its own gastronomic statement, from everyday home style to elaborate productions. They are fun to look through even if you don't read Italian. *Cucina Italiana* is the most traditional, and the best selling, of the food magazines. Its tone is classic, practical, not too well informed about wine, and boring. The photography is nothing to drool over. *Nuova Cucina* is "directed," it says on the cover, by actor–amateur chef Ugo Tognazzi. The photography is well done and the recipes usually work, but they always seem to be plugging some sponsor's product. *Grand Gourmet,* with its large-size format, glossy

"GOOD MEMORY PLATES"
·

Collectors of gastronomic memorabilia may be interested in the *Unione Ristoranti del Buon Ricordo.* Sponsored by the Touring Club Italiano, an automobile club serving the motorist, this association was created in 1964 to stimulate an interest in traditional foods. Each member restaurant features a regional specialty, and clients ordering this dish are given a hand-painted ceramic *Piatto del Buon Ricordo* (literally "Good Memory Plate") as a souvenir of the meal. The name and locality of each restaurant is printed around the circumference of the plate, and a drawing representing the specialty or relating to the restaurant decorates the center. Over two hundred different plates have been issued. Some members have dropped out, closed, or changed specialty, and collecting and trading the memento plates from the past or from the ninety-eight current members has become a pastime, like gastronomic stamp collecting. The hardest to find, from the Taverna della Giarrettiera in Milano, in production for only one year, may sell for more than $1,000. The *Collezionisti di Piatti del Buon Ricordo,* a club in Torino with a membership of over 5,000 collectors, can track down hard-to-find memento plates, and plate vendors and traders can often be found outside food and wine shows, swapping away. Some of the *Ristoranti del Buon Ricordo* are among my favorites, most serve above-average food, but some are inexcusably inferior and deserve to be kicked off their plates.

paper, and high price, has a nouvelle outlook and little to do with traditional Italian foods (no wonder, since the original edition is from Germany). The wine coverage is great, but the food styling is carried to extremes. Can a food magazine that makes a Rubik's

THE PROVINCIAL FEAST

∎

Adventurers curious about local cooking should attend a feast, called a *sagra*. For every regional, seasonal specialty in Italy, there is probably a feast somewhere to honor it: Winter festivals feature wild boar, sausage, truffles, and chestnuts and chestnut desserts; in spring homage is given to the strawberry, cherry, asparagus, and artichoke; summer festivals honor melons, peaches, hazelnuts; and in the fall freshly made olive oil, mushrooms, garlic bread, and the grape harvest are celebrated. Some feasts aren't tied to any specific season, but exist to heap praise on fried fish, snails, frogs, chickens, pasta, polenta, or whatever strikes the fancy of local residents. To recognize a feast in the making, look for signs posted on provincial roads, or festoons over the roadway, with the name of the town, the designated honoree, and the dates, usually two or three days that include a weekend. There will probably be music on Saturday night. It's considered bad luck not to stop for a *sagra del vino,* a wine festival. Food may range from inexcusable to sublime, with local volunteers dishing out plastic plates of overcooked flavorless greasy pasta; pink and green crescents of sun-ripened watermelon; crunchy fried whitebait, which look like guppies, served in a paper cone that absorbs the excess oil; or a three-course dinner with wine, all costing next to nothing. To connect with this bounty you may need to use the *scontrino* system, paying a cashier for a slip of paper which is then presented to the people dispensing the meal. You may pay a blanket fee to get into an area where each family unit fends for itself, its members standing on various lines and reserving places at the long communal tables. Observe the locals and act accordingly.

Cube out of mixed vegetables, or that weaves pasta, or that calls for a small glass of blood as a sauce ingredient be taken seriously? *Sale e Pepe* could use a better food stylist, wine consultant, and graphic artist. But in spite of these drawbacks, the content of the magazine is good, the articles interesting, the recipes inviting, easy to follow, and simple to prepare, and the travel feature, *"Viaggiare da buongustai,"* is filled with useful information. *La Gola* is beautifully presented, heavy on intellectual analysis, studded with an interesting selection of reproductions and photographs, and oriented toward literary gastronomes and book collectors. No recipes, food styling, or restaurant reviews, but the wine and cheese columns are terrific. *A Tavola,* a new monthly of "taste, flavors, invitations and encounters," features an attractive format and fine photography, in-depth restaurant coverage, and articles on a wide range of topics from table linens and flower arrangements to kitchen design and housewares. The entertainment articles feature lifestyles of the Italian rich and famous. The recipes, grouped in the back of the magazine, are clearly presented and range from simple to ultra-complex. *Etichetta* is a stylish, slick forum for photographers to present a visual image of "the material things according to Luigi Veronelli," a noted gastronome and wine expert. It also features new chefs, gifts, tableware, traditional products like saffron, goose sausage, *mostarda,* and regional travel—all from Luigi Veronelli's apparently sexist point of view, not always in the best of taste. The format is large, the glossy full-color photography is beautiful, the magazine is expensive, and the recipes are bare sketches—interesting, but not for the beginner. The female mouth seems to play an important role on this quarterly's covers.

REGION
BY
REGION

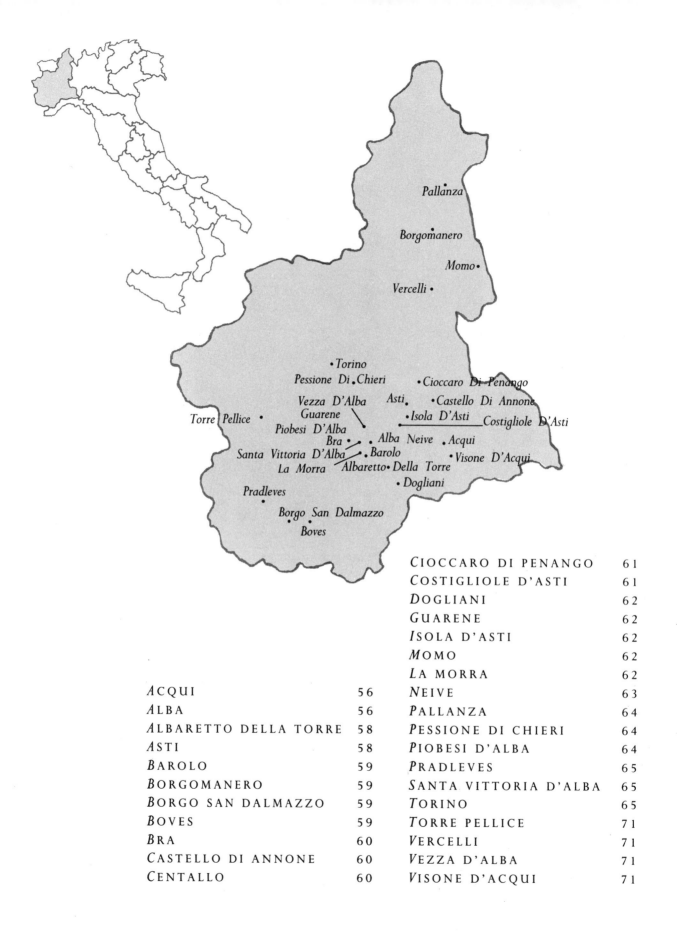

PIEMONTE

The northwest corner of Italy, Piemonte (from *pie,* "foot," and *monte,* "mountains") is separated from France by the Alps and from Liguria by the Apennines, which slope into hills as they stretch east to the alluvial plains of the Po Valley. Ruled by the Roman Empire and then the medieval Longobards and Franks, split into dukedoms, earldoms, and marquisates, bound to the royal House of Savoy in 1045, Piemonte expanded and contracted with the political power plays and trades of European nobility. French was the language, and France the primary influence.

Hot summers, cold winters, and lots of fog make up the climate necessary for this unique *cucina.* For the Piemontesi, dining seems more a procession than a meal. The traditional appetizers of marinated meats, vegetables, and mushrooms change with the seasons and may seem like a meal in themselves. *Bagna caoda,* available only in winter, is a variety of raw vegetables dipped in a "hot bath" of oil, anchovies, and garlic in a ceramic fondue-type arrangement. *Fritto misto* here consists of deep-fried meats, poultry, vegetables, fruit, and fritters.

The first course might be *agnolotti* (pasta stuffed with meat, egg, and cheese), or shoelace-size, irregularly cut *tajarin* pasta, simply sauced; or *risotto* made with rice from the lowlands, flavored with seasonal vegetables.

Meats are stewed in rich red wines.

Accompanying these full-flavored dishes are some of Italy's finest red wines, hearty and spirited to drink young, or complex, intense, and elegant with aging.

Traditional sweets feature a rich-tasting hazelnut in simple cookies, *torrone* (a honey-and-egg-white candy), and cake often accompanied by *zabaione.*

White truffles from other regions are a treat, but they will never touch the glory of those born under a cold moon in Piemonte. They are sold almost furtively in the markets at dawn—whole and in pieces, from marble- to baseball-size. Piemontese truffles are intensely scented, intoxicating, allegedly aphrodisiac, and addictive I'm sure—why else would one sniff of their unmistakable odor set me to scheming for a trip to Piemonte?

THE MENU

SALUMI

■

Salame al Barolo or *Salsicce al barolo* · pork and veal, marinated in rich red Barolo wine, spiced, and cured

Salamin d'la duja · soft mild salami, preserved in lard in a terracotta pot *(duja)*

ANTIPASTO

■

Bagna caoda or *calda* · raw vegetables dipped in a "hot bath" of olive oil, anchovies, and garlic. A winter-only appetizer that can also be a main course.

Capunet · small, finger-size stuffed cabbage leaves. In the summer, zucchini flowers are used instead of cabbage.

Insalata di carne cruda · a ground lean beef marinated with oil and lemon, topped with truffles in season

Insalata di pollo · chicken salad dressed in oil, lemon, and truffles

Vitello tonnato · roast veal with a tuna sauce

Antipasto Piemontese · marathon of appetizers, usually including all of the above plus salami, sausage, and marinated vegetables—a meal in itself

PRIMO

■

Agnolotti or *Agnellotti* · meat-stuffed miniature ravioli

Aia or *Agliata* · ribbon pasta with walnut garlic sauce

Cisrà · chick-pea soup

Fonduta · Fontina-based cheese fondue, served over toast or as a sauce, topped with truffles in season

Gnocchi di patate · potato gnocchi

Panissa or *Paniscia* · a *risotto* with beans

Polenta cunsa · polenta sautéed in butter with cheese

Ris an cagnon · soup with rice and Fontina cheese

Risotto alla Piemontese · simple *risotto,* with onions, butter, and cheese

Tajarin · homemade egg noodles

Tofeja · bean and pork rind soup

Zuppa canavesana · turnip soup garnished with gratinéed bread and cheese

SECONDO

■

Anatra farcita · duck stuffed with rice and sausage

Bollito misto · mixed boiled meats; served with *bagnet,* a green or red sauce

Brasato al barolo · beef braised in Barolo wine

Camoscio alla Piemontese · chamois stew

Finanziera · a stew of leftover meat, chicken livers, and sweetbreads; favored by the high-finance wizards of the 1800s

Fritto misto or *Fricia* · intricate progression of deep-fried foods: lamb chops, chicken, sausage, sweetbreads, brains, zucchini, eggplant, zucchini flowers, mushrooms, cubes of sweet semolina, peaches, and almond cookies

Lepre al sivè · wild hare, marinated in red wine and stewed

Puccia · stewed cabbage and pork, mixed with polenta and served with Parmesan. The next day, may be cut into slices and fried.

Tapulon or *Tapulone* · mule or donkey, stewed with wine and spices

CONTORNO

■

Cipolle ripiene ▪ baked onions
stuffed with cheese

Funghi ▪ mushrooms, served
grilled, stewed, or as a salad

FORMAGGIO

■

Bross ▪ bits of leftover cheese,
mashed and marinated in
grappa

Castelmagno ▪ unique, pungent,
rare

Formaggetta ▪ small, soft, tasty
white round, made from a
mixture of cow's and ewe's
milk

Raschera ▪ hearty, smooth

Ricotta ▪ soft, mild fresh cheese
made from whey, at its best
when freshly made

Robiola ▪ soft, creamy, rich,
delicate; from cow's or ewe's
milk

Tome ▪ smooth, firm

DOLCE

■

Amaretti ▪ almond cookies made
from regular (sweet) almonds
and a few bitter ones

Baci di dama ▪ chocolate-covered
almond cookies

Bonet ▪ custard pudding
containing chocolate, rum,
and *amaretti.*

Crumiri ▪ polenta butter cookies

Panna cotta ▪ rich, elegant
reduced cream sauce with
burnt-sugar topping. Makes
crème caramel seem like diet
food.

Pere (or Ciliege) al Barolo ▪ pears
or cherries cooked in Barolo
wine

Torta di nocciole ▪ hazelnut cake

Zabaione ▪ egg yolks whipped
with sugar and Marsala until
thick and golden, served with
dry cookies or as a dessert
sauce; named for San Giovanni
Bayon, patron saint of pastry
chefs, venerated in Torino at
the church of San Tommaso

THE *W*INE LIST

Most Piemontese wines are made with grapes found only in this region. Arneis, Dolcetto, Freisa, Grignolino, but most of all Nebbiolo grapes are frequently grown on small single-owner plots, and transformed into some of Italy's finest wines. Barolo and Barbaresco, ample and elegant, get most of the attention, but Barbera and Dolcetto are perfect for everyday drinking and stand up well to the gutsy, flavorful regional foods. Don't forget to end your meal with a glass of Moscato d'Asti, a delicate, barely alcoholic dessert wine that tastes like a combination of flowers and fruit.

Arneis dei Roeri, a soft, dry white, is best with fish and seafood. Top producers are Castello di Neive, Cornarea, Bruno Giacosa, Malvirà, Vietti, and Ceretto, who calls his Arneis, with its distinctive cutout label, "Blangè."

Barbaresco is one of Italy's truly great wines, a dramatic, elegant dry red. Made from the Nebbiolo grape and aged for at least two years—four for a *riserva*—Barbaresco is at its best after four to eight years, served with roast meat and fowl. The following fine producers make some special single-vineyard wines (listed in parentheses): Cantina del Glicine (Marcorino), Castello di Neive (Santo Stefano), Ceretto (Bricco Asili and Asij), Gaja (Costa Russi, Sori San Lorenzo, Sori Tildin), Bruno Giacosa (Santo Stefano), I Paglieri (Crichet Pajè), Marchesi di Gresy (Camp Gros), Produttori di Barbaresco, Prunotto (Montestefano), Vietti (Rocche di Castiglione Falletto).

Barbera, a rustic, hearty dry red, not intended for aging, is made in many areas of Piemonte. Drink this high-spirited wine with meat and fowl. Braida's Barbera, called La Monella, is a personal favorite.

Barbera d'Alba, a rich, smooth dry red, is made from Barbera grapes in the area outside Alba, and is paired with meat and fowl. The following top producers make Barbera d'Alba and special single-vineyard wines (listed in parentheses): Cantina del Glicine (Curà), Castello di Neive, Ceretto (Piana Brunate), Aldo Conterno, Giacomo Conterno, Clerico, Fratelli Cigliutti (Serraboella), Giacosa, Gaja (Vignarey), Podere Rocche dei Manzoni, Prunotto, Renato Ratti, Vietti.

Barbera d'Asti, a full, dry red, is made in the area outside Asti by top producers Scarpa and Rivetti.

Barolo, ruby colored, complex, rich, and long-lived, is called "the king of wine and the wine of kings" by the Piemontese. Made from the Nebbiolo grape, aged at least three years and at its best after eight, Barolo is served with meat, fowl, and game. The following quality producers also make special single-vineyard wines (listed in parentheses): Ceretto (Bricco Rocche, Brunate, Prapò, and Zonchera), Clerico (Ciabot Ginestra), Aldo Conterno (Bricco Bussia), Giacomo Conterno (Monfortino), Paolo Cordero di Montezemolo (Monfalletto), Bruno Giacosa (Collina Rionda), Mascarello (Monprivato), Bartolo Mascarello, Prunotto (Cannubi), Vietti (Bussia).

Brachetto d'Acqui is a light, sparkling semi-sweet red wine made from the Brachetto grape, served with *salumi* and desserts. At its best when produced by Braida and Villa Banfi.

Cortese di Gavi, also known as *Gavi,* is a rich, dry white made from the Cortese grape near the village of Gavi. It is a perfect companion to fish and seafood in all forms. Top producers are La Battistina, La Chiara, La Giustiana, La Scolca, and Tenuta San Pietro.

Dolcetto, made from the Dolcetto grape and, in spite of its name (which seems to imply sweetness), is a dry, fruity red. It is made in seven different DOC areas, often paired with fowl and hearty regional cooking.

Dolcetto d'Alba is a balanced, grapey, dry red. The following quality producers make Dolcetto as well as special single-vineyard wines (listed in parentheses): Castello di Neive (Basarin), Ceretto (Rossana and Vigna), Aldo Conterno (Cascina Favot), Paolo Cordero di Montezemolo (Monfalletto), Dogliotti (Campo Rosso), Gaja (Vignabajla), Bruno Giacosa (Basarin), I Paglieri, Marchesi di Gresy (Monte Aribaldo), Podere Rocche dei Manzoni, Renato Ratti (Colombè), Luciano Sandrone, Vietti (Bussia and Castelletto), Roberto Voerzio.

The pride and joy of a well-made wine

Dolcetto di Diano d'Alba is a balanced dry red, best made by La Porta Rossa.

Dolcetto di Dogliani is a well-balanced dry red made from three different vineyards of Chionetti (Briccolero, San Luigi, and La Costa).

Dolcetto di Ovada is a dry red of quality as produced by Dott. Pino Ratto (Vigneti Scarsi).

Freisa is a ruby-red still or slightly sparkling wine made from the local Freisa grape, and is served with poultry or hearty regional dishes. Top producers include Fratelli Cigliutti, Aldo Conterno, Dogliotti, Gaja, Scarpa, and Vietti.

Gattinara is an ample dry red made mostly from Nebbiolo grapes near the village of Gattinara, and served with roast and sauced meat, fowl, and game. Quality wines are produced by Antoniolo.

Grignolino d'Asti, made from the local Grignolino grape, is a delicate, pale-colored, dry red, to be drunk young and fresh, at the beginning of a meal. Quality wines are produced by Braida, Bruno Giacosa, Incisa della Rocchetta, Rivetti, and Scarpa.

Moscato d'Asti is a delicate, slightly sparkling, floral-scented white wine, a perfect accompaniment to fruit, dessert, or cookies, especially when made by Bera,

Rivetti, Dogliotti, I Vignaioli di Santo Stefano, Saracco, and Vietti.

Nebbiolo d'Alba is a full, dry red made from the local Nebbiolo grape, served with roasted and grilled meats, poultry, and cheese dishes. Quality producers, who also make single-vineyard wines (listed in parentheses) include: Ceretto (Lantasco), Gaja (Vignaveja), Bruno Giacosa (Valmaggiore), Malvirà, Marchesi di Gresy, Mascarello and Figlio (San Rocco), Prunotto (Ochetti), Vietti (San Michele).

Roero is a newly created DOC from the same growing area as Nebbiolo d'Alba. An ample, dry red, it is best made by Malvirà, Prunotto, and many of the Nebbiolo d'Alba producers.

Spumante, sparkling wines of high quality, some made according to *méthode champenoise*, are produced in Piemonte. Marone Pas Dosè is made by Cinzano; Banfi Brut is made by Villa Banfi; Bruno Giacosa Extra Brut is made by Bruno Giacosa; Riserva Privata Angelo Riccadonna is made by Riccadonna; Gran Cuvé Carlo Gancia and Crémant Riserva Vallarino Gancia are made by Fratelli Gancia; Contratto Brut and Riserva Novecento are made by Contratto; Riserva Montelera is made by Martini & Rossi; and Valentino Brut is made by Podere Rocche dei Manzoni.

Exemplary reds and whites classified as **vino da tavola** are made by some of Piemonte's finest winemakers. Rich red **Bricco dell' Uccellone** is produced by larger-than-life Giacomo Bologna. Chardonnay **Gaia & Rey,** an elegant white, and **Darmagi,** a rich, full red cabernet, are both made by Angelo Gaja, Piemonte's leading winemaker. **Opera Prima,** a ripe, elegant red, is made by I Paglieri. **Bricco Manzoni,** a deep red, is made by Podere Rocche dei Manzoni. **Villa Pattono,** a rich red aged in wood, is made by Renato Ratti.

REGIONAL SPECIALTIES

HAZELNUTS

The *tonda gentile della Langa*—the round gentle hazelnut of the Langhe region—is unique: rich, intense, smoky, with a skin that slips off more easily after roasting than the skin of regular hazelnuts. These special local hazelnuts appear in many sweets—combined with chocolate in *giandujotti,* suspended in honey and meringue *torrone,* or ground in the heady *torta di nocciole* (hazelnut cake), a world-class dessert when prepared with the *tonda gentile.*

For sources of *torta di nocciole,* see page 62; for *torrone,* see page 71.

CHESTNUTS

Although both *marroni* and *castagne* are called "chestnuts" in English, they are not the same. Fans of what was once known as "poor man's bread" (an accessible form of protein in the diet of poor Piemontese farmers) can easily tell the difference. *Castagne* grow inside a green, sea-urchin-like spiked husk, which always contains an odd number of chestnuts (either three, five or seven), each with one flat surface. *Marroni* always contain three nuts in each husk, but two of them atrophy and the remaining fruit fills the entire space, resulting in a rounder, bean-shaped chestnut. *Marroni* are richer, more flavorful, and are a specialty of the Val Susa, outside Torino. They are preserved in sugar syrup and made into *marrons glacés,* a local invention in spite of its French name (most of France's *marrons glacés* come from Piemonte or Campania, in the south). Chestnuts were traditionally preserved in the cellar under sand or in the woods under a pile of chestnut husks; or they were slightly fermented in water for nine days to enrich their flavor, then stored in stone grottoes.

For the best in *marroni,* see page 59.

TRUFFLES

The *tartufo* is a fungus that grows four to six inches below ground in parasitical symbiosis with the roots of walnut, oak, poplar, chestnut, hazelnut, and willow trees. Supposedly the harder the wood of the tree, the better and more intense the truffle's perfume. There are two distinct kinds of truffles. *Tuber melanosporum,* the black truffle, is found from December through March in much of Italy. It is usually served cooked and is almost tasteless. The black truffle owes its reputation to its kinship with the higher-priced, highly scented *Tuber magnatum,* the white truffle, which is found from late September through January in northern and central Italy. Pungent, gassy-scented, intense and haunting, it is at its best in Piemonte, fresh out of the ground, shaved on a special truffle slicer. The white truffle reaches stratospheric gastronomic heights when combined with eggs.

The search for white truffles involves stealth and secrecy. Selectively bred hounds help their masters find up to five pounds of truffles in an evening. This bounty is sold by the gram (at over $1,000 a pound), almost furtively, wrapped in wrinkled handkerchiefs or paper towels, at dawn in the markets in Nizza Monferrato, Canelli, Asti, and Alba, a cash-only ritual with its own style and pace, conducted in dialect. Unscrupulous truffle vendors will fill in wormholes, adding grams of high-priced dirt, or will toothpick together a broken truffle.

The largest truffle market takes place in Alba (see page 56).

CHOCOLATES

Piemonte is a region that takes its chocolate seriously. Locals don't let you forget that they were the chocolatiers of the royal House of Savoy, and that the Swiss came to Torino to learn the arts of blending, roasting, tempering, and forging the exotic import from the New World. Chocolates are frequently sold by the piece, and gift boxes are assembled according to the whim of the buyer. Chocolate hazelnut creams (*giandujotti*) are the specialty of Torino, but local *grappa*, *marroni* chestnuts, walnuts, and other natural ingredients flavor rectangles, leaves, truffles, barrels, hearts, shells, and snails of glossy dark or light brown chocolates.

Peyrano (page 68) makes sublime chocolates.

GIANDUJA: THE MARRIAGE OF CHOCOLATE AND HAZELNUT

How typical of the practical Piemontese to combine the expensive, exotic, imported cocoa bean with the smoky local hazelnut, cheap and abundant. The bitter intensity of chocolate is tempered by the nutty richness of the hazelnut, for a taste far more complex than the wimpy Swiss invention, milk chocolate. Almost all the great Torinese chocolate makers produce *giandujotti*, chocolate hazelnut creams, made with ground hazelnuts, sugar, and chocolate. With a slightly sticky texture, like peanut butter, this confection is piped (not molded) into traditional chubby wedge shapes and individually wrapped in foil.

Peyrano (see page 68) and Caffarel produce excellent *giandujotti*.

Many chocolatiers also make a soft chocolate hazelnut spread, *crema gianduja*, a Piemontese response to peanut butter and jelly, which is applied in a thick layer on freshly made bread—a taste trio of nuts, chocolate, and bread that isn't taken as seriously as it should be. See page 57 for the world's largest producer of chocolate hazelnut spread.

VERMOUTH

Vermouth has been a Piemontese tradition since the 1700s, created by a type of shop no longer in existence—a cross between the candy maker, bar-caffè, and pharmacy. Each store had its own special recipe, blending herbs, spices, and wine. In the 1800s vermouth became a commercial product, no longer artisanal but made in quantity by companies using traditional formulas of herbs, spices, roots, and barks (especially absinthe, or wormwood) infused in a neutral, nonaromatic wine and sweetened with sugar. The so-called medicinal function of vermouth was to prepare the stomach for the onslaught of a meal, a digestive call-to-arms. The classic vermouth, either white or red, is consumed before lunch or dinner: *liscio* (neat), *con ghiaccio* (on the rocks), with a splash of *seltz* (soda water) and *con una scorza di limone* (a twist of lemon peel).

To visit the Cinzano cellars or the Martini & Rossi museum, see pages 65 and 64.

GRISSINI

Yard-long breadsticks—gold and tan, hand-rolled and slightly knobby, sprinkled with pale semolina—frequently form the centerpiece of the Piemontese table setting. These are *grissini*, slim, featherweight, and all crunch. According to a recent conference on the history and nutritional value of this illustrious form of bread, in 1668 the Savoia court doctor, Don Baldo Pecchio, had the court baker whip up some crunchy, thin, and easily digestible breadsticks for the sickly Prince Vittorio Amadeo II, who suffered from "intestinal fevers." He ate his *grissini*, "miraculously" recovered, and went on to govern as the first Savoyard king.

The packaged commercial breadsticks found in other regions of Italy are barely related to the glorious fresh *grissini* of Piemonte. At least twice the length of breadsticks found in other regions, they are served whole, tied in a bundle with a napkin, or simply placed on the tablecloth. They also appear in unlabeled waxed-paper envelopes.

See pages 58 and 59 for fine *grissini*.

TERRACOTTA BEAN POTS

Tofeja, the elliptical terracotta clay bean pot, is one of the last vestiges of the Piemontese traditional crafts, still made in Castellemonte, north of Torino. The pots can be found at the exciting Porta Palazzo market in Torino. Artisanal and semi-industrial models can be found at La Mezzaluna in Torino (see page 70) and at most housewares stores in the region.

THE SILVERSMITHS OF SAVOY

Piemonte is a region of contrasts, from the poverty of Cesare Pavese's *The Moon and the Bonfire* to the splendor of the Savoy palace. The tradition of court artisan has almost completely disappeared, but Piemonte is still an important center for crafted silver. Moving into the twenty-first century, some companies have chosen to work with silverplate, or even stainless steel, combining technology with tradition. Design may range from Piemontese baroque to Milanese postmodern, but the emphasis is on quality.

For a variety of crafts, see below and page 71.

CITIES AND TOWNS

ACQUI

TABLEWARE
Ricci Argentieri
219 Corso Acqui
Tel. 0144/345912

Ricci Argentieri's classic designs in silver and silverplate tableware are found throughout Italy. For more information, contact the office in Acqui.

ALBA

Nestled in the valley of the Tanaro river, amid grapevine-covered hillsides parceled into single-owner plots, Alba is a charming town of medieval towers, medieval pageantry, and a sunset that stretches to the Alps.

INN
Cascina Reiné
Località Altavilla 9
Tel. 0173/42119
No credit cards
Price: inexpensive

Too good to be true is the only way to describe Cascina Reiné, a villa in the hills overlooking the city of Alba and the Tanaro Valley, and on a clear day, with a view of the Alps. Signora Giuliana Pionzo has opened a part of her home—three rooms, each with private bath, and one two-bedroom apartment—and her guests are in for a real treat of country-style hospitality on this working farm. An ample American-style breakfast is included. Reserve in advance and Signora Pionzo will prepare a meal for you, of her own farm-fresh poultry, fruit, and vegetables, and even homemade *gelato*.

BAR-CAFFÈ
Caffè Calissano
Piazza Risorgimento 3
Tel. 0173/43955
Closed Wednesday

The Caffè Calissano is a place to spend time in, for people-watching and for enjoying the decor of marble, brocade, and lace. The bar dates from the turn of the century, and there is a back room with sofas, a fireplace, and frescoed ceilings. The pastry and *gelato* are first-rate, and the selection of *grappa* and wine is impressive.

TRUFFLES
Piemonte's largest truffle market, and the most accessible to the nonprofessional, non-Piemontese buyer, takes place on Saturdays in October, November, and December, along via Maestra or via V. Emanuele, under the arcade, and in Palazzo Maddalena.

PASTRY
Pettiti
Via Vittorio Emanuele 25
Tel. 0173/49818
Closed Monday

Pettiti, the classic *pasticceria* in Alba, makes quality baked goods. The elegant bar, with its turn-of-the-century fixtures, is perfect for a quick coffee and pastry.

PASTRY
io . . . tu . . . e i dolci
Piazza Savona 12
Tel. 0173/497038
Closed Monday

"You and I and the desserts" is the name of Beppe Scavina's *pasticceria,* and it reflects his point of view. Beppe is involved with each item that comes out of his minute kitchen, and he practically custom-makes desserts for his clients. The cakes are meant to be eaten and aren't excessively decorated, although some of Beppe's more unusual custom Easter eggs and special orders are fanciful and imaginative. *Torrone, albesi,* chocolate hazelnut truffles, and chocolate-covered *goffi* ("clumsies") are all delicious. Beppe's enthusiasm for life is expressed in his desserts and in his attire—so don't be surprised if you find him behind the counter sporting a bow tie made of mirror or marble, or a skirt, or a pair of transparent nylon pants.

HAZELNUT CREAM
Ferrero
Piazza Ferrero 1
Tel. 0173/3131

Ferrero is the world's largest producer of chocolate hazelnut cream spread; Italy accounts for half their total yearly output (55,000,000 pounds) of Nutella, probably the most popular snack for school-age children. Not all their hazelnuts are local, and Nutella also contains powdered skimmed milk, cocoa, palm oil, and emulsifiers. It's kids' stuff and doesn't have much appeal for post-adolescent palates, but isn't too bad warmed up with a shot of rum and served over ice cream. To visit the factory, a hygienic high-tech production-line behemoth, write to Dott. Stalianò, c/o Ferrero, Pino Torrinese 10025, for an appointment.

WINE
Il Crutin
Via Cuneo 3
Tel. 0173/39239
Closed Monday

Il Crutin, "the wine cellar" in Piemontese dialect, has a vast assortment of local wines, grappa, and distillates, and quality regional products. Wine tastings can be arranged.

Who could resist this mouth-watering display at the bar?

RESTAURANT
Osteria dell'Arco
Vicolo dell'Arco
Tel. 0173/363974
Closed Sunday
Credit cards: American Express
Price: low moderate

Osteria dell'Arco has white stucco walls, archways, and is decorated with beautiful color photographs of the graceful local countryside. The menu is limited (not particularly regional) and changes daily. Pasta and desserts are homemade, portions are generous, the ambience is informal, and the wine list, of regional Piemontese and Italian offerings, is formidable for a restaurant of this size. Alberto Gallizio will make you feel welcome.

RESTAURANT
Vigin Mudest
Via Giacosa 4
Tel. 0173/43921
Closed Monday and August
No credit cards
Price: low moderate

Vigin Mudest serves traditional, predictable Piemontese *cucina.* But the listing, printed in red at the bottom of the menu, for their *an-*

tipasti misti freddi doesn't convey the excitement of fifteen different offerings of cold marinated salads, meats, vegetables, cheeses, and egg dishes. The locals always seem to be enjoying the homemade pasta, hearty meat and game dishes, and house desserts, but I have never been able to get past the *antipasto*. In season, truffles are served over fresh pasta—priced, according to a cardboard sign, by the grating, or *grattata*. The wine list offers some gems under the heading "Others" (*Altri*).

ALBARETTO DELLA TORRE

HOTEL
Albergo Bellavista
Via Umberto I 10
Bossolasco (close by)
Tel. 0173/793102
No credit cards
Price: moderate

RESTAURANT
Da Cesare
Via Umberto 12
Tel. 0173/520141
Closed Tuesday, Wednesday, January, and August
No credit cards
Price: expensive to very expensive

Da Cesare is the gastronomic version of a one-man band. Although wife Silvana, daughter Elisa, and son Filippo all work in the dining room, the heart and soul of this restaurant is Cesare Giaccone. His eyes light up when he discusses his food, a moody vision of re-gional dishes, at times inspired, at times bizarre, created with the finest local ingredients, extrava-gantly presented on large leaf-covered trays, but not decorated or fussed with. Hiding behind a huge, handsome, chestnut-colored mustache but cooking in sight of some diners through the glass kitchen door, Cesare skillfully pre-pares a personal, masculine *cucina*. Meats are roasted whole on a spit in the fireplace, or in a bread crust, or wrapped in foil, then surrounded by a layer of earth and baked. Woodsy mush-rooms, truffles, and game appear in season, and the pasta is hand-rolled and delicate. The hand-whisked *zabaione* is a poem in body language, a thrill to watch and taste, especially with the plate-size buttery hazelnut cookie. Ex-cited hoards of noisy German and Swiss gastronomic tourists flock to Da Cesare during truffle season, and you may be hard-pressed to hear a word of Italian. But I'd risk it for a taste of Cesare's *cucina*. The wine selection is splendid.

ASTI

Asti is a pleasant city featuring medieval monuments and in Sep-tember, a historic procession dat-ing from 1275, a horse race, and a wine fair called the *Douja d'or*.

HOTEL
Palio
Via Cavour 106
Tel. 0141/34371
Credit cards: all
Price: moderate

BREAD
Panetteria Gianchello
Corso Savona 104
Tel. 0141/53513
Closed Thursday afternoon

These beautiful, golden, irregu-larly shaped, slender, tasty hand-rolled *grissini*, a specialty of Panetteria Gianchello, are irresis-tible.

RESTAURANT
Gener Neuv
Lungo Tanaro 4
Tel. 0141/57270
Closed Sunday night, Monday, and August
Credit cards: American Express, Diners Club, Visa
Price: expensive

It seems that some of the greatest expressions of traditional *cucina Piemontese* are turned out by women, and Gener Neuv is a clas-sic example. The success of this fantastic restaurant is due to the hard work of the Fassi family—Piero offering selections from a splendid wine list to go with the *cucina* of his wife, Giuseppina, and daughters Maura and Maria Luisa. Local ingredients are wisely com-bined, perfectly executed, and simply placed on the plate. I can't imagine a better *finanziera* (lightly stewed cockscombs, sweetbreads, and mushrooms), and the rabbit dishes are exceptional. During their glorious season, Piero skill-fully slices wafers of intensely per-fumed truffles with abandon. Save room for a taste of ripe regional cheeses paired with intense Pie-montese red wines, and don't skip the dessert plate, decorated with a cocoa-dusted stencil of the res-taurant's logo, a cavalier.

BAROLO

BREAD
Panettiere Cravero
Piazza Castello 3
Tel. 0173/56134
Closed Sunday afternoon and
*   Thursday*

Panetteria Cravero, across the street from the castello di Barolo, makes splendid hand-rolled *grissini* and also sells an incredible goat's milk *robiola* cheese.

MEAT
Macelleria Canonica Pier Carlo
Via Roma 43
Tel. 0173/56131
Closed Sunday afternoon and
*   Monday*

Rosanna and Pier Carlo Canonica sell quality meats in their tidy butcher shop, and they make their own sausage and salami, a zesty blend of garlic, spices, pork, and veal, marinated in son Giovanni's Barolo wine. This is an example of the creative Piemontese *cucina,* combining local ingredients, mundane and sublime, to produce an improved version of a familiar food, in this case salami and sausage.

BORGOMANERO

HOTEL
Albergo San Rocco
Orta San Giulio,
Lago d'Orta (close by)
Tel. 0322/90222
Closed November through
*   February*
Credit cards: all
Price: low expensive

RESTAURANT
Ristorante Pinocchio
Via Matteotti 147
Tel. 0322/82273
Closed Monday
Credit cards: all
Price: expensive

Ristorante Pinocchio, once a place to go for a family outing, almost impossible for non-natives to find, seems to be suffering from delusions of nouvelle cuisine. Two different *degustazione,* each for a minimum of two diners, and selections from the somewhat fancy nonregional menu are nothing to write home about, and the wine list also has its highs and lows. But the *paniscia* (rice and vegetables) and *tapulon* (stewed minced donkey) served with polenta may be worth the trip. The eclectic decor of plaid wall-to-wall carpeting, wood paneling, and hanging lamps matches the menu.

BORGO SAN DALMAZZO

CHESTNUTS AND CANDIED VIOLETS
Agrimontana
Borgo San Dalmazzo
Tel. 0171/261157

Brothers Cesare and Enrico Bardini own this state-of-the-art factory, which produces the world's finest-quality *marroni* chestnuts preserved in syrup, as well as *crema di marroni,* a cream of riced chestnuts and cane sugar, and *marroni* in cognac. He is also responsible for the production of genuine candied violets (not the colored and sugared blobby-looking acacia flowers often passed off as violets). Each flower, grown outdoors, is hand-harvested. Its petals are individually coated with gum arabic, dusted with superfine sugar, soaked in sugar syrup for two days, and then dried in a warm oven. A drop of all-natural violet essence in the pale bentwood oval box delicately perfumes the candied flowers—a dainty pale mauve piece of romance.

BOVES

BREAD, SWEETS
Forno Bruno Baudino
Piazza Garibaldi 8
Tel. 0171/680208
Closed Sunday afternoon and
*   Monday*

If the Rododendro experience (see below) and its superior breakfasts aren't enough to lure you to end-of-the road Boves, probably the eighty-six different breads including fig, hazelnut, leek, chestnut, rye, Carlo Alberto (with walnuts, anchovies, and pepper—served to the soldiers when King Carlo Alberto came to review the troops—), and the hand-rolled *grissini,* all baked in a wood-burning oven, will be of no interest to you either. But who can resist Bruno and Piera Baudino's homemade chocolates—pralines and liquid centers—and jellied candies made with over forty varieties of fresh fruits?

RESTAURANT-INN
Rododendro
Frazione San Giacomo
Tel. 0171/680372
Closed Sunday night, Monday,
Tuesday lunch, Christmas, and
August
Credit cards: American Express,
MasterCard
Price: expensive

Mary Barale has a permanent place in the pantheon of female Piemontese chefs, having transformed her country-style *trattoria* into one of Italy's most illustrious two-star restaurants. Much of the regional *cucina* has disappeared from her kitchen, and many of the basic ingredients are French, but the Piemontese in her is irrepressible, especially in her abundant use of the local white truffle. Mary's pastry work is among the finest in all of Italy. I stopped eating other croissants after I tasted her elongated twists of featherweight puff pastry. I watched Marco Valinotti, able director, carve and serve a banana to a client with such grace and style that I wound up liking this restaurant in spite of its Frenchness. The wine list concentrates on fine Piemontese and French wines. The breakfast is a reason enough for an overnight stay in one of the Rododendro's few rooms.

BRA

Bra is the hometown of Arci Gola, which can be translated as "Superlative Gluttony" or "Extra-Large Throat." It's a gastronomical recreational club with over 15,000 card-carrying members, with political ties to the Italian Communist Party. They publish the magazine *Gambero Rosso* twice a year, filled with restaurant reviews and culinary itineraries, with an emphasis on quality wine.

INN
See Cascina Reiné in Alba (page 56)

RESTAURANT
L'Arcangelo
Strada San Michele 28
Tel. 0172/42163
Closed Monday and January
Credit card: American Express
Price: moderate

Arci Gola has taken over the restaurant L'Arcangelo, currently on its third change of ownership in three years. The young staff were trained by the previous, and most professional, chef in the restaurant's history, when the menu was sprinkled with classic dishes inspired by legendary chef Nino Bergese, considered by many to be the grand *maestro* of Italian high *cucina*. I hope that the young chefs of L'Arcangelo have learned their lesson well. The splendid wine list, well priced and heavy on the great local Piemontese reds, the quality Castelmagno cheese, and the countryside panorama aid, but do not substitute for, consistently good cooking.

The fixed-price lunch is an inexpensive choice.

CASTELLO DI ANNONE

HOTEL
See Palio in Asti (page 58)

RESTAURANT
Ristorante La Fioraia
Via Tagliata 26
Tel. 0141/60106
Closed Monday
No credit cards
Price: high moderate

Ornella Cornero runs the kitchen while her husband, Mario, is out in the markets, hunting down fine ingredients, bringing his personal selection of local wines to his wife's daily menu. Most dishes are traditional, well prepared, and interesting. The pasta is homemade, the *grissini* are crispy, the service is efficient. But the true star of this restaurant is the *brasato*, beef braised in Barolo and Barbera wines, served with silky mashed potatoes, crispy chunks of polenta, and one of the brownest, wine-rich sauces I've ever encountered. Worth a detour for braised-beef fans.

CENTALLO

HOTEL
Principe
Via Cavour 1
Cuneo (close by)
Tel. 0171/693355
Credit cards: All
Price: moderate

RESTAURANT
Due Palme
Tel. 0171/211366
Closed Sunday night and
Wednesday
No credit cards
Price: moderate

There are many restaurants that claim to be the gastronomic heirs of Nino Bergese, said to be the "cook of the century" in Italy, chef to noble Piemontese families, including King Umberto of Italy. When the Italian royal family went into exile, Bergese opened the Trattoria della Santa in Genova, but he frequently passed by Centallo on his way home to visit his family and stopped to eat at the Due Palme. He became friendly with owners Ernesta and Ettore Dalmasso, and revealed many of his secrets in their kitchen. Classic, regal *cucina* is unexpected in this country *trattoria* with simple table settings, but the appetizers garnished with tasty aspics offer a hint of the kind of food enjoyed by the Piemontese nobility. Ernesta has learned her lesson well, and skillfully prepares many dishes in Bergese's grand tradition. The *risotto mantecato* with its rich reduced sauce and whisked-in enrichment is bliss. The regional *finanziera* and the elegant duck with orange sauce are both splendid. The nobility never ever asked for seconds, but King Umberto made an exception for Bergese's *torta fiorentina* (chocolate layer cake), a tasty bite as prepared by Ernesta. The house wines, lusty Dolcetto and Nebbiolo, are both lovely with the *cucina*, but exigent enophiles can also drink something to write home about. Reservations are a must.

CIOCCARO DI PENANGO

HOTEL
Locanda del Sant'Uffizio
Cioccaro di Penango
Tel. 0141/91271
Credit cards: American Express, Diners Club, MasterCard
Price: moderate

Beppe Firato and his wife, Carla, who own and run the restaurant Beppe (see below), have beautifully restored a nearby seventeenth-century church complex. The Locanda del Sant'Uffizio has eighteen suites, large communal living rooms, a billiard room, gardens, tennis, and swimming, all set amidst the tranquility of the Monferrato countryside, north of Asti.

RESTAURANT
Beppe
Via Piano 11
Tel. 0141/91271
Closed Tuesday, the first half of January, and 10 days in August
Credit cards: American Express, Diners Club, MasterCard
Price: expensive

A meal at Beppe starts off with the house aperitif (local white wine and peaches) and light and crispy fried pastry, to take the edge off your hunger before proceeding to the Piemontese marathon of an *antipasto*. Homemade pasta and typical Piemontese dishes like *fritto misto* and *panna cotta* (custard) are well prepared, and the house wines, produced in Beppe's nearby Sant'Uffizio vineyards, are pleasant. Be sure to dine in the garden in summer.

COSTIGLIOLE D'ASTI

HOTEL
See Il Cascinale Nuovo in Isola d'Asti (page 62)

RESTAURANT
Guido
Piazza Re Umberto 1
Tel. 0141/966012
Closed Sunday
Credit card: American Express
Price: expensive

The location (in the basement of what looks like a bank), the stuffy formal ambience (paneled walls, Oriental rugs, draperies, heavy Piemontese antique reproductions), and the high ratings in most guidebooks had me worried that Guido was going to "nouvelle" out on me. Wrong. In spite of its appearance, this is a family affair: Lidia Alciati in the kitchen with her son Ugo, husband Guido in the dining room with sons Andrea and Piero. Their professionalism and commitment are overwhelming. The *cucina* is all Piemontese, with some of the most attractive and tasty dishes in the region. Mushrooms and truffles are used to perfection in season; all pasta is homemade and hand-rolled; the *stinco* (veal shank), baked for six hours, is tender, rich, and meaty: the local cheese is splendid; and the *piccola pasticceria* (small pastries) are not to be skipped. The mostly Piemontese wine selection is excellent, although other regions and countries are also represented.

DOGLIANI

PASTRY

Pasticceria Della Ferrera
Via Vittorio Emanuele 18
Tel. 0173/70587
Closed Wednesday

Hazelnut fans should flock to this simple bakery for the intensely nutty *torta di nocciole* (hazelnut cake) made with local hazelnuts; it's heavenly when eaten fresh. The pound cake with raisins (called *plum cake* in Italian) and the *baci di Dogliani*, two chocolate hazelnut cookies glued together with a chocolate filling, are also tasty.

GUARENE

INN

See Cascina Reiné in Alba (page 56)

RESTAURANT

La Villa
Località Castelrotto
Tel. 0173/361497
Closed Sunday night, Monday, and January
Credit cards: American Express, MasterCard
Price: moderate

La Villa, in the middle of Nebbiolo vineyards, is a classic regional restaurant. Isabella Monchiero is in the kitchen, husband Beppe is sommelier. Seasonal mushrooms, homemade *salumi* and pasta, fine local cheeses, and a large selection of Barolo, Barbaresco, and *grappa* make dining at La Villa a pleasant experience.

ISOLA D'ASTI

RESTAURANT-HOTEL

Il Cascinale Nuovo
Statale Asti-Alba
Tel. 0141/958166
Closed Sunday night, Monday, and August
Credit cards: American Express, Diners Club
Price: high moderate

The only farmlike part of Il Cascinale Nuovo ("The New Farm") is the freshly picked vegetables. Tennis courts, a swimming pool, four fully equipped suites with Jacuzzis and linen sheets, and one of Piemonte's rising stars in the restaurant scene are not what Old MacDonald was ee-ay-oh-ing about. Two Ferretto brothers, Walter in the kitchen and sommelier Roberto in the dining room, have teamed up to create a New Wave Piemontese *cucina*, aided by Old Wave Piemontese women (Mamma Silvana and two grandmothers) who speak up if a dish doesn't work out. The food is traditional but lightened up, and takes advantage of first-rate fruit, vegetables, eggs, and poultry raised by the family. The decor in pale wood, gray, and white, the elegant silver, the large white dinner plates, and the breadstick bundle wrapped in a napkin are as refreshing as the food. The Langhe salad of *porcini* mushrooms, Roccaverano cheese, and duck with balsamic vinegar is a winner, and desserts are beautifully presented. If you spend the night, breakfast is a treat of fruit nectar, pound cake or croissants, and preserves, all homemade.

LA MORRA

INN

See Cascina Reiné in Alba (page 56)

PASTRY

Pasticceria di Giovanni Cogno
Via Vittorio Emanuele 18
Tel. 0173/509192
Closed Thursday

Giovanni Cogno is a passionate baker. His plain hazelnut cake, and a version with chocolate chips, are more cookie-like than most, but both are clearly made with freshly toasted local hazelnuts. Chocolate hazelnut cookies (*lamorresi*) are given an adult treatment with Barolo, rum, or *grappa*. Whole-grain cornmeal cookies (*biscotti di meliga*) are delicately perfumed with lemon peel. All natural ingredients, no preservatives added, and Gianni Gallo's charming drawings on the labels are other good reasons for a visit to Giovanni Cogno's *pasticceria*.

RESTAURANT

Belvedere
Piazza Castello 5
Tel. 0173/50190
Closed Sunday night, Monday, January, and February
No credit cards
Price: moderate

The Belvedere, true to its name, has a view that will make you yearn to come back, a kind of visual and gastronomic *Three Coins in a Fountain* effect. Gianfranco Bovio is a winemaker, and ably takes care of provisions and the dining rooms, while his sister Maria Vittoria reigns in the kitchen.

The simple, clean lines of her traditional *cucina* never fail to ring true. Game pâté, mushrooms and truffles in season, hand-rolled and cut *tajarin* pasta, *agnolotti,* and richly flavored whole-grain cornmeal polenta, served with stewed or braised meats or game, are well prepared. Local cheeses are carefully chosen, and the wine list offers many pages of well-priced regional gems that will make enophiles go crazy. Finish your meal with a *grappa* and a lingering glance at the countryside, and you'll vow to return.

Claudia and Tonino's
La Contea restaurant in Neive
is an especially
wonderful treat.

MOMO

HOTEL
See Albergo San Rocco in Lago d'Orta (page 59)

RESTAURANT
Ristorante Macallè
Via Boniperti 2
Tel. 0321/96064
Closed Wednesday and July
Credit cards: all
Price: moderate

Sergio Zuin is in the kitchen with his mother, Speranza, and his wife, Silvana, runs the dining room of Macallè, one of the few traditional restaurants in the area that haven't gone nouvelle. The menu features regional specialties: homemade *salumi, risotto,* hard-to-find *paniscia* (vegetables and rice), donkey stew, game, homemade desserts, and rich *zabaione.* Fresh fish is served on Friday and Saturday. The wine list offers some pleasant surprises.

NEIVE

RESTAURANT
La Contea
Piazza Cocito 8
Tel. 0173/671126
Closed Sunday night and Monday
Credit cards: American Express,
  MasterCard
Price: high moderate

Every time I come back to Piemonte, I feel like a homing pigeon, heading for Neive, which has always been my local point of reference. Claudia and Tonino Verro's sense of warmth and hospitality creates the mood in this enchanting restaurant, with its patterned wallpaper, terracotta floors, wood-burning fireplaces ablaze, and Piemontese villa feeling. La Contea's front room is a local hangout, a *bar-tabacchi* that sells ropy-smelling cigarettes, where someone always seems to be drinking a *caffè* or a glass of wine or a *grappa*. Jars of homemade preserves and *bross* (cheeses mashed in grappa) sit on the shelves of large antique cupboards. Claudia has endured my questions and let me watch the action in her kitchen; she is a combination of traditional talent, professionalism won by pure hard work, a heart as big as all of Piemonte, and a vocabulary of Tuscan obscenities that makes the Florentine in me smile. Tonino has taken me to taste *grappa*, to market for truffles at dawn, and we have all sat up drinking Barbaresco and talking *cucina* until 3 a.m. What do I think of La Contea? I am moved by the *cucina*, by the strength of the traditional food that Tonino, Claudia, Gianni, and Maurizio offer in the three intimate dining rooms. I have never ordered anything, but have always let Tonino and Claudia put whatever they want on my plate. Their choices have never been disappointing. What a treat! Tonino's pairing of local wines with Claudia's cooking is an act of love. Spend the night in one of the charming guest rooms upstairs, and breakfast on hazelnut cookies and cake.

PALLANZA

Pallanza is a small, elegant tourist village on Lago Maggiore, a perfect base for exploring the area's ornate villas with their immense, well-planned, Italianate terraced gardens adorned with tropical, exotic, and local plants and trees. Villa Taranto, Villa Borromeo, and the Giardino Botanico of the Isole Borromee are settings that seem to call for white flannels, blazers, and linen lawn dresses.

HOTEL
Europalace
Viale delle Magnolie 16
Tel. 0323/506441
Credit cards: all
Price: low luxury

HOTEL
Italia
Viale delle Magnolie 10
Tel. 0323/50306
No credit cards
Price: moderate

RESTAURANT
Il Torchio
Via Manzoni 20
Tel. 0323/503352
Closed Monday and the second half of June
Credit cards: all
Price: moderate

Restaurants cater to tourists in this area—not the best climate for traditional *cucina* and attentive service. But Il Torchio, run by brothers Vittorio (in the kitchen) and Franco Gurian (sommelier) and their wives has concentrated on fine local lake fish and the bounty of the Milano market, transforming quality ingredients into fine food. The Piemontese wine selection is superb, with some great vintage wines for enophiles and Italian and French wines for locals bored with the fantastic regional reds.

PESSIONE DI CHIERI

MUSEUM
Martini & Rossi
Museo del Vino
Piazza L. Rossi
Tel. 011/9470345

The Martini & Rossi Museum, in the original Martini & Rossi cellars in Pessione, houses one of the world's most important collections of winemaking artifacts and traces the history of wine from the seventh century B.C. through its 3,000-year evolution. Apulian, Attic, Corinthian, Etruscan, and Roman objects, grape presses, carts, and vats, are beautifully displayed in the vaulted brick cellars that still retain some of the scent of wine.

PIOBESI D'ALBA

RESTAURANT-INN
Le Clivie
Via Camoreto 1
Tel. 0173/619261
Closed Monday
No credit cards
Price: moderate

Caterina Clivio has turned her nineteenth-century villa, surrounded by manicured gardens, into a charming seven-room inn. The dining room has vaulted frescoed ceilings, marble columns, and service by a uniformed "butler" in grand Piemontese style. Winemaker Bruno Ceretto's former cook is in the kitchen, preparing traditional seasonal dishes like meat-stuffed *caponet,* done in the summer with zucchini flowers and in the winter with cabbage, *bagna caoda,* and hand-rolled pasta. Truffles are served in season, fine local cheese is available, breads are homemade, and the cellar holds some fine Piemontese wines.

PRADLEVES

RESTAURANT
Tre Verghe D'Oro
Via IV Novembre 131
Tel. 0171/98516
Closed January and Tuesday in
winter
No credit cards
Price: low moderate

The Tre Verghe D'Oro is tucked in the Valle Grana, close to the village of Castelmagno, a mecca for lovers of full-flavored cheese. Seven generations of the Durando family have run this mountain lodge serving traditional Piemontese *cucina,* seasonal mushrooms, marinated meats, a lengthy but tasty *antipasto* series, potato *gnocchi* sauced with Castelmagno cheese, and a *fritto misto Piemontese* (order in advance) of fifteen delicately fried meats, vegetables, fruit—even *amaretti* cookies. Save room for a taste of hard-to-find fresh and ripe Castelmagno cheese, and conclude with a glass of Ginepy, an herbal digestive. The wine selection has its highs and lows. Spend the night in one of the thirty slightly seedy rooms and wake up to the music of the Grana River.

SANTA VITTORIA D'ALBA

VERMOUTH
Cinzano
Via Statale Santa Vittoria
Tel. 0172/47041

Cinzano makes one of the more popular vermouths. For an appointment to visit their cellars, call 011/57401.

TORINO

On the banks of the Po River, in sight of the Alps, stands Torino. The Roman colony of Augusta Taurinorum, the capital of Savoia, the center of the Italian Risorgimento, and the first capital of the newly united Italy, it is clearly a city of noble aspect, with spacious piazzas, elegant shops in covered arcades, and turn-of-the-century architecture. Its castles and palaces are a reminder of over 600 years of rule by the important and powerful family monarchy of Savoy. Great wealth and power in Torino is now clearly represented by Fiat, but gastronomic trends last longer than politics. Traditional bars in the city are always crowded, each filled with its own partisans, who stop in for a coffee, pastry, chocolate, cocktail, aperitif, or even a *marron glacé.* The Fiat plants have brought immigrants in from the south, and many restaurants offer *cucina Toscana,* frequently cooked by southern chefs who prepare pasta to perfection (unlike the way it's done in Toscana). Chocolates, tiny pastries, and the *bicerin,* a shot of coffee, sweetened hot chocolate, and whipped cream served in a special glass, are all part of the special Torinese gastronomic tradition, among the most interesting in Italy.

HOTEL
Villa Sassi
Strada al Traforo del Pino 47
Tel. 011/890556
Credit cards: all
Price: luxury

At the gates of the city of Torino, Villa Sassi has seen the passage of royalty and local luminaries for over 200 years. It has been turned into a luxury hotel, with ten rooms and two suites, overlooking manificent gardens and huge trees. This is what living like a king is all about.

HOTEL
Hotel Vittoria
Via Nino Costa 4
Tel. 011/534265
Credit cards: American Express,
MasterCard, Visa
Price: high moderate

The eighty-room Vittoria, located in the center of Torino, is a perfect hotel. All rooms are fully equipped; some are furnished in charming flea-market antiques, others in simple modern. The staff is friendly and helpful, and parking is available nearby.

BAR-CAFFÈ
Caffè San Carlo
Piazza San Carlo 156
Tel. 011/515317
Closed Monday

The Caffè San Carlo, which bills itself as "the living room of Torino," features gilt columns, mirrors, green-and-rust-veined marble tables, and a massive Murano glass chandelier, all authentic 1800s decor on the corner of Piazza San Carlo. Another smaller, frescoed tearoom and a more modern no-nonsense bar handle the stand-up business.

BAR-CAFFÈ
Caffè Torino
Piazza San Carlo 04
Tel. 011/545118
Closed Tuesday

Behind the old-fashioned bar, in a scallop shell shrine, stands the rampant bull, symbol of Torino from the Roman colony of Augusta Taurinorum. The ambience of this local institution is classic.

BAR-CAFFÈ
Al Bicerin
Piazza Consolata 5
Tel. 011/518794
Closed Wednesday

Although some other bars in Torino make the *bicerin*—a hot chocolate, coffee, and whipped cream beverage served in a glass—this is the bar to head for if you want a taste of the most authentic version in town. Watch out for the hoards of Torinese out for a Sunday afternoon stroll and a *bicerin,* and look for the *toro* water fountain in the corner of the piazza.

BAR-CAFFÈ
Antica Dolceria Baratti
Piazza Castello 29
Tel. 011/511481
Closed Monday

Baratti is a nice place to rest while you gawk at the vast assortment of wrapped candies and tiny pastries. The small turn-of-the-century bar is a gem.

BAR-CAFFÈ
Platti
Corso Vittorio Emanuele 72
Tel. 011/511507
Closed Friday

Platti seems to have the best sandwich selection of the Torinese bars. All the bread is homemade, the little pastries are attractive, and they make their own *marrons glacés* and *giandujotti* (chocolate hazelnut wedges).

MARKET
The Porta Palazzo market must be one of the largest food markets in Italy. Meat, poultry, and perishable goods are sold in pavilions, but the excitement and hustle of this market is outdoors, amidst piles of fruit and vegetables—local bounty bartered, traded, and sold with a flourish. Fresh hazelnuts, real *marroni* chestnuts, fantastic ripe peppers, and chains of braided garlic, along with a treasure of organic and synthetic goods—all are cleared away at 1:30 p.m. Lunch around the corner at San Giors or Tre Galline, both typical Torinese *trattorie.*

MARKET
Via Lagrange is Torino's gastronomic Fifth Avenue, the food street, with a fine selection of cheese, pastry, meat, produce, and some fancy take-out. Fine wine is available around the corner.

SPECIALTY FOODS
Salumeria Rosticceria Castagno
Via Lagrange 34
Tel. 011/544350
Closed Wednesday afternoon

Torino's Castagno shops are a local version of the Peck empire in Milano (see page 165), three high-quality specialty shops selling a beautiful selection of meat, cheese, and take-out. The salads in the windows of the corner shop, simply placed on trays and in baking dishes, are fresh-looking and attractive. *Nervetti* (calf's foot salad), peppers with *bagna caoda* sauce, *tavola calda* (hot table) items, and roast meats are sold to go.

MEAT
La Bottega del Maiale
Via Lagrange 38
Tel. 011/519934
Closed Wednesday afternoon

"The Pork Shop" seems to sell every cut of pork, and a wide selection of prosciutto and salumi as well.

CHEESE
La Baita del Formaggio
Via Lagrange 36/A
Tel. 011/547257
Closed Wednesday afternoon

All the special regional cheeses of Piemonte, like *castelmagno, toma, ricotta piemontese, robiole,* and *tomini* are sold here, as well as quality *parmigiano* and *provolone* produced in other regions.

Last-minute preparations for Sunday-lunch desserts

The salads, especially the aspics, at Steffanone are special, made with homemade mayonnaise and aspic. The Ligurian-style stuffed vegetables and *torta pasqualina* (vegetable tart) make a pleasant picnic lunch.

CHEESE
Toja
Via Torino 48
Tel. 011/9101271
Closed Wednesday afternoon

Toja doesn't always have all the great local cheeses, but when they do have them, the quality is high. *Brus, robiole* made from goat or cow's milk, *gorgonzola* from Novara, and squashed mountain *tomini* can sometimes be found.

WINE
Enoteca Casa del Barolo
Via Andrea Doria 7
Tel. 011/532038
Closed Wednesday afternoon

Gigi Molinaro has a splendid, vast selection of Piemontese wines, as well as a personal, more limited but nevertheless splendid, selection of wines from other regions, and *grappa*. Chilled whites are always available.

WINE
Il Salotto dei Vini
Via San Massimo 12
Tel. 011/830418
Closed Wednesday afternoon

Franca Ferraro's one-room wine shop has a good selection of wines and hides, down a spiral staircase, a comfortable wine cellar where she holds interesting tastings.

PASTA
Pastificio Defilippis
Via Lagrange 39
Tel. 011/542137
Closed Wednesday afternoon

Fresh and dry pasta, and flours and beans of all kinds, are the specialty of the Pastificio Defilippis. It'll make you wish you had a pot of boiling water waiting at home.

PRODUCE
Scanavino due
Via Lagrange 38
Tel. 011/511268
Closed Wednesday afternoon

Fruit and vegetables, local and imported exotics, and dried fruit and nuts are all attractively displayed in this chic modern produce shop on via Lagrange.

TRUFFLES AND GAME
Ottino
Via Lagrange 36
Tel. 011/544928
Closed Wednesday afternoon

Founded in 1919, Ottino sells truffles, mushrooms, game, poultry, eggs, and meat. In the fall this shop is in full bloom, with an array of feathered game birds and hairy animals, and the perfume of truffles in the air.

SPECIALTY FOODS
Steffanone
Via Maria Vittoria 2
Tel. 011/546737
Closed Wednesday afternoon

PASTRY

Pasticceria Falchero
Via S. Massimo 4
Tel. 011/830024
Closed Monday

No smoking allowed in Signor Falchero's pastry shop, where the air is brought in from the roof because it's better than street air for his pastry, the best in Torino. The miniatures are smaller, more original, and the selection is wider; the puff pastry is light and flaky; cookies, warm *cornetti*, mini-pizzas, custom cakes, and chocolates of the highest quality are made fresh daily.

PASTRY

Pfatish
Corso Vittorio Emanuele 76
Tel. 011/538765
Closed Monday

A complete line of Peyrano chocolates and fine pastries are specialties of this pastry shop, which starts with a silent "P."

CHOCOLATES

Peyrano
Corso Moncalieri 47
Tel. 011/650574

Antonio Peyrano founded his chocolate shop in 1915 in the chic suburbs of Torino. Giorgio and Bruna Peyrano run the family business today, with total control over every phase of the chocolate-making process. A blend of nine different cocoa beans is toasted over heat produced by burning olive wood, then ground with a porphyry stone mill. After aging for three months, the ground beans are melted, "slapped" (stirred and beaten) for seventy-two hours at 45° C, (113° F) tempered, and molded into ingots, awaiting transformation. A visit to the factory is a chocoholic's dream come true, surrounded by Willi Wonka machinery all devoted to the worship of the cocoa bean. The tan gift boxes are simple and sturdy, the type you never throw away, and a numbered edition of 5000 beautiful handmade layered wooden boxes, designed by Ettore Sottsass, is available to those of discriminating taste with money to burn.

GELATO

Pepino
Piazza Carignano 8
Tel. 011/542009
Closed Monday

Pepino was founded in 1884, across the street from Palazzo Madama, site of the first Italian senate. Did Cavour send someone across the street for one of Pepino's wrapped ice cream bars, the classic chocolate-dipped *pinguino* (penguin) in either mint, custard, chocolate hazelnut, or hazelnut, or the chocolate *tartufi*, or candied-fruit-studded *cassate*, or *amaretti*-flavored *spumoni*, or truncated *pezzi duri* in chocolate or vanilla, or the up to twenty fruit-flavored *gelati* offered in the summer? I like to think he did.

GELATO

A. Gioari
Via Mazzini 19/B
Tel. 011/533064
Closed Sunday afternoon and
*   Monday morning*

Homemade chocolates and *gelato* in innovative but very Torinese flavors such as *bunet*, *torrone*, and *gianduja*, and dainty cookie baskets filled with *gelato*, will be irrestible for ice cream lovers.

GELATO

–18
Via Accademia Albertina 25
Tel. 011/8396538
Closed Sunday

Eighteen degrees below zero Celsius (0° F) is the temperature at which sweet liquid base is transformed into the wonder known as *gelato*. Torino's newest *gelateria* specializes in fruit flavors, especially exotics like mango, papaya, passion fruit, melons, berries, and chestnut, as well as local flavors like hazelnut and chocolate-hazelnut.

RESTAURANT

Ristorante del Cambio
Piazza Carignano 2
Tel. 011/543760
Closed Monday and August
Credit cards: American Express,
*   MasterCard, Visa*
Price: expensive

The Cambio has been a classic in Torino since 1757. Crystal chandeliers, plush red velvet seating, a small entranceway bar with marble-topped and pedestaled tables—the one-time elegance of Torino has been preserved like an Egyptian mummy. The *cucina* doesn't seem to have changed much since then either, with its emphasis on Baltic sturgeon, Strasbourg foie gras, and other continental favorites. But the traditional dishes are nicely cooked; try the homemade pasta, *finanziera* (chicken liver and sweetbread stew), Barolo braised beef, and the Barolo-flavored *zabaione* served with cornmeal lemon cookies and amaretti-and-cocoa-stuffed peaches. Reserve the table where Cavour liked to dine, backed by a banner of faded green, white, and red bunting. On Friday evenings in the spring, the spirit of old-world Torino is re-created with chamber music and royal family menus—six- or seven-course meals—accompanied by local wines. The Cambio's wine list, with its vintage Barolo and Barbaresco going back to the 1960s, will please enophiles even more than the *cucina*.

RESTAURANT
C'era una volta
Corso Vittorio Emanuele 14
Tel. 011/655498
Closed Sunday and August
Credit cards: all
Price: moderate

"Once upon a time" is the name of this restaurant, one flight up, where you'll be served a traditional Piemontese dinner: one sitting, a fixed menu of eight *antipasti,* two first courses, *sorbetto,* two meat dishes, vegetables, and a taste of three desserts. Owner-sommelier Piero Prete welcomes all diners and selects interesting, reasonably priced wines that go well with his procession of a meal, served by waiters in red-and-white-checked shirts and blue V-neck sweaters. Conclude your dinner with a *grappa,* served from a cute little cask. The dining room, with its frescoed ceiling and ornate cornices, makes you feel like a guest at a private party.

RESTAURANT
Gatto Nero
Corso Turati 14
Tel. 011/590414
Closed Sunday and August
Credit cards: American Express, Diners Club
Price: expensive

The owners of Gatto Nero are from Montecarlo, a walled village outside Lucca, and produce their own extra virgin olive oil and splendid wines for their Tuscan restaurant, the city's oldest. The restaurant is modern, with a brick-wall rustic ambience and built-in shelves holding a large selection of wines. The *cucina* is a blend of Toscana, Piemontese, and fresh fish and vegetables prepared by their able cooks. The menu is quite large; the *degustazione* tasting of Gatto Nero's specialties includes a lightly dressed seafood salad, *melizza* (a mini-pizza on a slice of eggplant), homemade pasta with seafood, cooked to almost crunchy perfection, mushrooms in season, grilled meats, fish, or a *fritto misto* marathon. The *gelato* is from −18 (see page 68). The house wines are wonderful, especially the white and the red reserves that the family makes in Toscana.

RESTAURANT
Tre Galline
Via Bellezia 37
Tel. 011/546833
Closed Monday and August
No credit cards
Price: low moderate

Around the corner from Porta Palazzo, Tre Galline ("Three Hens") is one of the oldest restaurants in Torino. Marble-chip floors, painted wainscoting, coat hooks, typical high-hung *trattoria* paintings, and an all-local clientele set the mood. The menu features some fine local specialties—a variety of appetizers, *bagna coada* (anchovy-garlic dip with raw vegetables), Barolo braised beef, and mixed boiled meats served with four kinds of sauce. In season, truffles are sold by the *grattata,* or grating. The chef is from the south, and his pasta is perfectly cooked. Cheese lovers will want to try the *tomino elettrico* ("electric") cheese marinated in oil and spicy chili peppers. The house wine is without character, and wine bottles are displayed rather than listed on the menu. Coppo's Barbera or Grignolino goes nicely with the *cucina* of this classic gem of a *trattoria.*

RESTAURANT
San Giors
Via Borgo Dora 3
Tel. 011/5211256
Closed Monday, Tuesday, and July
No credit cards
Price: moderate

Around the corner from the Porta Palazzo market, up a flight of stairs in a seedy hotel, the San Giors (San Giorgio in Piemontese dialect) serves traditional Torinese *trattoria* food. The house specialty is *bollito misto*—mixed boiled meats served with a variety of sauces (including ketchup!)—and hard-to-find hearty *tofeja,* a bean and pork rind soup. The strictly local crowd seems to contain a high proportion of smokers in all three dining rooms of this no-frills authentic *trattoria.* A personal favorite!

RESTAURANT
La Smarrita
Corso Unione Sovietica 244
Tel. 011/390657
Closed Monday and most of
    August
Credit cards: all
Price: expensive

La Smarrita is the name of the bell that rang out for lost travelers, rung by the cavaliers of Tau, a chivalrous order that provided hospitality to stranded knights in central Italy in the 1300s. Waiters at the restaurant are garbed in the tunics of the cavaliers of Tau and provide succor to victims of the Torinese work ethic with the best food and wine in town. The decor is modern, the colors subdued, the lighting soft, and the acoustics better than in most restaurants. The *cucina* isn't particularly regional, although the Tuscan background of Moreno Grossi and his sister Franca shines through in the use of extra virgin olive oil. Fresh fish and vegetables are lightly cooked, barely sauced, treated with respect, and individual flavors and textures stand out. Mushrooms in season are a special treat. There's no printed menu or wine list, but Moreno will discuss your meal and help you to decide, and his sommelier, Antonio Dacomo, will choose a wine from their wonderful selection to complement your meal. The waiters are a bunch of cuties.

HOUSEWARES
La Mezzaluna
Via Lagrange 2/D
Tel. 011/5575181
Closed Monday morning
Credit cards: American Express,
    Diners Club, Visa

Torino's best housewares shop is named after the two-handled rocking knife that most Italian housewives use. The shelves are neatly arranged with the finest names in Italian products—Alessi, ICM, and Sambonet stainless, IVV glassware, Guzzini plastics, and Montana knives—as well as English jar labels, French pottery, German baking tins, and traditional terracotta bean pots. Owners Anna Calcagne and Paola Giubergia are passionate about cooking and equipment and are friendly and helpful. They'll wrap and send your purchases home if you want.

CANDLES
Colenghi
Piazza Solferino 3
Tel. 011/512550
Closed Monday morning
No credit cards

All sizes, lengths, and colors of candles, from birthday-cake size to decorative holiday tapers, spirals, fruit, vegetables, a sandwich on a realistic roll, and even custom-designed candles, are the specialty of Colenghi. They also make soap, including some serious-looking detergents and blocks of no-nonsense *Sapone Marsiglia* for removing oil-based stains from washables.

BAKERY EQUIPMENT
Siccardi
Via Principe Amadeo 22/B
Tel. 011/8397210
Closed Saturday
No credit cards

Siccardi is a bakery equipment shop for professional or ambitious bakers, and their selection of utensils is a joy to behold. Boards to shove bread into the oven; cake molds in chestnut, mushroom, pine-cone, corn-cob, and shooting-star shapes; cutters, molds, sifters in all sizes and meshes, pizza accessories, rolling pins, hand-carved wooden spoons, bowls, strainers, a pantographic seven-bladed crimped or straight-edged pastry cutter, and *rosetta* stamps that look like a cross between knuckle dusters and an Oriental martial-arts weapon.

BOOKS
Luxemburg Libreria
    Internazionale
Via Cesare Battisti 7
Tel. 011/532007
Closed Monday morning
No credit cards

The Luxemburg Libreria Internazionale has a large collection of Judaica, as well as a nice assortment of cookbooks in both Italian and English. They will send your books home if you wish.

BOOKS
Bloomsbury Books and Arts
Via dei Mille 20
Tel. 011/8398989
Closed Monday morning
Credit cards: American Express,
    Visa

Bloomsbury Books and Arts has a good selection of Italian cookbooks, literary and art books in English and Italian, and local pictorials. The ambience is inviting. They will send, a plus since books are heavy.

MUSEUM
Egyptian Museum
Via Accademia delle Scienze 6
Tel. 011/537581
Closed Monday

Housed in the Science Academy, the Torino Museo Egizio, the oldest Egyptian museum in the world—founded even before Cairo's museum—is breathtaking, and you don't have to suffer Egyptian hotels and food to see it. A vast collection of everyday Egyptian relics from daily life, from inkwells to pawns for an unknown board game, are displayed in case after case of fabulous and amazing objects. Cairo on the Po, open from 9 a.m. to 2 p.m.

FLEA MARKET
Balon
Porta Palazzo Market
Open Saturday

The Porta Palazzo market hosts the Balon flea market on Saturdays. Although the best stuff is snapped up early, and most interesting items are too big even to consider purchasing, I can always find something fun to bring home—tableware, glasses, old linens.

MUSEUM
Museo dell'arredamento
Palazzina di Stupinigi
Tel. 011/598844
Closed Monday and
  Friday

Built by famed architect Juvara in 1730 as a hunting lodge for Vittorio Amadeo II, rococo Villa Reale now houses the Museo dell' arredamento, a unique glimpse into noble Piemontese taste and lifestyles. The portraits, especially those of the small children, evoke another time and a different world.

TORRE PELLICE

RESTAURANT-INN
Flipot
Corso Gramsci 17
Tel. 021/91236
Closed Tuesday, 2 weeks in
  March, 2 weeks in October
Credit card: American Express
Price: moderate

Torre Pellice, in the Valle del Pellice, is gastronomically closer to Switzerland and France. The *cucina* at Flipot is based on regional traditions and the season, and offers fresh field greens and wild herbs cooked up in *frittate,* homemade pasta, local goose (in November), wild boar, chamois, deer, and trout, Sanato Piemontese veal, and farm-raised poultry. Cheese is purchased directly from the dairy; taste the *sairas,* a fresh ricotta with herbs that I've never found elsewhere. Walter Eynard, his wife, Gisella, and maître d' Marco Fornarone seem to have thought of everything, and the selection of fine Piemontese—and French and Californian—wines is impressive. Spend the night in one of the seven simple, clean rooms.

VERCELLI

TABLEWARE
Sambonet (factory)
Via XXVI Aprile 62
Tel. 0161/5971

Founded in 1856, this company makes high-quality silverplate. Designs for their tableware are classic as well as modern, and are found throughout Italy. Call Dr.

Bruno in Milano, 02/66800293, for an appointment.

VEZZA D'ALBA

TRUFFLES
Tartufingros
Piazza S. Bernardo 9
Tel. 0173/65553

Tartufingros wholesales truffles—fresh or processed as paste—throughout Italy, and exports their wares all over the world. The office and warehouse in Vezza d'Alba are well guarded, and owner Andrea Rossano travels with his briefcase of valuable samples handcuffed to his wrist. You can purchase truffles in season, truffled pâté, and other jarred truffle products.

VISONE D'ACQUI

HAZELNUT CANDY
Canelin
Via Acqui 123
Tel. 0144/593285
Closed Monday

There are no secret ingredients in *torrone,* according to Giovanni Verdese, a fourth-generation maker of this nougat hazelnut candy. Honey, sugar, and egg whites are cooked for eleven hours (instead of the three or four hours of other candy makers), lots of toasted local hazelnuts are folded in, and the mixture is poured into molds of 200-, 300-, 400-, and 500-gram blocks as well as a jumbo 1-kilo size. It's not difficult to find good *torrone,* but Canelin's is probably Piemonte's finest.

VALLE D'AOSTA

∎

The character of Valle d'Aosta, Italy's smallest region, has been formed by mountains, valleys, and rivers. The Aosta valley is separated from Switzerland and France by towering Alps, western Europe's tallest mountains, and bisected by the main valley of the Dora Baltea river, fed by torrential tributaries coursing down through smaller valleys. The Valle d'Aosta is dotted with archeological excavations, Roman monuments, medieval castles, Gothic churches, slate-tiled stone cottages, ski resorts, and grazing cows that outnumber the inhabitants of this bilingual (French and Italian) region.

The *cucina* is dominated by animal protein—meat and dairy products. Game comes from the mountain forests, cheese and butter from the cows that have summered in the high alpine pastures. Venison and chamois, a small goat-like antelope, are stewed or salt-cured and dried. *Mocetta*, traditionally a chamois prosciutto, is now more commonly made of beef. The local bread—called "black," *pane nero*—is made from rye flour and is the main ingredient in most of the traditional first-course soups. Pasta is nowhere to be found, although rice, *gnocchi,* and *polenta* appear as first courses. Many dishes are enriched with butter and Fontina cheese, a hallmark of the *cucina valdostana.* Meat is stewed with red wine and spices and served with polenta; trout is cooked in butter or red wine.

Regional cheeses can be exceptional. *Fontina,* made from whole unpasteurized milk, is still produced by small artisanal dairies, stored and aged by cooperatives, and stamped with the seal of the Consortium of Fontina Producers to guarantee quality. *Toma,* made from spring, summer, or fall milk, is found in varying degrees of ripeness ranging from delicate to putrid.

The dramatic finale to a typical meal is *caffè valdostano,* a mixture of coffee, lemon or orange peel, *grappa,* and sugar, sipped from the spouts of a *coppa dell'amicizia* ("friendship cup"), a steaming, squat wooden pot to be passed around among friends at the table.

THE MENU

SALUMI

Boudin ▪ potato-based blood pudding or sausage

Lardo ▪ salt-cured lard streaked with pork

Mocetta ▪ leg of chamois or ibex, cured like prosciutto

PRIMO

Fonduta ▪ creamy melted Fontina, milk, and eggs, served with polenta or toast rounds

Gnocchi alla valdostana ▪ potato gnocchi with Fontina sauce

Polenta concia ▪ polenta cooked with butter and Fontina

Riso alla valdostana ▪ rice cooked with onion, broth, butter, and Fontina

Seupetta di cogne ▪ rice cooked with broth, Fontina, butter, and stale rye bread

Zuppa alla ueca ▪ soup of vegetables, pork, barley, stale rye bread, and Fontina

Zuppa alla valpellinentze, or *alla valdostana* ▪ soup of cabbage, stale rye bread, Fontina and broth, sometimes topped with nutmeg

SECONDO

Trota al vino rosso ▪ trout cooked in red wine

Boudin ▪ sausage served with potatoes

Camoscio e polenta ▪ chamois stew, cooked with red wine and spices, served with polenta

Carbonada ▪ beef stew cooked with red wine and spices

Costoletta alla valdostana ▪ veal chop stuffed with prosciutto and Fontina

FORMAGGIO

Fontina ▪ large reddish wheel, delicate buttery flavor, compact and smooth

Reblec ▪ fresh curdled cream cheese

Robiola ▪ soft, creamy, rich, small round

Toma ▪ medium-size flat round, ranging from bland to feisty

Tomini ▪ small rounds of fresh goat or mixed-milk cheese or coated with herbs *(alle erbe)*

DOLCE

Frutta cotta ▪ seasonal fruit, especially the martin sec pear, cooked with red wine and spices

Tegole ▪ literally "roof tiles," round curved hazelnut cookies

THE *W*INE LIST

Italy's smallest region also has the smallest wine production; there's not much space for growing grapes between the Alps and the valleys traversed by torrential mountain streams. However, the people "of the valley," as they refer to themselves, ever industrious, have terraced south-facing slopes for growing limited quantities of native grapes. The wine that these dedicated winemakers produce is barely enough to fill the regional need, and is rarely found outside the Valle d'Aosta. *Valle d'Aosta* is a new DOC that covers fifteen different wines in almost all of the Aosta Valley's vine-growing territory. Among the best are:

Blanc de Morgex is a delicate dry white made from the local Blanc de Morgex grape, served with first-course dishes and fish. Costantino Charrere is a quality producer.

Chambave Rouge is a full dry red, made from Petit Rouge blended with other local grapes, served with meat and game from the mountains. The top producer is Ezio Voyat.

Enfer d'Arvier, the "Arvier Inferno," is a rich dry red made with the Petit Rouge grape, served with meat and regional *cucina,* produced by Co-Enfer.

Passito di Chambave is a sweet, aromatic golden wine, made from the Moscato grape, served with simple desserts or between meals, and at its best produced by Ezio Voyat and La Crotta di Vegneron.

Petit Rouge is a purplish, intense, dry red made from the Petit Rouge grape, served with meat, fowl, and regional *cucina.* Top producers are Institut Agricole Régional Aoste and G. Gabriele.

Pinot Noir is a lively, purplish, dry red, made from the Pinot Noir grape, produced by the Institut Agricole Régional Aoste, and served with sauced meats and stews.

Torrette is a robust, dry, ruby-red wine made from the Petit Rouge and a blend of local grape varieties. It is served with meat and hearty regional dishes, and produced by Filippo Garin.

Vin du Conseil is a straw-colored, rich, dry white made from the Petite Arvine grape, served with light first-course dishes and fish. It is produced by the Institut Agricole Régional Aoste.

*R*EGIONAL SPECIALTIES

FONTINA

Almost all the milk produced in the Valle d'Aosta, from a local breed of over 20,000 cows, is used in the production of Fontina cheese. Cows are trucked from their farms to Alpine mountain pastures for a summer of grazing on grass and herbs. Modern-day shepherds, milkers, and cheesemakers use essentially the same techniques that have been used for seven centuries. Fresh whole unpasteurized straight-from-the-cow milk is partially cooked, drained, dry-salted, and aged for at least three months in a cool, humid room. The best cheese is made with milk from cows that have been grazing in high mountain pastures on spring's tender alpine grass and herbs. The Cooperativa di Produttori Latte e Fontina, a cooperative of milk producers and cheesemakers, guarantees the quality of each rust-colored wheel, which may weigh anywhere from seventeen to forty pounds. They seem to have some kind of secret numbering system for coding the valuable high-altitude spring-milk Fontina. I have recently discovered that cheese numbers 10 through 453 indicate high-altitude grazing lands. Will I ever figure out the code for spring milk?

For more information about the cooperative, see page 81.

LARD

Lard (lardo), the subcutaneous fat from the dorsal, flank, or shoulder area, is probably the most flavorful part of the pig. The lard from the village of Arnad is cut into chunks, marinated in brine with mountain herbs and spices, and sold in jars that can keep—stored in a cool, dark, well-aired pantry—for a year or two. At its best, it has a rich, complex, buttery sweetness. It is *not* like eating raw bacon.

See page 78.

THE MARTIN SEC PEAR AND THE RENETTA APPLE

The *martin sec* pear and the *renetta* apple are typical products of the Aosta valley culture, with its emphasis on preserving food for the long, hard winters. The small, rough-skinned, rust-colored pear with gray freckles isn't eaten fresh, but preserved—or it is cooked with wine, a typical mountain dessert. The apple is a lumpy ovoid, rough-skinned, straw-colored, with red sun-spot "cheeks." The pulp is white, juicy, and sweeter than most apples.

For apples and apple products, see page 80.

CRAFTS

The isolation of Valle d'Aosta's mountain winters has inspired one of Italy's finest craft traditions. Five regional I.V.A.T. shops (Institut Valdtain de l'Artisanat Typique) sell handmade lace, hand-loomed woolen blankets, wrought-iron fireplace tools, and beautiful hand-carved wooden objects. Butter molds, graceful scoops, bowls, friendship cups for coffee, the *grolla,* a chalice-like cup for wine whose origin dates from the Crusades, and other artfully created items are far superior to the junk displayed in most tourist souvenir shops. The Aosta store (via Xavier de Maistre 1) has the largest selection and is open year-round (tel. 0165/40808). The smaller shops in village locations (Cogne, Valtournenche, Gressoney, and Antagnad) are open only during the summer and winter tourist seasons. They have no telephones and may lack a specific street address, but they aren't hard to find. No credit cards are accepted.

See also the Foire de Saint-Ours, page 78.

CITIES AND TOWNS

AOSTA

Aosta, situated along the strategically important road to the Alpine passes of the Grande and Piccolo S. Bernardo, was founded by the Romans in 25 B.C. The Roman and medieval monuments, wide piazzas, and small-town feeling in the center make this city a fun place to visit.

HOTEL
Hotel Europe
Piazza Narbonne
Tel. 0165/362214
Credit cards: all
Price: moderate

MEAT
Salumeria Anselmo
Via de Tillier 50
Tel. 0165/40187
Closed Thursday afternoon

Salumeria Anselmo has the best selection of meat and *salumi* in town. Their local homemade products—lard (lardo), sausage (boudin), cured chamois prosciutto (mocetta), and goose salami (salame d'oca)—are first-rate. A few take-out dishes are prepared daily. French, Italian, and a local dialect unlike both languages are spoken here.

CHEESE

Palmira Olivier
Via E. Aubert 36
Tel. 0165/34495
Closed Thursday afternoon

The small, crowded grocery store of Palmira Olivier has the best selection of Val d'Aosta's cheeses, in varying stages of ripeness, made from the milk produced in different months and from different pastures. Spring cheese, made from the milk of cows grazing on tender young wild herbs and grass, is said to be the best. *Fontina* and *tome* range in taste from delicate to decidedly pungent; freshly curdled *roblec* is more like a custard than a cheese; and *seras* is a kind of *ricotta* made with the whey left over after making *fontina*. These fine and hard-to-find cheeses are available at Palmira Olivier's shop.

*Cheeses aging
in salt brine*

WINE

Enoteca La Cave
Via de Tillier 50
Tel. 0165/40187
*Closed Monday morning in
    winter*
Credit card: American Express

La Cave is a family operation, with *mamma* Piera and her son Guido selling a surprising selection of quality wines and *grappa*. All the best local, limited-production, hard-to-find wines are usually available, as well as a wide choice of fine Italian wines from almost every region. Swiss enophiles come to La Cave to stock up on their favorites. Informal wine tastings are held on Saturday afternoons.

RESTAURANT

Cavallo Bianco
Via Aubert 15
Tel. 0165/3614
Closed Sunday night and Monday
*Credit cards: American Express,
    Diners Club, MasterCard*
Price: expensive

Tucked in a courtyard, the Cavallo Bianco is an old inn where travelers ate while their carriage horses were being replaced. This is one of those restaurants that does everything right. The table is beautifully set with white damask tablecloths, silver service plates,

and the most beautiful flowers I've seen in any restaurant in Italy. Regional and creative seasonal dishes are complemented by a variety of homemade breads. The traditional menu offers a choice of two different appetizers, first and main courses, followed by a superb and very special selection of regional cheeses, then dessert and *piccola pasticceria* (small pastries). Chef Paolo Vai combines traditional flavors with innovative skill and an artist's eye for detail, and the resulting dishes are tasty, well prepared, attractively arranged on the plate, yet faithful to the region's *cucina.* The à la carte menu offers fish and seasonal dishes, expertly cooked but for my taste less interesting than the traditional menu. Desserts are perfectly executed and dramatically presented, and the *piccola pasticceria* seem to disappear by themselves. Paolo's brother Franco will help select wines from their well-stocked cellar of local gems, wines from other regions, and some from France or California. Will their project for a twelve-room hotel be approved? One can hope.

CRAFTS
Foire de Saint-Ours
January 30–31

The Foire de Saint-Ours, an amazing crafts fair held on the last two days of January, is a 1000-year-old tradition in the city of Aosta. Hand-fashioned articles are displayed in the streets and piazzas, and prizes are awarded to local craftsmen celebrating their folk art traditions: carved wooden objects—butter molds, scoops, bowls, friendship cups for coffee, *sabots* (wooden clogs), woven baskets, buckets—along with tools, wrought iron, and lace items that are a pleasure to own. Animal sculptures, especially rabbits with graceful upright ears, are special. The yearly poster competition, open to all comers, has resulted in some stunning artwork, displayed during the fair in the Torre dei Signori di Porta S. Orso.

For more information, call the Assessorato Industria, Commercio e Artigianato (tel. 0165/303523).

ARNAD

MEAT
Marilena Bertolin
Via Nazionale 11
Tel. 0125/966127

"Lard?" my friends said to me when I proposed a taste of the barely-pink-streaked, creamy white *lardo,* a specialty that I had brought back from Arnad, a tiny village on the banks of the Dora Baltea river. "What about the cholesterol?" was the question I encountered most often when I pulled out my jar of Marilena Bertolin's lard. The cholesterol in a thin slice of lard is less than half the equivalent amount of butter, and lard contains fewer calories per gram than olive oil. And it is tasty. Sliced wafer-thin, on a slice of warm bread, slightly melty, lightly perfumed with herbs, and no tough muscular meat to chew, it can be exquisite. If you get hooked on lard, you'll probably be interested in the commemorative festival, with lots of tasting, that takes place at the end of August in Arnad.

CERVINIA

RESTAURANT-INN
Les Neiges d'Antan
Località Perrères
Tel. 0165/948775
Closed Monday, and May
**   through July**
Credit card: American Express
Price: high moderate

Situated three kilometers (less than two miles) south of the center of Cervinia, tucked in a ring of hills, Les Neiges d'Antan is a perfect stop for skier-gastronomes. The small hotel has thirty-two simple, functional rooms, plus a large living room with a fireplace and an impressive seven-speaker stereo system and collection of tapes. Husband-host Maurizio and wife-chef Carmen Bich, and their son, sommelier and *tisane* expert Ludovico, all unique individuals, run the hotel and the restaurant in personal style. The *cucina* is mostly regional, hearty mountain food like local *salumi,* wonderful hard-to-find cheeses, grilled meats, *polenta,* fruit cooked in wine and spices or preserved in alcohol, and homemade *gelato.* Wines are mostly Piemontese.

COGNE

HOTEL
Hotel Sant'Orso
Tel. 0165/74821
Credit cards: American Express,
**   Visa**
Price: moderate

RESTAURANT
Lou Ressignon
Via Bourgeois 23
Tel. 0165/74034
Closed Monday evening, Tuesday,
**   and September 15–30**
Credit cards: American Express,
**   MasterCard**
Price: low moderate

Skiers and hikers have always come to this typical Valdostano restaurant around midnight for a snack, or a *ressignon,* in the dialect of Cogne. Arturo Allera, ski instructor, sommelier, owner, and "simpatico" host, will welcome you into a cozy room with a blazing fireplace and walls decorated with mountain scenes and antlers. The so-called snacks are partially traditional, with some concessions to tourism (pasta, fondue, Swiss raclette, hot dogs). Stick with the *salumi*, especially the lard and *mocetta*, and first-course *soupetta* (a cheesy Fontina *risotto)* or perhaps *polenta alla valdostana* (polenta baked with butter and Fontina). Chamois or veal is stewed in red wine and spices and served with *polenta*. Conclude your meal with Arturo's fine local cheeses. The wine list offers some fantastic local wines as well as a small, personal selection from other regions. A few weeks after we first met, I bumped into Arturo leading a group of restaurateur-bicyclists, pedaling and tasting in the wine country of Friuli, searching for wines to send home.

COURMAYEUR

Courmayeur, once famous for its mineral waters, was the chic 1800s vacation spot of the royal Savoia family and the Piemontese nobility. It has always been a favorite of skiers and, especially, mountain climbers.

HOTEL
Palace Bron
Via Plan Gorret 37
Tel. 0165/842545
Credit cards: American Express, Diners Club, Visa
Price: expensive

HOTEL
Hotel La Brenva
Entrèves (close by)
Tel. 0165/89285
Credit cards: American Express, Visa
Price: high moderate

CHEESE
Le Bien Faire, La Maison du Fromage
Via Roma 120
Tel. 0165/844634
Closed Thursday afternoon
No credit cards

A nice selection of regional cheeses can be found at Le Bien Faire, on via Roma, the main drag of Courmayeur.

WINE
Goio
Avenue Mont Blanc 18
Tel. 0165/84282
Closed Thursday afternoon
No credit cards

Goio has a good wine selection and an impressive collection of *grappa*, arrayed in an almost dizzying floor-to-ceiling display.

RESTAURANT
La Maison de Filippo
Entrèves
Tel. 0165/89968
Closed Tuesday, May, and November
Credit card: American Express
Price: moderate

This is a quintessential rustic mountain restaurant, with attractive prints and paintings, cascades of red geraniums in the summer, a cozy fire in the winter, and a procession of a meal that seems endless. The fixed-price marathon includes an eight-course *antipasto* of bowls, platters, and trays of marinated cheeses, vegetables, anchovies, and cooked ham and sausage with boiled potatoes and cabbage, plus a cutting board of at least six slice-it-yourself *salumi*. Pace yourself to be ready for the first-course choices (try the *zuppa alla valdostana*) and a second course of traditional meat or game dishes. The onslaught continues with the cheese selection; marinated fresh, cooked, and dried fruit; homemade *gelato;* and if you still haven't had enough, a *caffè alla valdostana*. The house wine is pleasant, but a few quality bottles from local producers are also available. This restaurant is used to hungry skiers, and the service is swift and courteous. Dine outside in the summer under the Cinzano umbrellas.

RESTAURANT
Cadran Solaire
Via Roma 122
Tel. 0165/844609
Closed Thursday, October, and June
Credit cards: American Express, MasterCard
Price: expensive

When all the rustic local *cucina* is too much and you'd like a bit of sophisticated elegance, head for Cadran Solaire, in a beautifully restored seventeenth-century building. The terrace, with its 500-year-old ivy vine, overlooks via Roma, Courmayeur's main street, and is perfect for people-watching while sipping an aperitif. The emphasis here is on seasonal, somewhat trendy dishes, lightly cooked with plenty of fresh herbs. The desserts are tasty and highly styled. The wine list could improve—and probably will.

Across the street is Papier, the only shop in town that has anything tempting for the kitchen. Old copper molds, corkscrews, a cheese taster, salt and pepper shakers, and other attractive items are for sale, along with a wide range of other tasteful items including leather goods.

BOOKS AND PRINTS
Leo Garin
Scorciatoia La Palud
Tel. 0165/89164

If you fall in love with Courmayeur and the warmer southern slopes of the mountain you used to think of as Mont Blanc, head for Leo Garin, who sells a lovely selection of prints, paintings, and books of the Valle d'Aosta and Monte Bianco. Call for an appointment.

GIGNOD

RESTAURANT-INN
Locanda La Clusaz
Frazione La Clusaz
Tel. 0165/56075
Closed Tuesday
No credit cards
Price: moderate

This wonderful home-style Valdostano restaurant, in its farmhouse dating from 1040(!), offers simple heart-and-soul-warming *cucina*. Maurizio Grange serves the same food that his grandfather, who founded the restaurant in 1925, dished out. Homemade sausages *(boudins)*, butter, cheese,

A bowl of fruit on a granite counter makes a casual still life.

their own farm-raised beef, pork, vegetables, and honey, are the raw materials with which *mamma* Vittorina Fiou prepares her traditional dishes. Try the grain soup, *polenta* cooked over a woodburning fire, salt cod *(merluzzo)* on Friday, and *carbonada* (veal stew). Salads are dressed with Maurizio's own walnut oil. The fine selection of regional, Italian, and even French wines is a pleasant surprise in this rustic restaurant.

GRESSAN

FRUIT
Rodolfo Coquillard
Agrival
La Tour de Villa
Tel. 0165/552363

Rodolfo Coquillard organically grows apples on his seven-acre farm and sells the very best as fresh fruit, mostly to a list of friends who beg for a few kilos each year. The rest of the crop is

pressed, and the juice is turned into sweet fermented cider, apple gelatin, and special apple vinegar. The vinegar, called *agro di mele,* is made from the cider of organically grown apples, aged for eighteen months, and bottled in attractive glass bottles. The flavor is fruity, intensely apple-y, without the aggressiveness of most vinegars.

SAINT-CHRISTOPHE

RESTAURANT-HOTEL
Albergo Ristorante Casale
Regione Candemine 1
Tel. 0165/541203
Closed Sunday evening, Monday, and December
Credit card: American Express
Price: high moderate

Brothers Fulvio and Ugo Casale and their wives, Mafalda and Chiara, prepare and serve a fixed menu at their hotel restaurant, an abundant review of the entire *cucina valdostana*. Start with rye bread, butter, and local honey; continue with *salumi*, soups, *polenta*, meats, trout, cheese, and dessert. A fun meal in the anti-minimalist style. Fulvio and Ugo are both sommeliers and pair quality local wines with their regional *cucina*. Drink a *grappa* from the wide selection, and when you can feast no more, trudge upstairs to one of Casale's simple rooms.

CHEESE
Cooperativa Produttori Latte e Fontina della Valle d'Aosta
Croix Noire
St. Christophe
Tel. 0165/35714

You can buy Fontina directly from the cooperative five days a week.

VERRÈS

RESTAURANT-INN
Hotel Ristorante da Pierre
Via Martorey 43
Tel. 0165/99376
Closed Tuesday, except in July and August
Credit cards: American Express, Diners Club
Price: high moderate to expensive

Da Pierre has two warm rooms for winter dining—decorated with pewter plates and hand-carved wooden crafts on the walls—and for the summer, a patio with huge pine trees and pots overflowing with geraniums. The *cucina* is seasonal, and takes a more creative look at regional ingredients than do most restaurants: *salumi*, homemade pasta, salmon trout, game, and wonderful cheeses, especially the *bichette dans le nid* (baked goat cheese served on a bed of chicory lettuce). Enjoy one of the fine regional wines. Spend the night in one of the twelve fully equipped rooms, and visit the nearby castles of Verrès and Issogne. And if castles don't appeal to you, you can dance until dawn at the hotel's disco, Crazy Things.

LIGURIA

Liguria is a narrow arc of land stretching from France to Toscana. It is backed by the Alps and Apennine mountains, which form a barrier against the cold northern winds, and fronted by the *Mar Ligure,* whose sea air mitigates the winter weather—southern Mediterranean palms, giant oleanders, and orange and lemon trees thrive here, at the same latitude as Maine.

The western coast is known as the Riviera di Ponente, "the coast where the sun sets," and the eastern coast as the Riviera di Levante, "the coast where the sun rises." Historically, Liguria's contacts with the outside world were primarily by sea. The region was originally populated by the ancient Ligure and later ruled by the Greeks, Saracens, Romans, Venetians, Lombards, French, and Piemontese, and influenced, through trade, by Sicily, Spain, and northern Africa.

The cuisine of the seafaring Ligurians is dominated by the color green. Products of this warm Mediterranean climate include fresh herbs, tasty early-ripening vegetables, and delicately perfumed, sweet extra virgin olive oil—perfect with fish and essential to the preparation of *pesto,* the crushed basil sauce that put Liguria on the gastronomic map. *Focaccia,* a flatbread sprinkled with herbs and olive oil, or stuffed with cheese, is sold at most bakeries and may be offered along with bread in some restaurants. *La farinata,* a chickpea-flour crepe baked in a pizza oven, may be more difficult to pin down, because it's usually sold only in the morning. The *torta pasqualina,* a vegetable tart with thirty-three paper-thin layers of pastry, shows clear signs of northern African or Greek influence. *Cappon magro,* literally "lean capon," is a Christmas Eve tradition for a meatless dinner, a counterpoint to the next day's real capon and an architectural triumph; a pyramid of layered shrimp, lobster, oysters, fish, boiled vegetables, and sea biscuits, flavored with a sauce containing pine nuts, anchovies, and capers. Pastureless Liguria depends on courtyard animals, mostly chicken and rabbit, for its meat. Vegetable stuffings *(ripieni)* are piped into hollowed-out vegetables or simply baked and cut into squares. Pastry shops sell *torta genovese,* a yellow, egg-rich sponge cake (mysteriously known throughout the baking world by its French name, *genoise)* rarely found in restaurants. Most Ligurian meals end with fruit or nontraditional desserts.

It seems that the *cucina* of Liguria was styled for its navigators who, nauseated by the ever-present perfumes of the spices they traded, sought the fresh-tasting herbs and vegetables they missed during their long, dangerous sea voyages. Or was it formed by the Genovese, with their reputation for extreme parsimony? In any case, the Ligurian table is a a palette of greens and a wealth of pungent herbal flavors.

The scenic panorama that has made the Ligurian Riviera famous has attracted hoards of tourists, and restaurants on the coast frequently cater to unsuspecting travelers, serving mediocre food at best. Beware!

THE MENU

SALUMI

•

Salumi di suino • salami or sausage, usually found inland

ANTIPASTO

•

Acciughe marinate • fresh anchovies marinated in lemon juice

Acciughe sotto sale • salt-cured anchovies

Farinata • large chickpea-flour crepe, baked in an oven, served in wedges

Panissa or *Paniccia* • chickpea-flour polenta, served with onions

Sardenaira or *Pissadella* • anchovy, olive, onion, and tomato pizza

Torta pasqualina • "Easter tart," with thirty-three paper-thin layers of pastry, stuffed with chard, artichokes, ricotta, and whole hard-cooked eggs. (Cooks in a rush make do with eighteen layers of pastry). Everyday versions—only four layers of pastry—of this vegetable tart are made with zucchini, peas, fava beans, or winter squash.

Ciuppin • fish stew

Corzetti • hand-rolled pasta cut into disks with a wooden stamp that embosses a pattern, usually star-shaped, on the rounds

Corzetti alla polceverasca • figure-eight-shaped pasta served with butter, pine nuts, and herb, meat, or walnut sauce

Mesciua • soup of chickpeas, wheat, and beans, served with pepper and olive oil

Minestrone col pesto • thick vegetable soup containing pasta, served with pesto, pecorino sardo (sheep's milk cheese to be grated), and Parmesan

Pansoti or *Pansotti* • ravioli stuffed with cheese and borage or chard, served with a creamy walnut sauce

Pesto • a sauce made of fresh basil, pounded in a stone mortar with pine nuts, garlic, pecorino sardo, Parmesan, and olive oil

Riso col preboggion • soup made with rice and field greens, pesto, and grated Parmesan

Trenette col pesto • thin strips of pasta served with pesto. The authentic version should contain string beans and pieces of boiled potato.

PRIMO

•

Trofie or *Troffie al pesto* • homemade lightning-like squiggles of pasta, served with pesto, potatoes, and string beans

Tuccu (or *Tocco*) *de nuxe* • creamy paste of walnuts, garlic, bread, and at times, *prescinsoea,* a yogurt-like cheese

Tuccu (or *Tocco*) *di carne* • meat sauce, used with pasta

Tuccu (or *Tocco*) *di funghi* • mushroom sauce, used with pasta

SECONDO

Baccalà alla genovese • strips of salt cod in a tomato sauce

Bollito freddo • cold salad of boiled beef, sea biscuit, anchovies, capers, and olive oil and vinegar

Buridda • fish stew prepared with salt cod and dried mushrooms or with fresh fish

Cappon magro or *Cappun magru* • layered pyramid of mixed fish, sea biscuits, and vegetables, garnished with lobsters, shrimp, oysters, clams, mussels, and olives, in a sauce containing anchovies, garlic, and capers

Cima alla genovese • veal breast stuffed with veal pâté, brains, sweetbreads, peas, pine nuts, Parmesan, and eggs, wrapped in a cloth, boiled, chilled, and sliced

Condion or *Condiggion* or *Condijun* • salad of sea biscuits, tomatoes, cucumber, lettuce, and thinly sliced dried tuna or pressed mullet roe, dressed with olive oil and vinegar

Coniglio in umido • rabbit cooked with rosemary, bay leaves, white wine, pine nuts, and nutmeg

Frittata di bieta • pan-fried flan with chard

Frittata di carciofi • pan-fried egg and artichoke flan

Frittata di gianchetti (or *bianchetti*) • pan-fried egg flan made with tiny sardines or anchovies

Frittata di zucchini (or *fiori di zucca*) • pan-fried egg and zucchini (or zucchini flower) flan

Lattughe ripiene • braised lettuce stuffed with eggs, vegetables, fish, ground meat, or chicken

Scabecio • fried fish, marinated in vinegar, onions, garlic, sage, and rosemary; similar to the Venetian *saor*

Scorzanera • salsify (oyster plant) root, served braised or deep-fried

Stecchi alla genovese • either a mixture of veal sweetbreads, brains, breast, and mushrooms; or an artichoke wrapped with a dense béchamel sauce; both skewered and deep-fried

Stoccafisso in tocchetto • salt cod cooked with tomatoes, and dry mushrooms

Tomaxelle • braised veal rolls stuffed with ground meat, mushrooms, and potatoes or beans, served with Parmesan

Triglie alla genovese • red mullet baked with a sauce of fennel seeds, white wine, capers, and tomato paste

FORMAGGIO

Formaggella • fresh cheese found inland, rarely ripened

DOLCE

Castagnaccio • flat, unleavened chestnut-flour cakes with raisins

Pandolce genovese • Christmas yeast bread with candied fruit and pine nuts

Pasta genovese • the original *genoise:* yellow egg-rich sponge cake

THE *W*INE LIST

A rocky coast backed by steep mountains isn't the most hospitable environment for grapevines, and Liguria's small production of quality wines is destined to be consumed locally. Few restaurants on the much-touristed coast emphasize quality wine, and the house wines you find will probably be nothing special.

The DOC **Cinque Terre** wines, made with the Bosco, Vermentino, and Albrola grapes, can be a dry delicate white, perfect with fish and seafood. Or with a stroke of luck you may find *Sciacchetrà,* a legendary amber dessert wine that can also be served as an aperitif. Liana Rolandi is the top producer.

Granaccia di Quiliano is a non-DOC rich dry red made from the local Granaccia grape, served with meat and cheese. Scarrone is the best producer.

The **Riviera Ligure di Ponente,** a DOC area along the western Riviera, produces the following wines: **Pigato di Albenga,** a full dry white, and **Vermentino,** a delicate, fresh dry white, both served with fish and seafood; **Pornassio Ormeasco,** a rich spicy red; and **Rossese,** a soft dry red, served with fowl, rabbit, and regional *cucina.* Top producers are Anfossi, Bruna, Cascina Feipu dei Massaretti (Parodi), Colle dei Bardellini, and Lupi.

The DOC **Rossese di Dolceacqua,** made of local Rossese grapes, is a lush dry red, best when paired with meat, game, fowl, and rabbit. Croesi, G. B. Cave (Mandino), and Guglielmi are the best producers.

*R*EGIONAL SPECIALTIES

EXTRA VIRGIN OLIVE OIL

Ligurian extra virgin olive oil, made from a local olive called *la taggiasca,* is delicate, sweet, more golden than green. Some of Italy's largest commercial manufacturers of olive oil, usually labeled "pure" olive oil in the United States and simply *"olio d'oliva"* in Italy, are located in this region. Their oils are made of olives imported from Spain, Greece, or northern Africa and refined in Liguria, and are to be avoided. Read the label carefully and look for *olio extra vergine d'oliva,* which is made with the first "soft" pressing of olives. For more information on extra virgin olive oil, see page 30.

CHICKPEA CREPES

La farinata is a flat crepe made of chickpea flour, water, and salt, drizzled with olive oil and a sprinkle of black pepper, and ideally baked in a wood-burning pizza oven. The best *farinata* is sold in *friggitorie* (fry shops) or in restaurants with pizza ovens, and is usu-ally found in the morning, around 10 a.m. Some restaurants, rediscovering a neglected traditional gem, are serving slices of *farinata* covered with fresh rosemary as an appetizer with a glass of sparkling wine, a splendid idea.

Fine chickpea flour *(farina di ceci)* is produced by the Mulino di Pegli. For the tastiest *farinata,* see pages 91 and 95.

Local hardware stores in Liguria sell shallow round baking pans—in tin-lined copper or in less expensive aluminum—for making *farinata.*

SCIACCHETRÀ DESSERT WINE

This excellent legendary dessert wine—rich, amber, semi-sweet—is almost impossible to find, especially outside of the Cinque Terre, an isolated, inaccessible necklace of five small villages strung along the Ligurian coast north of La Spezia. Terraced vineyards on cliffs overlooking the sea are difficult to harvest, and ensure a small production.

The best examples I've found are produced by Liana Rollandi, available at the Enoteca Internazionale (see page 88) by the bottle or the glass.

WOODEN PASTA STAMPS

Wooden stamps are used to cut and emboss a pattern, usually star-shaped, on hand-rolled pasta. The resulting silver-dollar–sized pasta rounds are known as *corzetti*. The symbol, like a watermark or designer's initials, identifies its creator. The attractive stamps are hand-made and can be used to emboss a decorative pattern on cookie dough or butter if you're not interested in making *corzetti*.

See page 88.

REGIONAL PRODUCERS
∙

These are some of Liguria's quality producers of extra virgin olive oil and olive paste:

Dino Abbo	*Benza e Lupi*
Frantoio Costa 16	*Via S. Lorenzo 1*
Lucinasco	*Dolcedo*
Tel. 0183/52411	*Tel. 0183/280132*
Nanni Ardoino	*Laura Marvaldi*
Piazza de Amicis	*Mulino aldilà*
20r	*dell'acqua*
Oneglia	*Borgomaro*
Tel. 0183/23660	*Tel. 0183/54031*

CITIES AND TOWNS

AMEGLIA

RESTAURANT-HOTEL
Locanda dell'Angelo
Via XXV Aprile
Tel. 018/64391
Always open
Credit cards: American Express,
*   MasterCard*
Price: expensive

Not far from the Roman ruins of Luni, the Locanda dell'Angelo is one of the gastronomic high points of Liguria. Owner-chef Angelo Paracucchi works magic with coastal ingredients. Fish and seafood taste of the sea, and tender early vegetables are flavored with herbs, extra virgin olive oil from his native Umbria, and an occasional dash of balsamic vinegar. Light sauces enhance, never overwhelm, their dishes. The wine list is excellent, although local wines are mostly ignored. Desserts range from refreshing to decadent, and the after-dinner pastries are irresistible. Paracucchi is a true professional, and he has brought his personal vision of Italian *cucina* to Carpaccio, his restaurant in Paris. The Locanda dell'Angelo isn't the same when he's not in the kitchen. The restaurant, and the thirty-six-room hotel, designed in the late 1970s by architect Vico Magistretti, could use some touch-ups.

BOGLIASCO

HOTEL
See Colombia in Genova (page 90)

HOTEL
See Agnello d'Oro in Genova (page 90)

RESTAURANT
Il Tipico
Via Poggio Pavaro 4
Tel. 010/3470754
Closed Monday and November
Credit cards: American Express,
*   Diners Club, MasterCard*
Price: high moderate

Il Tipico, a *trattoria* grown into restaurant, has a handsome view of a not so handsome coastline. The Paoloni brothers Angelo and Aldo, and their wives, Graziella and Silvana, serve "typical," as their name proclaims, Ligurian *cucina* with an occasional hint of their Tuscan origins. Fresh fish, local seafood, and seasonal vegetables are flavored with a wide variety of herbs. *Risotto* is nicely prepared, and carnivores will enjoy the grilled *Fiorentina* (steak) or *capretto* (kid). Ligurian wines, mostly quality, are served by sommelier Marco Farnè. Service and *cucina* deteriorate on Sundays and holidays, when Il Tipico fills to capacity with Genovese families escaping the city for lunch.

CASTELNUOVO MAGRA

Castelnuovo Magra, on the border between Toscana and Liguria, has the air of another era, with its castle ruins and views of vineyards, olive trees, and the not-too-distant coast.

HOTEL
Villa Irene
Via delle Macchie 125
Ronchi (close by)
Tel. 0585/309310
No credit cards
Price: high moderate

RESTAURANT
L'Armanda
Piazza Garibaldi 6
Tel. 0187/674410
Closed Wednesday
No credit cards
Price: moderate

The perfumes and flavors of the food at this simple restaurant are straightforward, with no pretense. Carolina Ponzanelli, known as Armanda, presides in the kitchen of her *trattoria* with daughter-in-law Luciana, and son Valerio is in the dining room. *Salumi* are local. Essential dishes of the inland *cu-cina*—stuffed vegetables, polenta with cabbage and beans, and lamb, rabbit, tripe or baccalà—are all beautifully prepared and tasty. The herbs that grow in this unforgiving meager soil are almost grayish, less lush-looking than hothouse herbs, but intense. They enhance all the dishes that are served in this rustic restaurant. The wines, a fine selection of local and Italian gems, are a joy to drink, an added dimension to a wonderful meal. Reservations are a must.

CHIAVARI

CRAFTS
Franco Casoni
Via Bighetti 73
Tel. 0185/301448

Franco Casoni, woodcarver and sculptor, makes pasta stamps for *corzetti* (see page 87) at his workshop in Chiavari. He also carves female figures that grace the prows of Ligurian ships, and statuettes for traditional Ligurian crèche scenes.

CINQUE TERRE

The Cinque Terre, the "five lands" (Monterosso, Vernazza, Corniglia, Manarola, Riomaggiore), is an isolated necklace of five small villages strung along the coast north of La Spezia, linked only by the railway and a footpath along the cliffs overlooking the sea. Their culinary claims to fame include Sciacchetrà, a legendary, hard-to-find dessert wine, and *pesto*. Natives insist that their basil is sweeter and more aromatic than any other and that their delicate golden olive oil is the best suited to the lively green fresh-tasting sauce. During the summer, beaches are dotted with umbrellas and hotel rooms may be scarce, although an easily infiltrated network of boardinghouses provides rooms for those drawn to the blue water and picturesque rocky coastline. The twisting road to the Cinque Terre is hazardous at best, a real "cliffhanger." The train from La Spezia may be faster and less harrowing, as mountain tunnels occasionally open for a few seconds of bright, breathtaking sea views.

HOTEL
Porta Roca
Monterosso
Tel. 0187/817502
Credit cards: American Express, Visa, MasterCard
Price: low expensive

WINE
Enoteca Internazionale
Via Roma 62
Tel. 0187/817278
Closed Tuesday
Credit cards: all

Francesco and Laura Giusti's wine shop in Monterosso, the largest of the Cinque Terre towns, has an excellent selection of Ligurian wines, sold by the glass or the bottle. They sell authentic Sciacchetrà, the dessert wine, produced by Liana Rollandi, and quality extra virgin olive oil and local honey. The bench in front of the Enoteca Internazionale, always well populated by natives, is the best place to find out about rooms or apartment rentals. In fact, finding a place to stay may be the highlight of your trip!

PASTRY
Pasticceria Laura
Via Vittorio Emanuele 59
No phone
Monterosso
Closed Monday except in summer

If you need a dessert more substantial than *gelato* or fruit, stroll to Laura Desimoni's *pasticceria* for a taste of *la monterossina*, her layered chocolate cream tart.

RESTAURANT
Al Carugio
Via S. Pietro 9
Monterosso
Tel. 0187/817453
No credit cards
Price: moderate

Al Carugio serves regional *cucina* as straightforward as its nautical decor. The menu features marinated fresh anchovies, potato *gnocchi* sauced with pesto, nicely cooked *risotto*, homemade ravioli, and best of all, fresh seafood and fish from the Ligurian Sea—simply prepared, deep-fried, grilled, or baked. Finish with fresh fruit or *macedonia* (fruit salad). The wines are local, light, and go well with the simple menu.

RESTAURANT
Gambero Rosso
Piazza Marconi 7
Vernazza
Tel. 0187/812265
Closed Monday, November, and
*   weekdays December through*
*   March; open every day in*
*   summer*
No credit cards
Price: moderate

Vernazza, a sleepy fishing village awakened to the music of tourism, is probably the most characteristic of the Cinque Terre. The

Window-shopping for pastry while eating gelato —heaven on earth for dessert fans

Gambero Rosso, with its maritime look, serves fine local cooking. Lemon-marinated anchovies are well prepared, and will keep you busy while you wait (longer than you expected in the height of the tourist season) for tasty traditional first course *primi* like *troffie al pesto*, *pansotti al timo*, and *ravioli di pesce* (fish-stuffed ravioli). Main-course options include stuffed mussels, *acciughe alla vernazzina* (anchovies baked with potatoes and onions), or the day's catch, lightly grilled with fresh herbs, served with a wedge of local lemon. Olive oil and wine are also local, although quality wines from other regions also are available. Reserve a table outside in the summertime.

RESTAURANT
Gianni Franzi
Via Visconti 2
Vernazza
Tel. 0187/812228
Closed Wednesday, January, and
*   February*
No credit cards
Price: moderate

Chef Gianni, his wife, Dea, sister Lina, aunt Maria and other assorted family members run the restaurant Gianni Franzi, and have since 1960. Dine outdoors overlooking the harbor, or in the main dining room with its rough rock walls, on authentic *trenette al pesto*, *acciughe al forno* (anchovies baked with potatoes and tomatoes), *acciughe ripiene fritte* (stuffed fried anchovies), *zuppa di datteri* (clam stew), or stuffed mussels. Desserts are simple and homemade; wines are mostly local.

GARLENDA

RESTAURANT-HOTEL
La Meridiana–Il Rosmarino
Regione San Rocco 15
Tel. 0182/580271
Closed November and December
Credit Cards: all
Price: low expensive for the restaurant, luxury for the hotel

Il Rosmarino, the Hotel La Meridiana's restaurant, has set out to prove that hotel dining doesn't have to be horrible or outrageously expensive. The *cucina* is predominantly Ligurian, utilizing locally grown vegetables, extra virgin olive oil, fish from the coast, and lots of herbs. At times the results may seem a bit "nouvelle," but if you've eaten one too many *ripiene* or *farinate* and crave a bit of lighter cooking, you'll enjoy the food at Il Rosmarino. Flavors are basic, all ingredients are of the highest quality—fresh and local— and owner Edmondo Segre's passionate interest in food and wine seems to have inspired the kitchen staff to greater heights. The wine list has been carefully chosen and includes fine regional, Italian, and even Californian wines. The luxurious hotel La Meridiana, part of the Relais & Chateaux group, is splendid, with a swimming pool, eighteen-hole golf course, riding, tennis, sauna, and service with a capital S. Reservations are required for the restaurant.

GENOVA

Genova, Italy's most important port, sprawls along thirty kilometers (nineteen miles) of coast, from Voltri to Nervi, hiding its medieval origins in one of the nation's largest historic centers. Bombed heavily during World War II, parts of Genova still seem to be awaiting repair. The area along the port is seedy-looking, but the narrow lanes called *carugi* and the impressive Renaissance and baroque palaces give Genova a unique charm. Beware of August, when it seems that the entire city—for the most part without air conditioning— closes, probably due to the excessive heat.

HOTEL
Colombia
Piazza Acquaverde
Tel. 010/261841
Credit cards: all
Price: luxury

HOTEL
Agnello d'Oro
Vico delle Monachette 6
Tel. 010/262084
Credit cards: Diners Club, MasterCard, Visa
Price: moderate

BAR-CAFFÈ
Klainguti
Piazza Soziglia 102
Tel. 010/296502
Closed Sunday

Klainguti is one of Genova's best bars, even if its name doesn't sound very Italian. It was founded in 1828 by Swiss pastry chefs who emigrated to Italy at the turn of the century, and the pastry work has always been fine. Giuseppe Verdi—and "Sir John Falstaff," according to the handwritten note on a framed calling card—were great fans of this Genovese bar/pastry shop.

BAR-CAFFÈ
Romanengo
Via Orefici 31
Tel. 010/203915
Closed Sunday

Romanengo
Piazza Soziglia 74r
Tel. 010/297869
Closed Monday

There are two Romanengo shops on via Orefici. The original, at via Orefici 31, is Genova's oldest bar, founded in 1805. One room is lined with glass jars of colorful candy called *goccie al rosolio*, pastel beads of sugar enclosing a rose liqueur center; bottles of naturally flavored syrups including barley, tamarind, sour cherry, rose, and citron; and pots of honey, preserves, and fruit jellies. The old-fashioned wood-trimmed display counters contain trays of neatly aligned rows of hand-dipped chocolates, *marroni* chestnuts, and at Christmas, a major selection of whole, shiny, translucent, hypersweet preserved fruits. I was puzzled by a jar of thick white cream labeled *manna* (not to be confused with the food the Israelites ate in the desert). The salesperson described it as a *rinfrescante*, which means refresher, but Romanengo's *manna* is a sweet syrup, known for its mild laxative powers, made from the sap of a native ash tree.

The owner of the original shop sold it, then regretted his choice and founded a second Romanengo store, uphill from the original. Both have more or less the same selection of old-fashioned bottles, jars, and candied fruits, but some say that the second store's products are superior.

MARKET
Mercato Orientale
Via XX Settembre, next to the
church of Santa Maria della
Consolazione
Open Monday through Saturday
mornings

The name of Genova's market, the "Oriental Market," evokes images of exotic bazaars, silks and spices, of the days when the Genovesi explored the unknown seas. It is the prototypical market, a bit more "oriental" than most, and a perfect stop for picnic supplies. Flower vendors spill out onto the sidewalks of via XX Settembre, backed by a wall of plants and greenery, with buckets of fresh flowers at hard-to-resist prices. Vegetable, fruit, and fish stands are in the middle of the market, ringed by an arcade containing *alimentari* (groceries), meat, poultry, tripe stalls, bread bakeries, and *casalinghi* (housewares shops). The produce inside is impressive, choice, just picked, firm, and scented with garden loam. The fresh fish (the signs say *"Nostrane"*—"Local") is lively-looking and clear-eyed.

At Stand 181, Francesco Abis has an impressive selection of olives from the Riviera, and sun-dried tomatoes ready to be preserved under olive oil, sold by weight.

At Stand 186, Benedetta Dolcino's display of vegetables and herbs, a study in the color green, is a thriller. Artichoke and asparagus fans should plan a spring visit.

Gino and Sergio, Stand 100–101, have the freshest-looking fish.

Stand 176, Lo Chalet, offers exotic fruit, mushrooms, and a vast variety of shelled nuts.

Al Mulino, a bread bakery at Stand 34, makes a good *focaccia alla salvia* or *alla cipolla* (sage or onion flatbread) and interesting leaf-shaped whole-wheat breads.

At Stand 251, Ermanno Ubaldi sells housewares, including tin-lined *farinata* pans.

FRY SHOP
Antica Sciamada
Vico San Giorgio 14r
No phone
Closed Sunday

Antica Sciamada
Via Ravecca 19r
Tel. 010/280843
Closed Sunday

Genova is the *farinata* capital of Liguria, and two of the best shops for this tasty crepe are both called Antica Sciamada. The original, owned by Ornella Capra, is on vico San Giorgio. The second Antica Sciamada, on via Ravecca, is owned by Viviana Sturla.

GELATO
Cremeria Augusto
Via Nino Bixio 3r
Tel. 010/591884
Closed Saturday and August
10–31

The unassuming sign says "Illy Caffè Cremeria," and the ambience is archetypal busy bar, but the Cremeria Augusto serves the best *gelato* in Genova. The stainless-steel counter next to the door is punctuated with lids of inset *gelato* containers, and the pink granite bar holds a carousel of fresh ice cream cones. The list includes classics and seasonal fruit flavors, but the true stars are the custardy egg-yolk-rich *crema* (custard cream) and *panera,* which tastes like *cappuccino,* worth a detour for coffee fans. Sunday crowds confirm my enthusiasm for this tasty *gelato.*

SWEETS
Rosella
Via Berghini 59r
Tel. 010/503843

Soft, snow-white sugary rectangles of fondant—creamy candies made of water, sugar, and cream of tartar, cooked, then kneaded like dough and flavored—are created by the artisans of Rosella, using Santo Rosello's recipe from the 1800s. Fringed pastel papers are wrapped around the eight flavors: pale pink for raspberry, yellow for lemon, green for apricot, orange for orange, white for mint, blue for anise, light brown for coffee, and dark brown, almost black, for chocolate. For a factory visit, contact Mr. Pallavicini.

WINE BAR, RESTAURANT
Enoteca Bar Sola
Via Barabino 120r
Tel. 010/594513
Closed Sunday and August
Credit Card: American Express
Price: low moderate

A local crowd streams through the Enoteca Bar Sola to drink a glass of wine or beer, purchase a bottle of wine or olive oil or imported gourmet items, or to taste some of the specialties of the Sola family. Rita is in the kitchen, and her brothers Luigi and sommelier Pino are at the counter of their friendly bar. Stop in for a glass of fine local Vermentino and a taste of the fresh *focaccia* with sage or onion. The dining rooms, with dark wood trim, overhead fans, leather banquettes, and director's chairs, combine English and maritime styles. The *cucina* is pure Ligurian, however, with a large selection of regional cured meats, as well as imported products for locals bored with tradition, like caviar, Russian crab, and canned lobster bisque. Pasta, minestrone, vegetables, and *cima alla Genovese* (veal stuffed with a tasty forcemeat) are beautifully prepared, speckled with fresh green herbs. All cooking is done with local extra virgin olive oil. Hooray for one of Liguria's best wine lists, with wines priced by the bottle or glass.

RESTAURANT
La Fate
Via Ruspoli 31
Tel. 010/546402
Closed Sunday and August
No credit cards
Price: expensive

Candles, crystal, and silver grace the tables of this tiny restaurant, where owners Sandro Caponetto, wife Elena, and sister Silvana have taken traditional Ligurian *cucina* and restored it as carefully as they have their old tavern–wine shop,

Le Fate. Sandro searches out the best possible local ingredients, the freshest fish, the first early vegetables of the season, hard-to-find cheeses, and extra virgin olive oil that he flavors with herbs. Chef Angelo Guerra uses this bounty to full advantage. The *gnocchi con cagliata al pesto* (potato gnocchi dressed with pesto that has been lightened with a yogurty curdled fresh cheese) will thrill fans of the heady green super-basil paste. Humble fish like hake, anchovies, and salt cod are given equal billing with prawns, salmon, and monkfish. Predictably, herbs play an important role at Le Fate. Desserts are worth saving room for and have a menu all their own. Wines are splendid, carefully selected by Sandro.

RESTAURANT
Toe Drüe
Via Carlo Corso 44
Sestri Ponente
Tel. 010/671100
Closed for lunch; Sunday and
*   Monday; sometimes Tuesday;*
*   and August*
No credit cards
Price: high moderate

Don't attempt to drive to Toe Drüe in Sestri Ponente, because you'll never find it. Take a cab (your driver will probably have to ask for directions in Sestri) to this restaurant with its unpronounceable name, which means "thick-topped tables" in Ligurian dialect. The *cucina* is local, tavern-style, based on a knowledge that goes beyond the kitchen to the seas, tides, vines, and the phases of the moon. Gianni and Marialina Fer-

rando dish out food that looks and tastes the way it should—real, not dressed up. Toe Drüe has no black-tie waiters, cork-sniffing sommeliers, china, crystal, or silver, and the acoustics are horrible, but it serves the best, most genuine *cucina* in Genova, accompanied by a selection of wines that Gianni has unearthed from the vineyards of Liguria and Piemonte. I have never seen a printed menu in this restaurant, or a wine list, and I doubt that they exist. I leave my choices to Gianni and I've never been disappointed. If the wood-burning oven is lit, you'll get a taste of one of Genova's best *farinate*. Desserts are Piemontese, either *panna cotta* (a rich cream confection) or *bonet* (chocolate almond custard). Reservations are hard to come by at times, and are a must since the restaurant often closes at Gianni's whim.

RESTAURANT
Bruxiaboschi
Via F. Mignone 8
San Desiderio
Tel. 010/345032
Closed Sunday evening, Monday,
*   and August*
No credit cards
Price: moderate

Located in one of Genova's anonymous and not-too-easy-to-find suburbs, Trattoria Bruxiaboschi is staffed by the Sciaccaluga family and serves classic home-style Ligurian *cucina*. Along with the usual stuffed vegetables, flatbreads, and *minestrone* (vegetable soup), the menu offers homemade chestnut pasta, tasty mushroom dishes, lamb, tripe, and a varied

The sirens of the Ligurian coast sing of fresh fish and olive oil.

fritto misto that changes with the seasons but always includes *cuculli* (potato fritters). Conclude your meal with the *latte dolce fritto*, a cinnamon-spiced deep-fried custard. The lovely local and Italian wines complement the simple menu.

GRIMALDI INFERIORE

RESTAURANT-INN
Baia Beniamin
Corso Europa 63
Tel. 0184/38002
Closed Tuesday evening,
*   Wednesday, and October*
Credit card: American Express
Price: expensive

Baia Beniamin, a restaurant-inn with elegant service and eight rooms, is one of the places people begged me not to include in my book, for fear of never again finding a table in this almost unknown gem. But it didn't seem fair not to mention the hardworking partners, Oscar Falsirolli in the dining room and Carlo Brunelli in the kitchen, dedicated to light, mostly fish, partly Ligurian, *cucina,* beautifully prepared, nicely presented. The wines are excellent and carefully selected. The diners are mostly French, out for a splendid bargain at such an elevated gastronomic level. This is one of the most promising restaurants on the coast, a rising star.

LEIVI

RESTAURANT-INN
Ca' Peo
Strada Panoramica 77
Tel. 0185/319090
Closed Monday, Tuesday lunch,
*   and November*
Credit card: Visa
Price: expensive

Six kilometers (four miles) of winding country road lead to Ca' Peo, an isolated restaurant immersed in the olive-tree-covered hills above Chiavari. The *cucina* and wines are well worth the trip. Franco and Melly Solari's restaurant, tucked away in a town that none of my Italian friends had ever heard of, is an expression of devotion to Ligurian tradition. Vegetable fans will appreciate Melly's ethereal cooking, especially the homemade pasta stuffed with fresh fava beans and sauced with leeks, and the crispy wide deep-fried strips of zucchini. Fish from the nearby coast, local lamb, and fresh woodsy mushrooms are skillfully prepared. The dining room has an impressive view of the countryside and the distant coast. Tables are carefully set with service plates, crocheted doilies, and simple low flower arrangements. Sommelier Franco is determined in his quest for fine wines, and hosts a yearly competition for the best Ligurian wine, chosen by a panel of experts. Spend the night in one of Ca' Peo's modern rooms or two-bedroom apartments with terraces and a view of the sea, and you can taste all the winners without worrying about driving. The sunset is worth a detour.

LERICI

HOTEL
Il Nido
Via Fiascherino 75
Tel. 0187/967286
Closed November through mid-
*   March*
Credit cards: American Express,
*   Diners Club, MasterCard*
Price: moderate

RESTAURANT
Conchiglia
Piazza del Molo
Tel. 0187/967334
Closed Wednesday and December
Credit cards: all
Price: high moderate

Small and cozy in the winter, the Trattoria Conchiglia doubles in size in the warmer months with terrace dining. Start your meal with a varied *antipasto*, prepared by owner Massimo Lorate with whatever came in on the fishing boats, lightly dressed with local extra virgin olive oil. Fresh fish is grilled, skewered, or slowly deep-fried to a crunch. Chocolate sauce will probably cover your dessert of ice cream or nut cake. House wines are basic.

RAPALLO

HOTEL
Cuba e Milton
San Michele di Pagana
Tel. 0185/50610
Credit cards: all
Price: moderate

RESTAURANT
Trattoria ü Giancu
Via San Massimo 78
Tel. 0185/56189
Closed Wednesday, Thursday lunch, November, and December
No credit cards
Price: low moderate

Mamma Pasqualina in the kitchen and her son Fausto Oneto in the large dining room of ü Giancu ("white" in dialect, the nickname of the original owner) serve *cucina ligure* that will thrill vegetarians and traditionalists alike. The food is home-style, the wines are simple, and on Fridays the menu features vegetarian dishes so varied you won't miss the meat. The *formaggetta* cheese is homemade and tasty. Charming Fausto's English is perfect, learned from friends, he says. During the off-season they are closed early in the week; call to be sure.

RECCO

HOTEL
Stella Maris
Punta Chiappa (take a boat from Camogli)
Tel. 0185/770285
Closed October to April
No credit cards
Price: moderate

RESTAURANT
Focacceria
Via Roma 278
Tel. 0185/720019
Closed Wednesday; open evenings only mid-January to mid-February
No credit cards
Price: low moderate

The Focacceria is owned by the same family as, and shares its kitchen and street number with, the famous restaurant Manuelina. Manuelina is coasting along on its past glories—it is credited with inventing *focaccia col formaggio*, flatbread stuffed with melty *stracchino* cheese. The Focacceria's *cucina* is traditional, with all the classics, but stick to the *focaccia*, the house specialty, oozing cheese out of the tasty thin bread-dough crust. Prices are modest, and there's always a crowd waiting to be served.

VARESE LIGURE

SWEETS
Monastero Suore Agostiniane
S. Filippo Neri
Piazza Marconi
Tel. 0187/842179

The nuns of Varese Ligure make *scoette*, or *sciuette*, ("little flowers" in Ligurian dialect) from almond paste. These delicately painted pastel flowers and fruit are as graceful as porcelain, too attractive to eat. The nuns have temporarily suspended production, but they don't rule out resuming in the near future. Will it be possible to ring the bell at the main gate and wait for the wheel to turn, filled with a packet of lovely sweets from another world? The pears and peaches are personal favorites.

VOZE

Voze, almost four kilometers (2½ miles) inland from the coastal village of Noli, is a pleasant detour into olive country.

HOTEL
Punta Est
Via Aurelia 1
Finale Ligure (close by)
Tel. 019/600611
Credit cards: American Express, Visa
Price: moderate

RESTAURANT
Lilliput
Regione Zulieno 76
Tel. 019/748009
Closed Monday, January, and
  weekday lunch
No credit cards
Price: moderate

The *cucina* of Lilliput is Ligurian reexamined by Carlo Nan with patience and intellience, and nicely prepared. The *farinata* sprinkled with rosemary and black pepper is served with a glass of *Spumante* (sparkling wine) for openers. Warm vegetable *antipasti* and cold fish salads compete for the appetizer course. Pasta, potato *gnocchi,* and *risotto* are sauced with seafood, mushrooms, or herbs. Fish are grilled to perfection, and the wines are of equally good quality.

•Merano   •Bressanone

Bolzano

Santa Gertrude Val D'Ultimo

Appiano•

Cornaiano

Egna•

•Cavalese Masi

San Michele All'Adige

•Civezzano
•Pinzolo   •Trento

•Rovereto

TRENTINO–ALTO ADIGE

∎

Trentino and Alto Adige are geographically united by mountains, by deep valleys cut by streams coursing down from towering peaks; they are separated from Veneto by the dramatic Dolomite Mountains and linked to the rest of Europe by the Brenner Pass. But the hyphen between Trentino, the southern half of this fraternal—not identical—twin region, and northern Alto Adige (the South Tirol, the southern side of the Austrian and Swiss Alps) separates two distinct cultures. All street signs in Alto Adige are in both Italian and German, but the dominant language and culture of this region is Teutonic. Intertwined histories account for Alto Adige's traditional attachment to Austria. Trentino, which was governed for almost 800 years by the ecclesiastic principality of Trento, preceded and followed by brief periods of Austrian and Tirolian dominion, is far more Italian.

The *cucina* of Trentino is decidedly Venetian in spirit, with *polenta* playing an important role, frequently accompanied by mushrooms. In Alto Adige, regional dishes have German names, translated into Italian on most menus. Bread there is usually white or rye, often flavored with caraway or fennel seeds. Ham is the most likely appetizer, either cooked and served with freshly grated horseradish or marinated in brine with aromatic herbs and spices, then cold-smoked and aged to produce *speck*. No traditional pasta is found; dumplings and soups are the usual first courses. Meats are roasted or stewed; game is often cooked with fruit. Cabbage, sauerkraut, and potatoes are the traditional vegetables. Strudel, a sure sign of Austrian influence, is frequently found, made with a regional specialty of great importance, the apple. (Vast apple orchards carpet the fertile valleys of Trentino and Alto Adige.) Grapes for the crisp white and fruity red wines cover the hills, and German-speaking tourists in hiking boots and red knee socks dot the mountain paths. At times the tension between the Italian majority and a vocal minority of German separationists flares up in Alto Adige, but signs of strain are rarely evident in the velvety green pastures with their grazing cows, haystacks, and split-wood fences.

Watch out for off-season closings here; many hotels and some restaurants close down for a month or longer in the winter.

THE MENU

SALUMI

•

Speck • brine- and smoke-cured pork

PRIMO

•

Canederli • bread dumplings that can be plain or flavored with meat, liver, or brown bread

Minestrone d'orzo • barley soup

Ribel • buckwheat fritters

Smacafam • buckwheat polenta, baked with sausage

Spatzle • flour and egg dumplings

Zuppa acida or *sauerkrautsuppe* • sauerkraut soup

Zuppa di terlano • white wine–based cream sauce

SECONDO

•

Anguilla • eel

Biroldo • blood sausage with walnuts, pine nuts, and chestnuts

Camoscio alla tirolese or *Gemsenfleisch* • chamois cooked in vinegar, spices, and sour cream

Capriolo in salsa • venison cooked in red wine

Gulasch di manzo or *Rindsgulasch* • beef stew with herbs and spices

Lumache • snails

Tortino di patate e carne or *Grostel* • cake of leftover boiled beef, potatoes, and onions

Trota in blu or *Blau forelle* • alpine trout cooked in white wine vinegar, wine, herbs, and spices

CONTORNO

•

Crauti or *sauerkraut* • sauerkraut

Gnocchetti or *Spatzle* • potato or flour and egg dumplings

Verdura ripiena or *Gefultes gemuse* • tomatoes, zucchini, or peppers stuffed with ground meat and rice

DOLCE

•

Frittelle di mele or *Apfelkuchel* • apple fritters

Krapfen • fried sweet dough, filled with preserves

Strudel • strudel

Torta di polenta nera • buckwheat-flour cake served with whipped cream

Zelten • Christmas cake of rye flour, nuts, candied fruit, and cinnamon

THE *W*INE LIST

More than half the wine produced in Trentino and Alto Adige is DOC. Much of it is exported to Germany and Austria, and wine labels in Alto Adige are frequently in German. The crisp dry white wines are more widely known than the light fruity reds. The dessert wines can be hard to find, but worth the effort.

The *Südtiroler* or *Alto Adige,* DOC zone, in the province of Bolzano, includes nineteen different types of wine. Crisp, dry whites *Muller Thurgau, Chardonnay, Pinot Bianco, Pinot Grigio, Riesling Renano, Sylvaner,* and *Traminer Aromatico* are served with appetizers, pasta, and fish dishes. Dry red *Cabernet,* made from Cabernet Franc and Cabernet Sauvignon grapes, and fruity *Pinot Nero* are good choices with meat or regional cooking. Native red grapes are used to produce full-flavored *Lagrein Dunkel;* light, young *Schiava;* and fragrant rosé *Lagrein Kretzer*—all paired with sauced meat dishes. Semi-sweet golden *Moscato Giallo* and rosé *Moscato Rosa,* made with the flowery scented Moscato grapes, are fine with simple desserts and pastry. Top producers are Bellendorf, Cornell, Gojer, Lageder, Girlan, Schreckbichl (also called Colterenzio), and Tiefenbrunner (also called Schloss Turmhof).

The *Caldaro,* or *Lago di Caldaro,* a DOC wine from the province of Bolzano, is made from the Schiava Grossa, Gentile, and Grigia grapes. This native light, winy dry red is served with meat and fowl, and is produced by Bellendorf, Girlan, Kuenberg, Schreckbichl (also called Colterenzio), and Tiefenbrunner (also called Schloss Turmhof).

Light, crisp, dry, non-DOC white *Chardonnay* is paired with appetizers, fish, and seafood, and produced by Maso Cantanghel, Pojer & Sandri, J. Tiefenbrunner, and Zeni.

Müller Thurgau is a dry, aromatic, fruity white made with the Müller Thurgau grape, and served with appetizers, fish, and seafood. Top producers are Pojer and Sandri, J. Tiefenbrunner, and Zeni.

Pinot Nero is a warm, fruity red, served with meat and fowl, and produced by Maso Cantangel, Pojer & Sandri, and Zeni.

Santa Maddalena, a dry red with a bitter finish, made from local Lagrein and Schiava grapes. It is at its best served with meat, fowl, and regional *cucina,* and is produced by Bellendorf, Gojer, J. Hofstätter, Kettmeir, and Lageder.

The grapes for many quality *Spumanti* (sparkling wines), produced locally and outside Trentino–Alto Adige, are grown in this region. Both *champenois* and *charmat* methods are used with great success on Chardonnay, Pinot Bianco, Pinot Nero, or Pinot Grigio grapes. These delightful sparkling wines are served with appetizers or light first-course dishes. Top producers are Arunda, Équipe 5, Ferrari, Frescobaldi (Toscana), Antinori (Toscana), Marone Cinzano (Piemonte), and Vivaldi.

Teroldego Rotiliano is a rich, full, dry red made from local Teroldego grapes, grown on the Rotaliano plain of alluvial soil in the province of Trento. It is served with meat, game, and richly sauced dishes and produced by Barone de Cles, Conti Martini, Foradori, Istituto Agrario Provinciale San Michele all'Adige, and Zeni.

The *Trentino* DOC zone makes wines from twenty different grape varieties. Whites *Chardonnay, Müller Thurgau, Pinot Bianco.*

Riesling, Nosiola, and *Traminer* are crisp, dry and fruity—served with appetizers, fish, and seafood. Reds *Cabernet,* made with Cabernet Franc and Sauvignon, and *Marzemino* and *Lagrein,* both made from local grape varieties, are served with meat, fowl, and regional dishes. Top producers are Barone de Cles, Conti Martini, de Tarczal, Foradori, Istituto Agrario Provinciale San Michele all'Adige, Poli, and Simoncelli.

Some of Trentino–Alto Adige's finest winemakers produce *vino da tavola*—exemplary reds, whites, and rosés produced outside DOC zones. Pojer and Sandri make fruity white *Nosiola;* delightful *Schiava di Faedo* and *Vin dei Molini,* full-flavored rosés; and rich red *Cabernet.* De Tarczal makes red *Pragiara,* a rich barrel-aged blend of Merlot and Cabernet. The Istituto Agrario Provinciale San Michele all'Adige makes many fine experimental wines, including **Castel San Michele,** a rich Cabernet-Merlot blend. J. Hofstätter makes elegant white **de Vite** with a hybrid of Riesling and Schiava grapes. Tiefenbrunner makes **Gold-** **muskateller,** a rich dry white Moscato Giallo; **Feldmarschall,** a fruity white Müller Thurgau; and Vinattieri makes dry, crisp white **Vinattieri Bianco,** a blend of Pinot Bianco and Chardonnay.

REGIONAL SPECIALTIES

APPLES

Over 30 percent of Italy's apples are grown in Trentino and Alto Adige, and many valleys, including the famous Val di Non, look like one huge apple orchard. Almost all production is sold through cooperatives, so it's impossible to single out a particular quality farmer. Look for hand-lettered signs for *mele* on country roads.

SPECK

Speck means "lard" in German, but in Alto Adige it means pork flank, boned, cured in a spiced brine, smoked gently for a few hours daily, and aged for at least six months. The bad news about *speck* is that most of it is inferior stuff, produced industrially, with the smoking and aging process reduced to weeks. Quality artisanal *speck* is sold, probably to friends and relatives of its producer, before it ever leaves its chimney or smokehouse. See page 103 for one source of artisanal *speck.*

CRAFTS

The royal blue apron called a *grembiule,* which is worn by farmers in various parts of Italy, is practically a uniform in Trentino–Alto Adige, and the locals even wear them to church. You can buy simple or embroidered versions of this sturdy canvas apron in notions stores *(mercerie)* throughout the region.

Archeological excavations in the Val di Cembra have uncovered antecedents, over 2000 years old, of the *situla,* a container that has been adapted as an ice bucket for chilling wine. The *spumante* producers of Trentino have adopted the *situla* as their symbol. See page 107 for one source.

CITIES AND TOWNS

APPIANO

HOTEL
Schloss Korb
Missiano (close by)
Tel. 0471/63322
No credit cards
Price: low expensive

RESTAURANT
Zur Rose
Josef Innherhoferstrasse 2
Tel. 0471/52249
Closed Sunday and February
No credit cards
Price: moderate

Zur Rose is a rustic family-style restaurant serving well-prepared traditional *cucina,* with the assistance of a wine list that makes everything taste even better. Ricotta *gnocchi* with fresh herbs are lovely. Mushrooms are a seasonal specialty.

BOLZANO

HOTEL
Parkhotel Laurin
Via Laurino 4
Tel. 041/980500
Credit cards: all
Price: expensive

BAR-CAFFÈ
Edi Bar
Piazza Walther von der
* Vogelweide-Platz*
Tel. 0471/978330
Closed Sunday except in summer

Giorgio Grai, the wizard of wine (an enologist known as *l'ombra,* "the shadow," because he's so dif-ficult to get to), can sometimes be found at his bar in piazza Walther. Recently restructured by Afra and Tobia Scarpa, the "new" Edi Bar has a wine-tasting area and a room upstairs where quality products are presented, tasted, and compared, with results that are often surprising. The coffee is excellent, and you can sip a glass of one of Giorgio's hard-to-find wines at an outdoor table in the piazza.

RESTAURANT
Castel Mareccio
Via Claudia de'Medici 12
Tel. 0471/979439
Closed Sunday
Credit card: American Express
Price: high moderate

Medieval Castel Mareccio, surrounded by vineyards, is a five-minute walk from the center of Bolzano. The dining rooms, with vaulted ceilings and intimate lighting, are an attractive backdrop for the traditional and seasonal *cucina.* The frequently changing menu lists four *degustazioni* consisting of four courses and a well-chosen wine from the small but wonderful wine list.

RESTAURANT
La Belle Epoque
Via Laurino 4
Tel. 0471/980500
Closed all day Saturday and
* Sunday lunch*
Credit cards: all
Price: expensive

La Belle Epoque is a hotel restaurant that is making a big effort at quality *cucina.* They seem caught up in lots of sauce and "nouvelle"-type dishes—a distinct contrast to the traditional heavy—and mostly brown—food of the region. The lunch "snack" (a main course and two vegetables) and the more complete business menu are both well priced. The menu changes monthly, and the wine list presents some pleasant surprises. Dining under a canopy in the garden, with its tall trees and manicured lawn in the center of Bolzano, is a treat.

BRESSANONE

HOTEL
Elefante
Via Rio Bianco 4
Tel. 0472/22288
Closed mid-November through
* February*
No credit cards
Price: expensive

HOTEL
Temlhof
Via Elvas 76
Tel. 0472/22658
Closed mid-November to mid-
* December*
Credit cards: American Express,
* Diners Club, MasterCard*
Price: high moderate

RESTAURANT
Fink
Via Portici Minori 4
Tel. 0472/23883
Closed Wednesday evening and
* Thursday*
No credit cards
Price: moderate

The Ristorante Fink is Alto Adige's keeper of the flame in a region that seems to pander to the taste of Teutonic tourists. The building is 500 years old, and the restaurant has been around for a hundred of them. The traditional mountain *cucina* is well prepared and presented, and the wine list offers fine regional selections. Taste the *formaggio grigio* (onion-topped cheese).

CAVALESE MASI

RESTAURANT
Inn
Mas del Saügo
Baldessalon 1
Tel. 0462/30788
Closed Thursday except in summer
Credit cards: Diners Club, Visa
Price: expensive

Keep your eyes peeled for the wooden sign pointing toward a hard right after the stream, or you'll miss Mas del Saügo, a cabin in a clearing in the pines down a twisting but beautifully paved mountain road leading to a valley with a landscape out of *Heidi*. Four guest rooms and three intimate dining rooms await you in this personalized inn with its home-style clutter of prints, dried flowers, Venetian masks, lace, linens, dolls, and books and magazines. The cottage, with its stone walls, wide plank floors, and down quilt decor, has been carefully under-restored. The *cucina* isn't as thrilling as the rest of the experience, although a complete line of Giorgio Grai's wines, from Alto Adige and beyond, bolsters neophyte cook Donatella Zampoli's nontraditional fixed-menu meals. Breakfast is served to the music of lowing cows.

CIVEZZANO

HOTEL
Villa Madruzzo
Cognola di Trento (close by)
Tel. 0461/986220
Credit card: American Express
Price: moderate

RESTAURANT
Maso Cantanghel
Via Madonnina 33
Tel. 0461/858714
Closed Sunday and August
No credit cards
Price: high moderate

Maso Cantanghel is the name of Piero Zabini and Lucia Gius's working farm, which produces vegetables, fruit, wine, and even a little *grappa* for its restaurant. The dining room is tastefully furnished with prints, antiques, a collection of soup tureens, and six tables simply but elegantly set with linen, Ginori china, and stemware. The *cucina* is home-style, a fixed menu that wisely uses seasonal home-grown products. Mushrooms are a regional specialty and often accompany silky homemade pasta, or are cooked with tender boned rabbit. Lucia outdoes herself with the homemade *gelato* and a tray of dessert pastries that may include *torroncino* nougat (made daily), candied orange peel, meringues, buttery crumbly *sbrisolona*, and sugar-coated grapes. The wine list offers a splendid personal selection of local, Italian, and some French wines, but the house wine is wonderful.

CORNAIANO

HOTEL
Schloss Korb
Missiano (close by)
Tel. 0471/633222
No credit cards
Price: low expensive

RESTAURANT
Marklhof-Bellavista
Via Belvedere 14
Tel. 0471/52407
Closed Monday
No credit cards
Price: moderate

The Marklhof is a typical Tirolean *trattoria*. Its hunting-trophy decor and bilingual menu appeal mostly to German and Austrian tourists. Order, from the more exciting menu of daily specials, the home-smoked *prosciutto* served with horseradish and butter, game, or *grostel* served with a cabbage and *speck* salad. The buckwheat *torta* with whipped cream and the fruit desserts are tasty. The house wines are adequate. In the summer, dine on the terrace overlooking some of Alto Adige's choicest vineyards.

EGNA

HOTEL
Schloss Korb
Missiano (close by)
Tel. 0471/633222
No credit cards
Price: low expensive

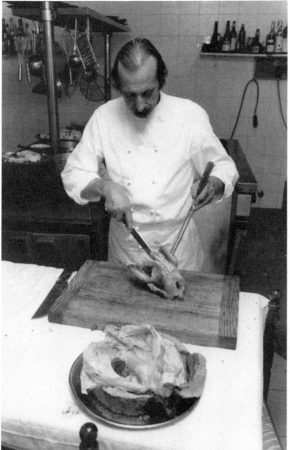

*Carving a
clay-baked pheasant*

RESTAURANT
Enoteca Johnson e Dipoli
Via A. Hofer 3
Tel. 0471/812923
*Closed Sunday evening and
Monday*
No credit cards
Price: moderate

The Enoteca Johnson e Dipoli has one of the most interesting wine lists in all Italy, a product of the intelligence and palate of Peter Dipoli, the guiding light of this wine bar forced to become a restaurant. The original decor, with floors, table, and curved bar of marble, and surprise frescoes in the bathrooms, is refreshing in the midst of this Tirolean village. More than twenty fine wines are served by the glass—in addition to milkshakes, fresh juice, and sandwiches—at the bar or in the adjacent no-smoking room on the ground floor. The upstairs dining room, complete with ceramic stove, seats eighteen and serves a reasonably priced six-course fixed menu in the evening. The wines—local, Italian, French, and even Californian—are splendid, an expression of Peter's commitment to quality.

MEAT
Macelleria Kofler
Piazza Umberto 132
Tel. 0471/81130
*Closed Thursday and Saturday
    afternoon*

The Macelleria Kofler makes a fine artisanal *speck,* beautifully smoked and spiced.

MERANO

HOTEL
Castel Labers
Via Labers 25
Tel. 0473/34484
Closed November to mid-March
*Credit cards: American Express,
    Diners Club, MasterCard*
Price: moderate

RESTAURANT-INN
Villa Mozart
Via San Marco 26
Tel. 0473/30630
Closed November to mid-March
No credit cards
Price: expensive

Andrea and Emmy Hellrigl's Villa Mozart is a ten-room *pensione* perfectly decorated in the Vienna Secession style of Josef Hoffman—all black and white—complete with linen, crystal, silver, marble bathrooms, sauna, and the most spectacular indoor swimming pool in Italy. I learned much about cooking from Andrea Hellrigl while staying at Villa Mozart. His great skill as a chef and his vision of food are unique. He is currently at the Palio in New York, transposing the *cucina* that he prepared for twenty diners at Villa Mozart to a large restaurant in an important metropolitan center. The kitchen at Villa Mozart continues in Andrea's style of lightened-up Tirolean cooking, dishes from other regions, and creative but not excessive *cucina*. The design purist's ambience is formal, the service precise. Wines are carefully chosen from a small, quality-oriented, temperature-controlled cellar. Breakfast, served until noon (strained juice, soft-boiled egg, homemade preserves, and six or seven types of fresh bread) and a fixed menu at dinner are included in the half-pension required of Villa Mozart's lucky guests.

RESTAURANT
Andrea
Via Galileo Galilei 44
Tel. 0473/37400
Closed Monday, January, and February
Credit cards: American Express, Diners Club
Price: expensive

Walter Oberrauch is the heir to Andrea Hellrigl, who left Ristorante Andrea to found Villa Mozart, in turn abandoned for the bright lights of Palio in New York. Walter, who worked with Andrea for many years, quietly absorbing the style and grace of his *cucina,* faultlessly prepares traditional dishes as well as those created by Andrea, efficiently served in a small, elegantly appointed dining room. Snails, wine soup, *canederli* (bread dumplings served in broth), game, parsley purée, and dessert ricotta *gnocchi* with fruit sauce are some of the specialties of this restaurant serving Alto Adige's most

professional *cucina*. The wine list concentrates on quality regional, Italian, and French selections.

HOUSEWARES
Brugnara
Via Roma 31/A
Tel. 0473/32755
Closed Saturday afternoon
No credit cards

The houseware stores of Merano—there are three big ones under the arcades on via Portici—offer a wealth of items for the kitchen and the table. But my favorite place to shop in Merano is this hardware store on via Roma, with its unexciting window display of rakes, hoses, lawn mowers, and picnic equipment. Walk to the back of the store, past bolts of chain and displays of tools, and up the stairs, and you'll find yourself surrounded by an unbelievable selection of utensils, a maze of tiny rooms filled with everything from milking pails to four sizes of melon ballers, *spatzle* makers, olive pitters, a variety of potato peelers, burner covers, toothpick holders, pastry brushes, and more. Expect to find something you can't live without.

PINZOLO

Pinzolo stands at the entrance to the breathtaking Val di Genova, a pristine alpine valley, not far from the Cascata di Nardis waterfalls and the mountain resort of Madonna di Campiglio.

HOTEL
Golf Hotel
Campo Carlo Magno (close by)
Tel. 0463/41003
Closed April to June, September to November
Credit cards: American Express, MasterCard, Visa
Price: expensive

HOTEL
Chalet dei Pini
Madonna di Campiglio (close by)
Tel. 0465/41489
Closed May, June, October, November
No credit cards
Price: moderate

RESTAURANT
Prima o Poi
Le Pozze 8
Saint'Antonio di Mavignole
Tel. 0465/57175
Closed Wednesday and June
No credit cards
Price: high moderate

The Recagni family—Luciano and Giorgia and daughters Enrica and Cristina—abandoned the Roman rat race for the Dolomite mountains, converting their vacation home, an archetypal mountain chalet, into Prima o Poi, "Sooner or Later." Ex-photographer Luciano dishes out his personal *cucina* composed of fresh seasonal ingredients. The fine *salumi* are brought in from Emilia, and trout-stuffed ravioli, vegetable soups, and just-picked mountain mushrooms cooked in a variety of dishes are specialties of this friendly family-style restaurant. The list of local wines is well chosen.

ROVERETO

HOTEL
Leon d'Oro
Via Tacchi 2
Tel. 0464/437333
Credit cards: all
Price: moderate

RESTAURANT
Ristorante Al Borgo
Via Garibaldi 13
Tel. 0464/436300
Closed Sunday evening and
Monday
Credit cards: American Express,
Diners Club, MasterCard
Price: expensive

Il Borgo is run by the Dalsasso family—chef Rinaldo in the kitchen, with wife Daniela, mother Rosa, and brother Carlo in the dining room. The *cucina* isn't traditional, and some dishes seem contrived, but the food is well prepared. All breads, including the appetizer flatbread with thinly sliced potatoes and herbs, are homemade. Mushroom dishes are a specialty, and fresh fish is nicely underdone. Wild berries and fruit bavarians are often served for dessert. The well-priced wine list, with local, Italian, French, and Californian wines, is a treat.

RESTAURANT
Mozart 1769
Contrada dei portici 36
Tel. 0464/430727
Closed Tuesday, Wednesday
lunch, and in August
Credit cards: American Express,
MasterCard, Visa
Price: high moderate

In 1769 Mozart performed his first Italian concert in Rovereto,

The recipe for bread is weighed out with time-worn utensils.

and this intimate, attractive, elegant restaurant's name calls attention to the event. The *cucina* is as light, innovative, and creative as Mozart's music must have seemed in 1769. Husband and wife Ezio and Erika Filizola, with chef Claudio Agostini, combine efforts, and the result, although it has almost nothing traditional about it, is simply delicious. Breads are homemade, fish and seafood are cooked to perfection, flavors are delicately balanced. There's even a selection of olive oils, almost unheard of in this northern region. Save room for the tasty desserts. The wine list is a thrill.

SAN MICHELE ALL'ADIGE

HOTEL
Villa Madruzzo
Cognola di Trento (close by)
Tel. 0461/986220
Credit card: American Express
Price: moderate

RESTAURANT
Da Silvio
Via Brennero 2
Tel. 0461/650324
Closed Monday
Credit cards: American Express,
Diners Club, MasterCard
Price: high moderate

In the land of Tirolean village–style construction, Da Silvio, built and frescoed by modern painter Riccardo Schweizer, combines modern design with a traditional Italian family unit, the Mannas: four brothers, a sister, two in-laws, and Mom. The *salumi,* brine-cured *carne salada,* and breads are homemade, and the *degustazione trentina* offers a tasting of traditional dishes. The *piatto Schweizer,* a heated block of granite on which meat, fish, vegetables, mushrooms, cheese, or fruit is grilled, can be purchased here, a weighty but useful souvenir. The wine list concentrates on quality local wines and distillates.

Spring's baby onions are hung on a greengrocer's medieval wall.

speck, wild salmon and trout, hearty soups, stewed venison, a variety of mushrooms, buckwheat *polenta,* and homemade *gelato.* The simple, flavorful food from Godio's high-altitude *cucina* (1950 meters, or 6,400 feet) is prepared with skill and passion. The excellent wine list offers some well-chosen local bargains. Reserve one of the eight slightly seedy rooms and spend the night. Mountain goats munching on Genziana's ornamental flowers may greet you in the morning.

TRENTO

Trento, with its Romanesque Duomo, Gothic Castello del Buonconsiglio, and Rinascimento palaces with frescoed facades, a traditional meeting place between the Latin and Germanic cultures, makes a pleasant base for touring the province of Trentino.

HOTEL
Villa Madruzzo
Cognola di Trento (close by)
Tel. 0461/986220
Credit card: American Express
Price: moderate

MARKET
Piazza Lodron
Open Monday through Saturday, 8 a.m. to noon

The piazza Lodron vegetable and fruit market distinguishes itself in the spring and especially in the fall, when mushroom vendors sell over twenty different types of mushrooms—after being patrolled by a communal expert mycologist (who doubles as a traffic cop).

SANTA GERTRUDE VAL D'ULTIMO

RESTAURANT-INN
Genziana
Via Fontana Bianca 116
Tel. 0473/79133
Closed Thursday evening, Friday, November, and December
No credit cards
Price: moderate

A steep, narrow road that I'd hate to deal with at night or in the winter winds through the mountains, pastures, forests, and alpine villages of Val d'Ultimo, and ends at Santa Gertrude. A Forst beer sign and a waterwheel stand in front of Giancarlo Godio's restaurant, which caters to three distinct types of customers: Teutonic tourists looking for steak and french fries, workers from the eyesore of an electrical plant across the road, and gastronomes making the pilgrimage to taste Godio's specialties in his two-booth, five-table dining room with no attempt at decor—or on the terrace, with faded plastic chairs and carvings of alpine flora and fauna. The menu features home-smoked

Mountain berries are found in the spring and summer.

RESTAURANT
Chiesa
Via S. Marco 64
Tel. 0461/985577
Closed Sunday evening and
   Monday
Credit cards: American Express,
   Diners Club, MasterCard
Price: moderate

The Ristorante Chiesa, in an attractive eighteenth-century palace with a beautiful garden, is a classic in Trento. It is known for its two distinct menus: one presents eight traditional dishes dating from the late 1400s, when they were served to Renaissance prince Bernardo Clesio, Cardinal of Trento; the other, La Mela Party, celebrates the apple with a series of six courses, all containing the apples of the Val di Non, concluding with an apple distillate. Both menus have their highs and lows, as does the wine list.

CRAFTS
Luigi Pegoretti
Via Lavisotto 139
Tel. 0461/822242

Luigi Pegoretti, a local artisan who works in copper and brass, makes traditional tin-lined cooking utensils, decorative items, and reproductions of the *situla* (bucket of Etruscan origin). He will also repair or re-tin worn-out cookware. No credit cards are accepted, but Luigi will take checks, and he will send your purchases home for you.

Pieve Alpago
Puos D'Alpago

Feltre Solighetto
Col San Martino Conegliano

Giavera Del Montello
Lovadina
Montecchio Precalcino Treviso
Trissino Vicenza Mogliano Veneto
Montecchia Di Crosara Mestre
Verona Venezia
Monteforte D'Alpone Padova
Valeggio Sul Mincio
Isola Della Scala

VENETO

Veneto, in northeastern Italy, is a topographical four-layer cake. The Alps, flanked by their foothills, separate it from the Tirolean culture. Fertile alluvial plains to the south are divided by the rivers Piave, Brenta, Adige, and the mighty Po, the Mississippi of Italy. Along the coast, lowlands and lagoonal islands rim the Gulf of Venezia and the Adriatic Sea.

Historically, *Venete* tribes, Roman colonization, barbaric invasions, Longobards, and subdivision into fiefdoms and dukedoms kept the mainland busy. Political refugees from all of the above fled to the lagoon, which looked eastward to the Byzantine Empire and to the Orient, with its spice and silk trade. The boundaries of the area that was once known as the *Tre Venezie*—comprising Veneto, Friuli–Venezia Giulia, and Trentino–Alto Adige—are roughly the same as they were in the fifteenth century, when it was a powerful, wealthy, expansionist maritime nation that had ruled for almost 400 years.

Politics ceded Veneto to Austria twice during its history, and signs of that dominion fill the shelves of pastry shops in much of this region. The *cucina* of Veneto is founded on rice and corn. *Polenta* (ground cornmeal) is cooked in a rounded cooking pot (*paiolo*), ladled into bowls, and sauced with hearty game stews; or cooled, sliced, and grilled or fried. It is present on almost every main-course plate in the region. Rice is served as a first course—as *risotto*, cooked with almost everything the countryside and lagoon have to offer, from field greens to baby peas, wild asparagus, fish, shellfish, and game. Lagoon menus feature fish and vegetables, whereas inland, game and poultry are more common—all times spiced with a hint of the Orient, of the power of the *Repubblica Veneziana*. Cheese is found in the mountains, but rarely turns up on the coast. The traditional sweet that seems to have taken Veneto, and the rest of Italy, by storm is *tiramisù*, a rich cocoa-dusted dessert flavored with *mascarpone* cheese and coffee.

The countryside of the Treviso area offers a number of possibilities for living like a doge in a Venetian country villa, with only a ten-minute commute by train to Venezia.

THE MENU

SALUMI

▪

Salumi di cacciagione ▪ various cold cuts made with game

ANTIPASTO

▪

Granseola ▪ crabmeat dressed with oil, lemon, and parsley

Pesce (or *Sarde* or *Sogliole*) *in saor* ▪ fish (or sardines or sole) sautéed and marinated in a sauce of cooked onion, vinegar, pine nuts, and raisins

PRIMO

▪

Bigoli ▪ homemade pasta, (with or without eggs), made with a special kind of spaghetti press

Bigoli con l'anara ▪ cooked in duck broth, sauced with duck

Bigoli in salsa ▪ sauced with oil, onions, and achovies

Casunziei ▪ ravioli stuffed with ricotta, beets, winter squash, or spinach

Pasta e fagioli ▪ bean soup with homemade pasta

Pastissada de manzo con gnocchi ▪ potato dumplings served with byzantine-spiced meat sauce

Polenta ▪ cornmeal pudding, as a side dish cooled, sliced, and either grilled or fried, served with butter and cheese

Risi ▪ rice

Risi e bisato ▪ cooked with eel, bay leaves, oil, and lemon

Risi e bisi ▪ cooked with peas and pancetta, served with butter and grated Parmesan

Risi in cavroman ▪ with a cinnamon-spiced lamb sauce

Riso con i bruscàndoli ▪ rice cooked with tender shoots of wild hops; found only in the spring

Risotto ▪ rice, sautéed, then cooked with broth and any number of enrichments

Risotto alla sbirraglia ▪ cooked with tender shoots of wild hops; found only in the spring

Risotto di mare or *di pesce* ▪ cooked with mixed seafood

Risotto nero ▪ cooked with cuttlefish and its black ink

Risotto primavera ▪ "springtime rice," cooked with tender spring vegetables: asparagus tips, baby peas, string beans, artichokes

Zuppa caoda ▪ baked squab, boned and layered with toasted bread, broth, and Parmesan cheese

SECONDO

Anatra col pien • stuffed duck, traditionally boiled, but sometimes roasted

Baccalà alla vicentina • salt cod, cooked with onions, milk, anchovies, and Parmesan cheese, served with polenta

Baccalà mantecato • poached salt cod, puréed with olive oil and parsley

Bisato alla veneziana • eel sautéed in olive oil, with bay leaves and vinegar

Bisato sull'ara • eel baked with bay leaves

Cape sante alla veneziana • sautéed scallops

Fegato alla veneziana • calf's liver cooked with onions, served with polenta

Gamberetti • tiny cooked shrimp, dressed with oil, lemon, and parsley

Moleche col pien • fried soft-shelled crabs

Polenta e osei or *Polenta e ucelli* • polenta served with skewered small birds and their roasting juices

Pollastro (or *Faraona*) *in tecia* • chicken (or guinea hen) cooked with onions and cloves, served with polenta

Seppie alla veneziana • cuttlefish cooked with its black ink and white wine

Torresani allo spiedo • bacon-wrapped spit-roasted pigeons flavored with rosemary, juniper berries, and bay leaves, served with polenta

CONTORNO

Asparagi in salsa or *alla bassanese* • steamed asparagus served with sauce containing hard-cooked egg, vinegar, and olive oil

Fagioli • beans

Radicchio • red chicory, eaten both raw and cooked

FORMAGGIO

Asiago • hard, sharp, cow's milk

Montasio • smooth, mild; sharper and harder when aged

Pecorino • fresh or aged, sheep's milk, distinct

Vezzena • smooth, fatty, bland

DOLCE

Baicoli • simple small cookies dipped in dessert wine

Forti • almond spice cookies from Bassano del Grappa

Fregolotta • crumbly almond cake

Frittole • round fritters containing raisins, pine nuts, and candied citron, found at Carnival time

Pandoro • eggy, rich, sweetened yeast bread, found at Christmastime

Tiramisù • mascarpone, eggs, ladyfingers, and coffee combined in a rich cocoa-dusted dessert

Zaleti • cornmeal raisin cookies

THE *W*INE LIST

Veneto is Italy's largest producer of DOC wine. *Soave* from the Verona area is the most popular Italian white wine in the U.S., but *Prosecco* is a local winner, light, sparkling, ethereal, served almost everywhere by the glass, pitcher, or bottle, and consumed almost like a soft drink. At times, some of Veneto's finer wines seem to be easier to find outside the region.

Amarone, also known as *Recioto della Valpolicella Amarone,* is a powerful dry red with a bitter finish, a DOC made in the province of Verona with semi-dried Corvina, Rondinella, and Molinara grapes. It is served with red meats and game. Top producers are Allegrini, Le Ragose, Masi, Giuseppe Quintarelli, Serègo Alighieri, and Fratelli Tedeschi.

Bardolino is a DOC from the Lago di Garda area. The *Rosso,* a blend of Corvina, Rondinella, Molinara, and Negrara grapes, is a light, dry red, served with meat, poultry, and rabbit. The *Chiaretto,* a rosé made from Corvina, Rondinella, and Molinara grapes, is lighter and more delicate, and is served with appetizers and first-course dishes. Top producers are Fratelli Tedeschi, Guerrieri-Rizzardi, and Le Vigne di San Pietro.

Bianco di Custoza is a soft dry white, a DOC from the Lago di Garda area, an aromatic blend of Trebbiano, Garganega, Tocai, and other white grape varieties. It is served with fish and seafood. Le Vigne di San Pietro is the top producer.

Breganze, a DOC area north of Vicenza, produces seven different wines. The *Bianco,* made with Tocai, *Pinot Bianco,* and *Pinot Grigio* are fruity, elegant whites. *Vespaiolo,* made from the local Vespaiolo grape, is a dry, fresh white. All are served with appetizers, fish, and seafood. *Rosso,* a blend of Cabernet Franc, Sauvignon, and Merlot, aged in oak, and *Cabernet* are rich and elegant dry reds, served with meat and sauced dishes. Ruby *Pinot Nero* is light,

fruity, and delicate, served with poultry. Non-DOC *Torcolato,* a semi-sweet golden dessert wine, is a rare treat, and costly. Maculan is the Breganze's top producer.

Elegant dry red *Cabernet* produced outside the DOC zones is usually a blend of Cabernet Franc and Sauvignon. It is served with meat and regional *cucina,* and is well made by Lazzarini's Villa dal Ferro and by Afra and Tobia Scarpa.

Non-DOC *Merlot,* a dry, elegant red, is produced by Lazzarini's Villa Dal Ferro, Col Sandago, and Afra and Tobia Scarpa.

Prosecco di Conegliano-Valdobbiadene, a DOC from northwest of Treviso, made of the Prosecco grape, is a light, fruity sparkling white that can be dry, semi-sweet, or sweet. *Cartizze* is a sparkling white made from the same grape, from the small microclimate within the *Prosecco* DOC area. Quality producers are Cantine Nino Franco, Carpenè Malvolti, Le Groppe, and Pino Zardetto.

Recioto di Soave, made from semi-dried Garganega and Trebbiano grapes, is a golden, smooth, delicate, flowery, and sweet dessert wine. It is best produced by Anselmi and Pieropan.

Soave, a delicate dry white DOC produced east of Verona, is made with Garganega and Trebbiano grapes. It's Italy's second most exported DOC wine—more than 52 million liters yearly, most of it not worth drinking. The following winemakers prove that Soave can be a wine of class, a perfect companion to appetizers, pasta with light sauces, vegetables, fish, and seafood: Anselmi, with his special cru Capitel Foscarino, Guerrieri-Rizzardi, Masi, and Pieropan.

Spumante, made with **charmat** or **champenoise** methods, is well produced by Nino Franco and Zandetto.

REGIONAL SPECIALTIES

VIALONE NANO RICE

Vialone nano, a local variety of rice, has a short, fat, almost oval kernel, with a small chip at one end which makes it look like a tiny tooth. It is widely grown in Veneto, and is perfect for *risotto,* one of the glories of this region's *cucina.* Rice paddies, flooded rectangular fields bordered by an intricate system of irrigation canals, are also home to carp and frogs, which are often cooked with this rice. See page 115 for a rice producer.

POLENTA

Polenta is the Italian version of cornmeal mush, a cheap starch that, when served with a bit of sauce, keeps the pains of hunger at bay. Historically, it was probably much coarser than the modern cornmeal, which is called *bramata.* (The outer 40 percent of the kernel is used for animal feed and the remaining 60 percent, the heart of the kernel, is ground to make the cornmeal.) *Polenta* is cooked with salt and water, stirred constantly for a long time, until it becomes a cohesive mass with the consistency of breakfast cereal. It is served freshly made as a side dish (like mashed potatoes) or cooled, sliced, and reheated with a sauce. In Veneto it is frequently grilled, and accompanies most main dishes. White *polenta* is more delicate, and usually accompanies fish or seafood (see page 114).

BELLINI

I can't imagine Veneto in the spring and summer without the Bellini, a refreshing combination of sparkling fruity Prosecco and white peach purée. It was originally created by Commendatore Giuseppe Cipriani, the founder of Harry's Bar, in the late 1950s, probably to take advantage of the tasty intensely perfumed white peaches of the Venetian lagoon. It can be found throughout the region, but is at its best in Venice, in the spring and summer months when the peaches are fresh. The quintessential Bellini is prepared at Harry's Bar (see page 122).

RADICCHIO

Radicchio is a winter vegetable, widely grown in Veneto in four major varieties. *Radicchio di Castelfranco* and *Radicchio di Chioggia* are leafy heads with green and red marblized leaves. *Radicchio di Verona* is a small purple lettuce-like ball. But best of all is *Radicchio di Treviso,* looking like a flower with elongated white-ribbed red petals, sold with about three inches of root attached. Known locally as *spadone* (big sword) it is at its glory in the cold winter months. Radicchio di Treviso is eaten raw, baked, fried, braised, or grilled and has a complex, slightly sweet and bitter flavor. Radicchio fans should plan to visit Da Domenico in Lovadina (page 116) or Tre Panoce in Conegliano (page 114) where homage is paid to this local specialty during its cool weather season.

COOKWARE

Bigoli freaks might want to look for a *torchio,* the press used to make this hearty extruded pasta. They can be found in housewares shops throughout the region.

CITIES AND TOWNS

COL SAN MARTINO

HOTEL
Villa Cipriani
Via Canova 298
Asolo (close by)
Tel. 0423/55444
Credit cards: all
Price: expensive

HOTEL
Sporting Ragno d'Oro
Via Diaz 37
Conegliano (close by)
Tel. 0438/24955
Credit cards: all
Price: moderate

RESTAURANT
Locanda da Condo
Via Fontana 69
Tel. 0438/898106
Closed Wednesday
No credit cards
Price: low moderate

The Locanda da Condo looks like a typical provincial family *trattoria,* complete with a bar in the downstairs entrance and a smattering of tables occupied by old men smoking strong-smelling cigarettes. However, the *cucina* has been renewed by Condo's son Enrico and his companion Sofia, who have blown their redecorating budget on studying with the great chefs of Italy and France. The *trattoria* decor hasn't been abandoned, and neither has the regional *cucina,* although there are plenty of creative, fresh dishes using seasonal local products.

Ultra-traditional specialties—white *polenta* sauced with mushrooms, bean soup, cooked sausage and smooth mashed potatoes, and boned guinea hen served with liver-anchovy sauce *(peverada)*—are nicely presented. Nontraditional but delicious: homemade vegetable pasta flavored and sauced with the same vegetable, and grilled meats. Conclude your meal with a selection of hard-to-find regional cheeses, like *taleggio di Soligo* and *carnia vecchio,* or with one of Sofia's desserts. The wine list is wonderful and includes many regional, and reasonably priced, gems as well as wines from other regions of the country. In the summer, dine outside on the terrace, under a cane mat ceiling that conceals the corrugated plastic roof.

CONEGLIANO

HOTEL
Sporting Ragno d'Oro
Via Diaz 37
Tel. 0438/24955
Credit cards: all
Price: moderate

RESTAURANT
Tre Panoce
Via Vecchia Trevigiana
Tel. 0438/60071
Closed Monday and August
Credit cards: American Express,
 Diners Club, MasterCard
Price: Moderate

Drive through lush vineyards to get to Tre Panoce, a restored farmhouse with a decor somewhere between country and kitsch. Armando Zanotto, looking more like a ship's captain than a chef, will welcome you to his restaurant, and you'll be served a glass of the house Prosecco and a bowl of fresh raw vegetables with a mustard dip. Armando offers a moderately priced tasting menu which I find large—nine courses plus small pastries—and not traditional enough for my taste. Homemade bread and herbal *grissini* are crispy; local *salumi, polenta,* and *chiodini* mushrooms, splendidly cooked *risotto,* eel with sour cherries, and duck with Prosecco grape sauce are all winners. The cheese selection is local and first-rate. A separate menu for homemade desserts should hint at the importance of this course: vanilla *gelato,* served plain or topped with fruit or chocolate sauce; fresh fruit ices; pastries; *tiramisù;* or refreshing sliced fresh fruit. Armando's wife, sommelier Ave, will help you choose a wine from their impressive list of regional and nonregional selections. Radicchio freaks will wonder how they survived without Armando's book *Il Radicchio in Cucina,* 617 recipes featuring the radicchio of Treviso and Castelfranco Veneto.

FELTRE

GRISTMILL
Molino Stien
Tel. 0439/2321

This modern mill produces quality *farina per polenta bramata* (cornmeal), both white and yellow. The corn is local because, as they informed me, it's the earth that gives the flavor to the corn, and the tastiest corn for *polenta* is, clearly, grown in this area of Veneto. The Molino Stien also makes flour from rye, barley, and oats.

GIAVERA DEL MONTELLO

HOTEL
Villa Corner della Regina
Cavasagra (close by)
Tel. 0423/481481
Credit cards: all
Price: expensive

HOTEL

Bellavista
Mercato Vecchio, Montebelluna
   (close by)
Tel. 0423/301031
Credit cards: all
Price: moderate

RESTAURANT
Agnoletti
Via della Vittoria 131
Tel. 0422/876009
Closed Monday, Tuesday, and the
   first half of July
No credit cards
Price: low moderate

Agnoletti has been a *trattoria* since 1780, a stopping-off place for changing carriage horses and having something to eat. The ambience is pure Veneto country, the waiters are surly, the menu is limited, and the wines are nothing special. Local *salumi* are good, but the reason for a visit to this restaurant is for a taste of mush-

A mushroom vendor lovingly offers her wares.

rooms *(funghi)*, preferably in every course. First-course soups, grilled meat, game, and anything with *polenta* are all good choices. Finish with local cheese and home-preserved figs with spices, honey, and alcohol, served with or without homemade *gelato*. Avoid this restaurant on Sunday, when, due to the weekly invasion of city folk, the quality of the cooking deteriorates.

ISOLA DELLA SCALA

RICE MILL
Riseria Ferron
Via Saccovener 6, Pilavecchia
Tel. 045/7301022

The Ferron family has been growing quality rice for *risotto* in their rice paddies and refining it in their mills outside Verona since 1650. They grow mostly *vialone nano semifino (semifino* refers to the size of the rice kernel, in this case large). The Ferron rice mill, or refinery, is a frenzy of activity, of cogged wheels, machine belts, tubes transporting the rice, wooden trays rocking back and forth to separate grain from chaff, a centrifuge grating the outer husk of the kernel, leaving a dusting of rice flour on the grains that will eventually thicken someone's *risotto*. In the back of the *riseria* stands an even more astounding object, looking distinctly like a Leonardo da Vinci invention; a series of large wooden metal-tipped pestles driven by wheels off a central axle, pounding into corresponding wooden bowls, each containing a few handfuls of rice. This amazing machine is powered by a seventeenth-century waterwheel, and the rice it produces is extremely rare, marked "*Lavorato con pistelli*" on the package, and impossible to find outside the area.

Isola della Scala holds a *fiera del riso*, a three-day festival held after the rice harvest, during the first weekend in October, with gastronomic competitions—a "*risotto-off*" for the best *risotto*, for professional chefs and for dilettantes. The contest for the restaurant chefs is called *Chicco d'Oro*, the "Golden Kernel." Finals are held in the old movie house, the Cinema Alba, decorated for the event with a huge poster of a grain of rice looking like a hugh tooth. The jury is served a bit better than the public, but tastes of competing *risotti* are available to all comers. *Risotto* with Taleggio cheese and field greens, *risotto* with winter squash and white truffles, and *risotto* with red radicchio and Jerusalem artichokes were past winners. Contact Diego Zarantonello (tel. 045/7300130) for more information about the festival.

LOVADINA

HOTEL
El Toulà
Via Postumia 63
Paderno di Ponzano (close by)
Tel. 0422/969023
Credit cards: all
Price: luxury

HOTEL
See Sporting Ragno d'Oro in Conegliano (page 114)

RESTAURANT
Da Domenico
Località Grave, via del Fante 23
Tel. 0422/881261
Closed Monday evening and
    Tuesday
Credit cards: American Express,
    MasterCard
Price: moderate

Anyone obsessed with red radicchio lettuce from Treviso, mushrooms, or asparagus should jump for joy and head for Lovadina during their respective festivals at this simple country restaurant: Domenico Camerotto, his wife, Sonia, and their children prepare and serve a meal of pure monomania—ten different dishes focused on a single vegetable. Serious asparagus worshippers will enjoy a procession of this relative of the lily, cultivated or wild, raw, fried, baked with eggs, wrapped, minced in *risotto*, puréed, julienned, in soup, or sauced with hard-cooked eggs. Mushrooms and Treviso lettuce get the same respect. Each dish is garnished with a little dyed mashed-potato flower. The wine selection is interesting and unusual. Da Domenico's decor is unstudied peculiar.

MESTRE

COOKWARE
Luciano Preo
Via Sernaglia 29/5
Tel. 041/933025

Barbecue fans may want to contact Luciano Preo for information about his amazing patented Turn-grill, a vertical rotating charcoal barbecue grill, especially adapted for cooking fish.

MOGLIANO VENETO

HOTEL
Villa Condulmer
Tel. 041/457100
Credit card: American Express
Price: high moderate

RESTAURANT
Enoteca La Sosta
Via Marconi 14
Tel. 041/5901428
Closed all day Monday and
    Tuesday lunch
Credit card: American Express
Price: moderate

Directly on the Terraglio, the main drag from Venezia to Treviso, Enoteca La Sosta has a large selection of fine Italian wines and *grappa*. The menu is limited to a few simple dishes, but good cheese and *salumi* are always available. The service is friendly, and wine is also sold by the bottle or case.

MONTECCHIA DI CROSARA

HOTEL
See Dei Castelli in Alte di Montecchio Maggiore (page 117)

RESTAURANT
Baba-jaga
Via Cabalao
Tel. 045/7450222
Closed Monday, January, and the
    first half of August
Price: high moderate

Chef Piero Burato's wife was studying for an important Russian exam. He was looking for a name for his about-to-open restaurant, and liked the sound of Baba-jaga, a Russian witch. But the magic at this countryside restaurant is in Veneto's dialect, with many creative dishes for locals tired of tradition. *Salumi, risotto,* and homemade pasta are stellar. Fish and meat are grilled over olive-wood charcoal. Some creative sauced dishes seem a bit trendy. Fresh black truffles are used with great abandon in season. Desserts are homemade, and wines are a pleasure. Dine outside on the shaded terrace in the spring and summer.

MONTECCHIO PRECALCINO

RESTAURANT-INN
La Locanda di Piero
Via Roma 34
Tel. 0445/864827
Closed Sunday, Monday lunch,
*   and August*
Credit card: American Express
Price: moderate

Piero Paoletti left the big-city bustle of Milano, where he owned two restaurants, for a simpler life on his wife Jole's native turf. But don't expect country cooking or a farmhouse ambience at their "inn" set in the flat, somewhat Midwestern-looking landscape of cornfields. The *cucina* is seasonal, most of the fruit and vegetables come from Jole and Piero's farm, and although some of the dishes are a bit trendy, the food is well prepared and tasty. The intensely

fruit-flavored dessert ices (*sorbetti*) are splendid. Quality local wines are available. Spend the night in one of the Locanda's four rooms. Dine on the veranda overlooking cornfields in the spring and summer.

MONTEFORTE D'ALPONE

HOTEL
Dei Castelli
Alte di Montecchio Maggiore
*   (close by)*
Tel. 0444/697366
Credit cards: all
Price: moderate

RESTAURANT
Riondo
Via Monte Riondo
Tel. 045/7610638
Closed Monday
Credit cards: American Express,
*   Diners Club*
Price range: high moderate

Riondo, perched on a hilltop in the middle of Soave vineyards, is a *trattoria* that has kept pace with the times. The *cucina,* mostly traditional—*salumi* served with *polenta,* homemade pasta, nicely done *risotto,* grilled Sorana beef, regional cheese, and *tiramisù*—is well prepared and accompanied by quality local wines. Drink a glass of Recioto di Soave by Anselmi for dessert. Dining on the terrace overlooking acres of grapevines is a treat in the spring and summer.

PADOVA

Padova is a charming city of Roman origins, with its university

founded in 1222, Giotto frescoes, Donatello sculpture, and Veneziana attitude. Its gastronomic center is located in the Piazze delle Erbe and della Frutta—twin piazzas, with produce in one and dry goods in the other, linked by a passageway of stalls selling cheese, meat, *salumi,* and fish.

HOTEL
Leon Bianco
Piazzetta Pedrocchi 12
Tel. 049/22514
Credit cards: all
Price: moderate

HOTEL
Villa Ducale
Via Martiri della Libertà 75
*   Dolo (close by)*
Tel. 041/420094
Credit cards: American Express,
*   Diners Club, Visa*
Price: moderate

WINE BAR
Enoteca Angelo Rasi
Riviera Paleocapa 7
Tel. 049/651709
Closed Monday and August; open
*   weekdays from 6 and*
*   weekends from noon.*
No credit cards
Price: moderate

Enoteca Angolo del Sommelier–
*   Bar Bologna*
Piazzale Santa Croce 13
Tel. 049/38993
Closed Wednesday
No credit cards
Price: moderate

Padova's restaurants are disappointing, but simple food like *salumi* (local and from other regions), a wide variety of *prosciutto,* goose salami, an array of cheeses, a choice of extra virgin olive oils, *grappa,* cognac, whiskey, and, most important, wine are easy enough to find at these two non-restaurants. Both the Enoteca Angelo Rasi and the Enoteca Angolo del Sommelier have splendid selections of local, Italian, French, and Californian wines, a commitment to quality drinking.

PIEVE D'ALPAGO

RESTAURANT-INN
Dolada
Località Plois, via Dolada
Tel. 0437/479141
Closed Monday except July and
August
Credit card: American Express
Price: high moderate

From the Lago di Santa Croce, follow the signs with the stylized snail to a very special inn run by very special people. The chef, Enzo Pra, and his wife, sommelier Rossana, have thought of every possible component of a fine dining or overnight experience, and have set about including them all at Dolada. Small two- or three-table dining rooms expand as needed by a clever system of sliding doors, but the mood is always intimate, elegant, studied. The decor is understated, the flower arrangements are low, the menu is embossed with the snail that helped to guide you to Dolada. Enzo's *cucina* is strong and masculine, contrasting flavors as op-

Fresh fish is displayed in its Styrofoam shipping cases.

posed to blending them. Very few dishes are traditional, other than the *broet de s'cioss e polenta* (snails cooked with celery, served with polenta), which may make snail haters change their minds. The marinated and home-smoked sturgeon may not be traditional, but it is tasty. Some dishes show signs of trendy ingredients like raspberry vinegar, but generally the menu is professionally executed with intelligence, moderation, and style. Save room for the splendid desserts. Rossana will help you choose a wine from her fine selection, which she ably pairs with Enzo's *cucina.* After a *grappa,* if

you're lucky you'll head upstairs to one of seven rooms, each a different color, with bathroom tiles, carpet, and bed linens of the same hue, equipped with TV, radio cassette player, refrigerator with splits of Ca' del Bosco *Spumante,* cocktail-table photography books to leaf through, and a bathroom with magnifying mirror, towel warmer, and even a Band-Aid. If you're truly lucky, you'll have a view of the full moon illuminating the entire valley, reflected in Lago di Santa Croce. Breakfast, served any time after 8, is world-class, and includes a local version of french toast, and butter so wonderful and sweet that you may eat it without bread.

PUOS D'ALPAGO

RESTAURANT-INN
San Lorenzo
Via 4 Novembre 79
Tel. 0437/4352
Closed Wednesday
Credit cards: American Express, Diners Club, Visa
Price: moderate

San Lorenzo is a simple inn *(locanda)* where Renzo Dal Farra, his wife, Mara, and his brother Aldo and their mother prepare traditional *cucina.* They have all clearly been influenced by nearby master Enzo Pra (see page 118) and his personal professional style. Local *salumi,* marinated fish, homemade pasta, and some nontraditional but interesting dishes are served with an eclectic wine list that places little emphasis on Veneto. The seven-course tasting meal offers a lot of food for the money.

SOLIGHETTO

RESTAURANT-INN
Da Lino
Via Brandolini 1
Tel. 0438/62150
Closed Monday and August
Credit cards: all
Price: high moderate

Da Lino is an immense, typical Veneto countryside restaurant with a successful formula that it's been repeating for years, to the point of tedium. Service is swift, but most of the dishes taste precooked and reheated. Mushrooms in season are a specialty, and fish is served on Thursday. The best choice is whatever you see turning on the spit in the fireplace. Jovial groups of celebrants pack this restaurant, and tapping on one's wine glass with a knife in unison seems to be a native custom.

TREVISO

Treviso, with its medieval and *rinascimento* palaces, arcade-lined streets, cobblestone lanes, and waterways coursing in and around the city, is a jewel.

The area's Palladian-style villas-turned-hotels offer a peek at a former era, and are perfect to use as a base for visiting the Venetian countryside.

HOTEL
El Toulà
Via Postumia 63
Paderno di Ponzano (close by)
Tel. 0422/969191
Credit cards: all
Price: luxury

HOTEL
Villa Corner della Regina
Cavasagra (close by)
Tel. 0423/481481
Credit cards: all
Price: expensive

HOTEL
Villa Condulmer
Zerman (close by)
Tel. 041/457100
Credit card: American Express
Price: high moderate

HOTEL
Villa Revedin
Via Palazzi 4
Gorgo al Monticano (close by)
Tel. 0422/740069
Credit cards: American Express, MasterCard, Visa
Price: low moderate

MARKET
The *pescheria* (fish market), located on the *isoletta,* the "little island" on the Botteniga waterway, is a typical daily Veneto market selling the bounty of the Adriatic.

SPECIALTY FOODS
Gastronomia Danesin
Corso del Popolo 28
Tel. 042/540625
Closed Wednesday afternoon

Picnic shopping is a pleasure at Gastronomia Danesin. They sell quality bread, cheese (especially local *asiago* and *montasio*), attractive salads, marinated vegetables, and regional specialties, such as quail with polenta, to go.

CRAFTS
Manu Fatti
Via Barberia 29
Tel. 0422/579887
Closed August
No credit cards

Lucia Tessari's lovely shop sells artisanal products, although not all her wares are Italian. Tuscan baskets and linens from Romagna are attractive and well priced.

RESTAURANT
Toni del Spin
Via Inferiore 7
Tel. 0422/543829
Closed Sunday and August
No credit cards
Price: inexpensive

I like the genuine *trattoria* ambience of Toni del Spin—the wooden floors, marble bar, beamed ceilings with large-bladed fans, the feeling that regulars are stepping up to the bar for their daily glass of wine. The blackboard menu features typical *cucina veneta*, such as *pasta e fagioli*, seasonal *risotto*, *bigoli*, *baccalà*, and poultry. The back room is lined with generally crummy wines, so Scarpa's fine wines look almost out of place here.

RESTAURANT
El Toulà da Alfredo
Via Collalto 26
Tel. 0422/40275
Closed Monday and August
Credit cards: American Express,
MasterCard
Price: expensive

This restaurant is the original El Toulà, founded by Alfredo Beltrame, who helped spread the message that regional *cucina* can be elegant as well as tasty. It became the first link in a chain of El Toulà restaurants. All feature the classic *cucina veneta*, with interregional and seasonal dishes on their interesting menu. Traditional *sarde in saor*, perfectly cooked *risotto* or *riso e fegatini* (rice and chicken liver soup), and the *frittatina con bruscandoli* (pan-fried flan with wild hops) are splendid, although Italians seem to prefer gazpacho, homemade pasta, marinated swordfish, or grilled vegetables. The Art Nouveau frescoes, pink tablecloths, and formal service are all part of the legacy of Alfredo Beltrame. Drink the Nino Franco Prosecco, one of Veneto's loveliest wines.

TRISSINO

RESTAURANT-INN
Ca' Masieri
Via Masieri 16
Tel. 0445/962100
Closed Monday lunch and Sunday
Credit cards: American Express,
Diners Club
Price: high moderate

What a joy to find a restaurant like Ca' Masieri, especially since it's become an inn. The *cucina* reflects the charming decor, a blend of clean modern design combined with the traditional country style. *Salumi* are tasty, *risotto* is beautifully prepared, pasta and *bigoli* are homemade. Meat, fowl, and fish are lightly sauced. Pasty and *gelato* are fresh and homemade. The wine list, studded with local and nonregional wines, is worth a detour. A welcoming fire burns in the hearth in the winter, and summer dining is on the terrace.

VALEGGIO SUL MINCIO

HOTEL
Victoria
Via Adua 8
Verona (close by)
Tel. 045/590566
Credit Cards: American Express,
Diners Club
Price: expensive

HOTEL
Aurora
Piazza delle Erbe
Verona (close by)
Tel. 045/594717
No credit cards
Price: inexpensive

RESTAURANT
Antica Locanda Mincio
Borghetto
Tel. 045/795059
Closed Wednesday evening in
winter, and Thursday
No credit cards
Price: moderate

On the banks of the Mincio river, immersed in the greens of ivy and weeping willows, the Antica Locanda Mincio (which dates from the 1700s) serves the traditional *cucina* of the area. Specialties include homemade *salumi*, hand-rolled pasta, freshwater fish, grilled chicken, and the homemade preserved peaches of Valeggio. The wine selection has its highs and lows.

VENEZIA

"Venezia": the sound of those three musical syllables, so different from the harsher English "Venice," won't prepare you for the fascination of this meeting place/port/Oriental bazaar where natives in costume seem to have been replaced by tourists in sneakers. Waterways are filled with the urban traffic of water buses and barges, but the back lanes are reserved for motorboats and gondolas, gracefully rowed by skilled *gondoliere*, a tradition passed down from father to son. Venezia is divided into six *sestieri*, or neighborhood districts: Cannaregio, San Marco, Castello, Santa Croce, San Polo, and Dorsoduro. Main routes (marked with yellow street signs pointing the way to major destinations), narrow passageways, and unexpected squares are numbered in zig-zag

MESTRE AND MARGHERA

.

Ugly Mestre and Marghera, Venezia's vital mainland link to the rest of the world, are the best places to leave your car before continuing on to the waterways of Venezia. Mestre's parking lots are less expensive, less chaotic, easier to execute, than Venezia's overcrowded lots at Piazzale Roma, which never seem to have room until a tip is pulled out. Trains leave Mestre every five minutes for Venezia. The food in the following two restaurants, frequented by locals and businesspeople, is better than almost anything in Venezia; the fish is fresher and the bill will be lighter.

Autoespresso, across the train tracks from Mestre, started out as a truck stop, serving simple food and lots of it. Then owner Franco Semenzato decided there was more to the restaurant business than feeding large numbers of people, fast. He removed tables, creating a more spacious environment, and added an impressive list of local and Italian white wines. Mother Savina and wife Luciana work together in the kitchen, preparing a minimalist *cucina* of grilled or lightly deep-fried fish, with no sauce. *Polenta* is white, more delicate than yellow, and better with seafood, Franco assured me, as he served a slice of it covered with minute pale pink shrimp coated with olive oil. Spaghetti is perfectly cooked, salads are dressed with your choice of extra virgin olive oil from Liguria, Toscana, or Lazio. A few meat dishes are available for fish haters. The wine list is wonderful, and distillates like *grappa,* armagnac, and malt whiskey are a specialty.

Valeriano's restaurant, a few steps from the train station, serves interesting well-prepared food. The fish *antipasto* is varied, and large enough to be a whole meal for some. Try to save room for the nicely cooked *risotto,* spaghetti, and simple fresh fish, prepared by Valeriano's wife, Maria, known as Gerry. The restaurant is always packed with locals, and reservations are a must. Not all the wines are thrilling.

HOTEL

Lugano
Via Rizzardi 11
Tel. 041/936777
Closed November through February
Credit cards: all
Price: low moderate

RESTAURANT

Autoespresso
Via Fratelli Bandiera 34
Marghera
Tel. 041/930214
Closed Sunday and August
Credit cards: American Express, Diners Club, Visa
Price: high moderate

RESTAURANT

Valeriano
Via Col di Lana 18
Mestre
Tel. 041/926474
Closed Sunday evening, Monday, and August
No credit cards
Price: moderate

or snail-shaped patterns, and make up a uniquely Venetian landscape where the vocabulary is a local dialect—*calle* or *ramo* means street; *fondamenta, rio, riva* are streets on a canal, and *campo,* literally "field," is a square, what the rest of Italy calls a *piazza.* The *cucina* of this once-great maritime nation is based on the fruits of the sea and the bounty of the rich alluvial soil of the Venetian lagoon. *Risotto,* made with locally grown rice, is a specialty, sauced with delicate seafood or tender greens. Fish is simply cooked—sautéed, grilled, fried. Cuttlefish (*seppia*) is stewed in its own ink. Calf's liver is transformed into *fegato alla veneziana*. The Cannaregio and Rialto markets display piles of fruit and vegetables from the lagoon and beyond. Quality wine served with reasonably priced food is hard to find in Venezia, a city with no wine cellars.

The hotels of Venezia are probably the most expensive in Italy, but few experiences can match the romance of a room with a view. These range from luxury to ultra-luxury:

Cipriani
Isola della Giudecca 10
Tel. 041/5207744

Gritti Palace
San Marco 2467, Campo Santa
  Maria del Giglio
Tel. 041/794611

Londra Palace
Castello 4171, Riva degli
  Schiavoni
Tel. 041/5200533

Monaco e Grand Canal
San Marco 1325, Calle
  Vallaresso
Tel. 041/5200211

Slightly less costly:
Carpaccio
San Polo 2765
Tel. 041/5235946

And actually moderate:
Santo Stefano
San Marco 2957
Tel. 041/5200166

BAR-CAFFÈ
Harry's Bar
San Marco 1323, Calle
  Vallaresso
Tel. 041/5236797
Closed Monday, January, and
  February
Credit cards: all
Price: expensive

Harry's Bar has been a classic in Venezia since Giuseppe Cipriani opened its doors in 1931. Although some consider it a fine restaurant, I'd rather dine elsewhere—but I can't think of a better place to stop off for a world-class Bellini. The nautical–private club ambience, tables with yellow cloths and barstools are a favorite with Italians and tourists, although you'll be hard-pressed to hear Italian spoken in the summer. The waiters are efficient, but for the 20 percent service charge they should be.

BAR-CAFFÈ
Florian
San Marco 56–59
Closed Wednesday in winter
Tel. 041/5285338
Price: expensive

Venetians hang out at Florian, located in one of the world's most wonderful squares, with an unbeatable view. In a local version of musical chairs, if you order your drink while the orchestra is playing, a service charge will be added to your bill.

BAR-CAFFÈ
La Boutique del Dolce
Santa Polo 890, Fondamenta Rio
  Marin
Tel. 041/718523
Closed Wednesday

Gilda Vio and Gino Riviani's little stand-up bar may not be in the same league as Harry's or Florian for most people, but it's my favorite spot in Venezia for breakfast. The *cappuccino* is well prepared, and they serve just-baked crispy croissants (called *brioche*), fresh

fruit tarts, cookies, and pastry. Sandwiches and savory pastry are of the same fine quality.

WINE BAR
Cantina Do Mori di Roberto
  Biscontin
San Polo 429
Tel. 041/5225401
Closed Sunday
No credit cards

The Do Mori is my favorite place for an *ombra* (or *ombretta*, "little shadow"), offering a close-up view of the real Venezia. Roberto Biscontin has his own boat for the *Festa del Redentore*, a festival of thanksgiving that takes place on the third Sunday in July. (The night before the festival there are fireworks, and the Veneziani picnic on their boats and stay up all night.)

WINE BAR
Vino Vino
San Marco 2007/A
No phone
Closed Tuesday
No credit cards

Another fine choice for wonderful *cicchetti*. The food comes from the kitchen of the Ristorante Antico Martini, and some of Italy's finest wines are sold here, by the bottle or by the glass. To make a special reservation, call the Antico Martini (tel. 041/5224121).

WINE BAR
Enoteca al Volto
San Marco 4081, Calle Cavalli
Tel. 041/5228945
Closed Sunday
No credit cards

CICCHETTI E L'OMBRA
(PICK-ME-UPS AND THE SHADOW)
·

The tradition of *cicchetti*—"pick-me-ups," little snacks in the style of Spanish tapas, something to munch on while drinking a glass of wine—is still strong in Venezia. *Cicchetti* (or *cicheti*) may range from a slice of bread and *prosciutto* to walnut-size meatballs, fried vegetables or zucchini flowers, whipped salt cod, or marinated sardines. The glass of wine is known as *l'ombra* ("the shadow"), since in the summer *gondolieri* used to grab some "shade" in the shadow of the *campanile* in Piazza San Marco. Although Veneziani might be horrified, *cicchetti* and a couple of *ombre* could easily substitute for lunch.

VENETIAN COOKIES
·

Venetian pastry chefs, influenced by the East, are said to have invented marzipan in 1500, created as a tribute to their city; *pane di San Marco* is *Marci Pan* in Latin, and *marzapan* in Venetian dialect. Cookies seem to be a local specialty, and they come in many shapes and flavors—S-shaped *buranelli* sugar cookies; light, delicate *baicoli*; cornmeal raisin *zaleti*; peppery cornmeal *peverini*; pine nut *pignoletti*. Both *pan dei Dogi* and *torta dei Dogi* are rich with honey, dried fruit, and nuts. The *fregolata* is a buttery crumble of cornmeal and almond shortbread.

Enoteca al Volto has one of Venezia's largest selections of quality wine.

WINE BAR
Ca' d'Oro
Cannaregio 3912, Calle Ca' d'Oro
Tel. 041/5285324
Closed Thursday and August
No credit cards

The Ca' d'Oro, in the untouristed Cannaregio neighborhood, is a local hangout. Everyone here seems to be smoking.

WINE BAR
Vini da Pinto
San Polo 367, Campo delle Beccarie
Tel. 041/5224599
Closed Monday
No credit cards

Da Pinto, with its no-nonsense decor of blond wood Formica, is one of my favorite places for *cicchetti*.

Don't miss the tripe or the *baccalà*.

WINE BAR
Cantina già Schiavi
Dorsoduro 992
Tel. 041/5230034
Closed Sunday
No credit cards

Locals stop off in this authentic Venetian bar for a glass of wine on the way home from work.

WINE BAR
Capitan Uncino
Santa Croce 1501, Campo San Giacomo dell'Orio
Tel. 041/721901
Closed Tuesday
No credit cards

Located in a wide, tree-lined square, Capitan Uncino ("Captain Hook") draws a neighborhood crowd. Go native and dawdle over a glass of the house wine.

PASTRY, BREAD
Panificio Colussi
San Marco 326
Tel. 041/5224628

San Luca 4579
Tel. 041/5222659

Closed Wednesday afternoon

Both locations of Colussi make all the typical Venetian cookies, and the bread is fresh and crusty.

PASTRY
Pasticceria Marchini
San Marco 2769, Ponte San Maurizio
Tel. 041/5229109
Closed Tuesday

Marchini is Venezia's only shop that sells nothing but pastry, all

Genuine handmade candied violets are flowers frozen in sugar.

their own production. Most of their specialties are traditional.

PASTRY
Giancarlo Vio
Dorsoduro 1192
Tel. 041/5227451
Closed Tuesday

Near the Accademia, *bar-cafè* Vio is a perfect stop for a coffee and a tempting pastry in the best Venetian and Austrian tradition. Go for the *sacher torte*.

TRADITIONAL JEWISH PASTRY
Giovanni Volpe
Cannaregio 1143
Ghetto Vecchio
Tel. 041/715178
Closed Wednesday afternoon

The word *ghetto* derives from *getar*, "to throw or cast" in Venetian dialect. The Cannaregio area, where the Jews were confined, was at one time the site of a foundry. Giovanni Volpe is the only permanently established baker in Venezia's Jewish ghetto who is turning out traditional pastry. Pointy *asime dolce* (fennel cookies), *zuccherini* (sugar cookies), S-shaped *bisce*, almond and almond paste *impade* cookies, and *tortiglione* (almond "snake") are sold in this grocery-bakery. The Italian matzoh (*pane azimo*) looks very different from the commercial American version. Signor Volpi learned to make the desserts from a Jewish baker, but isn't kosher or Jewish himself.

TRADITIONAL JEWISH FOODS
Comunità Ebraica
Cannaregio 1189, Ghetto Vecchio
Tel. 041/715012

The Jewish Center has a community baking oven—open one month a year, from the festival of Purim through Passover—for authentic *pane azimo* and traditional desserts. They send matzoh all over northern Italy and Europe, make essentially the same desserts as Volpi, and also organize fixed-price communal Passover dinners, usually attended by up to 200 people, where traditional Venetian Jewish *cucina* is served.

GELATO
Gelateria Nico
Zattere 922, Dorsoduro
Tel. 041/5225293
Closed Thursday and December 20–January 20

Soaking up the afternoon sun on the Zattere, overlooking the Giudecca, while eating one of Nico's tasty *gelati* is the essence of life in Venezia. There are other *gelaterie* on the Zattere, but Nico is the best.

GELATO
Paolin
San Marco 2962A, Campo Santo Stefano
Tel. 041/5225576
Closed Friday

Paolin makes what many locals feel is Venezia's finest *gelato*. There are only twelve flavors, all creamy and naturally flavored. Outdoor tables in the Campo Santo Stefano provide a ringside seat for some of Venezia's best people-watching, all for the price of a *gelato*. It's open till midnight in the summer.

RESTAURANT

Altanella
Giudecca 268, Rio de Ponte
Lungo
Tel. 041/5227780
Closed Monday evening, Tuesday,
and August
No credit cards
Price range: low moderate

Across the Canal Grande on the Giudecca, one of the last strongholds of a Venezia without mass tourism, Altanella is a favorite for its pure ambience and traditional *cucina*. The stained trilingual menu is filled with funny English typos, but the *cucina* makes no errors with simple boiled baby octopus, *sarde in saor* (marinated fresh sardines), well-prepared *risotto*, spaghetti, and deep-fried or grilled fish. Don't be put off by the inky, purply black sauce of *seppie in umido con polenta* (cuttlefish cooked with its ink, served with polenta)—it's one of the most glorious dishes of Venezia. The prices are miraculously low for Venezia. In fact, everything about Altanella is wonderful—except the wine.

RESTAURANT

Antico Pizzo
San Polo 814, Rialto
Tel. 041/5231575
Closed Sunday, Monday, and
August
No credit cards
Price: moderate

Around the corner from the Rialto fish market, the two wood-paneled dining rooms of Antico

Pizzo are always crowded with regulars who show up daily for the simple, well-prepared traditional *cucina* offered by Vittorio Marcolin and served by his brother Mario and Fabio Arban, co-owners. The *bigoli neri* (homemade pasta black with squid ink), *baccalà* (salt cod) "whipped" or cooked *alla vicentina* with onions and milk, and Venetian liver served with grilled *polenta* are tasty treats in this authentic *trattoria*. The wine, however, is unfortunate.

RESTAURANT

Le Carampane
San Polo 1911
Tel. 041/5240165
Closed Sunday evening, Monday,
and August
No credit cards
Price: moderate

Le Carampane is named after the neighborhood's "house of the Rapanti family," where in the fifteenth century prostitutes exposed their breasts to attract customers. Chef Gianni Bartolozzi's local clients pack this *trattoria* for the tasty, typical *cucina* of *sarde in saor,* and spaghetti sauced with fish or mussels. Fish and shellfish are simply stewed, grilled, or fried. Finish with homemade cookies and *crostatine* (tarts). The house wine is nothing to write home about. Dine outside in the summer.

RESTAURANT

Caffè Orientale
San Polo 2426, Calle dell'Olio at
Rio Marin
Tel. 041/719804
Closed Monday and January
Credit card: MasterCard
Price: high moderate

There's no Chinese food at the hard-to-find Caffè Orientale, with its attractive Josef Hoffman chairs and marble tables in two plant-lined dining rooms. A tiny terrace covered by a striped awning overlooks the rio Marin canal, and passing *gondolieri* stopping off for a glass of wine are greeted by name. The *cucina* is home-style, with Mom and an assistant in the kitchen, turning out lightly cooked fish and seafood, *risotto*, spaghetti, *gnocchi*, and unadorned grilled fish, served with a rectangle of *polenta*. Francesco markets every morning and gets much of the fish directly from fishermen. Freshly molted soft-shelled crabs are served in the spring, and tiny cuttlefish in August. Salads are dressed with extra virgin olive oil from Lake Garda. *Gelato*, fantastic *tiramisù*, and freshly made fruit salad are a wonderful end to the meal. There's not much of a wine selection, but they do have the Borgo Conventi wines from Friuli, to drink after a glass of the house Prosecco. Incurable romantics can gondola back to the hotel directly from the terrace.

RESTAURANT

Corte Sconta
Castello 3886, Calle del Pestrin
Tel. 041/5227024
Closed Sunday, Monday, January,
and often in July
Credit cards: American Express,
Diners Club, and MasterCard
Price: expensive

What a wonderful treat it used to be to eat under a grape arbor in the slightly squalid "Hidden Courtyard," sitting on wooden folding chairs and dining with paper napkins and placemats on stone tables. But the thrill, at least during the tourist season, is gone. Hoards of diners, famished for food of quality, descend on this ten-table restaurant and seem to have changed the perspective of the *cucina*. Successful dishes can be outstanding, like the *calimaretti con nero* (tiny tangles of squid in an inky sauce) served with grilled white *polenta*, but many dishes are less than perfect, and the summertime service can be surly. Finish your meal with lemony raisin polenta cookies *(zaleti)* or chocolate nut meringues *(brutti ma buoni)*, accompanied by a glass of their mediocre dessert wine. Skip the house wines and ask for some of the gems from Friuli. In the summer, English seems to be the only language spoken in this courtyard that didn't remain hidden for long.

RESTAURANT
Due Mori
Giudecca 558, Fondamenta del Ponte Piccolo
Tel. 041/5225452
Closed Sunday
No credit cards
Price: moderate

This large, simple restaurant on the Giudecca, with its paper tablecloths, napkins, and stemmed glassware, is a welcome newcomer on the Venetian restaurant scene. Chef Giuseppe Troili spent eight years in the kitchen of Harry's Bar, and his *cucina* at the Due Mori is a combination of classic *veneziana*, typical Harry's, and fantastic pizza, especially the egg-

plant, bell pepper, or zucchini versions. Service is swift and efficient, but the wines could stand lots of improvement.

RESTAURANT
Harry's Dolce
Giudecca 773, Fondamenta Sant' Eufemia
Tel. 041/5224844
Closed Sunday and Monday
Credit cards: all
Price: high moderate

Why bother eating at Harry's Bar, when almost all the best dishes— like the *pasta e fagioli* soup, fresh *taglierini* pasta, Venetian-style liver or cuttlefish served with *polenta*, the "Sandwich called Club," the "Salad called Chef," and the delicate buttery snail-shaped rolls—are served at Harry's Dolce? A fully equipped state-of-the-art central kitchen prepares the food served in both Harry's, and prices are at least 50 percent lower at the Giudecca restaurant. Reserve a table to dine under umbrellas overlooking the canal, with the bustle of Venezia in the background, or in the winter, in a cozy dining room with bentwood chairs, beamed ceiling, and marble-countered bar. The chocolate *torta* is an ample consolation for the weary. Fine (and expensive) whole cakes and *gelato* are sold to go, although the splendid coffee meringue pie *(torta meringata)* must be ordered in advance. The house wines don't help the *cucina*; the Bianco di Custoza by San Pietro seems to be the only semi-reasonably priced selection.

RESTAURANT
La Furatola
Dorsoduro 2870, Calle Lunga Barnaba
Tel. 041/5208594
Closed Wednesday evening, Thursday, July, and August
No credit cards
Price: moderate

Reservations are a must in this small out-of-the-way restaurant serving *cucina veneziana*, because it's hard to get a table and if the fish isn't fresh enough, they won't open. The *spaghetti alle vongole* (with clam sauce) is exquisite, main-course fish is simply cooked, and the dessert cookies served with hot *zabaione* are a fun conclusion to your meal. It seems strange that a restaurant that cares so much about its basic ingredients doesn't have wines that are better than the simple house Pinot Bianco and Cabernet from Veneto. Ask for one of the two tables on the terrace overlooking the canal.

RESTAURANT
Alla Madonna
San Polo 594, Calle della Madonna
Tel. 041/5223824
Closed Wednesday and part of August
No credit cards
Price: high moderate

Alla Madonna looks like yet another seedy tourist trap—it's within a stone's throw of the Rialto bridge, known for its views and knickknacks. Instead, this *trattoria* is packed with regulars, locals who lunch here daily on classic *cucina veneziana*. The menu is translated into English, with a few endearing typographical errors, although the most interesting dishes are laid out in a refrigerator case of fresh fish and a two-tiered unstyled display of the day's specials. The owner of Al Graspo de Ua, a famed restaurant across the Rialto from Alla Madonna, eats here on Monday and Tuesday, when his restaurant is closed. Wine, once again, is unfortunate.

RESTAURANT

Da Fiore
San Polo 2202, Calle del
Scaleter
Tel. 041/721308
Closed Sunday, Monday, and
August
Credit cards: American Express,
Diners Club, MasterCard
Price: high moderate

Da Fiore serves the best food in Venezia. The *cucina* is based on the finest-quality fresh fish and vegetables, given the simplest possible treatment. The flavors are sweet and direct. Chef Mara Zanetti and host Maurizio Martin's idea of a condiment is a drop of extra virgin olive oil and some chopped parsley. *Risotto*—made with special *vialone nano* rice and fish, shellfish, *porcini* mushrooms, or delicately perfumed local vegetables—is perfectly undercooked. Fish is fried with attention, and the results are almost greaseless. Seasonal soft-shelled crabs and baby cuttlefish are sensational. Save room for the S-shaped cook-

ies from Burano, served with a glass of amber-colored Recioto di Soave. Pieropan's Soave and the wines of Russiz Superiore are a treat to find.

RESTAURANT

Paradiso Perduto
Cannaregio 2540, Fondamenta
della Misericordia
Tel. 041/720581
Closed Monday
No credit cards
Price: moderate

Large, lively, and open late, "Paradise Lost" serves a typical *cucina veneziana* of sautéed seafood appetizers, fish pasta, and grilled or fried fish. The cover charge doubles on Sunday evenings, when there's live music. The wines of Collavini, especially the sparkling Il Grigio, are a pleasure to run into.

RESTAURANT-PIZZERIA

Alle Oche
San Polo 1552/A, Calle del
Tintor
Tel. 041/5227559
Closed Monday
No credit cards
Price: low moderate

Alle Oche is the Baskin-Robbins of pizza. Forty-one varieties are baked in their ovens, to the great delight of the young local crowd. Dine at the outdoor tables in front of the restaurant, the inside booths, or the rear garden. The "flying saucer"—two pizzas stuck together like a sandwich—is not

one of the better choices. Drink the beer.

HOTEL DINING

Cipriani
Giudecca 10, Fondamenta San
Giovanni
Tel. 041/5207744
Closed December through
February
Credit cards: all
Price: ultra-luxury

Arriving at the Cipriani, choice of crowned heads of state, with a view of San Giorgio Maggiore and the lagoon, is a special thrill. Rooms and suites are individually decorated, and opulent service is impeccable. Prices are for those who don't count the zeros on Italian banknotes. Lunch is served in the garden, overlooking the luxurious travertine marble swimming pool. The dining room is patterned with Fortuny fabric, the dishes are Limoges, and the same kind of attention has been paid to the *cucina* and wines. The menu offers tasty *risotto*, homemade pasta, *carpaccio*, and fresh fish, although they'll probably prepare anything within reason. Desserts are lovely, especially the famous bitter-chocolate *gelato*. Victor Hazan helped select the small, well-conceived, interesting wine list. The bar serves one of the best Bellinis in Venezia, and the Nonino *grappa frappè* is delicious but potent. Services for weary gastronomes include twenty-four-hour private launch service from Piazza San Marco, plus a sauna and fitness center. The hotel also has a cooking school (see page 42).

HOTEL DINING
Club del Doge—Gritti Palace
San Marco 2467, Campo Santa
  Maria del Giglio
Tel. 041/794611
Always open
Credit cards: all
Price: ultra-luxury

The fifteenth-century palace of magistrate Andrea Gritti, turned into a hotel, was the residence of Dickens and Hemingway (writers must have made more in the old days) during sojourns in Venezia. The luxury of being an honored guest in an actual palace is an unforgettable experience. Dine on an open-air terrace overlooking the Grand Canal, or in the antique-filled restaurant. Service is splendid, swift, and efficient. Skip the continental cuisine and concentrate on the well-prepared regional *cucina*. The wine list should be better. The cooking school (see page 42) offers some interesting classes.

HOTEL DINING
Londra Palace
Castello 4179, Riva degli
  Schiavoni
Tel. 041/5200533
Closed Tuesday
Credit cards: all
Price: luxury

The Londra Palace, with its 100 windows facing the lagoon, is smaller and more personal than the larger ultra-luxurious hotels of Venezia. The piano bar is comfortable and the barman makes a splendid Bellini. American Baroness Sylvia Von Block ably runs the restaurant. Chef Mirella Bettio is trying very hard, without too much success, although the grilled

vegetables are lovely. The small wine list is a gem.

HOTEL DINING
Monaco e Grand Canal
San Marco 1325, Calle
  Valleresso
Tel. 041/5200211
Closed Tuesday in winter
Credit cards: American Express,
  Visa
Price: expensive

Is the Monaco e Grand Hotel the least expensive hotel in Venezia that provides linen sheets? The furnishings are elegant, the location is ideal, and the restaurant, overlooking the Canal Grande and the Palladian facade of Le Zitelle on the Giudecca, serves some of the best food of any hotel in Venezia. The *cucina* is mostly traditional, service is efficient, and the fine wine list is a pleasure.

TABLEWARE
Rigattieri
San Marco 3532/35
Tel. 041/5231081
Closed Monday morning
Crdit cards: all

It's impossible for anyone interested in food presentation not to stop at the Rigattieri shop's windows and doorways, with its extensive display of objects from miniature copper molds to wonderful, huge, simple white serving pieces. Their Bassano ceramics are better than anything in Bassano (unless you're looking for ceramic-turbaned Indians holding telephones) and include beautiful centerpieces and ceramic tureens shaped like vegetables. The cabbage and squash are especially attractive. I love the specialized

service pieces, like the goose platter, the asparagus dishes, the poultry terrines, and anything for game. Liliana and Massimo Rigattieri are friendly, helpful, and will ship your purchases home for you.

GLASSWARE
Industrie Veneziane
Calle Vallaresso 1320
Tel. 041/5230509
Closed Monday morning
Credit cards: all

If Harry's Bar is your favorite place in Venezia, why not purchase their carafes at Industrie Veneziane, which also sells a wide selection of traditional eighteenth-century Veneziano blue, red, green, and pink gold-trimmed glassware, or the more contemporary designs of Nason-Moretti.

GLASSWARE
Barovier e Toso
Fondamenta Vetrai 28
Tel. 041/739049
Closed Saturday and Monday
  morning
Credit cards: all

Barovier e Toso is one of the oldest glassmaking firms of Venezia. Their modern serving pieces and glasses are mostly made to order, and many examples of their work are in the Murano Glass Museum.

GLASSWARE
L'Isola
San Marco 1468, Campo S.
  Moisè
Tel. 041/5231973
Closed Monday morning
Credit cards: all

L'Isola looks more like an art gallery than a glass shop, with its dra-

VENETIAN GLASS

.

The Veneziani rediscovered the art of making glass in the late 1200s, and maintained a monopoly on production through the sixteenth century. The glass produced on Murano is known for its color, intricate patterns, and light weight. Modern pieces with sleek lines and little decoration are created by the artisans of Murano, as are delicate, twisted, gold-trimmed pieces and reproductions of antiques from periods of former glory. Handmade artistry of this order is never inexpensive, so don't expect a bargain. All shops listed here are used to dealing with tourists and are thoroughly familiar with shipping procedures. Glass lovers visiting Murano will want to see the Museo dell 'Arte Vetraria, where examples of historical Egyptian, Roman, Venetian, and European glass and modern pieces are displayed.

matic lighting and sense of display. They have a complete line of the modern glassware by Carlo Moretti, who uses traditional Venetian glass-blowing techniques to create objects of great style. The simple elegance of his designs contrasts with the baroque intricacies of more classic local artisans.

GLASSWARE
Venini
San Marco 314, Piazzetta dei Leoncini
Tel. 041/5224045
Closed Monday morning
Credit cards: all

Venini is probably the most famous of the modern glassmakers, and the most innovative. This shop is the only place that sells their decorative pieces, bottles, and vases (some designed by Laura di Santillana and Gio Ponti), which are a joy to look at and justifiably expensive.

GLASSWARE
Pauly & Co.
Castello 4391/A, Ponte dei Consorzi
Tel. 041/5209899
Closed Monday morning
Credit cards: all

Pauly has shops in Piazza San Marco, but the shop in Palazzo Mozorini has more ambience, plus over thirty rooms of period glassware of intricate design, often complicated by painted gold filigree. Minimalists will be awed by the ornate chandeliers, mirrors, and glassware. The modern pieces are the least successful.

GLASSWARE
Salviati & Co.
Dorsoduro 195
Tel. 041/5222532
Closed Monday morning
Credit cards: all

Salviati also has shops in Piazza San Marco, but their most inter-

esting store is on the Grand Canal. Ornate designs and reproductions have been a specialty of Salviati for over one hundred years, and are overwhelmingly displayed in eight rooms. They offer free glass-blowing demonstrations on Murano.

GLASSWARE
Le Cose di Franca Petroli
San Marco 1799, Frezzeria
Tel. 041/5287116
Closed Monday morning
Credit cards: all

One-of-a-kind mouth-blown glass is designed by architect Franca Petroli. The colorful bowls and vases are unusual, expensive, and signed by both Franca and her glassblower.

GLASSWARE
L'Ixa
Campo San Stefano 2958
Tel. 041/5229656
Closed Monday morning
No credit cards

Tempting Murano glass pieces created from 1870 to 1960 are attractively priced and displayed in this wonderful antiques shop in Campo Santo Stefano. A window-shop here is a perfect excuse for a Paolin *gelato* (see page 124).

LINEN AND LACE
Jesurum
San Marco 4310, Ponte Canonica
Tel. 041/5223409
Closed Monday morning
Credit cards: all

In 1868 Michelangelo Jesurum reestablished the lace industry with a core of artisans who remem-

---

THE LACE OF VENEZIA

·

The arts of lacemaking and embroidery were brought to Venezia from the East, and the Venetians incorporated lace in royal, clerical, and aristocratic attire, creating a market for the delicately stitched or intricately manipulated threads, hand-crafted by nobles, nuns, and common women. The lace "schools" of the lagoon, each with their own special stitch or technique—the bobbin lace of Pellestrina, the Venice-Burano stitch of Burano, the net stitch of Chioggia—practically disappeared with the advent of machine-made lace.

---

bered the traditional skills. His original shop, in the spectacular 1150 Church of Sant' Apollonia, has a splendid selection of antique and modern lace tablecloths and contemporary, brightly colored table linens. I could get lost staring at the incredible antique lace cloths of a quality usually found in museums. Director Eugenia Graziussi will help you if you'd like to order something special. Prices are justifiably steep.

LACE AND LACEMAKING
Scuola dei Merletti
Piazza B. Galuppi, Burano
Tel. 041/730034
No credit cards

The Burano Lace School, founded in 1872, closed on its one hundredth anniversary due to a lack of interest in the painstaking work necessary to produce fine handmade lace and embroidery. It was reopened in 1981 with the help of the Burano Lace Consortium, and offers free courses taught by eleven master lacemakers. Modern and traditional lace or open-work embroidered table linens can be purchased or made to order.

LINEN AND LACE
Maria and Lina Mazzaron
Castello 4970, Fondamenta
dell'Osmarin
Tel. 041/5221392
By appointment only
No credit cards

Before World War II, all proper young women in Italy knew how to make lace and embroider. When they were fourteen, the Mazzaron sisters were sent to study lacemaking with the nuns, and they obviously learned their lessons well. Their private shop, on the first floor of a noble Venetian palace, offers linens that look and feel like heirlooms.

STATIONERY
Legatoria Piazzesi
San Marco 2511, S.M. del Giglio
Tel. 041/5221202
Closed Monday morning
Credit cards: all

The Legatoria Piazzesi, the "bookbindery" of the Piazzesi family, sells beautiful paper, hand-printed from a large collection of antique blocks. Directories, recipe files, table place cards, photo albums, stationery, covered boxes, and other items are made from or covered with this traditionally patterned paper.

STATIONERY
Paolo Olbi
San Marco 3653, Calle della
Mandola
Tel. 041/5237655
Closed Monday morning
Credit cards: all

Paoli Olbi sells handmade paper and leather notebooks with blank pages, photo albums, diaries, and stationary.

PRESERVES
Convento degli Armeni
Isola di San Lazzaro

The tiny island of San Lazzaro degli Armeni, close to Lido in the Venetian lagoon, was donated to Armenian refugees, who founded a convent with a printing house, a library of over 50,000 books, some dating from A.D. 900, cloisters, and rose gardens where petals and hips are collected to make rose preserves, which are available at the convent.

VERONA

Verona, a city of Roman origin, is located on the banks of the Adige river—hometown of Romeo and Giulietta, of the exciting open-air opera performed in a Roman arena, and of Vinitaly, the most important wine fair in Italy, held in the early spring.

HOTEL
Vittoria
Via Adua 8
Tel. 045/590566
Credit cards: American Express,
   Diners
Price: expensive

HOTEL
Touring
Via Q. Sella 5
Tel. 045/590944
Credit cards: all
Price: moderate

HOTEL
Aurora
Piazza delle Erbe
Tel. 045/594717
No credit cards
Price range: inexpensive

MARKET
Piazza delle Erbe

The central outdoor fruit and vegetable market, in piazza delle Erbe, takes place six mornings a week. The light in the piazza, reflecting off the pastel rust- and apricot-colored brick buildings, is best in the early morning, before 9, when the produce stands are stocked with crisp-looking vegetables and lively fruit, and the perfumes in the air make your nose prickle. The evening light is also wonderful, but the food stands will be closed, leaving only stalls selling touristy trinkets.

GELATO
Da Paolo
Via Risorgimento 1
Tel. 041/918429
Closed Monday, January, and
   August

Paolo makes the best *gelato* in Verona. His *gelateria* has all the clas-

A mid-afternoon break: **gelato** *and a stroll*

sics, like chocolate, hazelnut, and vanilla custard, which can be found everywhere, but his specialty is fruit flavors, especially tropical fruit. Paolo has been to the U.S., Mexico, South America, Africa, and the Orient, tracking down exotic fruits, turning them into *gelato*. He's at work on a book on the subject. You may find mango, lychee, passion fruit, fresh pistachio or date, pink grapefruit, or grayish quintessential banana *gelato* (the best I've ever had!), depending on what Paolo has managed to procure. The flavors, which change daily, are listed on a large sign behind the granite counter inset with stainless-steel ice cream tubs. No smoking is allowed—hooray!

RESTAURANT
Il Desco
Via dietro San Sebastiano 7
Tel. 045/595358
Closed Sunday
Credit cards: American Express,
   MasterCard
Price: expensive

The golden apricot marbleized stucco walls, beamed wooden ceilings, patchwork-inspired tapestries by Missoni, subdued lighting, and warm welcome by host Natale Spinelli set the stage for dining at Il Desco, one of Italy's most attractive restaurants and a

Wrapping strawberries at an outdoor market

liata (sliced beef) are nicely done. Watch the young chefs, wearing strange squashed-down toques, working behind the glass. The decor seems to have been carried out by three different decorators, each unaware of the others.

HOUSEWARES
Casa mia di Montaldo
Via IV Novembre 17
Tel. 045/914362
Closed Monday morning
No credit cards

This small maze of rooms with what looks like at least two of every houseware known to man, stacked on floor-to-ceiling shelves, is worth a slight detour on the way to Paolo's *gelateria* (see page 131). One room contains all-plastic toys and is especially strong on Lego. I can always find something of interest.

rising star on the gastronomic scene. The *cucina*, guided by Elia Rizzo, has little to do with tradition but uses a wide range of not-strictly-local meat, poultry, fish, and vegetables to great advantage. Tastes are balanced, herbs are used wisely, pasta is homemade, and cheese is served with fig bread. Desserts are glorious and have a separate menu. The wine list is splendid and clear, with a great selection of local and Italian wines.

RESTAURANT
La Torretta
Piazza Broilo 1
Tel. 045/592752
Closed Saturday lunch and Sunday
Credit card: American Express
Price: high moderate

La Torretta seems to be trying hard. The wine list is picking up, and the *antipasto* selection of vegetable salads is a lovely meal in itself. Pasta, homemade *bigoli*, and simple meat dishes like the *tag-*

VICENZA

HOTEL
Michelangelo
Via Sacco 4/A
Arcugnano (close by)
Tel. 0444/550300
Credit cards: American Express, Diners Club, MasterCard
Price: expensive

HOTEL
Cristina
Corso SS Felice e Fortunato 32
Tel. 0444/234280
Credit cards: all
Price: moderate

RESTAURANT

Da Remo
Via Caimpenta 14
Tel. 0444/911007
Closed Sunday evening, Monday,
*   and August*
Credit card: American Express
Price: moderate

Da Remo is a rustic farmhouse decorated in typical *trattoria* style. The *cucina* is also typical, featuring simple regional food of the Breganze area. Owner Mario Baratto is interested in hard-to-find traditional dishes, and it's a pleasure to find them on his menu. The rice and hops *(riso e bruscandoli)* may be worth the trip. Mushrooms are served in season. Wine is mostly local. Sunday lunch is a mob scene, interesting from a cultural point of view but not for the food, which is better when the kitchen isn't so stressed.

FRIULI–VENEZIA GIULIA

■

"There," pointing eastward, "over those mountains is Yugoslavia," the Friulani never fail to let you know. It's a boundary that most people aren't too happy about, since in the early 1950s a whole section of this region, Istria, was ceded to Yugoslavia in exchange for Trieste. Friuli–Venezia Giulia is a land of Alps, hills with some of the best wine-growing areas in Italy, plains, and lagoons, wedged between the Adriatic Sea, Yugoslavia, Austria, and Veneto. They all played musical chairs with this region after the rule of Romans, Longobards, Franks, the bishops of Aquileia, the dukes of Friuli, and the counts of Grado.

The traditional open hearth *(fogolar)* is an invitation to come in and warm up, an essential element in both restaurants and homes and an expression of the Friulani sense of hospitality and warmth. The *cucina,* influenced by many cultures but above all by poverty, is flavored by original combinations of spices, sweet and sour, and smoke. *Brovada,* its recipe dating from Roman Apicio's *De Re Coquinaria,* is usually offered with misgivings and apologies in case you don't appreciate turnips, fermented with the dregs of pressed grapes for a month, then grated and cooked. Roman legions were fueled by grain and beans, found here in the form of barley and bean soup. Dumplings *(gnocchi)* may be made of potatoes, winter squash, or stale bread, and the traditional pasta *(cialzons)* may be stuffed with smoked *ricotta,* herbs, or even sweet and sour combinations. *Polenta* may appear as a first or second course, or as a side dish. Meats, mostly pork, game, and courtyard animals, are usually grilled in the *fogolar* or roasted. Field greens and herbs flavor the *cucina friulana* of the hills and plains. Restaurants on the lagoon serve simply prepared Adriatic seafood to summer tourists. Cheese made by individuals who graze their herds in the mountains rarely reaches the city, and never leaves the region. More easily found *latteria* cheese is used to create *frico* or *fricco,* a tasty cheese fritter. It is made, I have been informed many times, by frying a bit of *latteria* until it's done, and then turning it over to complete cooking. Mine has never come out right. Strudel-type desserts reflect the Austrian influence in this region. The Friulani are *grappa* drinkers, not sippers, and even rinse their coffee cups with a shot of *grappa,* known as a *resentin.*

This is the region of Italy where I left my heart. Most tourists seem to have overlooked Friuli's Roman outposts; the star-shaped Venetian fortress of Palmanova; Villa Manin, the country estate of the last Doge of Venezia; the synagogue of Trieste; Udine, with its Venetian piazza and hilltop castle in the middle of town; Aquileia, with backyard Roman columns and a fourth-century mosaic the size of a football field. But could they all have overlooked the Friulani, the warmest and most hospitable of the Italians?

THE MENU

SALUMI
▪

Muset or *Musetto* ▪ cooked sausage made with ground pork and spices that may include coriander and cinnamon

Prosciutto affumicato ▪ raw ham smoked with juniper and fir, a specialty of the village of Sauris

Prosciutto crudo di San Daniele ▪ raw ham cured in the hills of San Daniele, thought to be the best in Italy

Salame friuilano ▪ cured pork sausage

ANTIPASTO
▪

Cvapcici ▪ unpronounceable meatballs from Trieste, made with veal, pork, and beef

Frico or *Fricco* ▪ fried cheese fritters

Salame cotto nell'aceto ▪ fresh salami cooked in vinegar, served with polenta

PRIMO
▪

Brodeto or *Brodetto* ▪ fish soup

Cialzone ▪ pasta stuffed with spinach and candied citron, or potatoes and cinnamon, or herbs and smoked ricotta, served with melted butter

Gnocchi ▪ potato dumplings

Gnocchi di pane ▪ made of stale bread

Gnocchi di susina ▪ stuffed with a prune

Gnocchi di zucca ▪ made with winter squash, served with grated smoked ricotta

Jota or *Iota* ▪ bean, cabbage, or *brovada* and polenta soup

Lasagne ai semi di papavero ▪ sweet poppy-seed lasagna

Minestra d'orzo e fagioli ▪ bean and barley soup

Paparot ▪ spinach and cornmeal soup

Ravioli di zucca ▪ squash-filled pasta, at times made from a potato dough

Ris e fasui ▪ rice, bean, and potato soup

Zuppa di pesce alla gradese ▪ soup of local Adriatic fish, made with vinegar and garlic

SECONDO

Baccalà alla capuccina • salt cod cooked with anchovies, raisins, pine nuts, and spices

Brovada • turnips marinated with grape‧skins left over from winemaking, cooked with pork sausage

Capriolo in salmi • venison stewed in a sauce of wine, herbs, and spices

Costine di maiale • roast pork ribs

Fasui cul muset • beans with pork sausage

Frittata alle erbe • pan-fried flan of eggs and field greens

Granzevola alla triestina • crab baked with bread crumbs, garlic, and parsley

Gulyas • (gulash) beef stew cooked with onions, herbs, and paprika

Toc de purcit • pork stewed with white wine, cloves, cinnamon, and other spices

CONTORNO

Radichietto • tender salad greens, sometimes served with beans

FORMAGGIO

Formaggio di malga • cheese found only in the mountain districts, made from the milk of cows grazing in Alpine pastures

Latteria • mild when fresh, more intense when aged, made from cow's milk

Montasio • mild, smooth, made from cow's milk

Ricotta • soft, mild, fresh, or smoked *(affumicata)*

DOLCE

Esse di raveo • S-shaped sugar cookies

Gubana • light, flaky pastry stuffed with nuts and candied fruits, or in its more authentic form, a puffy spiral-shaped yeast bread filled with nuts, cocoa, candied fruit, and liqueur

Presnitz • roll stuffed with raisins, nuts, and candied fruit

Putizza • similar to *gubana,* but moister and containing chocolate pieces

Strucolo • ricotta-raisin strudel

THE *W*INE LIST

Six major DOC production zones of Friuli, each producing wines named for up to thirteen different grape varieties, plus personal non-DOC wines labeled *vino da tavola,* may contribute to some confusion about the wines of this region. A Pinot Grigio or Tocai from Latisana or Aquileia won't have the same style as the wines of the same name from Colli Orientali dei Friuli and Collio Goriziano, also known as Collio. The flowery whites and rich reds are meant to be drunk young, although some producers seem to be coming up with wines, both red and white, of more lasting promise. Wineries are experimenting with native grape varieties, at times clonally rescued from near extinction, and the resulting lusty reds are worthy of their effort.

Wines from the *Colli Orientali del Friuli,* an area that stretches along the Yugoslavian border to the foothills of the Alps, are among the best in the region. The reds, especially elegant *Cabernet,* smooth *Merlot,* and hearty native *Refosco,* are fine with meats and game. *Pinot Bianco, Pinot Grigio, Riesling Renano,* and *Sauvignon* are delicate, fruity, dry whites that go well with antipasti, pasta, rice, and fish. *Tocai* is soft, aromatic, and special, in no way resembling the Tokay of Hungary and Austria. For dessert, *Verduzzo* and *Picolit,* both made from native grapes, are delicately perfumed and semi-sweet. Quality wines are produced by Abbazia di Rosazzo, Girolamo Dorigo, Giovanni Dri, Livio Felluga, La Viarte, Rocca Bernarda, Ronchi di Cialla, Ronco del Gnemiz, Vigne dal Leon, and Volpe Pasini.

Some of Italy's finest white wines are made in the area known as *Collio* or *Collio Goriziano,* outside the city of Gorizia, along the border of Yugoslavia. Whites are dry and fruity and are served with antipasti and fish dishes: *Pinot Bianco, Pinot Grigio, Sauvignon,* and *Traminer. Collio* is a delicate blend of Tocai, Malvasia, and Ribolla white grapes. Aromatic *Tocai,* at its best from this area, is served with fish and regional *cucina.* Reds *Cabernet* and *Merlot* are dry, light, and fragrant; they're perfect with meat and game. Quality producers include Borgo Conventi, Borgo del Tiglio, Ca' Ronesca, Livio Felluga, Gradimir Gradnik, Francesco Gravner, Jermann, Doro Princic, Puiatti, Radikon, Russiz Superiore, and Mario Schiopetto.

The *Isonzo* area, which follows the Isonzo River from the plains to the hills near the Yugoslavian border, produces fragrant dry reds *Cabernet* and *Merlot,* often paired with meat dishes. *Pinot Bianco, Pinot Grigio, Sauvignon, Riesling Renano,* and *Tocai,* all fine, crisp whites, are also produced in the Isonzo area by Stelio Gallo and Pier Paolo Pecorari. They're at their best with antipasti, first courses, and fish.

Fine *Chardonnay,* an elegant dry white served with fish, is produced by Abbazia di Rosazzo, Borgo Conventi, Jermann, Stelio Gallo, Gravner, and Puiatti.

Müller Thurgau, an elegant, fruity, dry white, splendid with fish and seafood, is produced by Ronco del Gnemiz, Mario Schiopetto, and Marina Danieli.

Pignolo, a uniquely Friulian grape, has recently been rescued from extinction (clonally!) and is now the basis for a robust, hearty red that pairs well with meat, fowl, and local rustic country cooking. It is ably produced by Abbazia di Rosazzo and Girolanio Dorigo.

Schioppettino is a ruby-colored full red from the native Ribolla Nera or Schioppettino grape. It is usually served with meat, fowl, and game and is produced by Ronchi di Cialla and Vigne dal Leon.

Tacelenghe or *Tazzelenghe,* literally "tongue-cutter" in dialect, is a direct reference to the tannic "bite" of this purple-ruby, lively red table wine made from a local grape variety. It is at its best with meat, fowl, and game, and produced by Girolamo Dorigo and Vigne dal Leon.

Exemplary red, white, and sparkling *vino da tavola* table wines are produced by some of Friuli's finest winemakers. Dorigo makes *Monsclapade,* a blend of red grapes aged in wood. Mario Schiopetto produces *Rivarossa,* a red, *Riesling Renano* and *Blanc des*

Roses, elegant rich whites. Abbazia di Rosazzo makes **Ronco delle Acacie** and **Ronco di Corte,** both blends of white grapes, and **Ronco dei Roseti,** a blend of mostly local reds, aged in new oak barrels. Livio Felluga's son Maurizio has created **Terre Alte,** a flowery blend of white grapes, and a personal favorite. Jermann makes **Vintage Tunina, Vinnae,** and **Engelwhite,** elegant whites, and **Moscato Rosa,** a rosé dessert wine, with great success. La Viarte ages its white **Liende** and red **Roi** in new oak barrels. Volpe Pasini makes **Zuc di Volpe,** a blend of red grapes. **Applause, il Grigio,** and **Ribolla Gialla** are sparkling whites made by Collavini.

REGIONAL SPECIALTIES

CURED GOOSE

In many parts of Italy, farmers too poor to raise pigs raised geese, which are easier to feed and ready to eat sooner. Each section of the goose was preserved in a different way—as salami, under rendered goose fat, smoked, or as sausages. Goose products were traditionally used by kosher Jews as a flavor substitute for pork. Sausage and salami were for personal use, and never made their way to the marketplace. But a few local producers have taken an interest in goose products, which can now be found in shops and restaurants.

The village of Viscone hosts a goose festival the second weekend in October, with gastronomic stands serving local specialties. Contact Fattoria dell'Oca Bianca (page 151) for more information.

GRAPPA

Grappa is made from pomace, the grape skins and pits left over after the winemaking process. It anesthetized generations of Friulani against cold and poverty. Local custom calls for rinsing the after-dinner coffee cup with a shot of *grappa,* thus adding a bit of leftover sugar and coffee to the aggressive alcoholic taste of this potent liquor. For more *grappa* information, see page 39; for a source of Friuli *grappa,* see page 141.

GUBANA

Gubana is a spiral-shaped yeast dessert cake, originally a specialty of Cividale but found throughout Friuli. There are two basic versions—one made with puff pastry and the other with yeast dough, both with essentially the same filling of nuts, cocoa, candied fruit, spice, and liqueurs. It is eaten sliced and sprinkled with *grappa* for dessert, but is delicious plain for breakfast. See page 141 for sources. Fear not if you fall in love with *gubana*—Carol Field's recipe for this traditional cake in *The Italian Baker* is a gem.

PROSCIUTTO CRUDO DI SAN DANIELE

It's easy to recognize a San Daniele *prosciutto*—it's the violin-shaped ham complete with hoof, which is never removed from the *prosciutto* that many feel is the tastiest in Italy. But what makes the *prosciutto* from the village of San Daniele so special? The procedure is practically the same one used to make the more famous Parma version. But there are differences. The raw hams, called *coscie* (thighs), are flattened and massaged with salt. The larger surface and thinner ham produced by flattening takes less salt and less time to cure. The hams are hung to age in well-ventilated temperature-controlled rooms, with windows that open to expose the hams to gusts of a cold northern wind known as the *bora.* See page 146 for sources.

PROSCIUTTO AFFUMICATO

Smoke is an important flavor in the *cucina friulana.* In some areas of Friuli, *prosciutto* is cured, then smoked with aromatic wood and spices in the hood of the *fogolar.* Is the chimney soot that has accumulated during decades of *prosciutto*-smoking really a determining flavor factor? See pages 142, 146, and 147 to taste some samples.

MOUNTAIN CHEESE

Cheese production in Friuli is the antithesis of big business. There are no cooperatives, no standardization, and the only way to sample the best is to head for the mountains and valleys of Carnia, to the wiggly back roads on the Touring Club map, on the lookout for signs that say *"Formaggio."* Country restaurants may have the cheese of a neighboring producer. See below for one source.

THE FRIULIAN "PANTRY"

Cjabot, Friulan dialect for "pantry," isn't a store. It's a kind of collection agency that sets standards of excellence and seeks out the best traditional products from the Carnia, an area known for its genuine, simple mountain *cucina. Grappa,* honey, cookies, smoked mountain trout, aged smoked *speck,* cheese, and stone-ground polenta are elegantly packaged with attractive graphics. Almost all products have unrecognizable names—*flum, fumat, gust zintil*—that don't even sound Italian, and all are of the highest quality. For more information, contact Gianni Cosetti, the world's greatest Carnia expert (see page 147) or call tel. 0481/80328.

CRAFTS

Attractive, reasonably priced traditional baskets and shopping bags called *sporte* are woven from corn husks. They are sold at markets and in shops throughout the region. See page 142.

BROVADA

You probably won't like *brovada;* the Friulani will tell you when and if it's offered to you. Turnips that have been exposed to a cold autumn moon are submerged for thirty days under the leftovers of the winemaking process, a treatment not unlike the one that turns cabbage into sauerkraut. Then they are sold, grated by produce vendors, to be cooked with local sausage *(muset* or *musetto).* If you fall in love with *brovada,* the regional dish of Friuli, made only in the fall or winter, you might want to purchase a traditional wooden turnip grater, although the food processor works better (see page 142).

CITIES AND TOWNS

AQUILEIA

DISTILLERY
Distilleria Aquileia
Via Julia Augusta 87/A
Tel. 0431/91091
Closed Sunday except July and
*   August*
No credit cards

If the Roman ruins or the football-field-size fourth-century mosaics aren't enough to lure you to Aquileia, stop in for a taste of *Sgnape dal Checo* and the pear cream produced by the Distilleria Aquileia, sold in the store outside the distillery. (Go easy on the free samples!) If you'd like to see the grappa-making process, visits to the distillery are possible Monday through Friday and on Saturday mornings.

CHIANSUTAN

CHEESE
Cocco Carnelus
Chiansutan
No address
No phone

Cocco Carnelus is passionate about two things: goat cheese and vintage Harley Davidson motorcycles. After Cocco left his native Friuli to work in Paris, city life became too much for him and he moved to Provence, where he tended sheep and goats and discovered his craft. He married and moved to the almost abandoned village of Chiansutan, where he and his wife raise and milk around a hundred goats and make two cheeses from their milk. One is a fresh *ricotta* that bears absolutely no relation to the insipid curd sold in plastic containers in the U.S. It has the pungency of goat cheese, with the sweetness of fresh country milk. Cocco's other cheese is a delicate, lightly smoked goat cheese. Both, in guidebook terminology, are worth a detour. The 1936 "Knucklehead" Harley rounds out the experience.

CIVIDALE DEL FRIULI

BAR-CAFFÈ
Caffè San Marco
Largo Boiani 7
Tel. 0432/71001
Closed Thursday

The Caffè San Marco in Cividale has good coffee, a clean bathroom and a row of phone booths in the back. The friendly cashier will supply directions with a smile.

PASTRY–GELATO
Pasticceria Gelateria Ducale
Piazza Picco 18
Tel. 0432/730707
Closed Monday

The best place for *gubana* also makes the best *gelato*. Pine nut *(pignolato)* is rich and nutty, meringue *(meringhe)* with a hint of lemon peel is tasty, and the fruit flavors, made with seasonal fruit, are delicious. The miniature *gubane* (see page 139) are irresistible, if you don't want to commit yourself to a full-sized one.

PASTRY
Vogric
Via Libertà 136
Tel. 0432/730236
Closed Saturday and Sunday

Vogric's makes a high-quality commercial *gubana* that seems to last longer than artisanal versions. It is found throughout the region and can also be purchased at the bakery.

A detail of the Roman mosaics in Aquileia

CORMONS

RESTAURANT-INN
La Subida
Località Subida
Tel. 0481/60531
No credit cards
Closed Tuesday, Wednesday, and February
Price: moderate

Josco and Loredana Sirk's La Subida is a rustic vacation center with seven apartments, some with *fogolar* hearths, in the woods outside Cormons. Tennis courts, swimming pool, and stables make this a perfect base for a family vacation. Their attractive restaurant, Al Cacciatore, serves simple, traditional *cucina*, nicely prepared. The all-Friuli wine list is carefully chosen and reasonably priced, and offers some gems.

RESTAURANT
Al Giardinetto
Via Matteotti 54
Tel. 0481/60257
Closed Monday evening, Tuesday, and July
Credit cards: American Express, MasterCard, Visa
Price range: moderate

The Zoppolatti family—mother Mariuccia and son Paolo in the kitchen, father Ezio and son Giorgio in the warm, rustic dining rooms—serve up some of the finest food in Friuli. Menus change monthly and offer traditional Austrian-inspired dishes like smoked pork loin served with grated horseradish, *ricotta* strudel with poppy seeds, prune-stuffed *gnocchi,* and goulash with *polenta.* Desserts are skillfully prepared and presented. The wine list offers a wide range of quality local wines. A monthly *menu degustazione* features a tasting of seasonal traditional dishes. Reserve in advance for a table near the hearth.

SALUMI
Lorenzo D'Osvaldo
Via Dante 40
Tel. 0481/61644

Lorenzo d'Osvaldo hand-cures and smokes 1,500 hams from little black Friulian pigs with a blend of juniper, bay, and fruit wood. The resulting *prosciutto affumicato,* produced from November to April, is lighter and more delicate than the more traditional and much smokier Sauris ham (see page 147).

CORTALE DI REANA

CRAFTS
Cooperativa Artigiana Cartocciai
    Friulani
Cortale di Reana
Tel. 0432/851434
Closed Saturday and Sunday

The Cooperativa Artigiana Cartocciai Friulani's crafts are sturdier and more attractive than the stuff sold in markets. Their inexpensive, durable baskets are a joy to own.

DOLEGNA DEL COLLIO

HOTEL
Wiener
Via Stazione 68
San Giovanni al Natisone (close by)
Tel. 0432/757378
Credit cards: American Express, Visa
Price: moderate

RESTAURANT
Al Castello dell'Aquila d'Oro
Via Ruttars 11
Tel. 0481/60545
Closed Monday, Tuesday, and most of August
Credit cards: American Express, Diners Club, Visa
Price: moderate

The Aquila d'Oro, "The Golden Eagle," situated in a castle of Roman origin, is probably Friuli's most attractive restaurant. Dine in one of the warm, intimate dining rooms in the winter, or on the shaded terrace overlooking gentle hills and vineyards in the spring and summer. The seasonal menu features creative, well-prepared, beautifully presented *cucina.* The desserts are all homemade and delicious, and the wine list offers a nice selection of fine local wines.

GORIZIA

RESTAURANT-INN
Locanda Sandro
Via Santa Chiara 18
Tel. 0481/83223
Closed Wednesday and holidays
No credit cards
Price: inexpensive

Elsa Peilizzon, who speaks Italian, German, English, Friulano, and Sloveno, runs this eight-room inn with its "visit to Grandma" feeling. The *cucina* is Gorizia family-style, and features hearty soups, stews, and a local version of hash-brown potatoes. The homemade desserts, especially the *sacher torta,* are delicious. The house wine is horrid. Bring your own, or drink the beer.

HOUSEWARES
La Casalinga di Paolo Ciampi
Piazza Vittoria 54
Tel. 0481/83216
Closed Monday
No credit cards

Paolo Ciampi's housewares shop seems to sell at least one of every houseware invented. His father used to make and sell his own turnip graters for *brovada* (see page 140), which may explain the presence of this hard-to-find item in Gorizia.

LAVARIANO

HOTEL
See Wiener in San Giovani al Natisone (above)

RESTAURANT
Blasut—Gnam Gnam Bar
Via Aquileia 7
Tel. 0432/767017
Closed Monday, and mid-August to mid-September
Credit card: Diners Club
Price: moderate

Since around 60 percent of the population of Lavariano is named Bernardis, most of them have dis-

*Cocco Carnelus makes
his famous goat cheese
in Chiansutan.*

tinguishing nicknames. Dante Bernardis is *Blasut,* "Shorty," which barely begins to describe the Tweedledee-like owner of this restaurant who propels himself through the dining room with contagious enthusiasm. Blasut and chef Andrea Bordignon search out the best local ingredients—delicately smoked *prosciutto,* farm-raised duck and goose, fresh herbs and vegetables, aged *latteria* cheese—and combine them with style and taste. The menu, which changes monthly, is presented with a glass of sparkling wine and a ruffle of cheese on a piece of whole-wheat bread, topped by a walnut, a meal-opener of great charm. Winter dishes are generally more exciting; summer dining takes place on a canopied patio with naïf frescoes. Fish is served on Fridays. The wine list offers a personal selection of quality, mostly Friulano wines. Ask to see the wine cellar and Blasut will jump for joy.

LEONACCO DI PAGNACCO

HOTEL
Boschetti
Piazza Mazzini 10
Tricesimo (close by)
Tel. 0432/851230
Credit cards: American Express,
   Diners Club, Visa
Price: high moderate

RESTAURANT
Da Toso
Via Pozzuolo 16
Tel. 0432/852515
Closed Wednesday
No credit cards
Price: moderate

Don't let the lively bar scene, the coat rack and poster decor, or the marble chip floor that looks like the original prototype for linoleum distract you from the hearth, which is what Da Toso is all about. This ultra-traditional *fogolar* fireplace, a low table with four legs (not the more modern brick constructions found in many homes and restaurants), is presided over by Giancarlo Toso and his wife, Alida. The menu never varies much, the pasta isn't very good, the soups are plain home-style, but the grill work is superb. White-aproned Toso pampers homemade sausage, veal, beef, pork, or liver, each cooked to perfection over the embers of a charcoal and wood fire in his *fogolar.* The house wines are decent, but they also have a limited selection of fine, fairly priced, quality local wines. Da Toso is always crowded, so be prepared for a wait if you haven't reserved in advance.

MANZANO

HOTEL
See Wiener in San Giovanni al Natisone (page 142)

RESTAURANT
Da Romea
Via Divisione Julia 15
Tel. 0432/754251
Closed Sunday
No credit cards
Price: inexpensive

Behind the nondescript facade and dining rooms of Da Romea, in a small, pine-paneled rustic dining room with a fireplace, Leda della Rovere prepares, with great skill, dedication, and passion, some of the finest *cucina* in Friuli. The strictly local clientele lunch in the main dining rooms, returning daily for Leda's light-handed treatment of quality ingredients combined with fresh herbs from the garden out back. The regular menu features a few traditional specialties, along with dishes from other regions. Reserve, at least a day in advance, the *Gusta' Furlan,* an inspired tasting menu of

regional dishes rarely found elsewhere—best in winter or spring—and hope that it includes deep-fried sage leaves, feather-weight *ricotta*-filled *gnocchi,* winter-squash bread, and Leda's apple, nut, and spice cake. The small, well-priced wine list offers some local gems.

OLIVE OIL
Abbazia di Rosazzo
Manzano
Tel. 0432/759429

Extra virgin olive oil isn't widely used in this northern region today, but historical documents that refer to olive cultivation on the Abbazia di Rosazzo's lands prompted Walter Filiputti to have the remaining olives analyzed. Pleased with the results, he worked with a nursery in Toscana to repropagate his native trees. They won't produce much oil for a few more years, but it's only a matter of time until extra virgin Friulian olive oil becomes a reality once again.

PALUZZA

TABLEWARE
Ceramica Dassi
Via Nazionale 44
Tel. 0433/775414
No credit cards

Rustic dinnerware of *graffito*—scratched-in patterns revealing the clay beneath the white glaze—and dishes with designs of local flowers are all hand-formed and -decorated by these traditional artisans of the Carnia, who make terra-cotta, majolica, and ceramic

crafts. Shipping must be separately arranged.

PAULARO

CRAFTS
Diomiro Blanzan
Via Roma 56
Tel. 0433/70078
Closed Sunday

Genuine *scarpets,* made of many layers of pressed fabric (not velvet), can be found at Diomiro Blanzan's shop, which sells native costumes for women and children, and wooden crafts of the Carnia.

PERCOTO

GRAPPA
Nonino Distillery
Via Aquileia 140
Tel. 0432/676263

Founded in 1897 by Orazio Nonino with a mobile still on wheels, the Nonino distillery, under the direction of Benito and Giannola Nonino and their daughters Betty, Cristina, and Antonella, produces some of Italy's finest *grappa.* Known for its elegant packaging and high-quality products, Nonino was the first to popularize the idea of *monovitigno,* one-grape-variety *grappa* distilled from the leftovers of the winemaking process, which they procure from some of the region's finest wineries. They also produce *ué,* distilled from grape must or juice, and le frute, distilled from fruits and berries. Visits to the distillery can be arranged.

The three Nonino sisters: fourth-generation distillers

rooms may serenade your meal. In the summer, dine under a canopy in the lush garden. The house wines are mediocre; ask to see the wine list if you're interested in quality.

RAUSCEDO

GRAPE NURSERY
Vivai Cooperativa di Rauscedo
Via Udine 39
Tel. 0427/94022

Some of Italy's finest vines come from the Cooperativa in Rauscedo, whose 250 nurseries produce 20,000,000 grape plants yearly—half the Italian production. A wide range of varieties and clones are grafted into over 1000 combinations by this unique nursery. If you'd like to visit, write or call director Dottor Sartore at least one week in advance.

REMANZACCO

FOGOLAR
L'Ottagono di Franco Pianalto
Via Ostelin 91
Tel. 0432/667598
Closed Sunday
No credit cards

The *fogolar* is the heart and hearth of the Friulian home, the center of the regional experience. It's for warming up, socializing, grilling, and much more.

Franco Pianalto specializes in the construction of the traditional *fogolar Friulano* hearth and the *spolerts*, a wood-burning brick oven with iron finishings.

PORCIA

INN
See La Primula in San Quirino (page 146)

RESTAURANT
Da Gildo
Via Marconi 17
Tel. 0434/921212
Closed Sunday evening, Monday, and August
Credit card: Visa
Price: moderate

You'll be hard-pressed to recognize any of the people in the photographs covering the walls of various dining rooms in this thirteenth-century palace. A menu exists, but no one orders from it. Gildo and his wife, Annamaria, serve a twelve-course marathon of nontraditional dishes. "If you don't like it, I'll take it away and give you something else," Annamaria will tell you. Dramatic presentations like the tower of *prosciutto* or the bouquet of seasonal fruit, complete with butterflies, make this restaurant a favorite with local families. On Sundays music from a wedding or first-communion celebration in one of the large private dining

SAN DANIELE

SMOKED TROUT
Friultrota di Dario Pighin
Via Aonedis 10
Tel. 0432/956560

Although smoked fish is not traditional, it certainly is tasty, and since the Friulani smoke meat and cheese, it seems like a logical extention of the regional palate. Dario Pighin raises salmon trout and trout, and smokes them with a special blend of beech and juniper. The flavor is smoky and complex, a treat to eat even if it isn't traditional.

PROSCIUTTO
Prolongo
Viale Trento 115
Tel. 0432/957161
Closed Saturday and Sunday

The artisans at Prolongo make only 7,000 prosciutti yearly, purchasing the hams in the fall, curing them in the special climate of San Daniele, without air conditioning. They'll sell you a whole prosciutto or just enough for lunch.

PROSCIUTTO
Prosciutti Daniel
Via Venezia 148
Tel. 0432/957543
Closed Saturday and Sunday

This factory makes over 100,000 prosciutti yearly, but most work is still done by hand. Their prosciutto is aged for up to fourteen months, hung in rows on stainless-steel S-hooks in rooms with controlled humidity and temperature and vents to let in the local winds. You

Leda offers her exceptional Friulan hospitality and a glass of wine.

can buy a whole prosciutto at the plant, or else head for the Bottega del Prosciutto, via Umberto 1 (closed Monday and Wednesday afternoon), to purchase a smaller amount of Daniel's fine product.

SAN QUIRINO

RESTAURANT-INN
La Primula
Via San Rocco 35
Tel. 0434/91005
Closed Tuesday and August
Credit cards: American Express, MasterCard
Price: high moderate

The kitchen of La Primula is staffed by Lidia, Daniela, and Andrea—mother, aunt, and son. Father and son sommeliers Roberto and Sandro are in charge of the dining rooms. Traditional and modern cucina are beautifully prepared—vegetables are green and crunchy, silky homemade pasta is simply sauced, fish from the nearby Adriatic is perfectly cooked. Fresh herbs and extra virgin olive oil flavor many dishes. The desserts and after-dinner pastries are worth leaving room for. The menu degustazione presents a selection, more traditional in the winter months, of dishes paired with wines chosen by Sandro to complement Andrea's cooking. The Canton family has been serving food in the same location since 1875, a fact that leaves me breathless.

SANT'ANDRAT DEL JUDRIO

HOTEL
See Wiener in San Giovanni al Natisone (page 142)

RESTAURANT
Osteria all'Armistizio
Piazza Zorutti 7
Tel. 0432/759017
Closed Monday and August
No credit cards
Price: inexpensive

Lunch at Armistizio is always the same: spaghetti with chicken liver sauce and *fogolar*-grilled meat or chicken, washed down with mediocre Tocai. A few seasonal specialties are also offered in this authentic classic, a tiny lunch-only *osteria* with a diner atmosphere.

SAURIS

SMOKED AND CURED MEATS
Prosciuttificio-Salumificio Wolf Petris
Via Dante Volvan
Tel. 0433/86054

Wolf Petris, located in the Carnia Alps, smokes up to 35,000 cured hams with juniper and beech. Their once small-scale artisanal output has been increased by popular demand, and they now make

a selection of good, traditional *salumi* in addition to their smoky *prosciutto*.

TAVAGNACCO

HOTEL
See Boschetti in Tricesimo (page 148)

RESTAURANT
Furlan
Via Nazionale 130
Tel. 0432/680395
Closed Sunday
No credit cards
Price: moderate

The Furlan family—Vincenzo on the *fogolar* grill, wife Nella in the kitchen, and daughter Nicoletta as sommelier—join forces in their home-style *trattoria*, easily recognized in the daytime by a small group of knee-high red plastic mushrooms with white spots on the front lawn. The menu is traditional. The house specialty, during the spring and fall, weather permitting, is a wide variety of mushrooms (*funghi*) cooked in an equally wide variety of dishes. Regional wines are the best choice on the well-priced wine list.

RESTAURANT
Al Grop
Via Matteotti 7
Tel. 0432/660240
Closed Thursday evening, Friday, and July
No credit cards
Price: moderate

Al Grop is nothing to write home about—unless you show up in the spring, when homage is paid to

the asparagus in practically every course of the meal, not counting dessert.

TOLMEZZO

Tolmezzo is the largest city in the Carnia and the gateway to this mountain area north of the Tagliamento river, which shares its Alps with Austria. The breathtaking natural beauty of this region, largely ignored by tourism, is enhanced by a wealth of artisanal crafts and a mountain *cucina* of alpine dairy products, smoked meat and cheese, and sweet and sour flavors.

RESTAURANT-HOTEL
Albergo Ristorante Roma
Piazza XX Settembre
Tel. 0433/2081
Closed Monday
Credit cards: American Express, Diners Club, Visa
Price: high moderate

Gianni Cosetti *is* the *cucina* of the Carnia. Many of the dishes he serves in his restaurant have names like *toc in braide, sope di urties e cais,* and *pita,* offering not a hint of their contents. The only thing I could understand when he handed me a menu, hand-printed on a wafer-thin slice of bark, was the wine list. The flavors are simple; the raw materials are the best that the Carnia can produce (and that only Gianni can track down). A sense of traditional pride enriches this rustic, beautifully executed *cucina* with an elegance few restaurants ever achieve. Dining at the Albergo Roma used to be by reservation only in a back room with all the charm of a high school gym. Recently Gianni has removed the gas stoves, replacing them with wood-burning ones (which cook better, he says), and in remodeling has created a one-room, seven-table restaurant next door to the unchanged bar, where the pattern in the floor tiles has been worn away by Friulani serious about their drinking. The hotel is clean, undistinguished, inexpensive, and convenient. The breakfast of local specialties is superlative, especially the fresh sweet butter. I couldn't imagine staying, eating, or breakfasting elsewhere in the Carnia.

The following area restaurants are recommended by Gianni, and prepare the Carnia *cucina* with a similar spirit. Although I haven't been to any of them, I trust Gianni.

Gianni Cosetti, the heart of Carnia, in his kitchen. His daughter Gabriella often helps out.

Locanda Maiolino
Via Cartiera 87
Ovaro
Tel. 0433/67102
Closed Sunday
No credit cards
Price: moderate

Salon
Via Casaletto 37
Piano d'Arta
Tel. 0433/9003
Closed Tuesday and November
Credit card: MasterCard
Price: moderate

Locanda alla Pace
Via Roma 38
Sauris
Tel. 0433/86010
Closed Wednesday and October
No credit cards
Price: moderate

TRICESIMO

RESTAURANT-HOTEL
Boschetti
Piazza Mazzini 9
Tel. 0432/851230
Closed Monday and January
Credit cards: American Express, Diners Club, Visa
Price: expensive

Boschetti, the restaurant that put Friuli on the gastronomic map, is rightfully considered a temple of regional *cucina*. The food is good.

The ambience is formal. Spacious damask-covered tables are decked out with seasonal centerpieces. The menu is composed of traditional specialties and local bounty—game and Adriatic seafood, a specialty of chef Vinicio Dovier. Past tendencies toward "nouvelle cuisine" have disappeared, replaced by simple dishes, beautifully executed—like pasta and bean or barley soups, or *polenta, ricotta e tartufi*, a world-class dish. The smaller dining room with its hearth is used during the winter; otherwise dining is in a large, formal, round, air-conditioned, chandeliered room with endless curtains. The wine list concentrates on quality local producers, but also includes many fine wines from other regions, as well as France and the U.S. Conclude your meal with a distillate from the large collection of *grappa*, scotch whisky, or cognac, especially if you're spending the night in one of Boschetti's thirty-two clean, comfortable, moderately priced rooms.

TRIESTE

Trieste is a port that looks longingly to the east, at the land it has ceded to Yugoslavia (or Jugoslavia, as it's written on signs throughout the area). The *cucina* of this province, known as Venezia Giulia, closely relates to that of Venezia, with its Adriatic seafood, eastern spices, coffee, and Austrian desserts. Coffee is stronger, fuller-flavored, in Trieste, home of Illy Caffè, one of Italy's finest commercial coffee roasters.

HOTEL
Duchi d'Aosta
Piazza dell'Unità d'Italia 2
Tel. 040/62081
Credit cards: all
Price: expensive

HOTEL
Albergo alla Posta
Piazza Oberdan 1
Tel. 040/68397
Credit card: American Express
Price: moderate

BAR-CAFFÈ
Caffè degli Specchi
Piazza Unità 7
Tel. 040/60533
Closed Monday

Trieste's best bar is Caffè degli Specchi, which has tables outside on piazza Unità for the best people-watching in Trieste, and interesting pastry. Try the *lettera d'amore* ("love letter"), two sheets of fried pastry with a whipped-cream filling.

BAR-CAFFÈ
Bar Tergesteo
Piazza Borsa 15
Tel. 040/60827
Closed Tuesday

The best coffee in Trieste is found at the Bar Tergesteo, in an arcade near the Stock Exchange. If you want a cappuccino, ask for a *cappuccino grande,* or you'll receive a cup of expresso coffee with a bit of foamy milk added.

FISH MARKET
Pescheria
Riva Sauro
Closed Sunday and Monday

Early risers may want to check out the 6:30 or 7 A.M. auction of the day's catch at Trieste's fish market, next to the Aquarium on the Riva Sauro. The market is open in the morning only.

BUFFET
Pepi Sciavo
Via Cassa Risparmio 3/B
Tel. 040/68073
Closed Sunday
No credit cards

The *buffet* is Trieste's version of Venezia's *osteria*—the traditional

place to stop off for little snacks and a glass of wine. The specialty of Pepi Sciavo is pork (*maiale*), either cooked or cured San Daniele, served with sauerkraut (*crauti*), mustard, and freshly grated horseradish (*cren*). Locals stop in for a midmorning snack, a light lunch, or a glass of wine before heading for home—it's open from 9 a.m. to 9 p.m.

PASTRY
La Bomboniera
Via XXX Ottobre 3
Tel. 040/62752
Closed Monday

Trieste's best pastry is found at La Bomboniera. The black-and-white–tiled shop, dating from 1850, bakes velvety cakes of Hungarian inspiration, and many of their tasty *torte* are sold by the slice. The six-layer *dobos torta* is a specialty, as are the homemade chocolates and marzipan.

GELATO
Zampolli
Viale XX Settembre 25
Tel. 040/64336
Closed Wednesday

Via Ghega
Tel. 040/64336
Closed Wednesday

Piazza Cavana 6
Tel. 040/303280
Closed Monday

A stroll down viale XX Settembre for a *gelato* is a local ritual, and Zampolli makes the most popular *gelato* in Trieste. Each of the three Zampolli *gelaterie* is separately owned by a family member, makes its own *gelato,* has its own following of adoring Triestini, and closes from December through February.

RESTAURANT
Da Stelio
Via Tonello 7
Tel. 040/307156
Closed Tuesday evening and
  Wednesday, and mid-July to
  mid-August
No credit cards
Price: high moderate

Friendly natives had to lead me to this difficult-to-find hole-in-the-wall one-room *trattoria,* with its eclectic decor of antlers and bullfighting posters. The Cigni family—Anny and her son Paolo in the kitchen, husband Stelio at the bar—make and serve the best fresh fish and seafood in Trieste. With no written menu, I let Stelio choose my meal, which proved tasty and typical enough until I got to the very special (and expensive) unpasteurized Iranian caviar and the flan topped with white truffles, obtained through secret sources in the port-frontier of Trieste. Fish is simply prepared and flavorful. The bar seems to be a neighborhood stopping-off point for a glass of Stelio's mediocre but genuine house wine, a slice of something to eat, and a little conversation. The crowd is strictly local, and reservations are a must.

RESTAURANT
Suban
Via Comici 2
Tel. 040/54368
Closed Tuesday
Credit cards: all
Price: high moderate

Since 1865, five generations of the Suban family have served the traditional *cucina* of Trieste in this suburban *trattoria.* Taste the *jota,* a soup with the Slavic flavors of cabbage, ham, and caraway, or the *palacinche* dessert crepes. Grilled meats are served with bell pepper sauce. *Strucolo* is the local version of strudel. In the summer, dine on the terrace overlooking Trieste and its urban sprawl. The house wines are pleasant, although the wine list has an interesting selection of fine regional, and some nonregional, wines. Italian families, at least two but sometimes three generations, populate the tables of this Trieste institution.

UDINE

HOTEL
Astoria
Piazza XX Settembre 24
Tel. 0432/505091
Credit cards: all
Price: expensive

HOTEL
La di Moret
Viale Tricesimo 276
Tel. 0432/471250
Credit cards: all
Price: moderate

BAR-CAFFÈ, GELATO, PASTRY
Volpe Pasini
Via Rialto 12
Tel. 0432/505191
Credit card: American Express
Closed Sunday

The Volpe Pasini shop specializes in *delizie,* which is translated in my

dictionary as "delights." And the vast assortment of products in the shop are truly delightful. The bakery has at least ten kinds of bread and homemade breadsticks, and the pastry shop's fresh cakes and cookies are tasty. There's a fine selection of different brands of coffee at the bar (including the unexpected Tri-Caffè from Toscana, see page 212), and the specialty section sells quality extra virgin olive oil, preserves, pasta, honey, chocolates, and life-size, realistically painted Sicilian marzipan fruit. The well-stocked *enoteca* sells fine wine by the glass, bottle, or case. *Gelato,* made with fresh fruits and natural flavors, is sold in the summer.

MARKET
Piazza Matteotti and piazza S.
  Giacomo

To understand what the *frittata alle erbe* is all about, visit the Piazza Matteotti market, where women under multicolored beach umbrellas sell field greens and herbs out of attractive (and unavailable) bent-wire baskets. Piazza S. Giacomo is also known as piazza delle Erbe.

CHEESE
La Baita Formaggi
Via delle Erbe 1/B
Tel. 0432/204276
Closed Monday afternoon and
  Wednesday afternoon
Credit card: Visa

La Baita has a nice selection of local cheeses—*latteria, montasio,* and *ricotta affumicata.* The nonlocal *parmigiano-reggiano* is first-rate.

In this region where almost no one takes credit cards, they take Visa.

FRUIT
Emporio Frutta
Riva Bartolini 9
Tel. 0432/501234
Closed Monday afternoon and
Wednesday afternoon

The Emporio Frutta sells a large assortment of attractive fresh, exotic, and dried fruit and nuts.

SPECIALTY FOODS
Tami Galliano
Riva Bartolini 10
Tel. 0432/502198
Closed Monday afternoon and
Wednesday afternoon

Across the street from the Emporio Frutta, this shop sells smoked Sauris *prosciutto.*

RESTAURANT
Alla Vedova
Via Tavagnacco 8
Tel. 0432/470291
Closed Sunday night, Monday,
and August
No credit cards
Price: moderate

Part of the charm of Alla Vedova is the decor: antler chandeliers and an attractive *fogolar* (hearth) and *spolerts* (brick oven for cooking traditional grilled meats). The squash or chestnut *gnocchi* are outstanding, but the rest of the menu is uninspired and the wine is mediocre to poor. However, this *trattoria* remains a favorite with locals from Udine, especially for dining outside in the summer.

Don't miss the extensive collection of African hunting trophies upstairs.

VERZEGNIS

TABLEWARE
Roberto Marzona
Via degli Artigiani 6
Tel. 0433/43076
Closed Sunday
No credit cards

Roberto Marzona works with seventy-seven local woods, forming them into plates, bowls, serving pieces, cutting boards, sugar bowls, and the *piattaia,* a traditional wooden dish rack. All pieces are handmade and signed.

VILLA SANTINA

TABLE LINENS
Carnica Arte Tessile
Via Nazionale 14
Tel. 0433/74129
Closed Sunday
No credit cards

Carnica Arte Tessile makes traditional hand-loomed tablecloths and napkins, as well as bedspreads, towels, and sheets, in cotton or linen.

VISCONE

CURED GOOSE
Fattoria dell'Oca Bianca
Via C. Battisti 6
Tel. 0432/991085

The Fattoria dell'Oca Bianca's specialties are made from the goose. Their *prosciutto d'oca* looks like a small San Daniele *prosciutto,* although it doesn't end in a hoof. The *petto d'oca affumicato* (smoked duck breast) and three varieties of *salame d'oca* (goose salami) are tasty. The kosher version is certified by the chief rabbi of Trieste. Their foie gras is one of Italy's finest.

ZOMPITTA

HOTEL
See Boschetti in Tricesimo (page 148)

RESTAURANT
Da Rochet
Via Rosta Ferracina 8
Tel. 0432/851090
Closed Tuesday
No credit cards
Price: low moderate

Follow the scent of barbecue and cross a little wooden footbridge over a clear stream to enter the world of Da Rochet. It's dominated by the sizzling music, the smoky perfumes, the choreography of the brothers and their wives—of Santina and Tite tending the sausage, pork, veal, trout, and chicken on one of Friuli's best hearth grills. The *salumi* and *risotto* (with mushrooms or asparagus in season) are good, but the star here is grilled meat or poultry, perfectly prepared. The mixed salad is a welcome sight. The house condiment is vegetable oil, although if you ask they'll bring olive oil. Dine outside under the trees in the summer, or in one of the cozy dining rooms. The wines could be better.

Ranco
Corgeno
Mapello
Bregnano
Bergamo
Iseo
Gardone Riviera
Milano
Cassinetta Di Lugagnano
Lugana Di Sirmione
Trescore Cremasco
Maleo
Goito
Mortara
Casalpusterlengo
Mantova
Cozzo Lomellina
Cremona
Canneto Sull'Oglio
Sermide
Montù Beccaria
Quistello
Villa Poma

LOMBARDIA

•

Landlocked Lombardia extends from the Alps to the fertile plains of the Po River, from Lago Maggiore to Lago di Garda. Mountains prevent the cold northern European weather from penetrating the lakes region, where Mediterranean vegetation—palms, oleanders, olive and lemon trees—thrives within sight of snow-capped peaks. Caught up in a continuing reshuffling of the political deck, Lombardia was part of the Roman *Gallia Cisalpina*, which included much of northern Italy, despoiled by barbarian tribes, united under the Longobards (Lombards), ruled by the Franks, reunited in the Lombard League, redivided among powerful provincial families—Visconti, Sforza, Gonzaga, Pallavincini, Scaligeri—invaded by Venezia, France, and the Spanish Hapsburgs, transferred to Austria, and absorbed by the Napoleonic Cisalpine Republic until the Austrians came back for another round!

Politics, and the thick fog that blankets and isolates much of Lombardia during the winter months, helped to maintain the separateness of each provincial *cucina*. Rice and *polenta* from the alluvial plains, butter, cream, and cheese from the mountain pastures, are the common denominators in what many people think of as northern Italian cooking. Pasta is fresh, and stuffed with fillings of winter squash, meat, cheese, spinach, or even raisins, candied fruit, and crumbled almond cookies. *Polenta* is made with cornmeal or buckwheat flour (*grano saraceno,* "Saracen grain"). Pork, veal, and cheese play an important role in the *cucina* of Lombardia. Vegetables rarely achieve stardom, although asparagus freaks will delight in the Lombardia spring. Traditional desserts are found in pastry shops, but rarely on restaurant menus. Don't miss *torta di tagliatelle,* a crunchy cake made with fresh egg pasta, almonds, and cocoa, or Mantova's *torta sbrisolona* ("big crumb"), a buttery, cookielike cake made with cornmeal and almonds.

THE MENU

SALUMI

■

Bresaola ▪ cured dried beef, dried in the mountain air, served sliced wafer thin, dressed with olive oil and pepper

Cotechino ▪ cooked pork sausage

Salame di Milano ▪ fine-grained pork salami

ANTIPASTO

■

Nervetti in insalata ▪ cold salad of calf's foot

Sciatt ▪ buckwheat cheese fritters (from the Alpine valley of the Valtellina)

PRIMO

■

Agnolini ▪ fresh pasta stuffed with meat, Parmesan, and spices

Buseca or *Busecca* ▪ Milanese tripe soup

Casonséi ▪ ravioli stuffed with sausage, Parmesan, and bread

Pizzoccheri ▪ buckwheat pasta served with potatoes, cabbage, butter, cheese, and sage

Polenta alla bergamasca ▪ polenta baked with sausage, tomato sauce, and cheese

Polenta e osei ▪ polenta sauced with small game birds, butter, and sage

Polenta taragna ▪ buckwheat polenta with butter and cheese

Ris e càgnon ▪ boiled rice with butter, Parmesan, and sage

Ris e coràda or *riso con coratella* ▪ rice and veal lung

Ris e ran ▪ soup with rice and frog's legs

Ris e spargitt ▪ soup with rice and asparagus

Riso al salto ▪ crispy pancake of risotto sautéed in butter

Risotto ▪ short-grained rice, sautéed, then cooked with broth and any number of enrichments

Risotto alla certosina ▪ with freshwater fish, shrimp, and sometimes frogs, peas, mushrooms, and rice

Risotto alla mantovana ▪ with sausage and onion

Risotto alla milanese ▪ with onions, saffron, and beef marrow

Risotto alla pilota ▪ with sausage

Risotto alla valtellinese ▪ with beans and cabbage

Tortelli di zucca ▪ fresh pasta filled with winter squash, *mostarda* (similar to chutney), and almond cookies, served with butter and Parmesan

Zuppa pavese ▪ broth containing a poached egg on fried or grilled toast, sprinkled with Parmesan

SECONDO

•

Asparagi alla milanese • boiled asparagus served with a fried egg, Parmesan, and melted butter (a kind of do-it-yourself Hollandaise sauce)

Cassoeula or *Cazzoeula* • various cuts of pork—usually sausage, ribs, feet—stewed with cabbage, served with polenta

Costolette alla milanese • breaded veal chop fried in butter, served with a lemon wedge

Foiolo • tripe cooked with butter and onions, served with grated cheese

Mondeghili • breaded meat croquettes fried in butter

Ossobuco • braised veal shank sprinkled with gremolata (chopped parsley, lemon peel, and garlic)

Rostin negaa • veal chops braised in white wine

FORMAGGIO

•

Bagoss • hard, aromatic, grainy

Bitto • soft and rich

Crescenza • soft, creamy, mild

Gorgonzola • rich, creamy, blue-veined, pungent, intensely flavored and scented

Grana • tasty, grainy texture, nutty flavor, similar to Parmesan

Mascarpone • rich, sweet, triple cream, white to pale yellow

Quartirolo • mild, soft, smooth

Robiola • soft, creamy, rich, eaten fresh or aged

Stracchino • smooth, soft, full-flavored (from *stracco*, dialect for "tired") made from the milk of cows weary from their long trek from alpine pastures

Taleggio • smooth, soft, ripe; similar to *stracchino*, but riper, more ample

DOLCE

•

Busecchina • boiled chestnuts and cream

Colomba pasquale • dove-shaped sweet yeast cakes with almonds, raisins, and candied fruits, found at Eastertime

Pan de mei or *Man de mej* or *Meini* • cornmeal yeast buns

Panettone • sweet yeast cakes with raisins, candied citron, orange, and lots of eggs, traditional at Christmastime

Polenta e osei • simple cake layered with apricot preserves, covered with almond paste, and decorated to resemble an unmolded bowl of polenta, topped with little chocolate game birds

Torta di tagliatelle • crunchy cake made with fresh egg pasta, almonds, and cocoa

Torta paradiso • delicate sponge cake

Torta sbrisolona • "big crumb" of cornmeal, almonds, and butter, more like a cookie than a cake

THE *W*INE LIST

The fertile plains and mild climate of the lakes region aren't ideal wine-growing country, although there are areas of Lombardia that do make fine wine. Locals, and especially the Milanese, tend to drink wines produced in other regions—reds from Piemonte and Toscana, whites from Friuli and Trentino–Alto Adige. But some of the sparkling wines are among Italy's best, and are easy to find in better restaurants.

The *Franciacorta* DOC includes red, white, rosé, and sparkling wines, produced south of Lago Iseo in the province of Brescia. The *Pinot Bianco di Franciacorta* is a still dry white, fruity and elegant, at its best with antipasti, fish, and vegetables, made with Pinot Bianco and Chardonnay grape varieties. The *Franciacorta Rosso,* ruby red, mellow, and dry, is made from a blend of Cabernet Franc and Sauvignon, Barbera, Nebbiolo, and Merlot, and is best served with regional *cucina* and meat. Quality producers are Fratelli Berlucchi, Ca' del Bosco, Cavalleri, and Bellevista. The *Spumante,* which can be white or rosé, and made from Pinot Bianco, Nero or Grigio, and Chardonnay, is one of Italy's finest sparkling wines. Look for Brut, Crémant, and Gran Cuvée by Bellavista; Brut, Pas Dosé, and Millesimé by Cavalleri; or Brut, Dosage Zéro, Crémant, Rosé, or gold-labeled Brut Millesimato by Ca' del Bosco, Italy's finest sparkling wines.

Oltrepò Pavese is a DOC that includes fifteen different wines—a large range of whites, reds, rosés, and sparkling wines—for the most part named after grape varieties. Reds *Barbacarlo, Barbera,* and *Rosso* are better than most, go well with the regional *cucina,* and are produced by Ca' Longa, Maga Lino, and Monsupello.

Riviera del Garda Bresciano is a large DOC zone near the Brescia side of Lago di Garda that includes red *Rosso* and *Chiaretto* rosé wines, both made from Gropello, Sangiovese, Barbera, and Marzemino grapes. They are served to advantage with first-course dishes and regional *cucina.* Top producers include Costaripa and Andrea Pasini.

Some of the *vino da tavola* produced in Lombardia is among the finest wine being made in Italy. Rich, elegant whites to be served with first-course dishes, fish, seafood and poultry, and luxurious reds, a fitting accompaniment to meat and sauced dishes, are a pleasure for all the senses.

Ca' del Bosco makes complex, smoky *Chardonnay;* splendid red *Maurizio Zanella,* a blend of Cabernet Sauvignon, Franc, and Merlot, a rich, harmonious red; and rich and full red *Pinero,* from Pinot Nero—all gems. Bellavista makes *Uccellanda,* an elegant oaky Chardonnay, and *Casotte* and *Solesine,* both wood-aged reds of finesse. La Muirighina makes *Riesling* and *Malvasia,* fruity fresh whites, and *Barbera di Montù Beccaria* and *Il Felicino,* made of Barbera, Croatina, and Rara grapes, rich hearty reds. Fine non-DOC *Spumante* are made by Carlo Zadra and Guido Berlucchi.

*R*EGIONAL SPECIALITIES

GOOSE SALAMI AND PROSCIUTTO

The goose presents farmers of the Oltrepò, "the area beyond the Po," with a shortcut version of pork *salumi,* which is made during the fall slaughter of the pigs, after the harvest. Geese are low-maintenance animals and fatten up quickly. The full-flavored meat is well suited to the traditional treatment for pork. See page 179 for a source—and a goose festival.

RISOTTO

Rice dominates the first course of Lombardia's menu. It is served in soups but reaches gastronomic glory as risotto (see page 29). This dish, which demands much stirring and fussing, the slow addition of broth, and a final enrichment of butter and *parmigiano,* is always served slightly *al dente* ("firm under the tooth"); each grain of rice remains separate. My favorite rice comes from the rich rice-growing flatlands southeast of Milano (see page 159).

POLENTA

Polenta is the Italian version of cornmeal mush (similar to grits), made of cornmeal, salt, and water cooked to the consistency of breakfast cereal in a traditional copper pot *(paiolo)* and stirred constantly for thirty minutes with a long-handled wooden spoon. Nontraditionalists in a hurry use instant polenta, which cooks up in 5 to 10 minutes—not exactly instant. Polenta is served freshly cooked as a side dish, or cooled, sliced, and reheated with sauce as a first or main course. (See page 163 for a fine producer.)

GORGONZOLA

Gorgonzola—ivory colored, run through with bluish mold, strongly scented—is one of Lombardia's greatest cheeses. It is made in a traditional, naturally fermented version as well as a sweeter, creamier, less aggressive style *(dolce)* that has fermented more quickly and is considered more palatable than the classic *gorgonzola,* said by detractors to smell like an adolescent's sneakers.

CITIES AND TOWNS

BERGAMO

Medieval Bergamo Alto, of pink-paved piazzas, and Bergamo Basso, which seems to be paved with parked cars, is only fifty kilometers (thirty miles) from Milano. Restaurants in the upper city tend to cater to tourists; lower-city restaurants seem to have abandoned tradition for fresh fish from Milano's market; and almost all restaurants in both parts of town are closed on Monday.

INN
Vigneto
Capriate San Gervasio (close by)
Tel. 02/90939351
Credit card: American Express
Price: moderate

WINE BAR
Vineria Cozzi
Via Colleoni 22
Tel. 035/238836
Closed Thursday
No credit cards
Price: inexpensive

In Bergamo Alto I head for the Vineria Cozzi for a sandwich *(panino)* prepared with interesting combinations like cured beef with walnuts, oil, and vinegar on a toasted roll, and I wait for owner Leonardo Vigorelli to surprise me with a wonderful local wine I've never heard of. Bentwood chairs, wine-bottle-lined walls, and locals in berets—serious about their drinking—make up the ambience of this old-fashioned authentic wine bar. Fine wine by the glass, freshly made sandwiches, and Leonardo's hospitality make this the best meal in town. And there's even outdoor dining, on the iron bench in front of the Vineria Cozzi.

BREGNANO

SILVERWARE
Sabattini Argenteria
Via Don Capiaghi 2
Tel. 031/771019

The fluid, exquisitely executed, award-winning silver objects, bowls, carafes, and serving pieces of Lino Sabattini are a pleasure to look at and to use. His designs are in the grand tradition of the table, executed in extra-heavy silver alloy. Sabattini lives, writes poetry, and works his metal magic in Bregnano, not far from Como, but his work can also be seen at his Milano showroom in via della Spiga (02/798449).

CANNETO SULL'OGLIO

INN
Il Sole (see page 162)
Via Trabattoni 32
Maleo (close by)
Tel. 0377/58142
Credit card: American Express
Price: low expensive

HOTEL
City
Via Cavour 54
Casalgrande (close by)
Tel. 0375/42118
Credit cards: all
Price: inexpensive

RESTAURANT
Dal Pescatore
Via Runate 13
Tel. 0376/70304
Closed Monday, Tuesday, the first half of January, and the second half of August
Credit cards: American Express, Diners Club
Price: expensive

Dal Pescatore seems to be doing everything right, with Bruna and her gentle daughter-in-law, Nadia, in the kitchen, Giovanni taking care of the provisions and the grill work. His son Antonio hustles between the kitchen, cantina, and dining room, judiciously choosing wines to complement the *cucina* of the Santini women, which is deeply rooted in the local tradi-

Perfectly ripened parmigiano is divided into wedges with a special blade.

tions. The elegantly appointed rustic stone farmhouse has three intimate dining rooms with large, well-spaced tables set with damask, silver, and crystal. Logs burning in the brick fireplace and indirect lighting create a feeling of warmth. Local ingredients of the highest quality—*salumi*, sturgeon from a pool in the back, freshwater fish from nearby rivers, and barnyard poultry—are the basis of the *cucina*, which combines tradition and intelligence. Homemade pasta, almost orange with duck eggs, *risotto* properly *al dente*; eel and provolone cheese, both grilled over wood; a flavorful chunk of country-style duck—all sit nicely on the plate, without the artistic excess of some fine restaurants.

Save room for the fine desserts, especially the buttery almond *torta di amaretto*. The wine list, like almost everything else here, is a joy.

CASALPUSTER-LENGO

CHEESE
Angelo Croce
Via Battisti 69
Tel. 0377/84236
Closed Monday afternoon

Gorgonzola fans should make the pilgrimage to Casalpusterlengo to taste the especially fine *gorgonzola malghese naturale* made by the Croce family. They use milk from cows grazing in Alpine pastures, and ferment their *gorgonzola* naturally (unlike most industrial producers), producing a full-flavored, complex cheese that's a pleasure to eat. The no-nonsense dairy store in Casalpusterlengo also sells smooth soft *taleggio,* mild *quartirolo,* packets of sweet fresh butter, and grainy-textured *grana,* sectioned into wedges with a wire cutter. There's no sign on the store; look for pale green Venetian blinds in the window.

CASSINETTA DI LUGAGNANO

HOTEL
Albergo Italia
Piazza Castello 31
Abbiategrasso (close by)
Tel. 02/9462871
No credit cards
Price: high moderate

RESTAURANT
Antica Osteria del Ponte
Piazza Negri 9
Tel. 02/9420034
Closed Sunday, Monday, and
*   August*
Credit cards: American Express,
*   Diners Club*
Price range: expensive

The Antica Osteria del Ponte—a small, rustic, charming Lombard country house on the banks of the Naviglio Grande, a thirteenth-century navigation canal—is the setting for the new Santin family gastronomic dynasty. Ezio and his wife, Renata, opened their restaurant with no previous experience, but quickly acquired, through passion and intelligence, a sense of professionalism and a style of understated opulence. The triple

taste sensation of white truffles, farm-fresh eggs, and foie gras typifies Ezio Santin's *cucina,* combining flavors and nearby Milano's market bounty to great advantage. At times the food gets a little too "nouvelle" for me, but the excellent cheese tray makes my doubts disappear. Desserts are amazing, the artistry of son Maurizio, a rising star in Italy's culinary lineup. Wines, both French and Italian, are more than up to the rest of the experience.

CORGENO

RESTAURANT-INN
La Cinzianella
Via Lago 26
Tel. 0331/946337
Closed Tuesday and January
Credit card: American Express
Price: high moderate

The Gnocchi family's restaurant keeps on improving. The *cucina* is light and innovative, composed of fresh, local, seasonal ingredients. Homemade pasta, *risotto,* lake fish, and Cinzia's homemade bread and pastry are well prepared. Her brother Maurizio, a champion sommelier, keeps enlarging the wine list, and his selections complement the *cucina.* Their father, Alfio, makes sure that everything runs smoothly. Save room for a taste of local, and impossible to find, Corgena *formaggina* cheese. Peaches from nearby Monate are some of the finest in Italy. Those spending the night in one of La Cinzianella's ten rooms may be tempted to do a tasting from the *grappa* collection.

COZZO LOMELLINA

RESTAURANT-INN
Castello di Cozzo
Via Castello 20
Tel. 0384/74298
Closed Tuesday, August, and
*   January*
No credit cards
Price: expensive

Padre Eligio, a figure of controversy in Italy, founded the Mondo X commune in the 1960s along Franciscan ideals of community and simplicity. His flock of mostly ex–drug addicts restored the abandoned castle, whose origins date from A.D. 800, and created this six-room inn and restaurant with its timeless air. Padre Eligio appreciates fine food and wine, and his disciples have produced some amazing *cucina.* Some dishes seem vaguely French, and plates are seriously stylized. But the *risotto* is first-rate, the homemade pasta is tasty, the dishes are well prepared, and the pastries at the end of the meal are splendid. The wine list offers quality Italian and French wines. Reservations are compulsory.

RICE
Filios Fratelli
Via Mulino 3
Tel. 0384/74112

Superfino Baldo, a new hybrid developed by the Italian Rice Board, is a rising star in the Italian rice lineup and a pleasure to cook with. It holds up under the tooth and contains just the right amount of starch for a perfect *risotto,* but is equally suited to salads, molded rice *timbales,* and soups. It has a full, grain-like flavor.

The Filios brothers produce six fine varieties of rice, but the best is their Superfino Baldo, which is almost impossible to find outside the tiny village of Cozzo Lomellina. But I spotted Filios' attractive mill-end plaid fabric sack of Baldo in some of the region's best restaurants, and even outside the borders of Lombardia. Their rice can be purchased at the farm from Tina or her sister-in-law, who are always around, or can be ordered (within Europe) by phone.

CREMONA

INN
See Il Sole in Maleo (page 162)

HOTEL
Astoria
Via Bondigallo 19
Tel. 0372/23322
Credit cards: all
Price: inexpensive

RESTAURANT
Cerasole
Via Cerasole 4
Tel. 0372/23322
Closed Sunday evening, Monday,
*   and August*
Credit cards: American Express,
*   Diners Club, Master Card*
Price: expensive

Medieval Cremona, with its Stradivarius Museum—testimony to the workshops producing superior stringed instruments—and charming Piazza del Comune, is home to Cerasole. This unusual restaurant is run by brothers Rino and Saverio Botte, who are from Basilicata, a region of southern Italy

wedged between Puglia and Calabria. Wives Lucia and Anna are in the kitchen, cooking up regional Lombard cooking as well as the Mediterranean tastes of their homeland. The menu offers goose liver pâté, *culatello* (the heart of the *prosciutto*), traditional stuffed pasta, and trendier sea bass ravioli, nicely cooked fish and vegetable combinations, and typically Cremonese stuffed duck. Cheese is carefully chosen and aged. Desserts, especially the unusually moist walnut cake served with a red wine and citrus parfait, are definitely worth saving room for. The well-selected all-Italian wine list contains some surprising gems.

GARDONE RIVIERA

RESTAURANT-INN
Villa Fiordaliso
Via Zanadelli 132
Tel. 0365/20158
Closed Sunday evening, Monday,
*   January, and February*
Credit card: American Express
Price: expensive

Villa Fiordaliso, probably the most romantic hotel in Italy, is a turn-of-the-century villa (a favorite of Clara Petacci, Mussolini's girl-friend) decorated with mosaic tiles, patterned marble, alabaster, inlaid wooden floors, Murano glass chandeliers, and columns everywhere. Diners have a view of a peaceful garden and the shores of Lago di Garda, where an occasional *bisse*—traditional flat-bottomed boat powered by four

standing rowers—crosses. Owner Pierantonio Ambrosi's experience at his first restaurant, Vecchia Lugana (see page 161), has made Villa Fiordaliso an almost instant success. Young local chef Mauro Botti's dishes are delicate, flavored with herbs and extra virgin olive oil from the Garda area. *Risotto,* homemade pasta, grilled or sauced meat and lake fish are well prepared, but the desserts look better than they taste. Presentations here are somewhat formal, served by black-uniformed waitresses with white eyelet aprons. The wine list offers an impressive selection of local wines, as well as a separate well-chosen listing of Italian and a few French wines. Spend the night in one of Villa Fiordaliso's four rooms, possibly with a columned and mosaic-floored balcony overlooking the lake, for fantastic breakfasting on homemade croissants and *cappuccino.* Dine in one of the four intimate dining rooms or on the lakeside terrace.

GOITO

RESTAURANT-INN
Al Bersagliere
Via Goitese 258
Tel. 0376/60007
Closed Monday and the second
*   half of August*
Credit cards: American Express,
*   Diners Club, Visa*
Price: expensive

A small shrine here commemorates Sargeant Antonio Pacinotti, who, in 1859, on a site behind the restaurant Al Bersagliere, near the chicken coops, invented the electromagnetic ring, prototype of the dynamo, transforming the current of the Mincio River into electricity. Possibly he celebrated his discovery at the Ferrari family restaurant, which had already been serving fine food for twenty years. The latest generation of Ferrari, brothers Massimo in the kitchen and sommelier Roberto, have continued the family tradition, with the same regional emphasis. Homemade *salumi,* hand-rolled pasta, almost orange with duck eggs, *risotto,* freshwater fish, and poultry are perfectly cooked, elegantly presented. Save room for the appealing desserts and fresh, buttery small pastries. The ambience is warm and inviting, the dishes intelligently prepared, and Roberto ably pairs wine from the extensive cellar with Massimo's *cucina.*

ISEO

HOTEL
Hotel Milano
Lungolago Marconi 4
Tel. 030/980449
Credit card: American Express
Price: moderate

RESTAURANT
Il Volto
Via Mirolte 33
Tel. 030/981462
Closed Wednesday, Thursday
lunch, and July
No credit cards
Price: low moderate

The smallest kitchen of all the restaurants listed in this book belongs to the Osteria Il Volto in sleepy Iseo, which seems less serious about its tourism than other larger lakes in Lombardia. A genuine tavern, its two small dining rooms furnished with rustic furniture and tables covered in blue-and-white-striped ticking, it's run by a group of friends—Roberto Sgarbi and his sister Anna Maria, Vittorio Fusari, and Mario Archetti. Armed with passion and an idea, the four friends have created a comfortable place to hang out, to eat something of quality made with fresh local ingredients, combined with simplicity, and paired with amazing local or Italian wines discovered during excursions to interesting wineries. A glass of Ca' del Bosco *spumante* will put you in a good mood while you examine the small but well-composed menu of delicate lake fish, steamed or combined with fresh pasta, country-style meats and poultry, and desserts like tart, cloudy, flowery-tasting strawberry gelatin, the essence of berry, or smooth, elegant *panna cotta* custard, or buttery, crumbly *sbrisolona.* Ask to see the wine cellar of this tiny gem of a restaurant.

RESTAURANT
Le Maschere
Vicolo della Pergola 7
Tel. 030/9821542
Closed Sunday evening and
Monday
Credit card: Visa
Price: moderate

The same people responsible for the fun experience at Il Volto have been let loose in a new locale. Wines will be the same, but what will Vittorio do in a bigger kitchen? I can't wait to find out, but I'm sure it'll be *fantastico.*

LUGANA DI SIRMIONE

HOTEL
Villa Cortina
Via Grotte 12
Sirmione
Tel. 030/916021
Credit cards: all
Price: luxury

HOTEL
Du Lac
Via 25 Aprile 60
Sirmione
Tel. 030/916026
Credit card: Visa
Price: moderate

RESTAURANT
Vecchia Lugana
Via Lugana Vecchia
Tel. 030/919012
Closed Monday evening, Tuesday,
and January
Credit cards: American Express,
Diners Club, Visa
Price: expensive

The Vecchia Lugana is one of Pierantonio Ambrosoli's fine restaurants. It's a rustic, carefully restored, old-style lakefront *trattoria* with some new ideas about cooking and wine. Traditional ingredients are given a lightened-up preparation, or are grilled over wood; pasta and pastry are homemade and hand-rolled; even simple dishes like *pasta e fagioli* soup are skillfully prepared. The menu changes with the seasons, and shows the influence of nearby Veneto. Help yourself to a colorful display of fresh appetizers, but don't skip the velvety pasta, prepared by Pierantonio's mother,

Alma. Regional cheeses and elegantly presented desserts, including fresh fruit ices, are delightful. The wine list and the incredible list of distillates and liquors clearly display Pierantonio's personal commitment to the Vecchia Lugana experience.

*M*ALEO

RESTAURANT-INN
Il Sole
Via Trabattoni 32
Tel. 0377/58142
Closed Sunday evening, Monday,
* January, and August*
Credit card: American Express
Price: expensive

The hotel situation in this area is depressing. Although the region abounds with interesting restaurants, there really was nowhere to stay until Franco and Silvana Colombani created twelve rooms at Il Sole, which I recommend as a base for local day trips. It's the most comfortable place around, and I can never resist a visit.

Every time I come back to Il Sole, I feel I've come back home. There's always something new that Franco and Silvana Colombani want to show me in their wonderful, warm, Lombard country house that's been an inn since 1464. But in spite of recently remodeled guest rooms that combine modern design with simple antique furniture, or new crystal stemware, or placemats by Missoni, or elegant service plates by Richard Ginori, everything impeccably Italian, Il Sole always feels the same. It's like visiting an ancestral hearth from a previous ex-

Wooden casks of balsamic vinegar age in their attic.

istence. Franco has total quality control over Il Sole's choice of raw materials—ripe fruit from a neighbor, butter from a nearby dairy, traditional (not creamy) *gorgonzola* from the Croce dairy, and fresh fish from Milano. Everything on the menu is comfort food, bubbling away on an old-fashioned stove in the corner of the room, filling the dining room with the warmth of good cooking. The *salumi* are flavorful, especially the splendid *prosciutto* and *pancetta*—cured pork that looks but doesn't taste like bacon. Silvana's soups are usually the best choice for a first course. Meat dishes, espe-

cially braised beef *(stracotto)*, are well prepared, home-style. Vegetables are all seasonal and varied. The *polenta*, made with four different grinds of cornmeal plus a bit of buckwheat flour, is unforgettably corny and substantial. Most Italian restaurants don't pay too much attention to cheese, but Franco ages *provolone* and *gorgonzola naturale* in his cellars, and the results are worth leaving room for. The grainy, eggy *sabbiosa*, a sand cake, is served with a silky custard; the crusty elderberry tart tastes just-baked; the ices are smooth and refreshing. The wine list reflects the unpretentious elegance of this restaurant, with a small selection of quality house wines, a medium-size selection of young, forward wines that go well with the food, and a large selection of older reserves, both Italian and French, wines for special occasions. Franco seats friends and unaccompanied diners at a long table in the middle of the main dining room, next to the fireplace, although private tables in both dining rooms are available. The Colombani dog, a wirehaired pointing griffon named Al, barks only at the butcher.

MANTOVA

Mantova, surrounded on three sides by the Mincio River, which widens enough to be called a lake, is the center of one of the major expressions of Italian regional *cucina.* Rich in courtyard animals and rice, influenced by nearby Emilia and Veneto, *la cucina mantovana* combines a wealth of flavors.

HOTEL
San Lorenzo
Piazza Concordia 14
Tel. 0376/327153
Credit cards: American Express,
*   Diners Club, Visa*
Price: expensive

HOTEL
Broletto
Via Accademia 1
Tel. 0376/326784
Credit cards: all
Price: moderate

RESTAURANT
Il Cigno
Piazza dell'Arco 1
Tel. 0376/327101
Closed Monday, Tuesday evening,
*   and the first half of August*
Credit cards: American Express,
*   Diners Club*
Price: expensive

Il Cigno, "The Swan," is located in a beautiful sixteenth-century palace with spectacular beamed wooden ceilings, in the heart of Mantova. Tano Martini provisions his restaurant with the finest fresh ingredients and wines, and his modest wife, Alessandra, transforms them into traditional dishes—some from the cookbook of the Gonzagas' court chef, Bartolomeo Stefani, others composed of remembered tastes, like the rich hand-rolled pasta stuffed with squash, or *polenta* with a melted dab of herb-perfumed lard, or duck cooked with its liver. All the desserts are good, but the rich, buttery, nutty *sbrisolona* is irresistible. Tano, a capable sommelier, will suggest a wine from his interesting and personal selection of quality Italian and regional wines.

MAPELLO

GRISTMILL
Azienda Aricola Scotti
Via Matteotti 16
Tel. 035/908115

Baronessa Scotti's farm in Mapello produces grain and corn to be stone-ground in a seventeenth-century watermill in nearby Zogno. The old-fashioned method of milling between two stones produces a coarser, fuller-flavored flour filled with bits of bran. The yellow *farina per polenta* makes a nutty, nicely textured *polenta,* and the whole-wheat *farina integrale* is fine for bread baking. An appointment can be made to view the mill in Zogno.

MILANO

Milano, capital of the Western Roman Empire and center for the new Christian religion, autonomous municipality, dominion of the Visconti and Sforza families, capital of the Dukedom of Milano and subject to the European chessboard of power, ruled by the French, Spanish, Hapsburgs, and the Austro-Hungarian Empire, has a true melting-pot mentality. The dynamic financial capital of Italy, Milano has a strong provincial *cucina,* but it's the only city in Italy where restaurants serve many kinds of foods, from American-style hamburgers to Japanese sushi, Neapolitan pizza, Tuscan *trattoria* offerings, and Sicilian seafood. The bounty of a metropolitan marketplace and its international point of view are combined with Old World or New Wave creativity, resulting in dishes that may range from misconceived to miraculous. Prices in Milanese restaurants tend to be higher than in the rest of Italy.

Milano has adopted the sandwich *(panino)* with true inventive style, and locals lunch on made-to-order grilled vegetable or goat cheese and smoky *speck* combination fillings, perfect for the work-conscious out for a quick lunch. The noontime one-dish meal or

*Waiting for lunch at a private
club in Milano*

fixed-price lunch presents a few different tastes or interesting specials, a light meal, and is offered by some restaurants whose business-oriented clientele don't want rich, heavy, sleep-inducing meals.

Dinner is the meal to unwind over after a hard day at work, but reservations are a must, especially since mysterious trade fairs may book up every hotel and restaurant in the city. Beware of the Milanese custom of abandoning town on the weekends, heading for the countryside. Most restaurants in the city close on Sunday, and you may be hard-pressed to find a place to eat. The restaurants that do stay open are indicated here.

HOTEL
Palace
Piazza della Repubblica 20
Tel. 02/6336
Credit cards: all
Price: luxury

HOTEL
Grand Hotel Duomo
Via San Raffaele 1
Tel. 02/8833
Credit cards: Visa, MasterCard
Price: luxury

HOTEL
Diana Majestic
Viale Piave 42
Tel. 02/203404
Credit cards: all
Price: expensive

HOTEL
Carlton Senate
Via Senato 5
Tel. 02/798583
*Credit cards: American Express,
   MasterCard, Visa*
Price: expensive

HOTEL
Ariosto
Via Ariosto 22
Tel. 02/490995
Credit cards: American Express
Price: high moderate

HOTEL
Manzoni
Via Santo Spirito 20
Tel. 02/705697
No credit cards
Price: high moderate

BAR-CAFFÈ
Biffi
Corso Magenta 87
Tel. 02/439570
Closed Monday

Biffi serves one of Milano's best breakfasts: a perfect, foamy *cappuccino* (or *cappuccio,* as it's often called locally) and a warm croissant. They also make one of the city's best *panettone.* The visit is a Sunday tradition.

BAR-CAFFÈ
Cova
Via Montenapoleone 8
Tel. 02/793187
Closed Sunday

Cova isn't only a famous tearoom, coffee bar, and meeting place on fashionable via Montenapoleone, where white-aproned, black-tied barmen serve chic Milanese at the stainless-steel bar. Cova also makes fine chocolates, gumdrops, hazelnut-chocolate *gianduia,* and *fruttini*—sugar fruit shapes that are elegantly boxed, hand-wrapped, and tied with a velvet ribbon. Austrian-influenced pastry work, including *sacher torte, rerhuken,* and *dobos,* and one of Milano's best traditional *panettone,* is giftwrapped in brocade and silk for Christmas but is available year-round. Bring your own surprise to insert in one of Cova's custom-made Easter eggs. Prices are scaled to the rest of elegant via Montenapoleone.

THE EMPIRE OF PECK

·

The golden sun—symbol of the Peck emporiums, reign of the four Stoppani brothers—never sets on the empire (they have a boutique in a department store in Tokyo). Their top-of-the-line outposts include Gastronomia Peck (below), Casa del Formaggio (below), Bottega del Maiale (below), Rosticceria (page 166), and La Bottega del Vino (page 166). The jewel of the empire, simply called Peck, is a restaurant located in a series of rooms under the Bottega del Vino (page 173).

BAR-CAFFÈ
Sant'Ambroeus
Corso Matteotti 7
Tel. 02/700540
Closed Sunday

Sant'Ambroeus is Milano's most traditional tearoom, with homemade pastry and chocolates to go elegantly wrapped in tulle. The golfball-size chocolate truffles and the ridged *sacher torte* are a chocoholic's dream, but skip the insipid, soft tea sandwiches. Black-bow-tied, white-jacketed bartenders preside over the shiny dark wood, lace-edged, doily-lined bar. The *cuppuccino* is creamier than most.

TEAROOM
Tecoteca
Via Magolfa 14
Tel. 02/8324119
Closed Monday

Tea from all over the world, and soothing herbal tisanes, are a specialty at the Tecoteca, a quiet tearoom in the Left Bank ambience of the Navigli area of Milano.

BAR-CAFFÈ
Taveggia
Via Visconti di Modrone 2
Tel. 02/791257
Closed Monday

The morning ritual of coffee and *brioche* (croissants) fresh from the oven, afternoon teatime, and pastries from Taveggia, with its unchanged 1930s decor, are classics in tradition-bound Milano. Open Sunday!

SPECIALTY FOODS
Gastronomia Peck
Via Spadari 9
Tel. 02/871737
Closed all day Sunday and
Monday afternoon
Credit cards: American Express,
Diners Club, Visa

This is a food shop to stroll through slowly, inhaling deeply. A triangular stand between the front doors sells almost 500,000 pounds of one of the store's specialties, *parmigiano-reggiano* cheese—golden, perfectly aged, with tiny crunchy crystals and rich, ample flavor. I never leave without a little chunk. Two massive display cases run the length of the shop, filled with a synopsis of all the Peck stores: platters of cold salads, aspics, pâtès, seafood, freshly made egg pasta in a variety of shapes, a butcher shop, take-out section, cheese, salami, and cured meats from all over the world, candy, cakes, coffee, and much more—an overwhelming array of edibles. An extensive selection of Italian and French wines and spirits in the back completes this gastronomic panorama. A self-catered meal from Peck always makes life a little easier and the flight home a little less sad.

CHEESE
Casa del Formaggio
Via Speronari 3
Tel. 02/800858
Closed all day Sunday and
Monday afternoon
Credit cards: American Express,
Diners Club, Visa

Remo Stoppani selects over 350 different types of cheese from all over the world—in wheels, wedges, loaves, teardrop-shaped globes tied with cord hanging from the ceiling, smoked brown circles, snow-white cones, flattened disks, balls soaking in whey—many almost impossible to find outside their areas of production. This is a cheese-lover's paradise, part of Peck's gastronomic contribution.

SALUMI
Bottega del Maiale
Via V. Hugo 3
Tel. 02/8053528
Closed all day Sunday and
Monday afternoon
Credit cards: American Express,
Diners Club, Visa

Angelo Stoppani is in charge of Peck's Bottega del Maiale, specializing in fresh and cured pork products. Festoons of salami; dozens of varieties of sausage; flat and rolled *pancetta* (bacon); *prosciutto* from Parma, Prague, and San Daniele; rendered, fresh, and flavored lard; smoked and fresh meats; and even snout, feet, and ears are sold in this "pig heaven."

ROTISSERIE TAKE-OUT
Rosticceria
Via C. Cantù 3
Tel. 02/8693017
*Closed Sunday afternoon and
    Monday*
*Credit cards: American Express,
    Diners Club, Visa*

Slowly spinning rows of poultry, quail, pigeon, duck, pheasant, chicken, and guinea hen rotate on the rotisserie under a wide copper hood, tanning in front of a wood-burning fire at the Rosticceria Peck. *Risotto,* baked pasta, roast meats, even whole pig, are portioned out to take away or to eat at the counter. The fryer section deep-fries poultry, meat, vegetables, *polenta,* and Sicilian rice balls. Pizza is sold by the slice. Avoid the 12:30 to 1:30 tidal wave of locals out for a fast lunch.

STAND-UP CAFETERIA
La Bottega del Vino
Via V. Hugo 4
Tel. 02/861040
Closed Sunday
*Credit cards: American Express,
    Diners Club, Visa*

The Bottega del Vino is a Milanese version of what fast food should be like, quality cafeteria-style. An interesting selection of hot dishes, cold salads, and freshly made sandwiches, displayed in a long wide glass case, can be accompanied by one of over 200 fine wines, ordered by the glass or bottle from the extensive list chosen by Mario Stoppani, the family wine expert. Wine can also be purchased by the bottle or case. Avoid the 12:30 to 1:30 lunchtime rush.

PRODUCE
L'Ortolano di via Spadari
Via Spadari 9
Tel. 02/866063
Closed Monday afternoon

L'Ortolano, on via Spadari, Milano's most elegant food street, sells every imaginable fruit, in and out of season, and a huge variety of salad greens and herbs, all casually but artfully arranged. Choose from untranslatable exotics like *alkikinger, mangoustan, carubi, cirimoia, stachis, corbezzoli,* and fresh dates.

BREAD
Garbagnati
Via V. Hugo 3
Tel. 02/860905
Closed Monday afternoon

The Garbagnati bakery, flanking part of the Peck Empire, sells tasty bread, rolls, and pastry in this convenient location.

BREAD
Cantoni
Piazza Giovane Italia 2
Tel. 02/4987561
*Closed Saturday and Monday
    afternoons*

The authentic turn-of-the-century family bakery of Bianca and Luigi Cantoni makes Milano's best whole-wheat bread, as well as home-style cakes and *panettone.*

SPECIALTY FOODS
Il Salumaio
Via Montenapoleone 12
Tel. 02/701123
Closed Monday morning

Calling this elegant shop on sophisticated via Montenapoleone "Il Salumaio," "The Salumi Vendor," is an understatement, like calling the Duomo a church. Il Salumaio sells the highest-quality, most aesthetically arranged ingredients for an instant banquet: *salumi,* cheese, layered *mascarpone torte,* salads, aspics, meat, pasta, pies, jars of olives, tiny onions, baby artichoke hearts, *porcini* mushrooms—all mouthwateringly displayed. Window shopping here may result in hypersalivation. A self-catered meal from Il Salumaio is a delicious way of prolonging your trip on the flight home.

WINE
*Enoteca Cotti and La Frasca di
    Cotti*
Via Solferino 42
Tel. 02/6555736
Closed Sunday

The Enoteca Cotti and its annex, La Frasca, in the heart of the Brera section of town, feel more like a neighborhood hangout than a wine store. Locals drop in for a chat with Luigi Cotti and a glass of wine before purchasing a bottle for lunch or dinner. Monthly wine tastings, featuring a winemaker and his or her wines, draw an interested group of Luigi's client-friends.

WINE
Enoteca Solci
Via Morosini 19
Tel. 02/573826
Closed Mondays
Credit cards: American Express,
  Diners Club, MasterCard

The Enoteca Solci has an impressive selection of over 1,000 Italian, French, and even some Californian and South American wines, a number of quality extra virgin olive oils from different regions, balsamic vinegar, honey, and a wide range of *grappa* from all over Italy. They will send purchases anywhere in Europe.

SUPERMARKET
Esselunga, "Long S," has locations throughout the city. It's the best American-style supermarket in Milano, stocked with fine Italian and some imported products. Prices are reasonable, wines can be excellent, and the delicatessen (*gastronomia*) offers a wide range of *salumi*, marinated salads, cheese, and olives. The small housewares section is well stocked with basics. Esselunga is studded with interesting inexpensive items like Domopak's baking-boiling bags, Frio's Ghiaccio Pronto—disposable plastic bags for making ice cubes, tubes of tomato paste, whole nutmeg sold with a tiny grater, instant aspic, Fini balsamic vinegar, and extra virgin olive oil. Closed Monday afternoon.

SANDWICH BAR
Paninoteca Bar Quadronno
Via Quadronno 34
Tel. 02/593089
Closed Monday

Playing with snails in Milano

THE MILANESE SANDWICH
·

Milano has created its own version of the sandwich (*panino*) as a snack or a lunch for those who can't take the time for a classic Italian meal. The *paninoteca* ("sandwich shrine") phenomenon began in Milano and has spread throughout Italy. Vegetable, cheese, fish, and cold-cut combination fillings are stuffed into partially cooked French bread rolls, then grilled to complete the cooking and to heat or melt the filling. Shrimp and crabmeat *panini* are often paired with Russian dressing (*salsa rubra* or *aurora*).

The rebirth of the sandwich as the *panino* took place at the Bar Quadronno, a gastronomic event of historic importance, especially for flocks of sandwich-eating teenagers, known as *paninari*, who dress like yuppies in designer sweatshirts, jeans, and Timberland shoes. This sandwich shrine won the Oscar of the sandwich world for their special *panino*, the "golden palm" *(palma d'oro)*, which is stuffed with cured beef *(bresaola)*, pressed mullet roe *(bottarga)*, pâté, and Russian dressing. Dagwood would approve.

Bar Quadronno is open from 7 a.m. to 2 a.m.

SANDWICH BAR
Barba del Corso
Corso Vittorio Emanuele 5
Tel. 02/804692
Closed Sunday

Navigating the crowd of coffee drinkers to get to the sandwich station in the back of this anonymous bar isn't easy, but it's worth the effort. Fresh rolls *(panini)* are stuffed with over forty different meat, cheese, fish, or vegetable fillings. Simple classics like *prosciutto* or salami, as well as double-deckers, extra-large *(robusti)*, and sometimes bizarre combinations are Barba del Corso's specialty. There's an extra charge for service at the tables outside, under the arcade. The bar is open from 8:30 a.m. to 1:30 a.m.

SANDWICH BAR
Bar de Santis
Corso Maenta 9
Tel. 02/875968
Closed Sunday

Roberto de Santis specializes in grilling French bread rolls filled with mild goat cheese flavored with either wine, onions, basil, or chili pepper. Other imaginative combinations and fillings, including tasty smoked herring, are stuffed into rolls in this popular *paninoteca*, but Roberto's cheese sandwiches are the new Milanese

classics. De Santis is open from 10:30 a.m. to 1:30 p.m., and from 6 p.m. to 1:30 a.m.

PASTRY, MARZIPAN
Freni
Corso Vittorio Emanuele 4
Tel. 02/804871
Closed Wednesday

The Freni window is a joy to behold. Miniature mushrooms, watermelon, fruit, vegetables, salami, cacti, rolls, frying pans with eggs, little animals—all are made from the Freni family's marzipan recipe, sculpted, and hand-painted with vegetable-based dyes by a staff of Sicilian marzipan artists. But the real reason for a pilgrimage to Freni is to taste the warm scallop-shaped *sfogliatelle* (ricotta-filled flaky pastry), a rich, elegant southern specialty.

PASTRY
Massimo di Crinò
Via Ripamonti 5
Tel. 02/55139
Closed Monday

Antonio Crinò named his pastry shop after his infant son for good luck, but luck has nothing to do with the splendid desserts that he turns out. He's been baking since he was thirteen, and his professionalism, dedication, and passion for quality are responsible for the excellent *panettone*, the best I've ever tasted. The secret is in the

all-natural ingredients—first-rate raisins, candied orange peel, egg yolks, Italian butter, less sugar than most, and forty hours of work from the dough to the final product. *Panettone* is baked from the end of September through March, when Antonino bakes *colomba*, dove-shaped Easter cakes for two weeks. *La veneziana*, similar to *panettone* but topped with almonds and sugar, is available the rest of the year. No preservatives are added to these tasty cakes, and I imagine that they won't last as long as more commercial versions, but in my home they disappear so quickly that they don't have time to grow stale.

PASTRY
Marchesi
Via Santa Maria alla Porta 13
Tel. 02/862770
Closed Monday, except before Christmas

A visit to Marchesi, with its Old World ambience of lace-trimmed aprons, silver, and doilies, where everything is a classic, feels like time warp. Nothing has ever changed. The chocolates and the pastry are wonderful, but rich yeast breads, like springtime *colomba* or winter *panettone*, are Marchesi's specialty. The traditional Christmas chantilly-cream-stuffed *panettone* is a Milanese classic.

Fine pastry and *panettone* can also be found at Cova, Taveggia, Biffi, and Sant'Ambroeus, listed as bar-caffès.

GELATO

Gelateria Ecologica
Corso di Porta Ticinese 40
Tel. 02/8351872
Closed August and November
through February

There's no sign outside Gelateria Ecologica but it's easy enough to find, with its permanent cluster of fans outside eating *gelato* with multicolored plastic spoons. All their *gelato* is made with seasonal organic fruit and natural ingredients. Daily specials are listed on a blackboard and may include date, rhubarb, and honey sesame. The *gelateria* is open from 1 p.m. to midnight, seven days a week.

GELATO

Passerini
Via Victor Hugo 5
Tel. 02/800663
Closed Wednesday

Passerini, on via Victor Hugo in the heart of gastronomic Milano, founded in the 1920s, is the city's most elegant ice cream parlor. Classic flavors of *gelato* are rich and creamy; the *gianduia* (chocolate hazelnut) is outstanding. Hollowed-out fruit is stuffed with frozen sherbet. *Gelato* snowmen and Santas, and thick hot chocolate topped with whipped cream, are winter specialties. Open from 7:30 a.m. to 8 p.m.

GELATO

Gelateria Umberto
Piazza Cinque Giornate 4
Tel. 02/5458113
Closed Sunday

Only seven kinds of *gelato,* all exquisite classic flavors, are prepared daily at Gelateria Umberto.

Personal favorites are the smooth creamy hazelnut, the intense coffee parfait, the *cassata alla siciliana* (a layered ricotta, candied fruit, and sponge cake dessert), and the white wine and candied fruit *sorbetto Romanov*, which must be ordered in advance. Free delivery, almost unheard of in Italy, is available for orders of more than 300 grams (about 10 ounces). Umberto is open from 9:30 a.m. to 7 p.m.

RESTAURANT

Aimo e Nadia
Via Montecuccoli 6
Tel. 02/416886
Closed Sunday and August
Credit card: American Express
Price: expensive

A lengthy cab ride to a suburb that looks like Yonkers is the prelude to the privilege of dining at Aimo e Nadia. The decor is modern without being sterile, softened by tones of brick, pale peach, and pink-flecked granite. Lighting, linens, flatware, glassware, and flower arrangements are discreet, complements rather than distractions from the food. The teamwork of husband and wife—Aimo procuring the finest raw materials and Nadia at work in the kitchen—is a lesson in harmony and respect. The *cucina* is composed of strong, decisive flavors spiked with herbs, taking full advantage of the best and freshest possible local ingredients, lightly cooked, simply combined. A seasonal vegetable, such as asparagus, zucchini flowers, mushrooms, or truffles, may dominate the menu during its brief period of excel-

lence, weaving its flavor through many courses of the meal, appearing in an antipasto salad, as *risotto* or with pasta, or combined with fish or meat. The cheese selection is the essence of Lombardia. The wine list is somewhat confusing, with many French and unknown Italian wines, reflecting the personal taste of the sommelier. The strength and sincerity of Aimo and Nadia Moroni and their *cucina* make dining at their restaurant an exceptional experience.

RESTAURANT

Alfredo Gran San Bernardo
Via Borgese 14
Tel. 02/3319000
Closed Sunday, December 20–
January 20, mid-July through
August
No credit cards
Price: high moderate

An extensive menu exists in this classic Milanese restaurant, but if you look at the other tables on your way to be seated, you'll notice that almost everyone is eating the same things: golden-yellow *risotto alla milanese,* or *riso al salto,* a crispy pancake of *risotto* sautéed in butter; the "true" *costoletta alla milanese,* a large pounded, breaded veal cutlet with the bone; and *cazzoeula,* a stew of pork sausage, ribs, forehead, and feet, stewed with cabbage, served with *polenta.* Most diners conclude with the soufflé, which is covered with chocolate sauce. The white-jacketed waiters are impatient, probably because they know what you're going to choose, and the service is speedy. The wine list offers a selection of fine wines as well as plonk.

RESTAURANT
L 'Ami Berton
Via F. Nullo 14
Tel. 02/13669
Closed Sunday, Monday lunch,
  and August
Credit card: American Express
Price: expensive

L 'Ami Berton, with its Art Nouveau greenhouse decor, beautiful brown-tendriled marble-chip floor, and planters separating the tables, creating a feeling of intimacy, serves nontraditional, light, simply prepared fish, seafood, and vegetables (meat dishes are a minority on the menu) coupled with a lovely selection of Italian wines. The homemade pasta is fabulous. Desserts are well made, but save room for the small chocolate-covered cube of intense coffee ice cream, served after coffee. Roberto Berton and his wife, Pia, in the kitchen (he's from Veneto, she's Tuscan) are the driving force behind this fine restaurant. In the summer you can dine outside, on the awning-covered sidewalk.

RESTAURANT
Asso di Fiori—Osteria dei
  Formaggi
Alzaia Naviglio Grande 54
Tel. 02/8399415
Closed Saturday lunch, Sunday,
  and August
Credit cards: American Express,
  Diners Club, MasterCard
Price: moderate

The informal Asso di Fiori ("Ace of Clubs") in the charming Navigli canal section of Milano serves close to 200 different types of Italian cheese, including fresh *mozzarella* and *burrata* that arrive daily from the south. Order the *degustazione,* a tasting of fifteen different cheeses, and choose from the interesting selection of fine Italian wines.

RESTAURANT
Aurora
Via Savona 23
Tel. 02/835498
Closed Monday
Credit cards: American Express,
  Diners Club
Price: high moderate

Mushrooms, truffles, and Piemonte cooking are the specialties of this turn-of-the-century restaurant. Tasty *bagna caoda* (raw vegetable dip), *risotto,* homemade pasta, boiled meats with a variety of sauces, salads dressed at the table with your choice of a large selection of olive oils and flavored vinegars, and homemade desserts and *gelato* are served to Aurora's chic Milanese clients. Cheese and wine are mostly Piemontese. The fixed-price menu at lunch and dinner offers a reasonably priced (for Milano) five-course meal, including wine. Drink the Ceretto Dolcetto. Lawn bowling and garden dining under the trees make Aurora even nicer in the warm months. Open on Sunday.

RESTAURANT
Osteria Battivacco
Via Bardolino 3
Tel. 02/8138825
Closed all day Monday and
  Tuesday lunch
No credit cards
Price range: high moderate

This typical old-fashioned Lombard farmhouse is in the middle of nowhere, a lengthy cab ride well past the suburbs of Milano, difficult to find even for locals. Owner Toni Cuman must be doing something right to get Milanese out of the heart of town. *Salumi* and cheese are first-rate. The *cucina* isn't traditional or regional, but nicely combines flavors, usually with restraint. Toni's selection of olive oils, wines, and distillates is formidable. The rustic dining rooms, with either fireplace or cast-iron stove, are cozy in the winter. Outdoor dining in the courtyard, near the ancient wisteria, is a treat in the spring and the sweltering summer.

RESTAURANT
Osteria dei Binari
Via Tortona 1
Tel. 02/8399428
Closed Sunday and August
Credit cards: American Express,
  Diners Club
Price: moderate

Near the Porta Genovese train station (hence *binari*—railroad platforms or tracks), this neighborhood *osteria* with its old Milano ambience serves mixed regional *cucina* with a bit of nouvelle tossed in. Piemonte, Liguria, and most of all Lombardia influence the menu of Osteria dei Binari, where bread, pasta, and desserts are homemade, the wine list wonderful, and the service swift. Lawn bowling (*bocce*) and garden dining under the trees are pleasant in the warm-weather months.

RESTAURANT

Calajunco
Via Stoppani 5
Tel. 02/2046003
Closed Sunday and August
Credit card: American Express
Price: expensive

Off the coast of Sicilia, on the Eolian island of Panarea, is a tiny bay called Calajunco, where Renato Carnevale used to dive for fish. His elegant restaurant, named after the bay, serves the *cucina*, lightened up for the modern palate, of Sicilia and Renato's islands. A hollowed-out mini-*mozzarella* filed with tomato and basil and dressed with olive oil, eggplant salad *(caponata)*, and a fried rice ball *(arancino)*, or another trio of tasty antipasti, will be served while you wait for your order in the evening, or can be your whole meal at lunchtime. Milano's fresh fish is served up in salads, with perfectly cooked spaghetti, and grilled, delicately fried, or sauced. The sliced fresh fruit makes a light conclusion to the meal, but it may be hard to resist the tiny *ricotta*-filled fried pastry. Choose from an ample selection of wines.

RESTAURANT

Casanova Grill
Piazza della Repubblica 20
Tel. 02/650803
Credit cards: all
Price: expensive

Frequented mostly by Milanese, the Casanova Grill, with its columns, plants, and subdued piano music in the evening, is hardly a grill. Located in the Palace (but with its own entrance), it proves that hotel dining doesn't have to be dull. The ambience is ele-

Backstage at Peck's restaurant

gant, service is doting, and linen tablecloths are set with large salmon-and-gold-trimmed service plates. The Mediterranean-oriented menu, supplemented by the specialties of chef Sergio Mei, is a treat for anyone who has been jet-lagged and overworked in workaholic Milano. Regional *risotto*, homemade pasta, simply grilled meat or chicken, nouvelle-inspired dishes, a fine selection of cheese, and tempting desserts and fruit ices are beautifully prepared, presented, and served. The wine list offers a fine selection of Italian wines.

RESTAURANT

Don Lisander
Via Manzoni 12/a
Tel. 02/790130
Closed Saturday evening, Sunday,
*   and most of August*
Credit cards: American Express,
*   Diners Club, MasterCard*
Price: expensive

Don Lisander, elegant and modern, with a beautiful garden dining area in the summer, feels like a patrician Milanese palace. The *cucina* of Maria Bani is Tuscan, sparked by her creativity. Husband Gioacchino Coppini supplies her with the best ingredients that

...y has to offer, and she does ...n justice. Pasta is hand—not ...machine—rolled. Fish, game, and the best Florentine-style steak in Milano are cooked to perfection, flavored with fresh herbs. Desserts and _gelato_ are homemade. Service is swift and formal. A wide selection of quality extra virgin olive oils are available, and the wine list offers some gems.

RESTAURANT
Franca, Paola e Lele
Viale Certosa 235
Tel. 02/305238
Closed Saturday, Sunday, Monday evening, and August
No credit cards
Price: expensive

The damask tablecloths and a few trendy diners are the only hints that there is more to this one-room _trattoria_ than meets the eye. Owner Lele, white-aproned and suspendered, is clearly proud of each dish that comes out of his wife's kitchen, and with good reason. Home-grown vegetables, poultry, eggs, and lightly salted homemade _salumi_, all from Paola and Lele's own farm outside Piacenza, are cooked with simplicity and artistry—no flowers, stars, braids, or trellis arrangements on the plates. The country-style _cucina_ of _salumi_, fine pâté, home-style chunky soups, duck, goose, but especially chicken of forgotten flavor, plus _gelato_ rich with orange egg yolks, is accompanied by classical music and quality local and often unusual wines. Lele's enthusiasm is infectious, and makes dining in this _trattoria_ in suburban Milano a treat.

RESTAURANT
Da Gianni e Dorina—Il Pontremolese
Via Pepe 38
Tel. 02/606340
Closed Saturday lunch, Sunday, and August
Credit cards: American Express, Diners Club, MasterCard
Price: high moderate

Tuscan restaurants with undistinguished food abound in Milano, but this restaurant is an exception. Dorina, expert sommelier, serves the _cucina_ from Pontremoli, close to the border between Toscana, Liguria, and Emilia-Romagna, showing the influences of all three regions with strong, determined flavors like _pesto_, whole kernels of wheat, and chestnut dominating the menu, accompanied by a wide selection of extra virgin olive oils, and a fine wine list of Tuscan and Italian gems.

RESTAURANT
Grand Italia
Via Palermo 5
Tel. 02/877759
Closed Tuesday and August
No credit cards
Price: inexpensive

Milanese restaurateur Cesare Denti, creator of Aurora and Osteria dei Binari, has opened a modest marble-tabled restaurant with his usual emphasis on quality. The menu includes pizza and _focaccia_ by the slice, interesting salads, a limited selection of first and second courses that change daily, and homemade desserts. The wine selection is good, and fine wines are available by the glass. Open on Sunday.

RESTAURANT
Gualtiero Marchesi
Via Bonvesin de la Riva 9
Tel. 02/741246
Closed Sunday, Monday, and August
Credit cards: American Express, Diners Club, MasterCard
Price: expensive

Gualtiero Marchesi, the first Italian chef to be awarded three stars by the Francophile Michelin guide, sent shock waves through the Italian food scene when he abolished pasta, and then when he reinstated it, cold, with caviar. Mercurial and innovative, with his roots in the Lombard and middle-European traditions, influenced but not overwhelmed by nouvelle cuisine, Gualtiero has developed his own personal, at times provocative, highly professional _cucina_, a landscape of grace, balance, and style. The large white textured menu with embossed logo and bright paintbrush strokes of color presents the framework within which Gualtiero composes a meal. Each course is represented on the menu by a different color: lightly prepared lively dishes like bright green _pesto_, _trenette_ (flat strips of pasta) and string beans, a personal version of _pasta e fagioli_, lamb and rosemary, truffled duck liver, fine fruit desserts, and attractive tiny pastries. The à la carte menu expands the color theme, increasing the choices. Three tasting meals—traditional Milanese, vegetarian, and pasta—are beautifully prepared. Lunch or after-theater diners will appreciate the one-course meal (_piatto unico_) of five different tastes, either fish or meat—a light and reasonably priced sampling of what Gualtiero's *cucina* is all about. The presentation, cheese selection, wine list, and ambience of this chic Milanese restaurant are all first-rate.

RESTAURANT

Nino Arnaldo
Via Carlo Poerio 3
Tel. 02/705981
Closed Saturday, Sunday, and
*   August*
Credit card: Visa
Price: expensive

Nino Arnaldo's minimalist Milanese decor is warmed by an enormous antique print of Roma, soft modern lighting, transparent wine coolers, and elegant locals dining on creative *cucina*, guided by Nino's wife, Lucia. Seasonal pan-fried flans *(frittate)*, homemade pasta or ravioli stuffed with a meat, vegetable, or fish filling, main-course meat and vegetable combinations and a few simple fish dishes, fine *gelato* and fruit ices, all with well-balanced flavors, are well prepared. Truffles and mushrooms are a specialty in season. The wine list is adequate.

RESTAURANT

L'Osteria
Alzaia Naviglio Grande 46
Tel. 02/8373426
Closed Tuesday
No credit cards
Price: low moderate

L'Osteria is a characteristic stucco-walled, marble-countered wine bar in the Navigli section of Milano. There are over 200 types of wine from all over Italy—with a few French, Alsatian, and even American wines available—to drink with the *salumi*, smoked game, salads,

raw vegetables *(pinzimonio)* to be dipped in extra virgin olive oil, and cheese. Desserts, mostly fruit tarts, cakes, and *semifreddo*, are unexciting.

L'Osteria is open evenings only (including Sundays), and all day on the last Sunday of the month, for the Naviglio flea market.

RESTAURANT

Peck
Via Victor Hugo 4
Tel. 02/876774
Closed Sunday and the first three
*   weeks in July*
Credit cards: all
Price: high moderate

This restaurant is the jewel in the crown of the Peck Empire (see page 165). Quality ingredients procured by the four Stoppani brothers, the princes of Peck, are used to full advantage. Needless to say, *salumi* and cheese are excellent, and the wine list is a joy to read. The six-course traditional Milanese tasting menu is reasonably priced; the *menu degustazione* offers somewhat fancier, although well-made, creative *cucina*. The ambience is modern and unpretentious.

RESTAURANT

Al Pont de Ferr
Ripa di Porta Ticinese 55
Tel. 02/8390277
Closed Sunday and two weeks in
*   August, open evenings only*
No Credit cards
Price: moderate

This restaurant's name is Milanese dialect for the iron bridge that spans the nearby Naviglio canal in the newly gentrified, once-bohemian quarter of town. Local

enophiles stop in for dinner, a snack, or a glass of wine from the selection of over 200 quality wines. Owner-sommelier Maida Mercuri is every bit as beautiful as her wine list. The food is simple, the *salumi* are fine, cheese is selected with great care. Swift service is not the highlight of this restaurant, but the genuine ambience, reasonable prices, and Maida's unfailing palate keep me coming back.

RESTAURANT

Al Pontell
Via Mameli 1
Tel. 02/733818
Closed Tuesday and August
Price: moderate

The specialty of Osteria al Pontell, a home-style Milanese *trattoria*, is *risotto*, and although they offer at least eight different kinds, most diners opt for the *risotto alla milanese* or the *risotto al salto*, a crispy pancake of *risotto* sautéed in butter, prepared *alla milanese* (with saffron) or stuffed with a variety of vegetable, cheese, and fish fillings. Classic Milanese dishes are well prepared, some desserts are homemade, and fresh fruit salad *(macedonia)* or ice cream is always available. The local wines aren't too interesting; drink the wines of Capezzana, Quintarelli, or Giacosa. Open on Sunday.

RESTAURANT

Al Porto
Piazzale Generale Cantore
Tel. 02/8321481
Closed Sunday, Monday lunch,
*   and August*
Credit cards: American Express,
*   Diners Club*
Price: expensive

Anna in the kitchen and husband Domenico Buonamici in the dining rooms of Al Porto prepare and serve some of the freshest fish in Milano. The classic *cucina* of this ex-tollhouse on the docks of Porta Ticinese, decorated with maritime paraphernalia, offers few surprises and no disappointments, just fish and seafood, fresher than in restaurants on the coast, simply cooked in traditional Italian style. The *tiramisù* is delicious, although some diners prefer to conclude their meal with a *gelato* at nearby Gelateria Pozzi. Italian, and some French, wines are featured on the fine wine list. Outdoor dining in the warm weather months. Reservations should be made a few days in advance.

RESTAURANT
Sadler–Osteria di Porta Cicca
Ripa di Porta Ticinese 51
Tel. 02/8324451
Closed Sunday and the second half of August
Credit card: American Express
Price: high moderate

This charming newcomer is on the banks of the Naviglio canal: a sleek, remodernized gray and pink *osteria* with gray polka-dot walls and large-bladed ceiling fans. Claudio Sadler, ex-chef of the gourmet society *Altopalato*, combines creativity and a knowledge of regional gastronomic history, resulting in an interesting, personal *cucina*. Some dishes try too hard, and may combine too many flavors, like duck breast with dates, cream, mustard and herbs, but most offerings are simpler and all are well prepared. Pasta is homemade and the cheese tray is

good, but desserts are the high point of the meal. Chocolate fans may want a double portion of the bittersweet *fondente di cioccolata* with coffee sauce. Claudio's wife, Vittoria, will suggest a wine from their interesting selection. The *menu degustazione* (tasting menu) suggests appropriate, moderately priced wines. Open evenings only.

RESTAURANT
Savini
Galleria Vittorio Emanuele
Tel. 02/8058343
Closed Sunday and August
Credit cards: all
Price: expensive

Savini, decorated with brocade, gilt mirrors, crystal chandeliers, and plush red velvet banquettes—the most elegant and traditional of Milanese restaurants—has been frequented by royalty and stars from the nearby La Scala opera house for over a hundred years. The *cucina* is continental, from the days of the Grand Tour, featuring smoked salmon or sturgeon, Iranian caviar, and superb *salumi*. All pasta is hand-rolled daily by a special pasta roller (*la pastaia*), not a machine. Milanese, Italian, and international classics like chateaubriand with béarnaise sauce and sole Mornay are listed on the menu, which varies daily, but this is the kind of restaurant that will make anything that you want. Vegetables will probably be overcooked. The wine list is wonderful, but only for those for whom price is no object.

RESTAURANT
La Scaletta
Piazzale Stazione di Porta Genova 3
Tel. 02/8350290
Closed Sunday, Monday, August, Christmas, and Easter
No credit cards
Price: expensive

Pina Bellini is reputed to be one of Italy's finest chefs, and her son Aldo is an amiable host and sommelier. However, they don't take reservations for one, and every time I've tried to reserve a table for either lunch or dinner I've met with rejection. I find it offensive to exclude all single diners from the Scaletta experience, possibly since I often eat alone. Signora Bellini says, "In the restaurant business, like the fashion business, there are two paths, haute couture and ready-to-wear. I follow the first path, and custom tailor my dishes to the client." If haute couture, nontraditional *cucina* is what you're looking for, head for La Scaletta, but not alone.

RESTAURANT
Sciuè Sciuè
Via Solari 6
Tel. 02/496029
Closed Monday, Tuesday lunch, and August
Credit cards: American Express, Diners Club
Price: moderate

Sciuè Sciuè may look unpronounceable (say shoo-ay, shoo-ay) but it's worth the effort, because this inviting southern Italian restaurant, with its colorful seafood *antipasto* display, serves perfectly cooked spaghetti, grilled meats and fish, and wonderful pizza. Conclude your meal with the *pastiera napoletana,* a whole-wheat kernel, ricotta, and candied fruit flan. The wine list has its highs and lows. Sciuè Sciuè is open on Sunday.

RESTAURANT
Masuelli
Viale Umbria 80
Tel. 02/584138
Closed Sunday
No credit cards
Price: low moderate

The Masuelli family have been operating this authentic *trattoria* in viale Umbria since 1930, serving the *cucina* of their native Monferrato, in Piemonte, along with Milanese specialties. Pino Masuelli works the two dining rooms, and his wife, Tina, is kept busy in the kitchen. The ambience is typical *trattoria,* with an old-fashioned metal-topped bar and wooden wainscoting. Each day of the week has its own special—Monday, mixed boiled meats; Tuesday, chick-pea soup with ribs, or Milanese meatballs *(mondeghili);* Wednesday, tripe and onion stew; Thursday, pork and cabbage stew; Friday, *polenta* and cod; Saturday, *gnocchi.* The Masuellis used to produce and bottle simple wine from their native Piemonte, but the wine list is expanding and a small, everchanging selection of fine, reasonably priced wines is offered. Reservations are a must, and are not easy to come by for this wonderful *trattoria.*

Giorgio Lucini designs menus in his minimalist, all-white office.

PIZZA
Pizzeria Il Mozzo
Via Ravizzi 1
Tel. 02/4984746
Closed Wednesday and August
No credit cards
Price: low moderate

A genuine Napoletano pizza chef and a large wood-burning oven are a guarantee of this pizzeria's quality.

PIZZA
Vecchia Napoli da Rino
Via Chavez 4
Tel. 02/2619056
Closed Monday and August
No credit cards
Price: low moderate

Father and son pizza makers Rino and Massimo Francavilla, who consistently place in the European

A pizzeria is only as good as its *pizzaiolo,* the freewheeling professional pizza chef whose artistic temperament may frequently influence the quality of his pizza.

World Pizza Chef competition, prepare fragrant original pizzas in their two wood-burning ovens.

HOUSEWARES

Medagliani
Via Razza 8
Tel. 02/655145
Closed Saturday
No credit cards

Medagliani is not a conventional store but rather a series of rooms in the center of Milano that contain over 6,000 items—a wide selection of no-nonsense tools for cooking, serving, and eating. They seem to have every possible size of every possible object that can pass through a kitchen. Handmade copper pots, some lined with stainless steel, flattened sauce spoons, uniforms, carts, cleavers, cruets, meat hooks, and two different models of the *prosciutto* vise await you in Italy's most important restaurant supply shop. Eugenio Medagliani, chemical engineer, painter, philosopher, historian, dreamer, and third-generation restaurant supplier, has combined his spheres of interest as designer of the *pentapiatto,* a white plate with a design of ridges that creates five separate sections, each to be filled with foods that balance harmoniously, both to the eye and in the stomach.

The shop will take a check, and will ship your purchases home for you.

PAPER ITEMS

Tipographia Lucini
Via Piero della Francesca 38
Tel. 02/3315825
Closed August
No credit cards

Giorgio Lucini prints the menus of Italy's gastronomic stars. For over sixty years the Lucini *tipografia* has been printing books, art prints, and more basic everyday jobs. But since Giorgio and his wife, Clara, are devout gastronomes, he prints wine lists and menus for friends who own restaurants. He chooses from over 400 types of paper, many handmade, and works with his clients to come up with a practical object. His eye for color and texture is as perceptive as his palate for taste. His work—books, prints, wine labels, menus, and wine lists—is simply beautiful. Giorgio has promised to design and print up menu forms, to be filled in for special meals, or place cards, or guest or recipe books, for those who would appreciate the work of a man I consider a print and paper artist in the grand Italian artisanal tradition. He does not accept any new work between October and January.

BOOKS

Il Collezionista
Via Madonnina 9
Tel. 02/866665
By appointment only
No credit cards

Carlo Scipione Ferrero and collaborator-organizer Maria Paleari Hennsler have created a paradise for bibliophile food lovers. Il Collezionista is Italy's only antique bookstore specializing in culinary texts, cookbooks, menus, and erotica. They also have a vast collection of cooking pictures and an interesting assortment of obscure utensils (ever seen a strand-forming press for making butter-nest garnishes?). The recently installed computer archive of over 4,000 gastronomic images available for publication provides instant access to a wealth of cooking and food-related drawings, etchings, paintings, and photos. Tall, handsome, charming, and cultured, silver-haired Carlo is a whirlwind of ideas. He works with his son, Guido (who wrote the historical tract on cooking for Alessi's spectacular book *La Cintura di Orione,* see page 178), is available for historical gastronomic research, and speaks perfect English.

TABLEWARE

G. Lorenzi
Via Montenapoleone 9
Tel. 02/792848
Closed Monday morning
Credit cards: all

Coltellinaio—one who makes, sells, or repairs knives and other cutting tools—is how the Lorenzi family define their profession. They've been supplying Milano with cutlery since 1919, from their Montenapoleone location since 1929, always selling nothing but the finest. Ivory and horn specialty sets—a pineapple carving set consisting of a corer of two knives, a truffle set of slicer, brush, and glass bell jar, or an elegant pair of chopsticks in an equally elegant case—are displayed like jewelry in glass cases. How have you lived without a *prosciutto* vise, *polenta* knife, urchin opener, sardine shovel, a set of horn *osso buco* spoons for digging out marrow, or a mother-of-pearl caviar

*Gastronomic experiences may appear
on a street corner.*

set, with serving pieces and individual spoons and knives? The knife selection is excellent. I love the look of the stainless steel mesh glove, perfect for clumsy oyster shuckers or knife wielders. And amidst all this elegance, the Lorenzi family still repairs and sharpens knives.

TABLEWARE
Richard Ginori
Corso Matteotti 1
Tel. 02/702286
Closed Monday morning
Credit cards: all

The well-equipped Richard Ginori store on the corner of corso Matteotti sells a complete line of Ginori china, as well as silver and crystal by leading Italian and European manufacturers.

TABLEWARE
La Botteguccia
Via della Pergola 11
Tel. 02/6887580
Closed Monday
No credit cards

The Botteguccia sells Ginori seconds and leftovers at highly reduced prices, although savings will be minimized by the cost of shipping.

HOUSEWARES
Picowa
Piazza San Babila 4/D
Tel. 02/794078
Closed Monday
Credit cards: all

Picowa has more than 3,000 objects for the kitchen on three floors filled with crystal, china,

LOW-PRICED DEPARTMENT STORES

•

Is it the high-design atmosphere of Milano that makes the housewares sections of its department stores seem more exciting than anywhere else in Italy? These all have good selections of glass, plastic, ceramics, and gadgets for the kitchen, at low prices.

Rinascente
Piazza Duomo
Tel. 02/88521
Closed Monday morning
Credit cards: all

Coin
Piazzale Loreto
Tel. 02/2826179
Closed Monday morning
Credit cards: all

Standa
Corso Buenos Aires 37 (and other locations)
Tel. 02/279297
Credit cards: MasterCard, Visa

Upim
Corso Buenos Aires 21 (and other locations)
Tel. 02/272477
Credit cards: American Express, Visa

stainless steel, wood, and plastic—furnishings for the kitchen, dining room, and garden.

COOKWARE
Alessi
Corso Matteotti 9
Tel. 02/795726
Credit cards: all

A classic postwar industrial success story, a blend of Italian technology, ingenuity, and design, Alessi has taken stainless steel and worked with it the way a sculptor works with marble. From Carlo Alessi's 1945 chrome-plated tea and coffee set, through Richard Sapper's cooking utensils created with the consultation of Europe's great cooks, a list of who's who in Italian design has shaped Alessi's tools for cooking and serving. Two exceptional books mark the Alessi commitment to the kitchen: The *Pastario* ("Pasta Atlas"), in Italian and English, with its meticulous and delightful illustrations of pasta, was published by Alessi when they introduced their pasta cooker-steamer. *La Cintura di Orione* is a chronicle of an encounter between design and function, a history of cooking from the equipment point of view, illustrated with an unbelievable richness of images of cooking utensils, with recipes by the cooks who consulted with Richard Sapper in the design of this series of elegant, expensive pots and pans.

The entire Alessi line is available in the Milano showroom, but many items are sold in housewares stores throughout Italy.

A Milanese shows off Italy's freshest fish.

GLASSWARE
Vetrerie di Empoli
Via Borgospesso 5
Tel. 02/708791
Closed Monday
No credit cards

The lovely rustic mouth-blown glassware, plates, bowls, platters, goblets, tumblers, and decorative pieces are just part of the pleasure of this wonderful shop, with its eighteenth-century frescoes from the school of Tiepolo. Shipping can be arranged.

GLASSWARE
Venini
Via Montenapoleone 9
Tel. 02/700539
Closed Monday morning
Credit cards: all

If you can't make it to Venezia for glass, head for via Montenapoleone, one of Milano's most elegant shopping streets, where Venini's modern mouth-blown colored glass, each piece a work of art, is sold.

TABLE LINENS

Jesurum
Via Montenapoleone 14
Tel. 02/6559785
Closed Monday morning
Credit cards: all

See page 129 for a description of Jesurum's hand-loomed table linens and handmade lace, which are also sold in this shop on chic via Montenapoleone.

FURNITURE

Alivar
Via della Chiusa, corner of via Crocifisso
Tel. 02/8351096
Closed Monday morning
No credit cards

Alivar produces classic designer dining-room chairs and furniture faithful to the original designs and quality materials of Le Corbusier, Breuer, Stam, Mies van der Rohe, Hoffmann, Gray, and Mackintosh, all for a fraction of the U.S. price. Reproductions of the Alvar Aalto cart, Mackintosh chairs, and Le Corbusier dining-room table are tempting.

GARDEN SUPPLIES

Centro Botanico
Via dell'Orso 16
Tel. 02/873315
Closed Monday
Credit cards: all

Be careful or you'll miss the entrance to the Centro Botanico, hidden in the Brera neighborhood. Walk through the courtyard and small garden, and up the stairs to the first floor, where you'll find frescoed rooms filled with books, plants, seeds, herbal creams, floral essences, dried flowers, tea, and honey. This shop offers gardening courses and caters to the needs of the urban gardener.

MONTÙ BECCARIA

INN

Il Castello di San Gaudenzio
Via Molino 1
Cervesina (close by)
Tel. 0383/75025
Credit cards: all
Price: low expensive

RESTAURANT

Al Pino
Via Mulino Folla 11
Tel. 0385/60479
Closed Wednesday and the second half of July
Credit cards: American Express, Diners Club
Price: moderate

A small house in the middle of Oltrepò Pavese vines, south of Pavia, is the setting for this tiny restaurant with the huge fir tree in the front yard. Pavese chef of worldwide experience Mario Musoni, his English wife-sommelier, Patricia, and their son Ivan team up to produce some of the best *cucina* in the province. Nontraditional, simply conceived dishes, usually an encounter between two distinct flavors, hallmark Mario's menu. Fresh-tasting *risotto*, probably one of the best in Italy, and a balanced menu of meat offerings and fresh fish from the Milano market on Fridays are perfectly cooked. Cheese fans will thrill to the taste of the rich, mottled blue *gorgonzola*, aged *parmigiano*, and goat cheese with basil. Local wines of La Muiraghina complement the amazing, unheralded *cucina* of the Musoni family.

MORTARA

SALUMI

Gioacchino Palestro
Via Roma 49
Tel. 0384/98387
Closed Monday through Friday afternoons

Gioacchino Palestro transforms goose into salami, sausage, *prosciutto*, pâté, cracklings, and raw foie gras in Mortara, the goose capital of Lombardia, southwest of Milano. His pork products, raw salami, *zampone* and *cotechino* sausages, and Piemontese lard-preserved sausage *(salam d'la duja)* are first-rate. But it is Gioacchino's goose products that have made him famous in the wine world. Coupled at wine fairs with La Monella, a hearty red produced by a friend, these excellent *salumi* have always been the tastiest bite around. Gioacchino has just won the newly created Premio Gancia di Gancia, awarded yearly to an artisan and his products of gastronomic excellence.

Mortara's goose salami festival, held the last Sunday in September, begins with a procession of 500 locals in medieval costumes, representing the court of Lodovico il Moro (who used to hunt in the area), followed by a monumental *gioco dell'oca*, a traditional board game played, for this occasion, with human pawns. Traditional goose products are sold at stands.

QUISTELLO

HOTEL
See Hotels San Lorenzo and Broletto in Mantova (page 163)

RESTAURANT
L'Ambasciata
Via Martiri di Belfiore 33
Tel. 0376/618255
Closed Wednesday, January, and
   August
Credit cards: American Express,
   Diners Club
Price: expensive

South of the mighty Po River, tucked in the village of Quistello, L'Ambasciata ("The Embassy") looks like a typical countryside *trattoria.* But look more carefully at the license plates on the cars in the parking lot and you'll notice that diners have come from all over Italy to sample the *cucina* of the Tamani family. The restaurant's decor is busy, with Oriental rugs, copper pots, murky paintings, and elegantly turned-out tables. Mama, Grandma, and Aunt prepare luxurious traditional dishes, and wine-steward brothers Romano and Francesco pamper diners and pour splendid regional and Italian wines. The menu changes with the seasons, and features local *salumi* (served with sweet and spicy *mostarda,* a regional version of chutney), *tortelli di zucca* (squash-stuffed handrolled pasta), sturgeon from the nearby Po, local duck, pheasant, guinea hen, and capon. Caviar and Scotch salmon are offered for Italians bored with regional family-style *cucina,* which is elevated to an art form at L'Ambasciata. Conclude your meal with the rich, deep orange–colored *zabaione* and the *torta di tagliatelle* (crunchy pasta cake).

RANCO

RESTAURANT-INN
Del Sole
Piazza Venezia 5
Tel. 0331/976507
Credit cards: American Express,
   MasterCard, Visa
Price: expensive

Ristorante Albergo del Sole seems too good to be true. The domain of the perfectionist professional Brovelli family, husband and wife Carlo and Itala, and their son Davide, this small, comfortable nine-room inn faces Lago Maggiore, twenty minutes from Milano's inconveniently located Malpensa airport. The *cucina* can be inspirational. Diminutive Carlo and his son work magic with local lake ingredients and the bounty of both Milano and nearby Piemonte, turning out both traditional and creative *cucina,* lightened up and artistically arranged. Two tasting menus and a small, well-chosen seasonal à la carte menu are offered. Don't miss the local white peaches of Monate and the exceptional little pastries. The wine cellar, under the able guidance of sommelier Itala, contains a personal selection of fine Italian, French, and even some American wines. Warm-weather dining on a terrace overlooking gardens and the lake is an unforgettable experience. One of the world's finest breakfasts is served in the morning, a further demonstration of the Brovellis' attention to detail.

SERMIDE

HOTEL
Riparande
Via Ripagrande 21
Ferrara (close by)
Tel. 0532/34733
Credit cards: all
Price: expensive

HOTEL
Europa
Corso della Giovecca 49
Ferrara (close by)
Tel. 0532/21438
Credit card: American Express
Price: moderate

RESTAURANT
Il Cenacolo
Via Fratelli Bandiera 17
Tel. 0386/61872
Closed Monday and Tuesday
No credit cards
Price: moderate

Warm, home-style, and almost impossible to find, not exactly in the center of downtown Sermide, Benso and Romana Bertolesi's restaurant has all the personal charm of a private villa. It's populated by rather interesting people who do not look like locals. Romana makes plain, down-home cooking—pasta, soups, *risotto,* poultry, or beef braised in rich, aged classics from Benso's cellar. The *cucina,* served by reservation only, is a perfect accompaniment to enologist Benso's homemade unfiltered sparkling wine. Fine local *salumi* and cheese and a bottle of wine are always available, but it's best to call to tell Benso and Romana that you're on your way.

TRESCORE CREMASCO

HOTEL
See Il Sole in Maleo (page 162)

HOTEL
Palace Hotel
Via Cresmiero 10
Crema (close by)
Tel. 0373/81864
Credit cards: all
Price: moderate

RESTAURANT
Trattoria Fulmine
Via Carrioni 12
Tel. 0373/70203
Closed Sunday evening, Monday, and August
Credit cards: American Express, Diners Club
Price: high moderate

What happened to turn this Lombard village *trattoria,* inconspicuously hidden behind what appears to be a neighborhood bar, into a culinary rising star? Gianni Bolzoni serves his wife's well-made traditional *cucina,* based on the freshest local ingredients in an area of rich, fertile farmland. The menu features fine *salumi* (including *culatello,* the heart of the *prosciutto*), homemade pasta, and vegetable soups. Farm-raised goose and duck are cooked with their livers and served with *polenta.*

Gianni manages to procure the impossible-to-find *salva* cheese, made with spring milk and aged two months. Desserts are splendid, especially the custard *gelato* and the egg-yolk-rich *zabaione* served with *sabbiosa* (sand cake). The personal wine list offers Italian and French quality wines that make this well-prepared food taste even better. On a recent visit I watched as three priests (said to be knowledgeable about where to eat well) removed their collars and proceeded to accompany Fulmine's tasty home-style *cucina* with Italy's finest wines. Divine providence.

VILLA POMA

HOTEL
Fini
Via Emilia est 441
Modena (close by)
Tel. 059/238091
Credit cards: all
Price: expensive, but will provide transportation to Concorde

HOTEL
Pico
Mirandola (close by)
Tel. 0535/20050
Credit cards: American Express, Diners Club
Price: inexpensive

RESTAURANT
Concorde
Piazza Romano-Mazzali 8
Tel. 0386/566667
Closed Monday
Credit cards: all
Price: expensive

Oil and diamond magnate Marino Chiavelli flew on the Concorde's inaugural flight from London to New York. The supersonic experience was an unforgettable thrill. And now Dottor Chiavelli is attempting to create a restaurant that offers the same kind of extraordinary peak, a leap beyond normal expectations. Concorde has the best of everything that money can buy, with an initial investment of over ten billion lire. On the plains of the Po River, housed in a restored seventeenth-century villa with a staff of forty, including twelve cooks in the kitchen and two wine stewards, this restaurant offers four distinct seasonal menus based on the fine regional raw materials. Thirty-four-year-old chef Paolo Simione, tall, dark, and handsome, has trained in the grand hotels of Europe. His *cucina* is clearly creative, professionally prepared, and combines flavors with flair. Pastry chef Pascal Piermattei bakes four types of bread and delightful desserts daily. Pasta is hand-rolled. Tables are set with damask, china, crystal, and silver. The wine list—over 250 wines from Italy, Europe, and California—is amazing, especially for such a new restaurant. And Dottor Chiavelli has begun construction on a hotel that promises to be of the same level, to be ready in 1992. I hope that this challenge of a restaurant-hotel doesn't disappear into the Po Valley fog.

EMILIA-ROMAGNA

■

S outh of the river Po, bordered by the Apennine Mountains and the Adriatic Sea, Emilia-Romagna is a crazy quilt of provincial spheres of influence. It's joined together by the Roman road, the *via Emilia,* a vital line of communication built by Marcus Aemilius Lep us in A.D. 187. Dominated by ever-changing powers—Etruscans, Romans, barbarians, Guelph-Ghibelline factions, Milanese, Venetians, the Este family, the papal state—the provinces of Emilia-Romagna maintained distinct gastronomic traditions, linked by a theme as important as the *via Emilia:* pasta. In this region pasta-making has become an art form; not only is it homemade, it is *tirata a mano,* hand-stretched (or rolled or thrown, depending on how you interpret the verb *tirare*). This is accomplished with a two-foot-long wooden rolling pin, not a metal machine. The resulting *sfoglia,* a yellow egg yolk–rich, almost paper-thin translucent sheet of pasta, is sliced into thin or wide noodles, triangles, squares, curled around a special comb, or cut and stuffed with meat, cheese, or vegetable fillings that vary from village to village. Pasta is served in broth or simply sauced, to allow the unmasked flavors to stand out.

Both Emilia and Romagna maintain their distinct traditions in spite of their hyphenated union. Emilia's *cucina* is characterized by richness and wealth, the product of a gastronomic paradise with fertile plains of fruit trees and grazing land for livestock, resulting in cream, butter, cheese, and *salumi.* Romagna, in the southeast, has a dual personality of Adriatic seafood and Apennine mountains grilled foods that relate closely to the *cucina* of nearby Toscana.

THE MENU

SALUMI

Coppa • salt-cured boneless ham from Piacenza

Culatello • the "heart" of the prosciutto, made from the choice rump, boned, cured for a year; precious, rare, and costly

Fiocco or *Fiocchetto* • cured ham made from the boneless round, left over after taking out the rump for *culatello*

Mortadella • large, sometimes huge, smooth pork sausage studded with cubes of fat and whole peppercorns

Prosciutto di Parma • salt-cured ham from a limited area near Parma, cured for at least ten to twelve months

Prosciutto Langhirano • salt-cured ham, aged in a specific area within the geographic boundaries of Parma ham

Salame di Felino • fine-grained salami from the village of Felino

Spalla cotta di San Secondo • cured cooked shoulder ham from the village of San Secondo Parmense

Zampone, Cappello da Prete, Cotechino, Salama da sugo • cooked pork sausages, which change name and shape in each province

ANTIPASTO

Bocconotti • vol-au-vents filled with chicken liver, sweetbreads, and sometimes truffles

Burlenghi • pan-fried unleavened pastry covered with a lard, rosemary, and garlic spread

Gnocco • deep-fried pastry, served with prosciutto, culatello, or fresh cheese

Piadina • thin rounds of stone-grilled bread dough, served with prosciutto

Scarpazzone or *Erbazzone* • flan containing spinach, onion, and Parmesan cheese

Tigelle • yeast dough rolled into thin circles and deep-fried or grilled; served at times with a lard, garlic, and rosemary spread

PRIMO

Bomba di riso • baked rice mold with a filling of pigeon, in a rich mushroom sauce

Cappellacci • fresh pasta stuffed with winter squash and cheese

Cappelletti • fresh pasta shaped like an Alpine soldier's hat, stuffed with rich meat and Parmesan cheese

Garganelli • homemade egg pasta formed into ridged quill shapes

Lasagne • homemade pasta layered with meat sauce, béchamel sauce, and Parmesan cheese

Lasagne verdi • lasagne made with fresh homemade spinach pasta

Passatelli • strand-shaped cheese and egg dumplings, served in broth

Pasticcio • baked pie crust filled with pasta and various sauces

Pisarei e fasò • tiny bread dumplings sauced with tomatoes and beans

Tagliatelle • flat strips of homemade egg pasta

Tagliatelle alla romagnola • with fresh tomato sauce

Tagliatelle con ragù or *alla bolognese* • with rich, lusty meat sauce

Tortelli • fresh homemade egg pasta stuffed with cheese and spinach, or with winter squash

Tortellini • fresh homemade egg pasta rings stuffed with meat and cheese, served in broth or with butter and cheese

SECONDO

Baccalà alla bolognese • salt cod cooked with garlic, parsley, and lemon

Bollito misto • mixed boiled meats: beef, pork sausages, tongue, pig's foot, and capon, all served with green sauce and *mostarda,* a fruit chutney

Brodetto • Adriatic fish stew

Capretto alla piacentina, kid cooked in white wine sauce

Costoletta alla bolognese • breaded veal scallop baked with prosciutto, Parmesan cheese, and tomato or meat sauce

Lumache alla bobbiese • shelled snails cooked with celery, leeks, carrots, and wine

Salama da sugo • aged sausage made from various cuts of pork, served with mashed potato purée

Stracotto • pot roast

Trippa alla bolognese • tripe cooked with bacon, garlic, and Parmesan cheese

Zampone • pig's-foot sausage, cooked and served with mashed potatoes or lentils, or with a sauce of whipped egg yolks with balsamic vinegar

CONTORNO

Asparagi alla parmigiana • asparagus served with Parmesan cheese and butter

Cardi alla parmigiana • cardoons served with Parmesan cheese and butter

Tortino di patate • baked layers of mashed potato, Parmesan cheese, and butter

FORMAGGIO

Mascarpone • rich, triple sweet cream

Parmigiano-reggiano • the king of Italian cheese, straw-colored, nutty, and unique

Pecorino • fresh or aged, sheep's milk, distinct

Ricotta • soft, mild fresh cheese made from whey

Squaquarone • fresh, soft, sometimes liquid

DOLCE

Bensone • simple lemon cake sprinkled with almonds

Burricchi • puff pastry squares with almonds

Pan speziale • Christmas dessert of candied and dried fruits, nuts, and spices

Savor • mixed fruit—apples, pears, peaches, quince—and squash, cooked with unfermented wine

Spongata • traditional Christmas cake of nuts, honey, and raisins, enclosed in a pie crust

Torta di taglierini • crunchy cake made with fresh egg pasta, almonds, and candied fruit, in a pastry shell

Zuppa all'emiliana or *zuppa inglese* • rum-soaked sponge cake, layered with custard, preserves, and chocolate

THE *W*INE LIST

Wine production in Emilia-Romagna has traditionally aimed for quantity, turning out beverages of little significance; but wineries Terre Rosse and Castelluccio are producing extraordinary wines, and others are taking notice. The region's most interesting wines are *vino da tavola,* not DOC.

Albana di Romagna is a delicate white, either dry or semi-sweet *(amabile),* and sometimes sparkling. It is Italy's first DOCG white wine, and is made from the Albana grape in the area east of the *via Emilia.* The dry white is well suited to first-course dishes, fish, and seafood. The *amabile* is served with dessert. Top producers include Fratelli Vallunga, Fattoria Paradiso, Tenuta Zerbina, and Tre Monti.

Colli Bolognesi is a DOC zone outside Bologna, where eight different wine varieties are made. The best are fruity **Riesling Italico** and full, dry **Sauvignon,** both whites, and **Cabernet Sauvignon,** an elegant dry red from the Monte San Pietro area, made by Terre Rosse.

The **Colli Piacentini** DOC zone, south of Piacenza, includes eleven wines, most named after grape varieties. Best among them are **Gutturnio,** a dry red served with rich regional dishes, and white **Sauvignon,** paired with first-course pasta and soups. Top producers are Count Otto Barattieri and La Stoppa.

More than 50 million liters of Lambrusco, purplish-red and sparkling, dry or semi-sweet, are made in four different DOC zones. The best is considered to be **Lambrusco di Sorbara.** I have tried to learn to love Lambrusco, and have been defeated. Locals seem to feel it's the best wine for their hearty rich *cucina,* but I have serious doubts. Top producers of Lambrusco are Cavicchioli and Contessa Matilde.

Pagadebit is a delicate dry white made from the nearly extinct Pagadebit grape in the province of Forlì, served with first-course dishes, and ably produced by Fattoria Paradiso.

Sangiovese di Romagna is a dry, grapy red made from the Sangiovese grape in a large area between Bologna and the coast. It is usually paired with rich first-course pasta and sauced meats. Top producers include Fratelli Vallunga, Fattoria Paradiso, Spaletti's Rocca di Ribano, Tenuta Zerbina, and Tre Monti.

Some of the best wines produced in this region come under the classification of **vino da tavola.** Exemplary reds and whites are made by innovative winemakers. Fattoria di Paradiso makes rich red **Barbarossa di Bertinoro.** Terre Rosse by Vallania makes **Malvasia** and **Chardonnay,** elegant whites. Castelluccio di Gianmatteo Baldi makes **Ronco Casone, Ronco dei Ciliegi, Ronco delle Ginestre,** all complex reds, and **Ronco del Re,** a full, rich white, expensive and almost impossible to find. Fratelli Vallunga makes elegant red **Rosso Armentano.** Conte Otto Barattieri makes sparkling white **Chardonnay** and red **Rosso di Vignazzo.** Stoppa makes rich red **Rosso di Rivergaro.** Tre Monti makes **Boldo** and **Favagello,** both Cabernet-Sangiovese blends, and **Tarsallo,** a dry sparkling white.

REGIONAL SPECIALTIES

PASTA

La sfoglia ("the sheet"), golden egg yolk–rich pasta, translucent, paper-thin, elastic and resilient, with an almost leathery texture, achieves glory in the *cucina* of Emilia-Romagna. Sliced into thin or wide noodles, curled around a special comb, or cut and stuffed with meat, cheese, or vegetable fillings, pasta attains true stardom in this region. Is the special quality of this pasta attributable to the body english of the pasta roller (known as the *sfoglina),* a talent acquired with decades of experience? Or to the effect of the porous wooden pin and board, or of the air in which it's made? I am still researching the question, with joyful dedication, every time I cross the gastronomic frontiers of Emilia.

BALSAMIC VINEGAR

Balsamic vinegar, *aceto balsamico,* is made from the juice of Trebbiano grapes, evaporated and concentrated in caldrons directly over fire, and aged in progessively smaller casks of oak, chestnut, cherry, ash, and mulberry. Lengthy aging—anywhere from twelve to over a hundred years—in attic storerooms exposed to winter cold and summer heat causes further evaporation. The result is deep brown, almost syrupy, rich, aromatic, sweet and sour, almost sherry-like in flavor, and costly, at least 40,000 lire (around $30) for a tiny 100-gram bottle (less than four ounces). Less expensive, younger balsamic vinegars are thin, lacking the traditional richness that this unique product acquires with barrel aging. It is meant to be used sparingly, by the drop, on meat, eggs, and *parmigiano.* Local balsamic freaks drink a small amount as a *digestivo,* claiming that it stimulates digestion.

Two main groups, each claiming to be the best, attempt to insure the quality of *aceto balsamico.* Commissions from the *Consorzio* of Modena and the *Confraternita* of Reggio examine balsamic vinegars produced within their specific geographic zones that have aged for at least twelve years, and only those that qualify carry the numbered *Consorzio* or *Confraternita* seals. A third group, the *Consorteria* of Spilamberto, holds a yearly competition to determine the best *aceto balsamico.*

REGIONAL PRODUCERS OF ACETO BALSAMICO

■

Italo Pedroni
Via Risaia 2
Nonantola
Tel. 059/567638

Giuseppe Giusti
Largo S. Giorgio 89
Modena
Tel. 059/235400

Mirella Leonardi Giacobazzi
Via Provinciale Ovest 43
Nonantola
Tel. 059/549065

Cav. Ferdinando Cavalli
Scandiano
Tel. 052/856659

Consorzio Produttori Aceto
Balsamico Tradizionale di
Modena
c/o Camera di Commercio
Via Ganaceto 134
Modena
Tel. 059/222529

PARMIGIANO-REGGIANO

Parmigiano-reggiano, the king of cheese, has been made the same way and in the same area for over 700 years. In the *Decameron* Boccaccio describes Bengodi, a make-believe paradise with a mountain of grated *parmigiano,* topped with people making pasta and rolling it down the slopes to coat it with the cheese.

Each wheel of *parmigiano* is made from around 640 liters (170 gallons) of fresh milk from two successive milkings (the evening milk is skimmed, but the morning milk is added whole). The milk is heated in copper cauldrons, stirred, drained in cheesecloth, pressed into a circular wooden mold to shape the cheese, and finally removed. The newly made cheeses are then soaked in brine and placed on wooden shelves to ripen. After a year the cheese is usually sold to an intermediary for further aging in special rooms that may hold up to 200,000 precious wheels of *parmigiano.* These cheese vaults are frequently managed by banks, who may loan money to the dairy or intermediary against eventual profits. Expert cheese testers tap the wheels of *parmigiano* with a hammer, and the resulting thuds sound out defects to the professional ear. Perfect *parmigiano-reggiano* is firm-textured, straw-colored with pale flecks, fragrant but not pungent, delicate, nutty, studded with crunchy granules (a product of the aging process), and unique. It is in no way related to the hyperprocessed foul-smelling stuff that comes pregrated in a jar, a state in which no cheese can survive naturally. Each dairy that makes *parmigiano-reggiano* stamps its number, assigned by geographical location, on the cheese it produces. Lower numbers are closer to the original production zone between Parma and Reggio, although the one- and two-digit dairies are no longer in existence.

For sources of *parmigiano,* see pages 189 and 200.

EMILIAN HAMS

Pork production is elevated to an art form in Emilia, and, typically enough, each town and province is convinced that its special pork product is the best. *Prosciutto di Parma,* probably the most famous of the Emilian cured hams, is made in a specific geographic area around Parma, of pork thigh meat that, by law, may come from only four regions (Emilia-Romagna, Lombardia, Veneto, and Piemonte). Fresh pork thighs are massaged with salt and hung to age in open-windowed rooms, basking in special local air. (The word *prosciutto* is a dialectical conjugation of the verb *prosciugare,* to dry out.)

PASTA ROLLING PIN

The one-handled wooden rolling pin *(matterello),* traditional in parts of Emilia for pasta making, can be found in housewares stores in the Bologna area. But this object will have no meaning for you until you have seen an actual demonstration of pasta rolling, a manual ballet performed with pasta, pin, and board, gestures executed with a familiarity that comes with

---

TOP PORK PRODUCERS IN EMILIA
■

Consorzio del Prosciutto di Parma
Via Marco dell'Arpa 8/B
Parma
Tel. 0521/208187

Del Porto Arturo
Via S. Michele Cavana
Langhirano Ponte
Tel. 0521/857388
(prosciutto Langhirano)

Pappino Cantarelli
Samboseto
Tel. 0524/90133
Closed Sunday, open shop hours
(culatello and other regional salumi)

Salumificio Boschi
Via G. Verdi 21
Felino
Tel. 0521/835801
(spalla di San Secondo and salame di Felino)

Garetti
Piazza Duomo 44
Piacenza
Tel. 0523/22747
Closed Thursday afternoon
(coppa)

Negroni
Via Aglio 4
Cremona
Tel. 0372/27241
(salame di Felino, coppa, culatello, mortadella, and more)

a lifetime of experience. In Bologna the wielders of the rolling pin roll out a circle of pasta; in Modena they form an oval.

CRAFTS

Linen cloth is decorated with traditional designs in parts of Romagna, and made into tablecloths, napkins, kitchen towels, aprons, bedspreads, and curtains. A paste of minerals, flour, and vinegar is applied to wood blocks, and then pressed onto natural, off-white, coarse linen. Indelibly printed red, green, blue, and most of all, rust-colored country-style patterns of grapes and grape leaves, griffins, roosters, fruits, and flowers are among the traditional designs. See page 197 for one source.

The glazed, richly colored earthenware pottery known as *faience* (French for Faenza) has been produced in Faenza since the end of the thirteenth century. Periods of glory for this majolica *(maiolica)* center were the sixteenth century for decorative items, and the eighteenth and nineteenth centuries for tableware. See page 196 for a museum, an exposition, and a source of reproductions.

CITIES AND TOWNS

ARGENTA

HOTEL
Villa Bolis
Via Corriera 5
Barbiano di Cotignola, near Lugo (close by)
Tel. 0545/79347
Credit cards: American Express, Diners Club
Price: moderate

RESTAURANT
Il Trigabolo
Piazza Garibaldi 4/5
Tel. 0532/804121
Closed Monday evening, Tuesday, and July
Credit cards: all
Price: expensive

Il Trigabolo, in the untouristed village of Argenta, is a restaurant that makes a personal statement. Together with chef Igles Corelli, owner Giacinto Rossetti has created a menu and wine list that follow the contours of his mind and palate. The *cucina* is provocative, nonregional, executed with great professionalism and the best ingredients that the international marketplace has to offer. The decor is low-key; tables are graced with fine stemware, flowers, and *pane ferrarese*, a local twisted bread. Attention is paid to presentation, but don't mistake the food for imitation "nouvelle." The *cucina* is original, and flavors are carefully balanced, contrasted in combinations that are more successful than they may sound. The food is exciting and delicious. Compact, mustachioed Giacinto is passionate about wine, and his selections, especialy the local wines, are a pleasure to drink. Desserts are splendid, especially the pastry, baked by a teen-aged chef with a promising career.

BIBBIANO

CHEESE
Dairy 193—Nuova Barco
Giancarlo Grisendi
Via 24 Maggio 56
Tel. 0522/875182

A visit to Nuova Barco is an instant lesson in *parmigiano*. If you're interested in seeing the cheese-making process, plan to arrive in the morning. All visitors can purchase a chunk for less than store price, and the dairy's always open, Giancarlo told me, because the cows don't go on vacation.

BOLOGNA

Bologna, the heart of Emilia (or of all Italy, according to locals) beats strongly, in spite of the cholesterol content of the extra-rich Bolognese *cucina*. This is the birthplace of the oversized *mortadella*, pink sausage studded with creamy cubes of pork fat, of *tortellini*, forcemeat-stuffed fresh pasta rings, and of *ragù alla bolognese*, richer and headier than a meat sauce—all triumphs of meat and spice, symphonies of flavors. The Bolognese seem to have been impressed by nouvelle cuisine, and many famous restaurants serve "creative" dishes. They are not mentioned here. The splendid medieval towers, Gothic churches, pleasant arcades, and eleventh-century university are a delightful setting for one of Italy's major pasta cults.

HOTEL
Grand Hotel Baglioni
Via Indipendenza 8
Tel. 051/225445
Credit cards: all
Price: luxury

HOTEL
Al Capello Rosso
Via Fusar 9
Tel. 051/261891
Credit cards: all
Price: expensive

HOTEL
Orologio
Via IV Novembre 10
Tel. 051/231253
Credit cards: all
Price: moderate

BAR-CAFFÉ, PASTRY
Roberto
Via Orefici 9/A
Tel. 051/232256
Closed Friday

No smoking is allowed in Roberto's wonderful bar-*pasticceria*. A glass of sparkling water, served on a coaster, is offered to all clients at this always-crowded bar near the market. The coffee is wonderful, triangular sandwiches *(tramezzini)* are fresh, glossy miniature rolls filled with quality *salumi* are tasty snacks, pastry is well made, and the service is rapid and friendly. And all these wonders

Precious balsamic vinegar is measured by the drop.

are available in a smoke-free ambience, rare indeed in Italy. Hooray for Roberto!

MARKET
The Bologna market is too dynamic to limit itself to a single piazza like most Italian cities. It sprawls through the streets—via Orefici, via Mercanzie, via Capraie, via Drapperie—perfumed with produce, packed with residents pinching, poking, sorting, intent on selecting the best before someone else grabs it up. The fruit is especially fine. Mornings only.

CHEESE
La Baita Freo
Via Pescherie Vecchie 3/A
Tel. 051/223940
Closed Thursday afternoon

La Baita Freo has the best selection of cheese in Bologna. Look for *squaquarone,* a fresh, soft, sometimes liquid cheese, and *parmigiano-reggiano.* Nonregional gems include three different ripenesses of *gorgonzola,* a wide selection of *pecorino* sheep's-milk cheeses, at least ten kinds of *mozzarella,* and layered cream cheese and salmon or herb *torte.*

SPECIALTY FOODS
Salsamenteria Tamburini
Via Capraie 1
Tel. 051/234354
Closed Thursday afternoon

The windows and glass display cases of Tamburini are a monument to the *cucina Bolognese,* a triumph of local products, and contain the ingredients for an instant banquet. Butter, cheese, and yogurt made from white buffalo *(bufala)* milk are all first-rate. The selection of *salumi* is overwhelming—choose from over thirty different *prosciutti di Parma, culatello,* and *coppa.* Salami, *zampone* ("big paw") sausage packed in a pig's shin and foot, and various sausages *(insaccati,* "sacked meats") are made by Tamburini using quality meat, salt, and pepper—no extraneous herbs or spices to distract from their intensely porky flavor. The cannon-size *mortadella* sausage is world-class. Thousands of golden handmade *tortellini* in various sizes flank a wood-burning fireplace, where chicken, quail, and large cuts of meat turn on a vertical merry-go-round of spits. The take-out section has over seventy-five prepared dishes and salads. Tamburini is irresistible.

BAKERY
Panetteria e Pastificio Atti
Via Drapperie 6
Tel. 051/33349
Closed Thursday afternoon

Atti's windows are lined with breads in all sizes, shapes, and hues of golden brown, plus homemade pasta, *tortellini, tagliatelle,* and vol-au-vents. Hand-written notes extoll the virtues of these fine products. Cookies, pastries, spiced *pan speziale, torta bolognese di tagliatelle, tagliatelle* cake, and apricot "ravioli" are among Atti's tempting specialties. A second location at via Capraie 7 sells the same fine products.

RESTAURANT
I Caracci
Via Manzoni 2
Tel. 051/20815
Closed Sunday and August
Credit cards: all
Price: expensive

I Caracci is Bologna's most elegant restaurant, with fifteenth-century frescoes on the vaulted ceilings, Empire decor, exquisite flower arrangements, linen, silver, and Ginori china. Waiters in cream-colored jackets are professional and swift. The *cucina* is pure, regional, and consists of perfectly executed classics as well as many hard-to-find specialties. *Tortellini,* small golden gems, are served in a pale but tasty capon broth that enhances the pasta's clever blend of cheese, meat, and spices. Hand-rolled *tagliatelle* are sauced with a rich, lusty Bolognese meat sauce. Meat dishes are well prepared. Desserts are caloric but tempting. The wine list is one of the city's best, with quality local and Italian wines.

RESTAURANT
Antica Osteria Romagnola
Via Rialto 13
Tel. 051/263699
Closed Monday and August
Credit cards: American Express,
*   Diners Club*
Price: high moderate

The Antica Osteria Romagnola feels like a local tavern, with marble tables, a wine-bottle-lined bar, and an attractive red and chrome slicing machine—in use, but displayed like a jewel. Owner Antonio Amura is from Napoli, and his *cucina* is a blend of sturdy Bolognese with southern-style vegetables and herbs. The vast *antipasto* of vegetable salads using seasonal bounty will probably be a complete meal for most diners. Eggplant fans will find their favorite purple-skinned vegetable treated with respect in practically every course. Meat, and fish on Friday, are nicely sauced; desserts are well done and not excessively sweet. The wine selection is good, and even the Lambrusco is drinkable.

RESTAURANT
Da Sandro al Navile
Via Sostegno 15
Tel. 051/6343100
Closed Sunday and August
Credit cards: American Express,
*   Diners Club, MasterCard*
Price: high moderate

Sandro Montanari's restaurant is in a farmhouse on the banks of the Navile canal in suburban Bologna. His wife, Silvana, rules in the kitchen and prepares all the pasta, a task of great importance in Bologna. The ambience is country, with low beamed ceilings, and walls covered with *trattoria* art, gastronomic awards, bottles, and lamps. The tables are set with salmon-colored tablecloths and the heaviest service plates I've ever seen, over six pounds of distressed bronze. Appetizers are interesting, but I can't resist concentrating on the pasta, tasting two or three traditional offerings, each one perfection. The main course is anticlimactic, but the *parmigiano* is worth saving room for. Sandro makes all the desserts—including sweet and gooey trifle-like *paciugo* or simple *ciambella*, a lemony ring-shaped cake. The wine list offers many older Tuscan, Piemontese, and French wines in addition to a few local gems.

Good wine and conversation cap a country lunch.

RESTAURANT

Il Santapaola
Via S. Donato 3
Tel. 051/67276
Closed Sunday evening and
*   Monday*
Credit cards: American Express,
*   Diners Club*
Price: high moderate

Dante Cesari, who practically invented the modern Bolognese restaurant, has recently opened Il Santapaola in the suburb of Quarto Inferiore. He seems to have spared no expense in the nontraditional decor. The *cucina,* however, doesn't resemble the decor, sticking fairly close to tradition. Pasta is splendid, especially *tortellini* served in broth, and the quintessential *lasagne* is worth a detour for lovers of this rich Bolognese specialty. The rich *costoletta alla bolognese* (veal layered with cheese and tomato sauce) is well prepared. Desserts are good, but nothing special. Food this good deserves a better wine selection.

A cook in her kitchen outside of Bologna

HOUSEWARES
Aguzzeria del Cavallo
Via Drapperia 12
Tel. 051/263411
Closed Thursday afternoon
No credit cards

Knives and unusual kitchen accessories are sold in this charming wooden-floored tack shop perfumed with leather and wax. Riding, hunting, and fishing gear are also sold, and have been for the last 205 years, by the Bernagozzi family.

COOKWARE, TABLEWARE
Schiavina
Via Clavature 16
Tel. 051/2233438
Closed Thursday afternoon
Credit cards: American Express,
* MasterCard, Visa*

It seems only logical that the Bolognese would furnish their kitchens and set their tables with the finest. Schiavina has an interesting selection of Italian and imported cookware, crystal, wooden objects, china, and accessories.

*B*ORGO CAPANNE

HOTEL
Santoli
Via Roma 3
Porretta Terme (close by)
Tel. 0534/23206
Credit cards: American Express,
* Diners Club, Visa*
Price: expensive

HOTEL
Bertusi
Via Mazzini 105
Porretta Terme (close by)
Tel. 0534/22072
No credit cards
Price: moderate

RESTAURANT
Trattoria La Volta
Via Comunale della Pieve
Tel. 0534/60401
Closed Tuesday and January
Price: low moderate

La Volta is a rising star on the road known as the Porrettana. Giovanni Valdisseri presides in the rustic dining room, and his wife and sister-in-law work together in the kitchen. The *cucina*'s inspiration is Emilian, although nearby Toscana makes its presence felt, especially in the use of extra virgin olive oil. The *salumi* are local and the pasta is hand-rolled, freshly made, not to be skipped. *Tortellini* are lovely. Mushrooms and truffles are served in season. Desserts are simple and well prepared. Many Tuscan products have traveled the Porrettana with wine merchant–coffee roaster Andrea Trinci (see page 212). The wine selection is intelligent, a pleasure to drink from.

*B*RISIGHELLA

HOTEL
Terme
Viale delle Terme 37
Tel. 0546/81144
No credit cards
Price: moderate

RESTAURANT
La Grotta
Via Metelli 1
Tel. 0546/81829
Closed Tuesday and January
Credit cards: American Express,
* Diners Club, Visa*
Price: inexpensive to moderate

La Grotta is located in a genuine stone grotto, a spectacular backdrop for a special restaurant. The *cucina* is original, the result of a collaboration between chef Antonio Casadio and owner-sommelier Nerio Raccagni, who reminds me of a munchkin. He speaks rapid-fire Italian, as if he can't communicate his passion for everything local fast enough. Three fixed-price menus change daily, offering traditional, light, or more complex meals, created with the best fresh seasonal produce, meat, and fish. The simple, beautifully prepared dishes that exit from the minuscule kitchen are tasty. Nerio seems to know the name of each farmer responsible for each item in the restaurant. The dishes are beautiful hand-painted Faenza pottery (see page 189), and the placemats are rust-dyed, from Gambettola (see page 197). Save room for some of the special cheeses, unavailable elsewhere. Most people seem to enjoy the cereal coffee, which tastes like dirty water to me. Wines are wonderful, beautifully selected, and enhance the *cucina*—especially those of Castelluccio.

OLIVE OIL
Cooperative Agricola
* Brisighellese*
Frantoio Sociale per Olive
Via Firenze 30/A
Tel. 0546/81103

Cholesterol-loving Emilians practically scorn the use of full-flavored extra virgin olive oil, but it is used to advantage in the cooking of Romagna. A small amount of quality oil is produced in the Brisighella area by a local farmers' cooperative. It can be purchased here or at La Grotta (page 193).

CASALECCHIO DI RENO

HOTELS
See Grand Hotel Baglioni; Al Capello Rosso; and Orologio in Bologna (page 190).

RESTAURANT
Biagi
Via Porettana 273
Tel. 051/572063
Closed Sunday evening and Tuesday
No credit cards
Price: low moderate

The Ristorante Biagi, just off the Casalecchio exit of the *autostrada* a few minutes south of Bologna, looks like an annex of the AGIP gas station next door. The decor is quintessential *trattoria*, tidy, with small copper kettles of flowers on the tables. The *cucina* is classic, pure Bolognese, perfected by years of experience. Stick to the local specialties and do not miss the exquisite tiny *tortellini* (ten to the soupspoon), served in a tasty broth that lets the splendid tastes and textures of this dish sing out. The *cotechino* or *zampone* (cooked pork sausages) and the *costoletta alla bolognese* (breaded fried veal topped with melted cheese, wrapped with prosciutto) are served with mashed potatoes that are the essence of comfort food. Finish your meal with the superb homemade *gelato*, either egg yolk–rich custard *(crema)* for the intrepid or light lemony ice *(sorbetto di limone)* for the faint-hearted. Wines aren't up to the rest of the experience. Postcard collectors will be thrilled by the souvenir card of Ivano Biagi in the kitchen with his *tortellini* crafters.

CASTELFRANCO EMILIA

RESTAURANT-INN
Gaidello Club
Via Gaidello 18
Tel. 059/926806
Closed Sunday, Monday, and August
No credit cards
Price: moderate

The Gaidello Club isn't really a club. It's three rustic apartments in a restored farmhouse plus a reservations-only fixed-menu restaurant, all on a working farm in the flat Emilian countryside, owned and run by Paola Bini. The restaurant is in a carefully restored hayloft, and the setting is perfect for the meal that unfolds, with its family-type service and home-style *cucina*. Rustic unpuréed soups and pasta are delicious. Featherweight *gnocco* and *crescentina* (fried breads) are served with tasty *salumi* and onions marinated in balsamic vinegar. Chicken, rabbit, guinea hen, vegetables, and fruit all come from the farm and are full-flavored. Fresh fruit tart and *frutta sotto spirito* (liquor-soaked cherries, grapes, and apricots) are topped with whipped cream. Wines are from the farm, and not up to the quality of the *cucina*. The apartments are an ideal base for touring the area, and you'll be close to Nonantola, home of one of the area's great restaurants (see page 197).

CASTELVETRO

HOTEL
Canalgrande
Corso Canal Grande 6
Modena (close by)
Tel. 059/217160
Credit cards: all
Price: expensive

HOTEL
Green Park
Via Giardini 440
Casinalbo (close by)
Tel. 059/511200
Credit card: Visa
Price: moderate

RESTAURANT
Al Castello
Piazza Roma 7
Tel. 059/790276
Closed Monday
Credit cards: American Express, Diners Club, MasterCard
Price: high moderate

Located in a castle, this restaurant serves classic regional *cucina* with a Modenese accent. The *salumi* are served with whole-wheat fried pasta pillows *(crescenta fritta)* and crunchy purple pickled onions, a sensational trio of tastes. Homemade pasta is fine, especially the *tortellini*. The *fritto misto*—a procession of deep-fried seasonal vegetables, meats, flowers, and even a fried rice pudding—is nicely done. Meat dishes are anticlimactic, but the *parmigiano* is splendid. Finish with strawberries and balsamic vinegar, a local classic combination, made with owner Mario Pelloni's vinegar. Visit the attic across the street, where he makes his wonderful vinegar, for sale—along with preserves, pickled onions, and other fine homemade products—in La Vecchia Dispensa, "The Old Pantry," adjacent to the restaurant. Local wines are disappointing, and the non-locals are expensive. Dine under canvas umbrellas on the terrace when the weather is nice.

CASTROCARO TERME

HOTEL
Prati
Via Samori 6
Tel. 0543/767531
Credit cards: American Express, MasterCard, Visa
Price: moderate

HOTEL
Eden
Via Samori 11
Tel. 0543/767600
Credit cards: American Express, MasterCard, Visa
Price: moderate

RESTAURANT
La Frasca
Via Matteotti 34
Tel. 0543/767471
Closed Tuesday, January, and July
Credit cards: American Express, Diners Club, MasterCard
Price: expensive

La Frasca is considered one of Italy's gastronomic temples, but I found Gianfranco Bolognesi's restaurant a series of contrasts, not all of them harmonious. The intimate rustic stone dining rooms have odd touches of sophistication. The table is set with silver candelabra, long-stemmed glassware, and Faenza pottery dinnerware. The tone is hushed and formal. The *cucina* has, until recently, been exclusively creative, composed of overly delicate perfumes, occasionally using quality local products. Large and small tasting menus give a perspective of this inventive, somewhat bland, but perfectly executed *cucina*. The third and newest of the fixed menus is called *Sapore di Romagna*, "The Tastes of Romagna," and it features samples of hearty regional food, professionally prepared. Enjoy *garganelli* (handmade pasta with a rich, velvety *ragù* sauce), stuffed rabbit, and other decisively flavored dishes. The cheese is especially fine, and desserts are beautifully presented. Gianfranco's wine cellar is one of Italy's finest, and his regional selections are impeccable. A small gift shop sells beautiful rust-stamped table linens and Faenza ceramics.

CAVRIAGO

HOTEL
Posta
Piazza Cesare Battisti 4
Reggio nell'Emilia (close by)
Tel. 0522/32944
Credit cards: all
Price: low expensive

HOTEL
Ariosto
Via San Rocco 12
Reggio nell'Emilia (close by)
Tel. 0522/37320
Credit cards: all
Price: moderate

RESTAURANT
Picci
Via XX Settembre 2
Tel. 0522/57201
Closed Monday, Tuesday, and August
Credit cards: American Express, MasterCard
Price: high moderate

Raffaele Piccirilli, known as Picci, is crazy about mushrooms and goose. He has composed a menu based on his passions, with three tasting meals. Two are studies in monomania, devoted to mushrooms and goose products, which turn up everywhere but dessert. The third menu is seasonal. They are all good excuses for avoiding the seemingly exhaustive options of Picci's five-page menu. *Salumi* are first-rate, and mushroom dishes, usually available spring through fall, are well done. Grilled lamb chops with Picci's own balsamic vinegar are a splendid combination. The wine list is as exhaustive as the menu, and Italian, French, and even Californian, but especially regional, selections are fine, although the Lambrusco is, as usual, disappointing.

COLLECCHIO

HOTELS
See Park Hotel Stendahl and Button in Parma (page 198)

RESTAURANT
Ceci
Villa Maria Luigia
Tel. 0521/805489
Closed Thursday, most of August, and January
Credit cards: American Express, Diners Club, MasterCard
Price: expensive

Villa Luigia, surrounded by manicured lawn and massive trees, is an elegant restaurant in the grand Parma tradition. The daily menu is aimed mainly at locals bored with familiar dishes, but the regional *cucina* is well done. *Culatello,* the heart of the *prosciutto,* is pale pink, sweet, and delicate. The homemade stuffed pasta—*tortelli* and *anolini*—are glorious, and the *stracotto* (beef braised for two days in red wine) is tasty. A nontraditional "fantasy" of grilled vegetables was a welcome sight in this region that regards anything without cholesterol with suspicion. The *parmigiano-reggiano* is fantastic. Desserts are hypercaloric, although the small pastries *(piccola pasticceria)* are irresistible. The wine list is strong on Friulian white wines and Piemontese and Tuscan reds.

FAENZA

MUSEUM
**Museo Internazionale della
  Ceramica**
Via Campidori 2
Tel. 0546/21240
Closed Monday

The Museo Internazionale della Ceramica documents the history of the ceramic arts of all ages and countries, and its fine collection includes beautifully displayed examples of prehistoric, pre-Columbian, Italian Renaissance, and Faenza pottery as well as more modern pieces by Chagall, Matisse, and Picasso.

EXPOSITION
**Manifestazione Internazionale
  della Ceramica d'Arte**

**Contemporanea/Mostra
Antiquariato di Ceramica**
Palazzo Esposizioni
Corso Mazzini 92
Tel. 0546/22294

Faenza hosts one of Europe's most important modern ceramics competitions in July (odd-numbered years) and an antique ceramics exposition in late September (even-numbered years). For more information call the Palazzo Esposizioni.

TABLEWARE
Gatti di Dante Servadei
Via Pompignoli 4
Tel. 0546/30556
No credit cards

The best reproductions of traditional Faenza pottery are made by Dante Servadei. The Gatti studio, where he has always worked, was founded in 1928, and all work is still done by hand. Traditional designs from the eighteenth century are beautifully executed; the carnation *(garofano),* acorn *(ghiande),* and vine-leaf *(foglio di vite)* patterns are personal favorites. Dante welcomes visitors to his workshop-showroom, so that they can see the process involved in the creation of his lovely *faenza* pottery. The store in piazza della Libertà (closed Monday) doesn't have the same selection and lacks the excitement of the workshop.

FORLIMPOPOLI

HOTEL
Grand Hotel Cervia
Lungomare Grazia Deledda 9
Cervia (close by)
Tel. 0544/970500
**Credit cards: American Express,
  Diners Club, MasterCard**
Price: expensive

HOTEL
Nettuno
Lungomare D'Annunzio 34
Cervia (close by)
Tel. 0544/72325
**Credit cards: American Express,
  Diners Club, Visa**
Price: moderate

RESTAURANT
Al Maneggio
Selbagnone
Tel. 0543/742042
Closed Monday
**Credit cards: American Express,
  Diners Club, MasterCard**
**Price: high moderate to
  expensive**

Forlimpopoli is the birthplace of Pellegrino Artusi, the Italian Fanny Farmer. And even though Artusi's house has been turned into a bank, the gastronomic reputation of the city lives on, thanks to Bruna Sebastiani in the dining room and her husband, Giorgio, in the kitchen and in the cellars of this seventeenth-century countryside villa. The menu takes advantage of the finest products that Romagna has to offer and treats them with respect. The home-style salami is wonderful. Homemade pasta, especially with field greens like *strigoli* (poppy stems), is a treat to find, a sign of Giorgio's dedication to his regional *cucina.* The *manzetta brasata* (braised beef) is tasty, and the cheese is a hard-to-find local treasure. Wines are a complement to the *cucina,* and include fine regional and Italian selections.

GAMBETTOLA

TABLE LINENS
Antica Bottega Pascucci
Via Verdi 18
Tel. 0547/53056
No credit cards

The Pascucci family has been hand-stamping cloth for seven generations in Gambettola. The workshop smells decidedly of the vinegar used in the printing process (see page 189). The shop has a fine selection of ready-made items, but you can also special-order a hard-to-find size or a pattern chosen from their collection of antique hand-carved pearwood blocks. A small catalogue, with designs numbered for easier identification, is available.

IMOLA

HOTEL
Villa Bolis
Via Corriera 5
Barbiano di Cotignola, near Lugo (close by)
Tel. 0545/79347
Credit cards: American Express, Diners Club
Price: moderate

RESTAURANT
San Domenico
Via Sacchi 1
Tel. 0542/29000
Closed Monday
Credit cards: American Express, Diners Club, Visa
Price: expensive

In spite of chef Valentino Mercatilii's expertise and Gianluigi Morini's splendid cellars, I didn't like dining at San Domenico. It seemed so formal, smug, and condescending, so unlike what I look for in a restaurant, that I never went back for a second try. The menu proudly declares its dedication to the "culinary traditions of the antique noble families of Italy," who, Mr. Morini informed me, ate the best, most luxurious food that money could buy, paying no attention to region or season. I found the food insipid, a bit too precious. Breads and pastry, baked twice daily, were the high points of the meal. The wine list is one of Italy's finest—incredible wines at incredibly high prices. Mr. Morini has opened a San Domenico restaurant in New York, dividing his time and part of the kitchen brigade between Imola and the Big Apple. Will this alter the San Domenico experience?

RESTAURANT
Osteria del Vicolo Nuovo
Via Codronchi 6
Tel. 0542/32552
Closed Monday
No credit cards
Price: moderate

Lack of pretention and an excellent, extensive, well-priced wine list attracted me to the unknown Osteria del Vicolo Nuovo. The *cucina* is creative, which seems to be a tradition in Imola, but the *salumi,* cheeses, sandwiches, and soups are tasty. The daily six-course tasting menu is reasonably priced, and the wine suggestions are interesting.

NONANTOLA

HOTEL
Canalgrande
Corso Canal Grande 6
Modena (close by)
Tel. 059/217160
Credit cards: all
Price: expensive

HOTEL
Green Park
Via Giardini 440
Casinalbo (close by)
Tel. 059/511200
Credit card: Visa
Price: moderate

RESTAURANT
Osteria di Rubbiara
Via Risaia 2
Rubbiara
Tel. 059/549019
Closed Sunday evening, Tuesday, and August
Credit cards: American Express, MasterCard
Price: moderate

It's impossible to hide my enthusiasm for the Osteria di Rubbiara, opened in 1862 by host Italo Pedroni's great-great-grandfather. I love the little grocery store out front, the *acetaia* next door, where Italo makes some of the best balsamic vinegar in Emilia (winner of the Spilamberto Palio in '77, '79, and '81), and the room downstairs where he makes eleven different types of fruit *liquore,* following Grandmother Claudia's recipes. The kitchen is powered by his wife, Franca, and his mother, Irma, who roll out some of the tastiest pasta I've ever eaten—alone worth the trip. Italo served his last *antipasti* five years ago, he told me, because they were ruining appetites, detracting from the stellar first courses. Mom's paper-thin hand-rolled pasta is simply treated to butter and a sprinkling of *parmigiano,* or elegantly dressed with a *ragù* that's more than just another meat sauce. Meats are anticlimactic, but don't skip the *frittata all'aceto balsamico* or the plain boiled potatoes, elevated to glory by Italo's balsamic vinegar. Clean your plate or Mom will be upset, and watch out for the bathrooms: *Dann'* is for women, *Ann'* is the men's room. Italo's own wines are well suited to the *cucina*, but a small selection of more elegant wines is also available. Reservations are a must.

PARMA

Parma, important jewel on the necklace of the *via Emilia*, greatly influenced culturally and artistically by France, had moments of glory as the dukedom of Maria Luigia, ex-Empress, wife of Napoleon II. Pastry, *prosciutto, parmigiano,* and pasta are the essence of Parma's gastronomic tradition. The *parmigiana* treatment—sprinkled with grated *parmigiano-reggiano* cheese and butter, and baked until brown and crisped—is given mostly to worthy vegetables. Unfortunately some restaurants in town seem to be thriving on past laurels.

HOTEL
Park Hotel Stendhal
Piazzetta Bodoni 3
Tel. 0521/208057
Credit cards: all
Price: expensive

HOTEL
Button
Strada San Vitale 7
Tel. 0521/208039
Credit cards: all
Price: moderate

MARKET
Piazza della Ghiaia
Open weekday mornings, and all day Saturday

The components of Parma's elaborate *cucina* can be found in the exciting outdoor and covered market in Piazza della Ghiaia and in the nearby grocery shops, festooned with fragrant *salumi* and decked out with shining chubby forms of *parmigiano-reggiano.*

SPECIALTY FOODS
Salumeria Garibaldi
Via Garibaldi 42
Tel. 0521/35606
Closed Thursday afternoon and August

The Salumeria Garibaldi has a good selection of local *salumi,* and has all three traditional cuts of pork leg: *culatello,* the heart of the prosciutto; *fiocchetto,* the other part of the prosciutto, minus the *culatello;* and roasted *stinco* shin. The take-out section offers some great picnic options.

CHEESE
Otello Dall'Asta
Via E. Copelli 2/E
Tel. 0521/33788
Closed Thursday afternoon

Otello Dall'Asta sells lovely *parmigiano-reggiano,* selected from different dairies. He usually has three or four different years of cheese available, as well as *tenero,* which is unripened, fresh, sweet *parmigiano,* found only in this area. Although they're probably wonderful, Otello's other cheeses seem like a distraction from his splendid, fragrant *parmigiano-reggiano,* which is what this shop is all about.

RESTAURANT
Cocchi
Via Gramsci 16
Tel. 0521/91990

Closed Saturday and August
Credit cards: all
Price: high moderate

Ristorante Cocchi serves classic regional *cucina* with a Parma accent. *Salumi,* especially *culatello* and *spalla di San Secondo* (cooked shoulder ham) are wonderful. Homemade, hand-rolled pasta is well done, and second-course *trippa alla parmigiana* (Parma-style tripe) and *bollito misto* (mixed boiled meats), served at lunch only, are tasty. Salads are dressed with a selection of extra virgin olive oils. Corrado Cocchi and son-sommelier Daniele preside in the dining room, and the wines they offer are fine, well suited to this typical restaurant.

RESTAURANT
La Greppia
Strada Garibaldi 39
Tel. 0521/33686
Closed Thursday, Friday, and July
Credit cards: all
Price: expensive

The menu of Maurizio Rossi's restaurant, La Greppia, is filled with nouvelle-inspired inventions for locals bored with the same old home-style cooking. But the regional dishes that I'm looking for are also prepared here. Choose the excellent *culatello* (heart of the prosciutto) or any of the handmade stuffed pasta. *Stracotto* (braised beef, cooked for eight hours) can be cut with a fork. The wide selection of vegetables is a welcome surprise in this meat-oriented region. Desserts are interesting, especially the green tomato tart, and the wines are fine.

A glorious display of hand-rolled pasta with its creator

RESTAURANT
Antica Osteria Fontana
Via Farini 24/A
Tel. 0521/26037
Closed Sunday and July
No credit cards
Price: inexpensive

Join the students and locals at the bar, or sit down at the tables of the Antica Osteria Fontana and order some of their first-rate *salumi* tucked into tasty sandwiches. The *principe,* "prince," sandwich of young *grana* cheese and *prosciutto* is a popular choice. Quality wines, reasonably priced, are sold by the glass or the bottle.

TOSCANINI MUSEUM
Casa di Toscanini
Via R. Tanzi 13
Tel. 0521/35964
Closed Monday

One of the few calorie-free experiences in Emilia. For a nice pause from eating, visit the birthplace of Arturo Toscanini, a small museum filled with souvenirs and relics of the grand *maestro*'s musical career.

PIACENZA

Piacenza is a lively, bustling agricultural center south of the mighty Po River, on the gastronomic frontier that divides Emilia from neighboring Lombardia. Rose-colored brick piazza dei Cavalli, with its equestrian statues and impressive town hall, Il Gotico, is worth a visit. *Pisarei,* tiny dumplings dressed with beans and tomato sauce, are a local specialty not to be found elsewhere. The market, held on Wednesday and Saturday mornings in piazza del Duomo, hums with a special excitement and seems to electrify the whole city.

HOTEL
Il Sole
Via Trabattoni 32
Maleo (close by)

Tel. 0377/58142
Credit card: American Express
Price: expensive

HOTEL
Grand Albergo Roma
Via Cittadella 14
Tel. 0523/23201
Credit cards: all
Price: high moderate

BAR-CAFFÈ, PASTRY
Pasticceria Daniel Durand
Corso Vittorio Emanuele 82
Tel. 0523/23656
Closed Sunday

The pastry in my favorite bar in Piacenza is made by Frenchman Daniel Durand, a fan of bicycle racing and a friend of American cyclist Greg LeMond. This explains the miniature bicycle on the bar and the French and American flags in the entrance. The croissants *(cornetti)* are always fresh, and the tiny two-bite sandwiches are irresistible.

SPECIALTY FOODS
Garetti
Piazza Duomo 44
Tel. 0523/22747
Closed Thursday afternoon

The Garetti brothers and their wives proudly make and sell tasty *salumi*. Their sausage, *prosciutto,* and *pancetta* are first-rate, but gastronomic heights are reached with their splendid *coppa,* made from a cut of pork near the neck, and their *salame piacentino,* a special family recipe created three generations ago by the founder of their gastronomic dynasty. Takeout cold salads are interesting.

RESTAURANT
Antica Osteria del Teatro
Via Verdi 16
Tel. 0523/23777
Closed Sunday and August
Credit cards: American Express,
*   Diners Club, MasterCard*
Price: expensive

The Antica Osteria del Teatro has always been a duet featuring host-sommelier Franco Ilari and his former chef, Georges Cogny. A brilliant French chef who paired with Franco for the first years of the restaurant, Monsieur Cogny added a decidedly francophile spirit to the menu. But he has since moved to Farini, where he has founded a place of his own, Locanda Cantoniera. The kitchen at the Antica Osteria del Teatro is now headed by co-proprietor Filippo Chiappini-Dattilo, who is young, local, intelligent, and highly skilled, and who has brought a breath of life to this formal (but not uncomfortable) restaurant. The 1400s palace setting has been carefully restored, revealing wooden ceilings, stone, and brick. Honey-colored walls, indirect lighting, and modern but comfortable seating in three dining rooms create an intimate ambience. The à la carte menu features a perfectly executed innovative *cucina,* a bit precious at times. A tasting menu has been joined by a regional menu, cooked with professionalism. Cheese is local, and fine. Desserts are memorable. Franco Ilari's wines, especially the unknown, hard-to-find locals, are a pleasure.

PORTO GARIBALDI

HOTEL
Villa Bolis
Via Corriera 5
Bariano di Cotignola, near Lugo
*   (close by)*
Tel. 0545/79347
Credit cards: American Express,
*   Diners Club*
Price: moderate

RESTAURANT
Il Sambuco
Via Caduti del Mare 30
Tel. 0533/327478
Closed Monday
Credit cards: American Express,
*   Diners Club, MasterCard*
Price: expensive

Il Sambuco is one of the few reasons I can think of to go to the coast of Emilia-Romagna. Fish is fresh and lively, well prepared by Achille Maccanti with the assistance of his mother, Gina. The grilled seafood is splendid. Sometimes the *cucina* strays from the classics, but tastes are well combined. The selection of extra virgin olive oils is impressive. Desserts are delicious, especially the homemade fruit ices. The wine list is, without a doubt, the best on Emilia-Romagna's coast, focusing logically on white wines, and Il Sambuco also offers a wide choice of whiskeys and *grappa.*

REGGIO NELL'EMILIA

CHEESE
Dairy 122—Due Madonne
Ernesto Gabbi
Via Abramo Lincoln 3
Tel. 0522/512151

Outside the city of Reggio nell'Emilia, at the end of a dead-end street with no street signs, Ernesto Gabbi's dairy makes and sells quality *parmigiano.* Prices are reasonable and they're always open.

RUBIERA

RESTAURANT-HOTEL
Arnaldo—Aquila d'Oro
Piazza XXIV Maggio 3
Tel. 0522/62124
Closed Sunday and August
Credit cards: American Express,
*   Diners Club*
Price: moderate

It's hard to resist a restaurant that subtitles itself a *clinica gastronomica.* Housed in a fifteenth-century gem of a country house, with wooden beams, terracotta floors, and frescoed friezes, Ristorante Arnaldo offers a charming setting for a marathon of a meal. Regional *cucina* triumphs, hearty and heavy. The *salumi* are tasty, especially the *prosciutto di Parma* and *mortadella. Tortellini,* served in a purist's broth, and the morel mushroom lasagna are specialties. A serving cart is crowded with a selection of six or seven different roast meats, including guinea hen (*faraona*) cooked in a strange red crust. The *bollito* misto (mixed boiled) meats are served with green sauce and *mostarda*—spicy pickled whole fruit, an acquired taste. The vegetable cart, with its bowls of raw and cooked seasonal produce, to be dressed with olive oil and vinegar, is a welcome sight. Desserts may tempt the intrepid, and the *spazzacamino* ("chimney sweep") tisane guarantees that you'll digest everything you've eaten. Choosing a fine wine may be difficult. Thirty-six reasonably priced, attractive, modern, air-conditioned rooms make this "clinic" a comfortable base for touring the area.

SALA BAGANZA

HOTELS
See Park Hotel Stendhal and Button in Parma (page 198)

RESTAURANT
Da Eletta
Via Campi 3
Tel. 0521/833304
Closed Monday, Tuesday, and the second half of August
Price: high moderate

Eletta Violi, who cooked at Cantarelli (see below), continues with her impeccable *cucina* in Sala Baganza. Husband Ivan selects fine local *salumi* from farmers working with traditional methods: *culatello, spalla di San Secondo,* Langhirano *prosciutto,* and salami from Felino. Pasta is rolled out by hand, and the *cappelletti* and *anolini* (stuffed pastas) and *tagliatelle* are worth a detour. Meats are cooked home-style, with rich, earthy sauces. Save room for dessert. The great difficulty of dining at Trattoria da Eletta is deciding what to skip—I always want to taste practically everything. The wines are an asset

to the meal, and reservations are a must.

SAMBOSETO

HOTEL
I Due Foscari
Piazza Carlo Rossi 15
Busseto
Tel. 0524/92337
Credit cards: Visa, MasterCard
Price: moderate

SPECIALTY FOODS
Cantarelli
Località Samboseto
Tel. 0524/90133
Closed Sunday
No credit cards

Peppino Cantarelli created a legendary restaurant here, one of the first to emphasize quality wines with simple home-style regional Italian cooking, prepared by his wife, Mirella. They officially closed the restaurant at the end of 1982, but Peppino still sells his excellent *prosciutto, salame di Felino,* and *parmigiano,* as well as his own wine. Taste the *culatello* and you'll begin to understand why this unassuming grocery store still attracts a faithful following, who return to stock up on Peppino's fine regional products and to get a glimpse of the restaurant, looking somewhat diminished, that formed some of Italy's finest palates.

TREBBO DI RENO

RESTAURANT-HOTEL
Il Sole–Antica Locanda del Trebbo
Via Lame 67
Tel. 051/700102 or 700290
Closed Sunday
Credit cards: all
Price: high moderate

Il Sole, also called Antica Locanda del Trebbo, is a rising star on Emilia's restaurant scene. The 120-year-old inn has recently been restored by new owners, a trio of experienced professionals who seem to be doing everything right. Beamed ceilings and terracotta floors are a pleasing backdrop for the *cucina* of regional and innovative specialties. *Salumi* are well chosen. All pasta is hand-rolled daily. Thursday's menu is devoted to beautifully prepared fish at its freshest. Desserts and *gelato* are homemade, and hard to resist. Chef Luigi Moretti prepares traditional specials at lunch, but cuts loose in the evening with dishes of his own invention in addition to the classics. His wife, Paola, and partner, Guido Paolato, complement the well-prepared *cucina* with wines of distinction, both local and from the rest of Italy. Dining outdoors is a pleasure in the summer. Sample the *grappa* collection, and then spend the night in one of Il Sole's twenty rooms.

Pieve Fosciana

Castelnuovo Di Garfagnana
Abetone
Ponte A Moriano
San Giorgio A Colonica
Pieve Santo Stefano ·Pietrasanta
Montecatini Terme ·Prato
Forte Dei Marmi ·Camaiore
Ponte Attigliano
·Lucca
Viareggio
Borgo A Buggiano
·Sesto Fiorentino
Fucecchio
Artimino ·Firenze
Pisa
Montelupo Cerbaia ·Impruneta
Castelfranco Di Sopra
San Casciano In Val Di Pesa
·Greve Sansepolcro
Lari
San Giovanni ·Valdarno Anghiari
Panzano Gaiole In Chianti
Colle Di Val D'Elsa

Siena ·

Sinalunga
Montefollonico
San Vincenzo ·
Trequanda
·Pienza

Cetona ·

Saturnia
Fonte Blanda ·

TOSCANA

∎

Toscana seems to have the best of everything: art, architecture, archeological wonders, soft rolling countryside, mountain forests, and pastures—all less than a couple of hours from the coast and the Tyrrhenian Sea. Three tonalities of green—olive, cypress, and grapevine—color the landscape, mostly unchanged from the background of Renaissance paintings. Political loyalty is a temporary sentiment in Toscana. Beginning with the Etruscan Confederation in the eighth century B.C. a series of invasions, power struggles, and alliances by Romans, Lombards, Medici, Guelphs (backed by the Vatican) and Ghibellines (backed by the emperor) kept the Tuscan provinces suspicious and separate, alike only in their accent, with its aspirated "c," and in their condiment of choice, *olio d'oliva extra vergine*.

The *cucina toscana* is dominated by bread and oil. Bread appears in every course, from appetizer to dessert, even as a snack. *Schiacciata*, literally "crushed," is flattened dough baked with olive oil, or in the fall, sweetened with sugar and studded with purple wine grapes, just as it's depicted in Etruscan frescoes. Bread is also enriched with egg yolks and orange rind, and dusted with a heavy layer of powdered sugar, for a carnival dessert. Unsalted country loaves are paired with *companatico*, defined as anything that's eaten with bread, from *prosciutto* to preserves. Bread is sliced into thick slabs, grilled, rubbed with garlic, and dipped into extra virgin olive oil, or skewered between pieces of sausage and pork liver punctuated with bay leaves. *Ribollita* and *pappa*, hearty country soups, are thickened with stale bread.

All through Toscana the olive tree's once gnarled, ancient trunk has been cut back, after the disastrous freeze of 1985, reduced to what looks like a shrub with silvery gray-green leaves. Its fruit, hand-harvested in the late fall, stone-crushed, and pressed between woven mats, is transformed into murky green extra virgin olive oil, peppery tasting and almost effervescent when fresh, more transparent and less pungent when the sediment filters out after a month or two. The flavor of this special oil is felt throughout the *cucina toscana*.

Prosciutto, salami, or sausage made from pork or wild boar, and *crostini* (liver pâté appetizers) start off most traditional meals in Toscana. Meat and poultry are either roasted, grilled, or fried, and the accompanying lemon wedge is the Tuscan idea of a sauce. Vegetables are simply cooked or eaten raw, but always dressed with extra virgin olive oil. Traditional desserts are uncomplicated cakes and cookies flavored with spices, nuts, or dried fruit, served with a glass of *vin santo*, an aromatic dessert wine.

I live in Toscana, and I love the proud simplicity of its *cucina*. I am captivated by the Tuscans, the countryside, the light, and the oil. Living and traveling in Italy, I've discovered new foods—some so elegant, harmonious, and beautifully prepared that I've wondered what can I possibly eat at home after this kind of experience? Simple: bread and oil.

THE MENU

SALUMI

∎

Finocchiona ▪ pork sausage flavored with fennel seeds

Prosciutto di cinghiale ▪ salt- and air-cured wild boar ham

Salame toscano ▪ pork sausage studded with pepper and cubes of fat

Salsicce fresche (or secche) ▪ fresh (or dried) sausage of pork or wild boar

Soprassata or *soppressata* ▪ head cheese; cooked sausage made from pig's head, with spices and lemon peel

ANTIPASTO

∎

Crostini ▪ traditional minced chicken liver canapés

Crostini di milza ▪ canapés of minced sautéed spleen

Donzelle or *Donzelline* ▪ fried dough balls

Fettunta or *Bruschetta* ▪ slab of toasted country bread rubbed with garlic and dipped in tasty extra virgin olive oil, sprinkled with salt and pepper

PRIMO

∎

Acquacotta ▪ vegetable mushroom soup served over toasted bread and topped with a poached egg

Cacciucco ▪ coastal fish stew with tomatoes, chili pepper, and red wine

Carabaccia ▪ onion soup

Cavolo con le fette ▪ cooked black cabbage on garlic bread, moistened with cabbage broth and liberally dressed with olive oil

Garmugia ▪ springtime vegetable soup made with tender fava beans, peas, artichokes, asparagus tips, and bacon

Gnocchi di ricotta ▪ dumplings filled with ricotta and spinach

Infarinata ▪ vegetable soup thickened with cornmeal

Minestra di farro ▪ emmer and bean soup

Panzanella ▪ summer salad of tomatoes, basil, cucumber, onion, and bread, dressed with olive oil

Pappa col pomodoro ▪ tomato soup thickened with bread, enriched with olive oil at the table

Pappardelle sulla (or alla) lepre ▪ homemade egg pasta noodles with a wild rabbit sauce

Penne strascicate ▪ quill-shaped pasta "dragged through" a meat sauce

Pici ▪ hand-rolled egg pasta that looks like thick, short spaghetti

Ravioli or *Tortelli* ▪ ravioli filled with spinach and ricotta

Ribollita or *Minestra di Pane* ▪ hearty winter vegetable soup thickened with bread, enriched with olive oil at the table

Risotto nero ▪ rice cooked with cuttlefish and its black ink, and, at times, Swiss chard

Zuppa di fagioli ▪ vegetable soup dominated by beans

FORMAGGIO

∎

Pecorino ▪ fresh or aged, made from sheep's milk

Raveggiolo ▪ soft, fresh, made from sheep's-milk whey, delicate and hard to find

Ricotta ▪ soft, fresh, mild, made from whey

SECONDO

Arista • roast pork loin with garlic and rosemary

Asparagi alla fiorentina (or alla Bismark) • asparagus topped with melted butter, a fried egg, and cheese

Baccalà alla livornese • salt cod cooked with garlic, tomatoes, and parsley

Bistecca alla fiorentina • T-bone steak at least two inches thick, charcoal-grilled

Cibreo • stew of chicken livers, unlaid eggs, and cockscomb

Cieche (or Cèe) alla pisana • tiny baby eels cooked with garlic and tomatoes, served with Parmesan cheese

Fritto misto • mixed fried foods, usually chicken, rabbit or lamb chops, and vegetables: zucchini, zucchini flowers, artichokes, potatoes, winter squash, green or ripe tomatoes, mushrooms, and *polenta*

Lombatina • veal chop, usually grilled

Peposo • peppery beef stew

Pollo alla diavola or *al mattone* • chicken flattened with a brick, grilled with herbs

Scottiglia • mixed stew of veal, game, and poultry, cooked with white wine and tomatoes

Spiedini di maiale • pork loin cubes and pork liver spiced with fennel, skewered with bread and bay leaves, and grilled or spit-roasted

Stracotto • pot roast

Tonno con fagioli • tuna served with white beans and raw onion

Totani (or seppie) all'inzimino • cuttlefish (or squid) cooked with Swiss chard and tomatoes

Triglie alla livornese • red mullet cooked with tomatoes, garlic, and parsley

Trippa alla fiorentina • tripe cooked with tomatoes, served with Parmesan cheese

CONTORNO

Fagioli al fiasco • boiled white beans (once cooked in a *fiasco*, wine flask, slowly, in the ashes of the country hearth)

Fagioli all'olio • white beans served with olive oil

Fagioli all'uccelletto • white beans cooked with tomatoes, garlic, and sage

Frittata (or tortino) di carciofi • pan-fried (or oven-baked) artichoke flan

Pinzimonio • raw seasonal vegetables dipped in lively extra virgin olive oil, salt, and pepper

DOLCE

Biscottini di Prato, or *cantucci* • dried almond cookies, served with dessert wine

Bongo • filled cream puffs with chocolate sauce

Brigidini • anise wafer cookies

Buccellato • simple anise raisin cake

Castagnaccio • baked unleavened chestnut-flour cake containing raisins, walnuts, and rosemary

Cavallucci • spiced cookies

Cenci • "rags" of fried dough dusted with powdered sugar

Frittelle di riso • rice fritters

Meringa • frozen meringue with whipped cream and chocolate chips

Necci • chestnut-flour crepes baked in special terracotta forms

Panforte and *Panpepato* • medieval candied fruit, nut, and spice cakes

Ricciarelli • marzipan almond cookies

Schiacciata alla fiorentina • orange-flavored cake covered with powdered sugar, found at carnival time

Schiacciata con l'uva • grape- and sugar-covered bread dessert of Etruscan origin, served in the fall

Zuccotto • chocolate and whipped cream–filled spongecake dome

THE *W*INE LIST

The wines of Toscana are dominated by Sangiovese, a local grape that forms the backbone of traditional reds: Chianti, Brunello di Montalcino, Vino Nobile di Montepulciano, and Carmignano. Wine in Toscana is red; white wines have never been given much consideration. But modern winemaking techniques have drastically improved the quality of many whites, including traditional Vernaccia di San Gimignano and Bianco di Montecarlo. Many wineries are making high-quality non-DOC whites, although there is also a tendency toward dry, insipid wines to drink chilled in the summer.

Innovative Tuscans and non-Tuscans (it seems as if all the enologists responsible for interesting new wines are from outside Toscana) are experimenting with traditional grapes as well as nontraditional Cabernet Sauvignon, Chardonnay, and Sauvignon. They are using the French technique of *barriques,* 225-liter oak casks, for aging both reds and whites. The results are largely positive, and have contributed to a renewed interest in both traditional and innovative wines of quality.

Bianco di Pitigliano is a clean, delicate, dry white DOC from the south of Toscana, made of Trebbiano, Greco, Verdicchio, and Malvasia grapes. It is served with fish and the coastal *cucina* of southern Toscana. The best, La Stellata, is produced by Lunaia.

Bianco Vergine della Valdichiana is a soft, dry white DOC, made of Trebbiano, Malvasia, and Grechetto grapes south of Arezzo. Served with fish and vegetable dishes, it's at its best produced by Avignonesi.

Brunello di Montalcino, a DOCG from south of Siena, is made of the Brunello or Sangiovese Grosso grape. It's a full, harmonious red and one of Italy's finest wines—served with meat, fowl, game, and mixed grills. Top producers are Altesino, Case Basse, Cerbaiona, La Chiesa di Santa Restituta, La Casa by Tenuta Caparzo, La Gerla, Lisini, Poggio Antico, Poderi Emilio Costanti, Tenuta Caparzo, Tenuta Il Poggione, Mastrojanni, and Villa Banfi.

Carmignano, a DOC zone west of Firenze, produces **Carmignano,** a dry, elegant red, served with meat and regional *cucina,* and **Vin Ruspo,** a fresh, fruity rosé, served with appetizers and first-course dishes. Both wines are made with Sangiovese, Canaiolo, Cabernet, and a small percentage of Trebbiano and Malvasia grapes. Top producers are Fattoria di Ambra, Fattoria di Bacchereto, Podere Lo Locco, Villa Capezzana, and Villa di Trefiano by Contini-Bonacossi.

Chianti is made of Sangiovese, Canaiolo, Malvasia, and Trebbiano grapes in seven distinct zones that cover most of central Tuscany. Over 1,000 wineries produce Chianti, ranging from simple rustic table wine to elegant balanced dry reds well worth aging. The DOCG *(denominazione di origine controllata e garantita)* sticker on the neck of the bottle guarantees the wine's quality. *Chianti* is served with regional *cucina,* and with meat and poultry dishes.

Chianti Classico, produced in the area between Siena and Firenze, is the most famous of the seven Chianti zones. Members of a powerful consortium of producers label the neck of each bottle with a black rooster *(gallo nero)* as a further guarantee of quality. But the "G" of DOCG stands for "guaranteed," and the consortium's role has been partially superceded by government-appointed commissions. Not all wineries in the Classico area have chosen to join the consortium, and the lack of a *gallo nero* doesn't mean that a wine isn't good. The best wines in Chianti Classico are produced by Badia a Coltibuono, Capannelle, Castellare, Castell'in Villa, Castello dei Rampolla, Castello di Cacchiano, Castello di Fonterutoli, Castello di Gabbiano, Castello di Querceto, Castello di Uzzano, Castello di Volpaia, Fattoria di Felsina, Fattoria di Vistarenni, Fontodi, Fattoria di Ama, which makes **Castello di Ama** and special crus **Bellavista, San Lorenzo,** and **Casuccia,** Podere Il Palazzino, Isole e Olena, Monsanto, Monte Vertine, Monte Firidolfi and Panzano by Castelli di Grevepesa, Peppoli, Podere Capaccia, Poggio al Sole,

Poggio Bonelli, Giorgio Regni, Riecine, Savignola Paolina, San Polo in Rosso, Vecchie Terre di Montefili, Villa Antinori, Villa Cafaggio, and Villa Calcinaia.

Chianti Colli Aretini is made in the hills outside Arezzo, and produced by Villa Cilnia and Villa La Selva.

Chianti Colli Fiorentini is made to the south and east of Firenze, and is produced by Fattoria Il Corno.

Chianti Colli Senesi is made in a large area from San Gimignano southward, and produced by Fattoria L'Amorosa, Avignonesi, Il Poggiolo, Le Portine, Montenidoli, and Poderi Emilio Costanti.

Chianti Montalbano is from the area where Carmignano is grown, west of Firenze, and produced by Fattoria di Artimino, Fattoria di Bacchereto, and Tenuta di Capezzana by Contini-Bonacossi.

Chianti Rufina is made east of Firenze, produced by Castello di Montesodi, Castello di Nipozzano, and Selvapiana.

Galestro is a recently created summer white wine, made with Trebbiano and Malvasia grapes, light and dry, at its best chilled and served with light pasta, vegetable, and fish dishes. It is produced by Marchesi Antinori, Marchesi de' Frescobaldi, and Ruffino.

Grattamacco, not far from the Tuscan coast, makes two non-DOC wines. The ***Bianco,*** made from Trebbiano and Malvasia grapes, is fruity, harmonious, and dry, served with appetizers and first- and main-course vegetable and fish dishes. The ***Rosso,*** made from Sangiovese, Colorino, and Malvasia Nera grapes, is full, lively, dry, and is served with meat, fowl, game, and regional *cucina*. Both wines are produced by Meletti Cavallari.

Montecarlo, a DOC from outside Lucca, made of Trebbiano and a wealth of French and Italian grapes, is elegant, full, and dry, one of Toscana's finest whites. It is served with fish in all courses. Top producers are Fattoria del Buonamico, Fattoria del Teso, and Romano Franceschini.

Morellino di Scansano, a DOC, is made near Grosetto from Morellino, a strain of the Sangiovese grape. It is

Sealed wooden casks of Vin Santo

an elegant, balanced red, served with meat, game, and regional *cucina*. Top producers are Erik Banti, Sellari Franceschini, and Le Pupille.

Rosso delle Colline Lucchesi (or ***Colline Lucchesi),*** a DOC from east of Lucca, is made of mostly Sangiovese grapes. This dry, lively red is served with meat and hearty regional *cucina*. The best is produced by Fattoria di Fubbiano, and Tenuta Maria Teresa.

Rosso di Montalcino or ***Rosso dei Vigneti di Brunello*** is a DOC from the Montalcino area, made from the Brunello grape and aged less than noble Brunello di Montalcino. It's a full-bodied, lively red, served with meat, poultry, and regional *cucina*. Top producers are Altesino, Case Basse, La Chiesa di Santa Restituta,

Lisini, Mastrojanni, Poggio Antico, Tenuta Caparzo, Tenuta Il Poggione, Val di Suga, and Villa Banfi.

Dry sparkling **Spumante** is a break from Tuscan tradition. Using the *champenoise* or *charmat* method and Pinot and Chardonnay, or local Brunello, Vernaccia, or other native grape varieties, the following wineries have come up with a quality product. Marchesi Antinori makes **Antinori Brut Nature,** Tenuta Caparzo makes **Caparzo Brut Rosé,** Guicciardini-Strozzi makes **Cusona Brut,** Villa Cilnia makes **Le Bizze,** Teruzzi e Puthod makes **Sarpinello,** and Contini-Bonacossi's Villa di Capezzana makes **Brut di Capezzana.**

Vernaccia di San Gimignano is a DOC from the hills of San Gimignano, made with the Vernaccia grape. This traditional Tuscan white is subtle and dry, served with fish and shellfish. Top producers are Falchini, Fattoria di Pietrafitta, Guicciardini-Strozzi, Montenidoli, Pietraserena, and Ponte a Rondolino.

Vino Nobile di Montepulciano is a DOCG from the hills outside Montepulciano, south of Siena. Prugnolo Gentile, a clone of Sangiovese, is the backbone of this full, elegant red, served with meat, poultry, and game. Top producers are Avignonesi, De Ferrari Corradi, Fassati, and Tenuta Trerose.

Vin Santo Toscano is a lively aromatic wine, usually made from semi-dried Malvasia or Trebbiano grapes, sealed in small casks for at least three years. The resulting wine may range from dry to sweet, and is usually served for dessert. Fine *Vin Santo Toscano* is produced by Avignonesi, Artimino, Castellare, Castello di Ama, Fattoria del Buonamico, Castello di Volpaia, Badia a Coltibuono, Contini-Bonacossi, Frescobaldi, Isole e Olena, Poggio al Sole, Pomino, and Santa Cristina by Antinori.

Tuscan winemakers, not content with the traditional DOC wines, have turned to making *vino da tavola* to express themselves. Usually complex, many are aged in small oak casks and are frequently made with familiar grapes.

Chardonnay seems to be the white grape of the moment in Toscana, and many wineries have come out with interesting and very different Chardonnays.

Castello di Ama makes **Colline di Ama,** a crisp white Chardonnay, and **Bellaria** from Pinot Grigio. Ruffino makes **Cabrèo,** a rich oaky Chardonnay. Villa Cilnia's Giovanni Bianchi makes **Campo del Sasso,** a pleasant, well-balanced white. Tenuta di Capezzana makes a crisp, fruity **Chardonnay.** Villa Banfi makes **Fontanelle Chardonnay,** elegant and silky. Marchesi de' Frescobaldi make **Il Benefizio** with Pinot Bianco and Chardonnay grapes, an elegant, smoky white. Podere Capaccia makes **Spéra,** a Tuscan "sunbeam" of a white. Teruzzi e Puthod make oak-aged **Terre di Tufo.** Avignonesi makes **Marzocco,** a rich Chardonnay, one of Toscana's best whites. Fontodi makes **Meriggio,** a well-made Chardonnay; Vecchie Terre di Montefili makes **Vigna Regis,** an interesting, mouth-filling blend aged in oak; and Tenuta Caparzo makes **Le Grance,** a balanced Chardonnay.

Sangiovese, also called Sangioveto, is the most Tuscan of grapes, and is used alone or blended with nontraditional varieties in the red *vino da tavola.* Almost all are aged in new French oak. Vacchie Terre di Montefili makes **Bruno di Rocca** from Cabernet Sauvignon and Sangioveto, a rich, dry red. Tenuta Caparzo makes **Ca' del Pazzo** from Cabernet Sauvignon and Brunello, a Sangiovese clone. Ruffino makes **Cabrèo** from Cabernet Sauvignon and Sangiovese. Isole e Olena makes **Borro Cepparello,** an all-Sangiovese rich red. San Polo in Rosso makes **Cetinaia** with only the red grapes of Chianti, Canaiolo, and Sangiovese, and the result is a complex lively red. Fattoria di Vistarenni makes **Codirosso** with all Sangiovese. Castello di Volpaia makes **Coltassala** with Sangiovese and Mammolo. Castello di Fonterutoli makes **Concerto,** a blend of Sangiovese and Cabernet. Fattoria di Felsina makes **Fontalloro,** a rich, ripe Sangiovese. Fattoria di S. Giusto a Rentennano makes **Percarlo,** a red of unusual proportion and finesse. Fontodi makes **Flaccianello della Pieve,** a highly successful all-Sangiovese red. Contini-Bonacossi makes **Ghiaie della Furba** of Cabernet Sauvignon, Franc, and Merlot, a rich fruity red. Avignonesi makes **Grifi** with Sangiovese-clone Prugnolo and Cabernet. Podere Il Palazzino makes all-Sangiovese **Grosso Senese.** Castellare makes single-vineyard **I Sodi di San Niccolò** from Sangioveto, Canaiolo and Malvasia grapes. Monte Vertine makes **Le Pergole Torte,** one of Toscana's first all-Sangiovese reds aged in French oak. Villa Cilnia makes *Le Vignacce* from a blend of reds. Altesino makes elegant *Palazzo Altesi* with Brunello or Sangiovese Grosso, and *Alto Altese,* made with the addition of Cabernet. Podere Capaccia makes *Quercia Grande,* an all-Sangiovese wine of promise. Fattoria del Buonamico makes *Rosso di Cercatoia* from Sangiovese blended with other grapes. Badia a Coltibuono makes a long-lived *Sangioveto* from all Sangiovese. Castello dei Rampolla makes *Sammarco,* a heady blend of Cabernet and Sangiovese. Marchese Incisa della Rocchetta makes *Sassicaia,* one of Italy's great reds, from Cabernet Sauvignon. Marchesi Antinori makes *Solaia* from mostly Cabernet with a little Sangiovese. Villa Banfi makes *Tavernelle* from Cabernet Sauvignon. Marchesi Antinori makes elegant, harmonious *Tignanello* from Sangiovese blended with Cabernet. Vinattieri makes *Vinattieri Rosso* from Sangioveto and Brunello, aged in French oak, a rich, heady red.

REGIONAL SPECIALTIES

EXTRA VIRGIN OLIVE OIL

Quality *olio extra vergine d'olive,* extra virgin olive oil (see page 30), is a Tuscan specialty. The olive trees' silver leaves and gnarled trunks dominate the landscape of much of Toscana, although many trees were turned into shrubs by the freeze of 1985. The finest oil is made with hand-picked olives, quickly transported to the olive mill, where they are washed, picked over, crushed with millstones, and separated. There are distinct zones with individual taste characteristics. The oil of the Lucchesia, the area surrounding Lucca, is golden, delicate, fruity, and well suited to fish and lightly flavored dishes. The oil from the Carmignano area is green, full-flavored, balanced, and a personal favorite. I also love the oil from the Chianti area, green, intense, mouth-filling, to be used as a dressing. The oil of the Valdarno area is strong, green, and peppery. The southern part of Toscana yields a dark, strongly flavored oil that is best used uncooked. The southern coastal area produces a delicate golden oil with a peppery aftertaste.

The olive trees in most of Toscana have barely recovered from the 1985 freeze and aren't producing much oil. Genuine Tuscan olive oil should have *prodotto e imbottigliato,* "produced and bottled," written somewhere on the label, which means that the olives are grown by the oil producer, a guarantee of quality. All oils with only *imbottigliato* on the label can be made with olives from other regions, or other countries, and are not necessarily Tuscan.

Frantoio di Santa Tea
Santa Tea
Tel. 055/868117

Piero Gonnelli's family has milled olives at their *frantoio* in Santa Tea near Reggello, for over 400 years. In 1962 they were the first olive mill to experiment with a system of centrifugal pressure. For three years oil was made with both the traditional press and the newer method; today only the latter is used. Green olives, which can't be pressed effectively with the older system, are used in the Santa Tea's extra virgin olive oil, which is green, fruity, and peppery when fresh.

The oil can be purchased directly from the mill.

Giovanni Giachi
Via Campoli 31
Tel. 055/821082

Alberto Giachi, a third-generation olive oil merchant from San Casciano, in the heart of Chianti, works with his brother Francesco and his uncle Renato, selecting olives from local farmers. Their oil is considered one of the best reasonably priced quality extra virgin olive oils made. The Giachi label states *selezionato e imbottigliato,* "selected and bottled," because they choose, but do not raise and harvest, their own olives.

*Giant terracotta jars of
olive oil*

OIL-PRODUCING WINERIES

·

Olive trees grow well in the same climate as grapes, and fine oil is made by many wineries, including Antinori (Pèppoli), Avignonesi, Caparzo, Castello di Ama, Castello di Volpaia, Contini-Bonacossi, Fattoria di Felsina, Grattamacco, Marchese Incisa della Rocchetta, and Villa Banfi.

Antinori (Pèppoli)
Piazza degli Antinori 3
Firenze
Tel. 055/298298

Avignonesi
Via di Gracciano del Corso 91
Montepulciano
Tel. 0578/757874

Caparzo
Località Torrenieri
Montalcino
Tel. 0577/848390

Castello di Ama
Lecchi in Chianti
Tel. 0577/738066

Contini-Bonacossi
Via di Capezzana 100
Seano di Carmignano
Tel. 055/8706005

Fattoria di Felsina
Castelnuovo Berardenga
Tel. 0577/3555117

Incisa della Rocchetta (Sassicaia)
Tenuta San Guido
Bolgheri
Tel. 0565/762003

Meletti Cavallari
Località Grattamacco
Castagneto Carducci
Tel. 0565/763840

Villa Banfi
Piazza Mincio 3
Roma
Tel. 06/421901

BREAD

Tuscan bread, sold throughout Italy, is made without salt. When freshly baked, the crust is crisp and the inside *(midolla)* is moist. Wood-burning ovens traditionally were used to bake bread in the country, and they weren't fired daily, so the bread had to last. *Pane toscano* is at its best after a day, actually improving in texture and flavor. There are many different theories to explain the unusually fine breads baked in some areas—better water, special microclimates, the material or shape of the oven, the type of wood firing the oven, and the type of flour are some of the rationalizations for particularly fine breads. Of course, nothing has ever been proved scientifically.

BEANS

The most famous beans in Toscana, a region of bean eaters, are *cannellini,* but the small, slightly flattened white beans known as *piattellini* are considered superior by Tuscan legume lovers (usually from the area of Pisa or Lucca). The less starchy center of this compact bean remains firm and whole after cooking. They are sold at shops selling beans, grains, and seeds (called *civaie*) or in vegetable stores, but may not be so easy to find.

CHESTNUT FLOUR

Chestnut flour *(farina di castagne)* is used in many Tuscan desserts. Some of the best flour is made in the Garfagnana area, north of Lucca. Chestnuts from high-altitude forests are placed on straw mats in drying rooms and subjected to a smoking-drying process that lasts thirty to forty days. The chestnuts are then stone-ground to produce an extremely fine flour. Many of the mills in the Garfagnana region are still water-powered.

PECORINO

Pecorino is the most Tuscan of cheeses, a tradition going back over five hundred years, when shepherds crossed the region with their flocks, moving them between mountains and valleys according to the seasons. *Pecorino* is made with all sheep's milk, or with a combination of cow's and sheep's milk. Freshly made cheese called *marzolino* ("little March") or *pecorino fresco* is sold in the spring and is often eaten with raw fava beans *(bacelli).* Cheese held for aging is frequently rubbed with tomato or ashes, coloring the rind orange or dark gray. The combination of pears and *pecorino* is considered so great that a local saying warns about telling the farmer how well they go together, for fear he'll never part with them again.

SALUMI

Tuscan bread is said to be saltless in order to accommodate the savory tastes of the full-flavored local *salumi.* Fennel is an important ingredient in *finocchiona,* a specialty of the Chianti area. It was often served by farmers when prospective buyers came to taste their new wine, because Italians rarely drink without eating something, and fennel alters the palate, enhancing many flavors. The verb *infinocchiarsi,* to "fennel up"

or cheat, comes from this palate-co[...] the cunning Tuscan farmers.

CHIANINA BEEF

Texas has its longhorns, and Toscana's [...] from *la Chianina,* a local breed of larg[...]ite cattle. The perfect Florentine T-bone *(bistecca alla fiorentina),* at least two inches thick, should be grilled over a wood or charcoal fire, and ideally will be *Chianina* beef. But this prized cut of a prized breed of cattle isn't easy to find. See page 235 for one source.

VIN SANTO TOSCANO

Concluding a meal with a glass of amber-colored, aromatic, velvety *vin santo* is a local tradition that's easily adopted. The Tuscan dessert wine was supposedly given its name by Cardinale Bessarione, who, when served a glass after a banquet in 1440, was so impressed that he declared, *"Questo è Xanto!"* ("This is holy!") and ever since it's been known as *vin santo.* To make this special wine, grapes are partially dried on straw mats, or hung from rafters, then pressed and sealed in small barrels for at least three years in attics exposed to the summer heat and winter cold. Exactly what goes on in the wooden casks is unknown, but the resulting wine—sweet, semi-dry, or dry—may range from dreadful, when made by unscrupulous wineries, to glorious.

The best *vin santo,* precious and difficult to find, is made by Avignonesi, Isole e Olena, and Castello di Ama. Other fine winemakers (see page 208) also make this delightful finish to a meal, a bit less successfully.

CRAFTS

Rustic pottery is found throughout Toscana. Industrially manufactured or handmade by artisans, terracotta clay dinnerware and cooking utensils are produced in a wealth of traditional patterns and shapes. See pages 216, 217, 228, and 234 for source.

Large terracotta jars—four feet high, unglazed on the outside—are the traditional storage containers for olive oil in Toscana. The village of Impruneta is famous for its pots (see page 232). The wide-mouthed, top-heavy *orcio,* either plain or festooned, is kept in a cool, dark room, and the oil is ladled out when needed.

CITIES AND TOWNS

ABETONE

RESTAURANT-INN

La Capannina
Via Brennero 256
Tel. 0573/60562
Closed Tuesday evening and
*   Wednesday*
Credit cards: American Express,
*   Diners Club, MasterCard*
Price: moderate

Restaurants in mountain resorts tend to confuse quantity with quality, and most famished skiers or hikers don't seem to mind. However, at La Capannina Luigi Ugolini and Romea Politi don't make that mistake—or many others for that matter. Their *cucina* is based on the bounty of the forest and mountains—mushrooms, chestnuts, freshwater fish, herbs, and splendid cheeses. The fresh *ricotta*, of an unbelievable richness and natural sweetness, is served for dessert with chestnut-flour crepes *(necci)*, an acquired taste. Some dishes tend toward "nouvelle" and are less successful than the home-style cooking. Olive oils and wines are wonderful. La Capannina has seven modestly priced rooms, convenient for a stay in the mountains.

AGLIANA

Even my most detailed guidebook, which lists every unheard-of wonder in every unknown village in Toscana, makes no mention of Agliana. But this place merits a pilgrimage, especially for coffee, chocolate, and wine lovers. The stars of Provincial Highway 376, which connects Pistoia and Prato, are an artisanal coffee roaster and a master chocolate maker next door to each other, and a wine shop called Trinci down the road. Fine Tuscan bread, tasty *salumi*, and quality *gelato* are also made in this village of gastronomic significance.

HOTEL

Il Convento
Via San Quirico 33
Pontenovo, outside Pistoia (close
*   by)*
Tel. 0573/152652
Credit cards: MasterCard, Visa
Price: moderate

HOTEL

Villa Santa Cristina
Via Poggio Secco 58
Prato
Tel. 0574/595951
Credit cards: all
Price: moderate

COFFEE

Tri Caffè Torrefazione
Via Provinciale 376
Tel. 0574/718258
Closed Saturday
No credit cards

Andrea Trinci is Italy's finest artisanal coffee roaster. His father, Ercole, was a coffee roaster, and Andrea and his sister Chiara grew up amid the haunting, intense perfume of fine *arabica* beans from Central America, toasted to the color of a monk's robe over the heat (not the flame or smoke) of burning acacia wood. The *caffè* produced is special, served in many of Italy's best restaurants, and even at Le Cirque in New York.

WINE

Trinci
Via Provinciale 154/g
Tel. 0574/751125
Closed weekday mornings and
*   Sunday*
Credit cards: American Express,
*   MasterCard*

Andrea Trinci's fine sense of smell has served him well. His love of wine started as a hobby, and his passion and knowledge inspired him to open a "small" wine shop downstairs in the same building as the coffee roaster. He has recently transferred to more comfortable quarters down the street, and his selection is, as always, fantastic, with an impressive array of the best Tuscan, Italian, and foreign wines produced. There's not a single bottle that I wouldn't be thrilled to drink. And he delivers to Firenze.

CHOCOLATES

Roberto Catinari
Via Provinciale 378
Tel. 0574/718506
Closed Sunday and Monday
No credit cards

The first time I tasted Roberto Catinari's innocent-looking chocolates I took a delicate bite and dribbled the entire liquid center all over my sleeve. I selected a different shape the next time around, and once again was surprised by a liquid filling, the specialty of Italy's best chocolate artisan. *Maestro Roberto* fills many of his chocolates, each differently shaped, with *grappa, vin santo,* and fruit liqueurs. Once you've learned to pop the whole *cioccolatino* into your mouth, you'll be in for a treat. The rich, almost smoky flavored chocolate shell is coated inside with a crunchy, wafer-thin layer of crystallized sugar that contains the liquid center—not strong enough to be intoxicating, but exhilarating due to the pure quality and intense flavors of the ingredients. The covered cherries are exceptional. Chocolate hazelnut creams *(gianduja),* a large variety of all-handmade chocolates, and a small selection of chocolate keys, tools, and horseshoes are also for sale. Easter eggs and Christmas *panforte* are available in season.

BREAD
Castino
Via Calice 18
Tel. 0574/711433
Closed Wednesday afternoon

Angelo Giusti, known as "Castino," is a wonderful baker, perennially dusted with a coat of flour. His bread is sold in an anonymous grocery store, owned by his family, next door to his oven, and the scent of fresh bread perfumes the air. His wood-burning oven is over a hundred years old, and the bread baked in it, fragrant and wheaty, is made from Tuscan flour, starter, and a small amount of yeast. Bread rises in a room over the still-warm oven. On Saturdays bread is baked three

times to satisfy the local demand, since Castino's bread is known to last longer and taste better than most.

SALUMI
Macelleria Marini
Via Selva 313
Tel. 0574/718119
Closed Wednesday and Thursday afternoons

Adriano and Patrizia Marini make some of the finest *salumi* in the area. Locally grown pigs are transformed into tasty *prosciutto,* salami, *finocchiona,* and fantastic spiced *pancetta.* The wonderful *coppa,* a smaller version of the chunky pork sausage called *soprassata,* is not for the squeamish—it's made from head. All products are made by hand and contain salt, spices, and meat. *Prosciutto,* hung upstairs in well-aired rooms, ages for a year if Adriano and Patrizia aren't sweet-talked into selling it earlier.

GELATO
Bar Anisare
Via Roma 93
Tel. 0574/718490
Closed Tuesday

Surely all the people seated at the sidewalk tables or milling outside the Bar Anisare can't be local. The reputation of "Il Cinese," who is not from China and doesn't even look Oriental, has traveled because his *gelato* is made from all-natural ingredients. Most colors are pale, but the flavors are intense. The largest selection is available on summer weekends, with a splendid assortment of fresh fruit flavors. Nut, banana,

and citrus fruits, plus a rich, eggyolky custard *(crema)* and a slightly gummy, almost black, dark chocolate will thrill winter *gelato* fans.

RESTAURANT
Osteria
Via Provinciale 58
Tel. 0574/781450
Closed all day Monday, Tuesday and Wednesday evenings, and August
No credit cards
Price: high moderate

The Osteria del Contadino serves country-style food, simple and Tuscan; but with a generous selection of Andrea Trinci's superb wines, the plain *cucina* is given a boost. Homemade pasta, grilled meats, extra virgin olive oil, and field-greens salad all taste better with wonderful wine.

ANGHIARI

INN
L'Oroscopo (Ristorante Paolo e Marco)
Via Palmiro Togliatti 66, Pieve Vecchia
Sansepolcro (close by)
Credit cards: American Express, Diners Club
Price: moderate

RESTAURANT
Castello di Sorci
Via S. Lorenzo 21
Tel. 0575/789066
Closed Monday
Price: inexpensive

Located in a farmhouse outside the Castello di Sorci ("Mouse Castle"), this archetypal *trattoria* serves an astounding inexpensive fixed-price meal. Diners are served, or assaulted on Sundays and holidays, with an *antipasto* of *salumi* and chicken liver canapés *(crostini)*. Pace yourself for two *primi,* usually pasta and a soup or *gnocchi,* and a main dish of roasted meat, served with vegetables. Desserts, if you're still interested, are homemade. All the mediocre red and white wine you can drink, mineral water, and even an after-dinner *caffè* and a *digestivo* are included in the price.

ARTIMINO

HOTEL
Paggeria Medicea
Viale Papa Giovanni XXIII
Tel. 055/8718081
Credit cards: all
Price: high moderate

RESTAURANT
Da Delfina
Via della Chiesa 1
Tel. 055/871874
Closed Monday evening, Tuesday, and August
Credit card: American Express
Price: high moderate

Delfina was the cook at the hunting lodge of Artimino, and when sportsmen were lucky, she turned their bounty into tasty Tuscan *cucina.* She still presides in the kitchen at her rustic country-style restaurant, but her son Carlo has taken over most of the work—with great skill, enthusiasm, and intelligence. The *cucina* is strictly local, tied to seasonal ingredients from the vegetable garden, courtyard, and fields. Wild herbs and flowers play an important role in Delfina's dishes. The vegetable soup is thickened with bread *(ribollita)* and then is pan-fried, an unusual treatment that Carlo says is the "real" way. Call the chestnut-flour dessert by its dialectical name, *ghirighio* (pronounced GHEE-REE-GHEE´-OH) and Carlo will jump for joy. The wines are local, from one of the great winemaking areas of Toscana. The lusty Carmignano reds are wonderful.

BORGO A BUGGIANO

HOTEL
Grotta Giusti
Via Grotta Giusti 17
Monsummano Terme (close by)
Tel. 0572/51165
No credit cards
Price: moderate

RESTAURANT
Da Angiolo
Piazza del Popolo 2
Tel. 0572/32014
Closed Monday, Tuesday, and August
Credit card: American Express
Price: moderate

Luckily the food is far better than the coral, white, and olive-green decor of this gem of a fish restaurant nowhere near the coast. Angelo is in the kitchen, and his partner, sommelier Roberto, presides in the dining room. Almost everything on the extensive menu is made without sauce, and the clean, extra-fresh taste of the shellfish and fish, treated with respect, is a treat. Carnivores will be content with the meat selection. Desserts are simple, and the wine list is wonderful.

CAMAIORE

HOTEL
Ariston
Viale Colombo 355
Lido di Camaiore (close by)
Tel. 0584/906633
Credit cards: American Express, Visa
Price: expensive

HOTEL
Villa Iolanda
Viale Pistelli 127
Lido di Camaiore (close by)
Tel. 0584/64296
Credit cards: American Express, Diners Club, Visa
Price: moderate

MEAT
Danilo Bonuccelli
Via Vittorio Emanuele 9
Tel. 0584/981391
Closed Wednesday afternoon

Danilo Bonuccelli is known beyond the borders of Toscana for his *salumi.* His specialties include local versions of *soprassata* and *biroldo* (blood pudding). Best of all is Danilo's *lardo* (unrendered lard), tasty pork fat barely streaked with meat, more flavorful than butter, to be served in thin slices on saltless Tuscan bread, a treat for those who fear no cholesterol. (Note that local residents call via Vittorio Emanuele via de Mezzo.)

WINE
Dioniso di Giuseppe Pighini
Via Vittorio Emanuele 187
Tel. 0584/981105
Closed Monday morning
Credit card: American Express

Giuseppe Pighini, known to almost everyone as Nebraska, got tired of "seeing the morning from the wrong side of the pillow," as the saying goes, when he owned the Enoteca Nebraska (see below), and so he opened a wine store that I wish was around the corner from my house. All the fine wines from the Enoteca Nebraska are here, as well as a nice selection of *grappa* and fruit liqueurs.

WINE BAR
Enoteca Nebraska
Via Nocchi 72/c
No telephone
Closed Tuesday and October
No credit cards
Price: inexpensive

The Enoteca Nebraska is unique. The unheated, unrestored farmhouse opens around 5 or 6 p.m. and quickly fills up with locals who look like Hell's Angels, and who come to taste the reasonably priced, unusual selection of wines that Tiziano Franceschini has to offer. They mix with sophisticated summer people who come over from the nearby fashionable beach resorts, and everyone hangs out over stemmed glasses until 2 a.m. The *salumi* (served on paper plates) are quality, and the local extra virgin olive oil is light but olivey. "Nebraska," one of the original owners, has left to open

a wine shop with regular hours, but Tiziano seems to be managing.

RESTAURANT
Emilio e Bona
Via Lombricese 22
Località Candalla
Tel. 0584/989289
Closed Monday
Credit card: American Express
Price: moderate

Overlooking a woodsy ravine by a mountain stream, Emilio e Bona looks like the kind of place where Snow White would hang out. Three large millstones dominate the dining room of this former olive oil mill where Luigi (Emilio was his father) and his wife, Bona, serve simple, well-prepared food. Start with *polenta* tiles served with a rabbit mousse. I love the greaseless mixed fry *(fritto misto)* of bread dough, sage leaves, potato croquettes, and chicken, rabbit, or lamb chops. Freshly made *bomboloni* (light, hole-less doughnuts), served with hot chocolate sauce, are my son's favorite dessert anywhere. But if perfectly fried food isn't your style, try *pasta alla Bona* (creamy ricotta and spinach–dressed homemade pasta), *carpaccio* (thinly sliced raw beef served with wild mushrooms, artichokes, or truffles), roast veal, or anything grilled over the wood-burning fire in Bona's spotless kitchen. Luigi will bring you a glass of sparkling wine while you wait for your meal, and will help you to choose from the mostly Tuscan wine selection. This is home-style cooking at its best.

CASTELFRANCO DI SOPRA

HOTEL
Castello di Sammezzano
Leccio (close by)
Tel. 055/867911
Credit cards: all
Price: expensive

HOTEL
Villa Rigacci
Vaggio (close by)
Tel. 055/8656718
Credit cards: all
Price: high moderate

RESTAURANT
Vicolo del Contento
Via Mandria 38
Tel. 055/964277
Closed Monday, Tuesday, and
August
Credit cards: Diners Club, Visa
Price: high moderate

The Vicolo del Contento is a food lover's "easy street." Angelo and Lina Reditti have moved from the village to a carefully restored brick barn in the neighboring countryside, and the improved setting makes dining even more pleasant. Angelo's *cucina* is based on the best ingredients that his father can get his hands on. In the kitchen, together with his mother, who makes all the pasta and pastry, Angelo works wonders. Quality meat and super-fresh fish are simply cooked and graced with impeccable vegetable sauces that are bright and full-flavored. *Gnocchi* made with vegetables, fish, or *ricotta,* are ethereal. The olive oils are the best that Toscana has to offer. Lina gracefully suggests and serves wines from their wonderful selection. Desserts are well prepared, but I like the homemade *gelato* best, and the cookies that Mom makes are irresistible.

CASTELNUOVO DI GARFAGNANA

PASTRY
Pasticceria Enzo Petreschi
Via Ludovico Ariosto 1
Tel. 053/62190
Closed Tuesday

Enzo Petreschi's bakery makes lovely pastries. His intensely flavored unleavened *castagnaccio*, cake made with chestnut flour, is exceptional—flatter, and consequently less leaden, than most.

CERBAIA

HOTEL
See Firenze, pages 217–219.

RESTAURANT
La Tenda Rossa
Piazza del Monumento 9–14
Tel. 055/826132
Closed Wednesday
Credit cards: American Express,
   Diners Club
Price: expensive

La Tenda Rossa is a family-run restaurant obsessed with quality. Capable sommelier Silvano Santandrea and his wife, assisted by a host of in-laws and offspring, offer one of the Florentine countryside's most interesting nontraditional dining experiences. The decor is modern, with diffused lighting, planter-dividers that create intimate dining zones, and tables elegantly set with silver, crystal, china, and linen. The menu is innovative. Goose liver, lightly cooked fish, and tasty local meats are well prepared, flavored with lots of fresh herbs, local extra virgin olive oil, and white truffles in season. Pasta is homemade and tasty. Mushrooms are always splendid. Alas, there are too many concessions to puréed mousse cuisine, and some dishes tend to get faddish. The wine list is a personal favorite; there's always something new and wonderful that Silvano ably pairs with his wife's *cucina*.

CETONA

RESTAURANT-INN
La Frateria di Padre Eligio
Convento di San Francesco
Tel. 0578/238015
Closed Tuesday and January
Credit cards: American Express,
   MasterCard
Price: expensive

The Frateria was created by Padre Eligio, a controversial priest who has probably cured more drug addicts than anyone else in Italy, but who has a penchant for fine wine and red underwear. His hardworking flock has restored both the Castello in Cozzo Lomellina (see page 159) and La Frateria di Padre Eligio, and they now staff both restaurants. La Frateria is located in a spectacular thirteenth-century Franciscan convent with stone walls, brick floors, and vaulted ceilings. Walnut tables are set with hand-embroidered linens; the menus are hand-painted. The total effect is mystical, special, otherworldly. The *cucina* has its roots in Toscana, based on excellent local ingredients produced by the restaurant's working farm, but the menu is hardly regional. The olive oil is one of the area's finest, the preserves are tasty, and the pastry is first-class. Prices are high, more acceptable as a charitable contribution than as payment for a meal. (Note: Credit cards are not accepted at the inn.)

POTTERY
Pippo and Antonio Mencaglia
Piazza Garibaldi 55
Tel. 0578/238153
No credit cards

Pippo and his wife, Antonia, produce beautiful artisanal pottery. Dinnerware, serving pieces, and baking dishes are handcrafted, fired in their own kiln, and most of their work is custom-decorated to suit their clients. Many of the prettiest pieces are painted with wildflowers. Pippo throws in an extra place setting when you buy a set of dishes for six. You can even reorder more dishes from home, if you send a photo of your pattern. The workshop is always open, and they will take checks.

COLLE DI VAL D'ELSA

RESTAURANT-HOTEL
Arnolfo
Piazza Santa Caterina 2
Tel. 0577/920549
Closed Tuesday and from
   January 10 to February 10
Credit cards: American Express,
   Diners Club
Price: high moderate

Chef-owner Gaetano Trovato's tiny restaurant is named after

Colle di Val D'Elsa's native son Arnolfo di Cambio, architect and sculptor. The *cucina* is as original as Arnolfo's work must have seemed in the thirteenth century. Based on tradition but highly creative, some of the finest food between Firenze and Siena is prepared by Gaetano with the best and freshest ingredients that his territory can provide. Pasta is homemade, soups are stellar, and hard-to-find *Chianina* beef is always on the menu. Cheese fans should leave room for the sheep's-milk ricotta. Desserts are tempting. The wine list is a true joy and enhances the dining experience at Arnolfo, always a pleasure.

POTTERY
Vulcania
Via Mason 42
Tel. 0577/920089
Closed Saturday and Sunday
No credit cards

Traditional dark brown casseroles and pans with a lighter brown interior, as well as matching or bright red dinnerware, are manufactured by Vulcania in Colle Val d'Elsa and sold directly from the factory. The pottery is available in most housewares stores, as are their bean pots *(fagioliere)*.

FIRENZE

Firenze was founded in hilltop Fiesole by Etruscans who seem to have known better than to settle in the Arno Valley, with its frigid winters and torrid summers. The Romans colonized the city on the banks of the silver Arno. From the Comune's founding in 1115, Firenze flourished for over 500 years as a center of art, architecture, finance, and culture. Etruscan frescoes and excavations have revealed many details of daily life, including the use of utensils like the rolling pin, pasta strainer, and cheese grater, and typical dishes that are still part of the Florentine menu: wide pasta, grilled meats, and *schiacciata con l'uva* (a grape and honey cake). By the year 1200 the character of the Florentine *cucina* was already dominated by bread, in the form of *panunto* or *fettunta* (garlic-rubbed bread dipped in olive oil), early versions of bread-based soups, and *schiacciata alla fiorentina* and *pan di ramerino,* two dessert breads. Renaissance feasts for kings, popes, and the Medici family became food marathons. Catherine de' Medici, a true gourmand, took her own cooks and a supply of local ingredients to a distant and uncivilized France when she married Henry II. She also took another local invention, *la forchetta,* a two-tined instrument adapted from the Roman *lingula,* a spear-like utensil used to transfer food from serving dish to plate, and refined by the already famous Florentine goldsmiths. But the food found in most restaurants today isn't that of kings or the Medici but of the *contadini,* the farmers or peasants—simple, austere cooking that reflects the Tuscan emphasis on bread, beans, and olive oil. Soups, especially the trio of *pappa, ribollita,* and *panzanella,* dominate the first courses, while meats are usually grilled or fried. *La Fiorentina* can refer to the local soccer squad or to a T-bone steak at least two inches thick, charcoal-grilled rare. The Florentines, insultingly called "bean eaters" by their neighbors, are said to lick plates and ladles when beans are served. The *pinzimonio* style of eating raw vegetables dipped in fresh, peppery extra virgin olive oil, salt, and pepper is generally limited to the winter. All other vegetables in Firenze will be deep-fried or overcooked. Traditional desserts are a bit austere, but fine non-Tuscan desserts and *torte* are found in most restaurants.

The city is currently attempting to deal with a traffic problem—a siege of buses, cars, and pigeons—struggling against those who'd like to turn this unique Renaissance gem into a polluted parking lot. Tourism has spawned pizza-by-the-slice stands and restaurants that dish out mediocre food and crummy wine for a clientele who will never return. I haven't been thrilled by too many eateries in the city. But don't get me wrong—I live in Firenze, and I love it. Note: Street numbers of commercial establishments appear in red; this is indicated by an "r" (*rosso,* red) in the address.

HOTEL
Grand Hotel and Excelsior
Piazza Ognissanti
Tel. 055/278781 or 294301
Credit cards: all
Price: luxury

HOTEL
Regency
Piazza Massimo d'Azaglio 3
Tel. 055/245247
Credit cards: all
Price: luxury

STAYING IN A FLORENTINE VILLA

▪

The Florentines built beautiful villas in the surrounding countryside to escape the city's sweltering summers. Some have been turned into lovely small hotels, perfect as a base for touring the region and for excursions into Firenze. Most are expensive, but less costly than comparable accommodations in the city.

Villa Casalecchi
Castellina in Chianti
Tel. 0577/740240
Closed November through March
Credit cards: all
Price: expensive

Villa Casalecchi, with sixteen rooms, a suite, and three apartments in the former stables, is furnished in Tuscan style and surrounded by a magnificent park.

Badia Montescalari
Via Montescalari 129
Figline Valdarno
Tel. 055/959596
Credit card: American Express
Price: expensive

Seven simply restored, antique-filled, austere rooms in Badia Montescalari, an eleventh-century abbey, complete with stables, are a fine choice for those who'd like to see the Chianti area on horseback.

Villa Le Barone
Via S. Leolino 19
Panzano
Tel. 055/852215
Closed November through March
Credit card: American Express
Price: expensive

The sixteenth-century Villa Le Barone has twenty-five rooms and a beautiful pool in a large park with a spectacular view. Guests are required to eat at least one meal a day at the villa's restaurant.

Villa Rigacci
Strada Rigacci 76
Vaggio
Tel. 055/8656718
Credit cards: all
Price: moderate

More like a friend's country house than a hotel, the Villa Rigacci's ten rooms are tastefully furnished. Horseback riding in the Tuscan countryside or hanging out at the pool may distract you from visiting the city.

Villa Sangiovese
Piazza Bucciarelli 4
Panzano
Tel. 055/8544577
Credit card: American Express
Price: expensive

The recently restored Villa Sangiovese has sixteen rooms, and there are three apartments in the farmhouse next door to the nineteenth-century villa.

Conte Girolamo and Contessa Simonetta Brandolini d'Adda
Via Ugo Foscolo 72
Firenze
Tel. 055/223064
Price: outrageous

If you'd like to experience Italy in the height of luxury, you might consider renting a villa of your own, or a farmhouse, or a city apartment. Count and Countess Brandolini d'Adda offer expensive, unusual rentals, tastefully decorated, fully equipped, with maid service—a glimpse of *la dolce vita*, Tuscan noble style.

HOTEL
Loggiato dei Serviti
Piazza S. S. Annunziata 3
Tel. 055/263592
Credit cards: all
Price: expensive

HOTEL
Park Palace
Piazzale Galileo 5
Tel. 055/222431
Credit card: American Express
Price: expensive

HOTEL
Porta Rossa
Via Porta Rossa 19
Tel. 055/287551
Credit cards: all
Price: moderate

HOTEL
Pitti Palace
Via Barbadori 2
Tel. 055/282257
Credit cards: American Express, Visa
Price: moderate

BAR-CAFFÈ, PASTRY
Bar Pasticceria Marino
Piazza N. Sauro 19r, at Ponte alla Carraia
Tel. 055/212657
Closed Monday

The best continental breakfast in Firenze is found at this inconspicuous bar. Owner pastry-chef Marino makes fresh croissants (called *brioche* or *cornetti* in Firenze) all morning long, available plain or filled with (hot!) custard or preserves. He bakes an extra batch at 5 p.m., and the bar soon fills with locals waiting for a fresh *brioche*. The cappuccino also is well prepared.

BAR-CAFFÈ, COFFEE
Manaresi
Via de'Lamberti 16r
Tel. 055/87335
Closed Sunday

Manaresi roasts the best coffee in Firenze and sells it, with or without caffeine, in different qualities, whole or ground to order. The bar serves freshly ground, freshly made *caffè* and all its classic variations, beautifully prepared. The *caffè* is so good that most knowledgeable locals order a double *(doppio)*. On Wednesday afternoons, only the bar section is open.

BAR-CAFFÈ
Rivoire
Piazza della Signoria 5r
Tel. 055/214412
Closed Monday

Rivoire is the best of the people-watching bars in Firenze, with indoor seating as well as outdoor tables in Piazza Signoria, one of the world's most beautiful squares. The sandwiches are fresh, the pastry is fair, and the chocolates are wonderful, especially the bitter chocolate rectangles individually wrapped in royal blue paper and tin foil. The chocolate Easter eggs, custom-stuffed with a surprise of your own choice, are the best in Firenze. Thick hot chocolate *(cioccolata calda)* topped with whipped cream is a winter specialty.

BAR-CAFFÈ
Giacosa
Via Tornabuoni 83r
Tel. 055/296226
Closed Monday

Giacosa, under the same ownership as Rivoire but with a different pastry chef, serves the same fine coffee and chocolates. Florentines flock here for the quick stand-up lunch *(pranzo in piedi)*. Counter service is crowded, elbow room only. The Negroni, a Campari and gin cocktail named for the count who loved them, was invented at Giacosa, and is still in demand during the cocktail hour.

SPECIALTY FOODS
Procacci
Via Tornabuoni 64r
Tel. 055/211656
Closed Sunday

Procacci's window display of miscellaneous Anglo-Saxon expatriate items like English tea tins and jars of Scotch marmalade doesn't even hint at the specialty items in this understated shop. Delicate oval glazed rolls are spread with salmon or anchovies, but the cognoscenti turn up here for the truffle sandwiches *(panini tartufati)*. Help yourself from the glass display case and sip a glass of white wine or *Spumante* at the bar. Weary shoppers can recover at one of Procacci's two tiny tables.

MARKET
San Lorenzo Market
Piazza del Mercato Centrale
Open Monday through Saturday mornings, and Saturday from 4 to 8 p.m.

The ground floor of the huge nineteenth-century cast-iron San Lorenzo market is filled with stalls, most selling perishables that need refrigeration. Meat, poultry, fish, and general grocery *(alimentari)* stalls abound.

*Torquato
sells his vegetables in
Piazza Santo Spirito*

Medium-size Sant'Ambrogio is a gem. The building, with its iron trim and more stainless steel than marble, houses the perishables and an inexpensive take-out stand. The outdoor market sells some of Firenze's finest produce, piled up in mounds, as well as clothes, housewares, plants, herbs, and vegetable seedlings. Teresa Dutto's corner stand sells fresh produce from her family's farm, and has for more than fifty years.

MARKET
Santo Spirito
Piazza Santo Spirito
**Open Monday through Saturday
    mornings**

Piazza Santo Spirito has a small neighborhood market. Four large fruit and vegetable stands sell a wide range of produce at one end of the piazza, while at the other end, closer to the Santo Spirito church, four or five farmers set up tables, offering their seasonal harvest of fruit, vegetables, herbs, and flowers.

Torquato is my favorite farmer here. No strawberries in December, no grapefruit from Israel, just peak-of-the-season, fresh-from-the-garden vegetables, fruit, eggs, chicken, and rabbits to order, all raised by Torquato and his wife. The flavors aren't as good as they used to be because the land has been ruined by chemicals, says this farmer with a palate that remembers, but his produce is among the best in Firenze. As if all this weren't enough, Torquato also provides excellent, original advice on how to cook everything he sells. He has promised to collaborate with me on a cookbook, and I can't wait.

Mario Conto (banco 300, tel. 055/298501) is one of the stars of the ground floor, with his fabulous, and expensive, selection of the first early vegetables and fruits of the season, known as *primizie*. In general, his fruits and vegetables are the biggest, best, and most exotic. Mushrooms and a wide range of wild salad greens, herbs, and exotic fruit are beautifully displayed along with sidelines of beans, olives, and nuts. His stall faces Pispoli, who sells the best meat, and Luciano Baccetti, whose selection of well-priced quality cheeses always draws a crowd. Nearby, Signora Panerai, the cookie lady, sells *biscotti* of every shape and size, including crispy chocolate-cream-filled logs that thrill my son, Max.

Gianni Fancelli (upstairs at banco 16, tel. 055/263028) has the best selection of fresh herbs and salad greens, both wild and cultivated, and berries, all highly seasonal. It's a pleasure to see so many different baskets of fresh, lively looking, unfamiliar types of salad.

MARKET
Mercato di Sant'Ambrogio
Piazza Ghiberti
**Open Monday through Saturday
    mornings**

SPICES
Bizzarri
Via della Condotta 32r
Tel. 055/211580
Closed Wednesday afternoon

Bizzarri, founded in 1842, sells chemical supplies, no-frills cosmetics, and spices, whole or ground. It's always a thrill to breathe the strangely scented air in this shop with its huge, dark, glass-doored wooden cupboards.

WINE
Alessi
Via dell'Oche 27r
Closed Wednesday afternoon

Alessi's *enoteca* is hidden downstairs, behind their floor-to-ceiling assortment of candies, cookies, and seasonal sweets like Easter *colomba* and chocolate eggs and Christmas *panettone* and *panforte.* The back room is dedicated to fruit syrups, liqueurs, *grappa,* and sparkling wines. But the best part of the shop is downstairs, where wine is displayed according to region. Some areas are smaller than they should be, but the Toscana room is terrific, and features a large range of Chianti Classico, Brunello, and the new-style Tuscan table wines. Not all the wines are fantastic, but the selection is the best in Firenze.

WINE AND OIL
Vino e Olio
Via de'Serragli 29r
Tel. 055/298708
Closed Wednesday afternoon

Renzo Salsi's neighborhood wine and olive oil shop is a personal favorite. Wines are well priced, and the Tuscan selection is won-derful. Renzo usually has at least five or six different extra virgin olive oils for sale. Informal Saturday afternoon wine tastings are attended by locals, when Renzo's wife makes chicken liver *crostini.*

SUPERMARKET
Esselunga
Via Pisana 130
Tel. 055/706556

Viale de Amicis 89/b
Tel. 055/604442

and other locations

Closed Wednesday afternoon

Esselunga ("Long S") is the best American-style supermarket in Firenze, stocked with fine Italian and some imported products. See page 167 for a description.

TRIPE
Pinzauti
Piazza Dante
No phone
Closed Wednesday afternoon

Boiled tripe *(trippa),* looking very much like a worn-out bathing cap, is sold warm at stands in strategic locations in Firenze, ready to be turned into Florentine-style tripe or stuffed into a crispy roll. Major stainless-steel stands are to be found at the San Lorenzo central market, the Porcellino market, and best of all, at the corner of via Tavolini and via dei Cerchi, at Piazza Dante, manned by Signor Pinzauti. Open from 9 a.m. to 1 p.m., and from 5 to 7:30 p.m.

PIZZA
Pizzeria alla Marchigiana
Via del Corso 60r
Tel. 055/214961
Closed Tuesday

Warning! Most street pizza is tourist food, and to be avoided. But high-quality pizza-by-the-slice possibilities do exist in Firenze. Pizzeria alla Marchigiana, for example, serves squares of tomato, *mozzarella,* mushroom, or *prosciutto* thick-crust pizzas. The house beverage is *spuma,* a locally produced carbonated drink of uncertain and undistinguished flavor. The wad of paper napkins they place your slice on provides inadequate insulation from the hot molten cheese when this pizza comes straight from the oven. Open from 9 a.m. to 2 p.m., and 3:30 to 9 p.m.

BREAD, PASTRY, PIZZA
Forno Sartoni
Via dei Cerchi 34r
Tel. 055/212570
Closed Wednesday afternoon

The Forno on via dei Cerchi sells bread, rolls, sandwiches, and pastry, all baked on the premises. The crowd in the back is waiting for pizza or *schiacciata*—flat pizza crust dressed with a bit of oil, a local favorite—to come out of the oven, and it is well worth the mob scene and the wait.

WINE, SANDWICHES
Vini e Panini i Fratelli
Via dei Cimatori 38r
Tel. 055/296096
Closed Sunday

This closet-size hole in the wall is the original Florentine version of fast food. Crummy Chianti by the short, squat *osteria* glass, essential sandwiches of *salumi,* and chicken liver *crostini* are the unchanging menu for a stand-up lunch or snack. Hanging out on the corner of Firenze's main pedestrian drag substitutes for decor.

PASTRY
Pasticceria Sarti
Via Senese 147r
Tel. 055/20164
Closed Sunday, Wednesday
   afternoon, and most of August

Sarti makes the best "squashed" desserts in Firenze. The *schiacciata alla fiorentina,* an orange and egg–flavored pre-Lenten cake coated with a generous layer of powdered sugar, is excellent. So is the *schiacciata con l'uva,* bread dough baked with grapes and sugar, a dessert of Etruscan origins.

PASTRY
Gualtieri
Via Senese 18r
Tel. 055/221771
Closed Monday

The *torta iris* isn't made with iris corms, bulbs, leaves, or even flowers, but the moist, delicate crumb of this white iced loaf cake makes it a favorite at this fine *pasticceria.*

GELATO
Badiani
Viale dei Mille 20r
Tel. 055/50149
Closed Tuesday

Badiani is the original Florentine source for fabulous *Buontalenti,* the egg yolk–rich flavor named for Francesco de' Medici's personal *gelato* maker. Fruit flavors are good, but the rich chocolate, smoky, intense nut, and combination flavors are fantastic. The location is a bit out of the way, but this is considered the best *gelato* in Firenze.

GELATO
Frilli
Via S. Niccolò 57
Tel. 055/23621
Closed Wednesday and August

Disguised as an unassuming dairy store *(latteria),* Frilli makes fine *gelato* and the city's best *semifreddo* (gelato base with whipped cream folded in). The selection is limited and excellent.

GELATO
Frullati
Via de'Renai 25r
No phone
Closed mid-November to March

This tiny, tidy hole in the wall sells only ten flavors of *gelato.* Five fruit flavors are made of fresh seasonal fruit, and are probably the best in Firenze. The non-fruit flavors are good, but not as exceptional. Refreshing fruit smoothees *(frullati)* are also a specialty. The most difficult thing about this *gelateria* is finding it open—afternoons and evenings only.

GELATO
Festival del Gelato
Via del Corso 75r
Tel. 055/294386
Closed Monday

It may not be the best *gelato* in town, but it's fun. The sound system, disco lighting, central location, and one hundred flavors, some looking too brightly colored to be true, are all part of the Festival experience. Gray, slushy-looking *turbo,* turquoise *laguna blu,* and other oddities share space with rice, rose, and a case full of classic, original, and unusual combination flavors.

RESTAURANT
Acqua al Due
Via dell'Acqua 2r
Tel. 055/284170
Closed Monday
No credit cards
Price: moderate

There's always a crowd waiting for a seat at one of Acqua al Due's communal tables and a crack at this ex-vegetarian restaurant's two different tastings. Start with the *assaggio di primi,* a series of first courses, usually four pastas and a rice dish, and conclude with the the *assaggio di dolce,* a tasting of desserts including fruit tarts, fudge-like chocolate cake, and *tiramisù.* The wines could be better.

RESTAURANT
Acquacotta
Via dei Pilastri 51r
Tel. 055/242907
Closed Wednesday
No credit cards
Price: low moderate

Acquacotta is a simple, home-style *trattoria.* The food is reasonably priced and well prepared. The house specialty is *acquacotta,* rich vegetable soup served over toasted bread and topped with a poached egg. Some, but not too many, of the wines are wonderful.

RESTAURANT
Angiolino
Via Santo Spirito 36r
Tel. 055/29927
Closed Monday
No credit cards
Price: moderate

Everything is always the same at Angiolino. Waiters, decor, wine, and *cucina* are Tuscan. Stick to the regional *salumi, crostini,* and soups—skip the pasta, which is overcooked in true Florentine fashion. Tripe fans will be in heaven, but demanding enophiles will have a hard time with the wines.

RESTAURANT
Belle Donne
Via delle Belle Donne 16r
Tel. 055/262609
Closed Saturday and Sunday
No credit cards
Price: low moderate

Right in the center of town, inconspicuous except for the knot of people waiting outside for a vacant seat, the Belle Donne is a favorite with many Florentines, especially for lunch. Marble tables seat four, placemats are made of coarse ocher-colored butcher paper, and service is unfriendly at times. The blackboard menu is below the window, and it's wise to take a look before you're seated. The *cucina* is Tuscan, with a few concessions for locals bored with home-style dishes. The mixed green salad and interesting vegetables will please most diners. Desserts are simple, homemade, and tasty. Mustachioed Mario Bussi always promises that he'll improve the wines.

RESTAURANT
Bibe
Via delle Bagnese 1r
Tel. 055/2049085
Closed all day Wednesday and Thursday lunch
No credit cards
Price: high moderate

Outside the city, on the Bagnese River, Bibe has grown a bit more sophisticated with the latest generation, the fifth of the Scarselli family to reign in this typical Tuscan *trattoria*. They now make original herbal *liqueurs*, preserved fruits, and improved desserts, but otherwise the menu is unchanged. Classics are executed with time-honed expertise, and beautifully made country soups, grilled or fried poultry, meat, and nontraditional desserts are always tasty. The new wine list is welcome; the selection is well thought out and includes wonderful Tuscan wines. The charming country store entrance is filled with groceries as well as fine local cheeses and *salumi*. The fish tank with the piranha will entertain children of all ages waiting for their food.

RESTAURANT
Il Biribisso
Via dell'Albero 28r
Tel. 055/283335
Closed Sunday, Monday lunch, Saturday in summer, and August
Credit cards: American Express, Diners Club
Price: high moderate

Biribisso is an attractive, exciting board game—too exciting for the fifteenth century, when it was illegal—and the name of Firenze's newest restaurant. The decor is attractive and unusual. The *cucina* is creative with Tuscan inflections; the tastes are herby and refreshing. The restaurant has recently changed ownership, and signs point to a big improvement in the food and especially in the wines.

RESTAURANT
Cantinetta Antinori
Piazza Antinori 3r
Tel. 055/292234
Closed Saturday and Sunday, holidays, and August
Credit card: American Express
Price: high moderate

Cantinetta Antinori, in the beautiful fifteenth-century Palazzo Antinori, was created as a showplace for the Antinori wines. The simple *cucina* is mostly Tuscan, with some concessions for the Florentine regulars who frequent this restaurant. Some dishes are splendid, especially the *pappa al pomodoro* and *ribollita* bread soups, stellar tripe, and *calamaretti all'inzimino* (squid stewed with Swiss chard), served on Fridays. *Pecorino* and *caprino* cheeses and extra virgin olive oil from the Antinori estates are first-rate. Conclude your meal with Mattei's authentic *biscotti di Prato* (rich almond cookies) or the nontraditional, beautifully prepared cakes and other desserts. The Antinori family has been making wine for over 600 years, and the Cantinetta's all-Antinori wine list is wonderful. All wines are available by the bottle or the glass.

RESTAURANT
La Capannina di Sante
Piazza Ravenna, on the corner of Ponte Verrazzano
Tel. 055/688345
Closed Sunday, Monday lunch, and part of August
Credit cards: all
Price: expensive

Short, curly-haired Sante Collesano learned about seafood while fishing the waters off his native Sicily. His restaurant serves fine, fresh, simply prepared fish. The multi-course *antipasto* includes beautifully boiled octopus (*polpo lesso)*, baby shrimp, and Sicilian-style fresh anchovies baked with bay leaves and pine nuts. Pasta is nicely cooked, and whole fish are either grilled or baked, usually to perfection. Finish your meal with fresh fruit. The wine selection has drastically improved recently.

RESTAURANT
Il Cibreo
Via dei Macci 18r
Tel. 055/2341100
Closed July 15 through August
Credit cards: all
Price: expensive in front, moderate in back

Fabio and Benedetta Picchi serve traditional, hard-to-find Tuscan dishes at their restaurants near the Sant'Ambrogio market. The main restaurant, on via dei Macci, with its wooden wainscoting, white tablecloths, and short-stemmed wine glasses, offers an ample menu that starts off with an assortment of Tuscan *antipasto* tastes, including chicken liver spread and tripe and chickpea salad. First-course soups are fine, and the rustic meat dishes are more successful than the fish. Desserts are made by local baker Giulio Corti, and chocoholics will be thrilled by the dark brown wedge that's a cross between icing and a brownie. The wine selection has lots of lows, and most of the whites are to be avoided. If Fabio likes you, he'll sit at your table and discuss your menu.

Behind Cibreo's kitchen, with an entrance around the corner, a smaller, casual, crowded restaurant dishes out most of the same *cucina* served in the front room. Glasses have no stems, seating is communal, and prices are much lower here.

Fabio and Benedetta have recently opened an old-fashioned grocery store, around the corner from both restaurants, that seems as if it's been there forever. They carry quality gourmet-type food and lovely wines at expensive prices.

RESTAURANT
Coco Lezzone
Via del Parioncino 6r
Tel. 055/287178
Closed Wednesday evening and Sunday, and Saturday in summer
No credit cards
Price: expensive

Coco Lezzone, "smelly cook" in Florentine dialect, serves typical Tuscan dishes in the original tiny, white-tiled front room and in a newer, larger dining room in the back. The soups are good, and the roast pork *(arista)* is tasty. The meat croquettes *(crocchette)* are made with ground filet and cooked in a tomato sauce. Tender, tiny *primizie*, the first vegetables of the season, are a specialty, but they are usually overcooked, in the local tradition. Service is swift, and you may finish your meal in less than thirty minutes. Don't order the house wine.

RESTAURANT
Enoteca Pinchiorri
Via Ghibellina 87r
Tel. 055/242777
Closed Sunday, Monday lunch, and August
Credit cards: American Express, Visa
Price: very expensive

The Enoteca Pinchiorri is considered by many to be Italy's brightest gastronomic star. It's a beautiful, tasteful restaurant that seats fifty, with all the trappings of elegant dining—hand-painted Richard Ginori china, Riedel crystal, damask tablecloths, attentive service. But the *cucina,* either innovative or *ritrovata* ("found again"—who lost it?), has never swept me away. Although the food is skillfully prepared by chef Annie Feolde and a large staff of young professionals, I have never eaten anything truly memorable here. The spectacle of waiters whisking domed silver covers from plates in front of diners, in unison, strikes me as silly.

The best part of the meal is the wine, every drop a pleasure. Unless you have a specific preference from the wine books (surely they are too big to be called lists), your sommelier will serve you the wine that he, or Giorgio Pinchiorri, feels you merit. Important people drink better wines at the Enoteca. Giorgio is passionate and obsessive about his collection. Some of his wines can't be found elsewhere, and the cellar, which he owns privately, is absolutely breathtaking, with a vast and truly impressive selection of vintage Italian, French, and Californian wines. The Sauterne room, the Romanée-Conti hand-numbered double magnums, and the stacked pyramids of stupendous Tuscan wines can bring enophiles to their knees. If this sounds like your idea of fun, reserve a table, grab a gold credit card or a pile of cash, and hustle off to the Enoteca Pinchiorri.

RESTAURANT
Garga
Via del Moro 48r
Tel. 055/298898
Closed Saturday lunch, Sunday,
and August
Credit card: American Express
Price: moderate

Garga was probably Firenze's tiniest restaurant but a recent move up the street has expanded the possibilities of this delightful trattoria. Giuliano Garga's *cucina* is Tuscan, with a few new twists due to the influence of his Canadian wife, Sharon. Fresh-tasting pasta, lovely mixed field greens dressed with fantastic extra virgin olive oil, and nicely done meat and fish dishes are featured on their menu. Sharon's cheesecake has become a classic. Some wines are fine.

RESTAURANT
Il Guscio
Via dell'Orto 49r
Tel. 055/223737
Closed Saturday lunch and
Sunday
No credit cards
Price: low moderate

Il Guscio, "the shell," is a tiny two-room *trattoria* that feeds the San Frediano neighborhood at lunch and a young local crowd of regulars in the evening. The *cucina* is home-style, with Tuscan classics and a few original pasta dishes, nicely cooked. The menu is limited and changes daily. Wines are simple, service is quick and friendly, and prices are low.

RESTAURANT
Monkey Business
Chiasso dei Baroncelli
Tel. 055/288219

Closed Tuesday
Credit cards: all
Price: moderate

What will the hypertraditional Florentines think of Monkey Business, hidden in an alley off Piazza della Signoria? The decor is tropical jungle, complete with a life-size elephant in the entrance, the *cucina* has been inspired by exotic South American with a bit of trendy Tex-Mex and Cajun thrown in, plus a few concessions to unadventurous Italians. Manager Luciano Ioppoli is a pro and has chosen some wonderful wines for his restaurant. The kitchen is manned by a Sardinian and a Tex-Friulian, an amazing combo, and the food is well prepared, although it's not the same as most of New Orleans, Texas, or South America. Will Luciano's attempt at creating a no-smoking area be successful in a country that takes its cigarettes seriously? One can hope.

RESTAURANT
Da Noi
Via Fiesolana 40r
Tel. 055/242917
Closed Sunday, Monday, and
August
No credit cards
Price: expensive

Da Noi, a six-table restaurant near Santa Croce, owned by co-workers Bruno Tramontana and Sabine Busch, husband and wife, approaches the concept of *cucina* from a very personal point of view. The decor is understated and elegant, with attractive art, nicely appointed tables, and a warm, intimate ambience. Bruno, from the Garfagnana area north of Lucca, prepares a creative *cucina*, but his Tuscan-ness shows through in the food's simplicity. He works in tandem with Paolino Casu in the kitchen. Their basic ingredients are local, seasonal, treated with respect. Pasta is frequently homemade, soups are fresh and full-flavored, crepes are stuffed with tasty fillings. Meat, poultry, and fish are lovely—lightly cooked, perfumed with herbs and wines, or even home-smoked—and vegetables are nicely done, green and lively. Plates are simply arranged, anti-decorative. Sabine is a charming hostess who will recite and explain the menu in at least five languages, and can suggest wines from one of Firenze's finest personal selections. She also makes all Da Noi's terrific, not-too-sweet desserts, the best in the city. Pastry, *gelato,* ices, and other desserts are splendid, unusual, and worth the calories. Eating at Da Noi is always a thrill. Reservations are a must, and should be made well in advance.

RESTAURANT
Omero
Via Pian dei Giullari 11r
Tel. 055/220053
Closed Tuesday and August
Credit cards: American Express,
MasterCard
Price: high moderate

A five-minute cab ride up a narrow winding road leads to the hamlet where Galileo Galilei was exiled. His house is across the street from Omero, a quintessential Florentine country *trattoria,* with a quintessential Tuscan view of olive trees, cypresses, and hills. The *cucina* is home-style, pure, and never strays from the simple Florentine specialties. *Salumi* are local and tasty. First-course stars are bread soups (*ribollita* in the winter and *panzanella* in the summer), homemade *ricotta* and spinach–filled *ravioli*, and *pappardelle*—wide strips of pasta sauced with wild boar or wild rabbit. Meats, chicken, and rabbit are grilled over a real charcoal fire or deep-fried in fresh oil. Omero prepares the Florentine specialty *bistecca alla fiorentina* to perfection—charcoal-grilled T-bone steak at least two inches thick, and rare. Seasonal vegetables are eaten raw (*in pinzimonio*) or deep-fried. Ask for *carciofi senza pastella*, featherweight artichokes fried without batter. *Pecorino* cheese, fresh or aged, is always a good choice, an excuse to dig into Omero's stellar wine list of Tuscan reds. Desserts are lackluster, although the *meringa* is tasty and sweet. On your way out, buy a piece of first-rate *pecorino* or *salumi* from Alvaro, the small grocery store in the entrance.

RESTAURANT, TAKE-OUT
Osteria di Giuseppe Alessi
Via di Mezzo 26r
Tel. 055/41821
Closed Sunday
No credit cards
Price: inexpensive

Giuseppe Alessi, who used to own a highly rated restaurant outside Firenze and has written an Etruscan cookbook, has opened a take-out diner with six tiny marble-topped tables not far from Santa Croce. His sign defines the *cucina* as old-fashioned, rustic, and Tuscan, but the food is mostly undistinguished, as are the wines. Cheese, however, is local and wonderful. Prices are low.

Giuseppe is about to open the second part of his restaurant, called Lo Studiolo, next door. It won't be fancy, he swears, although the food will be more elaborate, and there'll be tablecloths, bottled wines, seating for fifty, and probably higher prices.

RESTAURANT
Pane e Vino
Via Poggio Bracciolini 48
Tel. 055/683746
Closed Sunday, holidays, and August
Credit cards: all
Price: high moderate

Inconveniently located and open only in the evening, the Enoteca Pane e Vino is nevertheless worth a visit. The *salumi* and cheeses are tasty, a good choice, but the dishes that are actually cooked aren't always successful. The wine list, which rotates over 400 wines, offers a wide, reasonably priced, quality selection. After 10:30, many locals stop in for one of Pane e Vino's homemade desserts and a glass of fine dessert wine. Claustrophobics should reserve one of the two ground-floor tables and avoid eating downstairs.

RESTAURANT
Pennello
Via Dante Alighieri 4r
Tel. 055/94848
Closed Sunday evening, Monday, and August
No credit cards
Price: moderate

Pennello, also known as Casa di Dante, serves home-style *cucina*. It's a typical Tuscan *trattoria*, complete with paintings of dubious worth and sassy waiters. But Pennello's main feature is a large display of platters, bowls, and trays containing a vast assortment of self-service *antipasti*—marinated fish, vegetables, and salads—that makes a delightful meal for many diners. Pasta is generally overcooked, but the fresh *tortelloni* filled with cheese and spinach are tasty. Meat dishes are simple. *Baccalà*—salt cod cooked with tomatoes and garlic—is served on Fridays. Cooked fruit desserts or classic *crème caramel* are the best dessert choices. Wines should be better.

RESTAURANT
Le Quattro Stagioni
Via Maggio 61
Tel. 055/218906
Closed Sunday, Saturday in summer, and August
Credit cards: American Express, Diners Club, MasterCard
Price: high moderate

Le Quattro Stagioni looks like a typical tourist trap. Instead, it's one of the city's best restaurants. Owner-chef Piero Giannacci's *cucina* is classic and well prepared. The varied menu offers some Tuscan dishes and a nice interregional selection for the regulars who turn up six days a week. Pasta, *risotto*, and light vegetable *gnocchi* are wonderful. Fish and meat are nicely cooked, and the fingernail-size deep-fried baby shrimp and tiny cuttlefish (*moscardini*) are greaseless and crunchy.

*Florentine fast food: Chianti and
crostini at a stand-up bar*

Desserts are homemade, simple, and tasty. The raisin and pine nut–studded custard, hidden on the middle shelf of the dessert cart, disappears quickly. The wine selection is limited but lovely. I always enjoy eating at this timeless restaurant.

RESTAURANT
I Raddi
Via d'Ardiglione 47r
Tel. 055/211072
Closed Tuesday
Credit card: American Express
Price: low moderate

Luciano Raddi, an ex-boxer and participant for the past twenty-seven years in *calcio in costume,* the medieval madness disguised as football, has taken to the kitchen of I Raddi with his wife and children. Their simple *trattoria* serves plain, home-style Florentine dishes. Soups are tasty, pasta is usually overcooked, stewed meat dishes are good. Desserts are sometimes homemade. The wine selection is limited, with no high points.

RESTAURANT
La Rucola
Via del Leone 50r
Tel. 055/224002
Closed Sunday and Monday lunch
Credit card: American Express
Price: expensive

It's not easy keeping track of Luciano Ghinassi, but it's worth the effort. Fans of his past restaurants are flocking to La Rucola. The decor is simple, rustic, and attractive, and the menu of unusual Tuscan dishes is well prepared. Five first and second courses are changed daily, and the desserts are fine. Luciano is paying more attention to the wines than he used to, and some quality selections are available.

RESTAURANT
Lo Strettoio
Via Serpiolle 7
Tel. 055/403044
Closed Sunday and Monday
No credit cards
Price: expensive

The Martini Benassai family traditions were gastronomic. Recipes, cooking techniques, and wines were discussed, flavors compared and confronted, with a specific aim: the educated palate. Andrea Benassai learned his lesson well, and has created a restaurant in the olive mill of his family's seventeenth-century villa in the countryside, a twenty-minute ride through Firenze's northern suburbs. Lo Strettoio is furnished with family antiques and mementos—lace handkerchiefs line the bread baskets, and no two tables are alike. The Tuscan country villa ambience is reflected in the *cucina,* composed of Andrea's remembered tastes. Many of the basic ingredients, local and strictly seasonal, come from neighborhood farmers, and extra virgin olive oil and a deep, rustic red wine are the restaurant's own production. The *antipasto* is a winner, a lengthy multiple-choice test of tastes: my answer is "all of the above" to fried dough balls *(coccoli),* *semolina* lozenges, *polenta* cubes, rich braised sweet and sour onions, game pâté, Tuscan tripe, salads, aspics, and more. I rarely get to the first course of beautifully cooked pasta, flavored with herbs and vegetables. Meats and courtyard animals are nicely done, and desserts are homemade. Wines are wonderful, and the Tuscan selection is a pleasure to choose from. This hard-to-find restaurant is worth the cab ride if you're celebrating a special occasion.

PIZZA
Borgo Antico
Piazza Santo Spirito 6r
Tel. 055/210437
Closed Sunday
No credit cards
Price: low moderate

Borgo Antico is in piazza Santo Spirito, and always crowded. They make a decent pizza, baked in a wood-burning oven. The garlic and chili pepper special is a personal favorite. Drink the beer.

PIZZA
Al Pescatore
Via Ponte alla Mosse 54
Tel. 055/353974
Closed Monday
Credit cards: American Express, Diners Club, Visa
Price: moderate

Al Pescatore, a seafood restaurant, makes a decent pizza in a wood-burning oven. The whale-shaped chocolate-covered ice cream *(balena)* is a favorite with kids.

TABLEWARE
Richard Ginori
Via Rondinelli 17r
Tel. 055/10041
Credit cards: all

This is the biggest and best of the Richard Ginori shops. Two large windows on via Rondinelli formally display the latest output of the nearby Sesto Fiorentino factory (see page 241). Inside, the complete Ginori production is displayed: place settings of seventeenth-century, Empire, Art Nouveau, and modern porcelain dinnerware. Superchef Gualtiero

Marchesi has designed his own set of dishes to suit his culinary philosophy. Recent reproductions of architect Gio Ponti's designs are stunning. The shop also sells Murano glass, Broggi and Ricci silver, some Alessi stainless steel, and many fine non-Italian items, like Riedel and Baccarat crystal.

HOUSEWARES
La Ménagère
Via dei Ginori 8r
Tel. 055/213875
Credit cards: all

La Ménagère has the best selection of quality housewares in Firenze. Founded in 1896, it looks like an old-fashioned general store, with wooden floors, long counter, and tall cabinets filled with stainless-steel cookware. La Ménagère is such a gold mine that it will take a while to examine all the rooms, shelves, stands, racks, and display cases filled with mostly Italian products. Choose from Richard Ginori porcelain, Bellini ceramics, Sambonet and Alessi stainless, IVV glassware, Guzzini plastics, Style picnic sets, Montana knives, and a wide assortment of rolling pins, sifters, wooden spoons, custom doormats, tin olive oil cans, pasta guitars and hand-cranked machines, a wind-up spit rotisserie, and every nonelectric *caffettiera* imaginable. The selection of cookware is exceptional, in copper, stainless, iron, enamel, and practically every other heatproof material known to man. They won't ship, but they will pack your purchases for shipping. La Ménagère's wonder-

ful ornate 1914 cash register is reproduced on their sturdy plastic bags.

HOUSEWARES
Eurostovil
Via Nazionale 81/85r
Tel. 055/214389
Credit cards: all

Eurostovil has a large selection of 110-volt coffee machines, for use in the U.S., including all models of the Pavoni, the Rolls Royce of coffee machines. Their dinnerware isn't Italian, but they sell Zani & Zani stainless-steel serving pieces, Montana knives, and glassware by IVV and Carlo Moretti of Murano.

TABLEWARE
Loli's Emporium
Via Guicciardini 122r
Tel. 055/212646
Credit cards: all

Loli Baffetti's keen sense of design is responsible for the eye-catching windows of her Emporium, filled with tasteful, elegant modern objects. One-of-a-kind pieces created by European artisans and Italian design classics are dramatically displayed in this shop near the Pitti Palace.

POTTERY
Sbigoli
Via S. Egidio 4r
Tel. 055/2479713
Credit cards: all

Sbigoli sells a wonderful selection of terracotta pottery, in a wealth of sizes and shapes. Unglazed garden pots, rustic no-lead bakeware, and a lovely selection of hand-decorated dinnerware, pitchers, egg cups, mugs, and attractive serving pieces are reasonably priced and hard to resist. I love the green and white, or green and yellow spatterware, "blessed" with a sprinkling of color. Choose from traditional patterns, or create your own with owner Valentino Adami. Shipping makes this pottery more convenient to purchase, but less of a bargain.

TABLE LINENS
Loretta Caponi
Borgo Ognissanti 12r
Tel. 055/213668
Credit cards: all

If you've always dreamed of owning heirloom linens but no one has left you any, head for Loretta Caponi. The selection of hand embroidery is unique, exceptional, eccentric, and justly expensive. Loretta loves the creativity of custom orders and has designed table linens to match her clients' whims, from dinnerware and wallpaper to villa gardens. Placemat sets known as *servizi all'americana* are embroidered and appliquéd with hunting, fishing, fruit, or floral themes, each mat and napkin decorated with a different scene or design. A lemon series uses at least ten shades of green and yellow, depicting lemons in bloom, on the branch, and sliced into halves, quarters, wedges, and slices. Brightly colored waterfowl and marine life sets are also knockouts. Linen tablecloths can be ordered with hand fagoting, handmade lace inserts, or trimmed

with hand embroidery. Damask cloths can be made in any size up to almost 24 meters (eighty feet) long. The three-dimensional mimosa-pattern cloth with a scalloped hem is a classic. Practical Loretta says that almost all her linens can be machine-washed. Prices are steep.

TABLE LINENS
Biagini
Via della Vigna Nuova 41r
Tel. 055/294733
Credit cards: all

Biagini has a nice selection of quality machine-stitched table linens and will make up tablecloths and napkins in any size you need. They usually have a few spectacular antique pieces that seem fairly priced.

STATIONERY
Il Torchio
Via dei Bardi 17
Tel. 055/2342862
Credit cards: American Express, MasterCard, Visa

Il Torchio has a nice selection of blank books bound with handmade Florentine paper. They're perfect for recipes, wine labels, guestbooks and albums. Il Torchio's artisans will lovingly recover a special book, or make up custom orders in the paper and leather combination of your choice.

CERAMIC TILES
Riccardo Barthel
Via dei Fossi 11r
Tel. 055/283683
No credit cards

The rustic tiled kitchen is Riccardo Barthel's specialty, and most of the tiles sold in his shop are handmade. Feast your eyes on reproductions of classics or simple solid-colored tiles, to be combined with a vast selection of contrasting borders. There are also some antique Neapolitan and Sicilian tiles. If you can't afford to buy a whole room, the patterned tiles make nice trivets.

SILVER TABLEWARE
Argenteria Il Leone
Via S. Giovanni 13/15r
Tel. 055/27848
No credit cards

Until two years ago, Il Leone had no showroom, and orders were taken in a corner of the workroom, over the racket of tiny hammers pounding away. But the fourteenth-century building's ground floor has been restored, revealing brick arches and beamed ceilings, creating a labyrinth of workrooms, each devoted to a different phase of the silversmithing craft. Lathes for shaping and buffers for polishing are used on Il Leone's silver and silver-plated pieces, but all other work is done by hand. The showroom is filled with glass display cases of plain, hammered, and chiseled trays, serving pieces, bowls, ice buckets, leaf-shaped candy dishes, and decorative items, but Walter Caselli assured me that he will custom-make or reproduce practically anything. His prices are the lowest in Firenze.

TABLEWARE
Parenti
Via Tornabuoni 93
Tel. 055/214438
Credit cards: all

Parenti, founded in 1865, has an interesting selection of tableware and silver. Many items are second-hand—not old enough to be antique, the granddaughter of the original Parenti told me. But I was impressed by silver or silverplate knife trays, berry spoons, potato rings, oyster forks, lamb bone holders, *osso buco* marrow scoops, sugar tongs, tea strainers, grape shears, and champagne stirrers.

BOOKS
BM Bookshop
Borgo Ognissanti 4r
Tel. 055/294575
Credit card: American Express

The BM Bookstore carries only new books, both hardcover and paperback, and has a wide variety of beautiful photographic books on Italy. They also sell English-language cookbooks and wine books, and can always be counted on for the latest edition of Burton Anderson's wine guide.

BOOKS
Paperback Exchange
Via Fiesolana 31r
Tel. 055/2478154
No credit cards

The Paperback Exchange sells some new paperbacks and accepts used paperbacks in exchange for credit on used-book purchases. They also sell English-language regional Italian cookbooks.

SHIPPING SERVICE

■

Fracassi International Forwarders
Via Santo Spirito 11
Tel. 055/263340

And now that you've bought it all and can't even bear to think about packing it up and dragging it home, call Fracassi. They will pick up your purchases, pack them, and ship them home, by air or sea. Their service may be costly, but everything will arrive intact.

ESSENCES
Officina Profumo–Farmaceutica di Santa Maria Novella
Via della Scala 16
Tel. 055/216276
No credit cards

The chapel entrance of the Officina Profumo–Farmaceutica di Santa Maria Novella sets the stage for the pharmaceutical-herbal-floral essence specialties, displayed in tall, dark oak cabinets. A visit to what feels like a medieval drugstore is a most astounding experience, and is accompanied by a unique, haunting scent. Fainting salts, strange tasting *liquore* and digestive tonics, as well as skin creams, soaps, shampoos, and potpourri are all made with original seventeenth-century formulas.

FONTE BLANDA

HOTEL
Corte dei Butteri
Via Aurelia Nord km. 157
Tel. 0564/885546
Credit cards: American Express, Visa
Price: moderate; very expensive in July and August

RESTAURANT
Bar Trattoria Uccellina
Via Aurelia km. 163.2
Tel. 0564/596000
Closed Wednesday
No credit cards
Price: moderate

The truckers whose rigs fill the parking lot of the Bar Trattoria Uccellina along the via Aurelia share this restaurant in the summer with tanned tourists visiting the coast or one of Toscana's most beautiful parks. The *cucina* is uncomplicated and abundant. Pasta is homemade, and toothsome spaghetti is laced with a meaty sauce of wild boar *(cinghiale)*. Pork ribs or chops are tasty, roast meats are generally overcooked, game is offered in season, and vegetables are lackluster. Finish your meal with seasonal fruit or ice cream bars. The coppery-colored white wine, sold by the carafe, won't satisfy exigent palates, but it slips down nicely in the summer.

FORTE DEI MARMI

HOTEL
Augustus
Viale Morin 169
Tel. 0584/80202

Credit cards: all
Price: luxury

HOTEL

Astoria Garden
Via Leonardo da Vinci 16
Tel. 0584/80754
Credit cards: all
Price: moderate

RESTAURANT

Lorenzo
Via Carducci 61
Tel. 0584/84030
Closed Monday except in
summer; closed November and
December
Credit cards: all
Price: expensive

Reservations are hard to come by in handsome, tanned Lorenzo Viani's newly redecorated restaurant in Forte dei Marmi. The light, well-prepared fish dishes are as elegant as the clientele. Lorenzo painstakingly hunts down the freshest seafood, which the kitchen treats with respect. Pasta and *risotto* are nicely cooked. Seasonal vegetables and herbs flavor most dishes. Desserts are simple, and the wines, the best in fashionable Forte, are worthy of the *cucina*.

FUCECCHIO

HOTEL

Il Convento
Via San Quirico 33
Pontenovo, outside Pistoia
Tel. 0573/152652
Credit cards: MasterCard, Visa
Price: moderate

RESTAURANT

Le Vedute
Via Romana-Lucchese 121
Ponte a Cappiano
Tel. 0571/297201
Closed Tuesday and most of
August
Credit cards: American Express,
Diners Club
Price: moderate

Le Vedute is where the managers of all the tanneries in the Arno Valley take their important guests. It's a large classic restaurant but the *cucina* is mostly fish and shellfish, decidedly unusual for inland Fucecchio. Most food is simply treated. Pasta is homemade and nicely cooked, and mushrooms are served in season. The menu is interesting, and dishes are well prepared. The wine list is wonderful, and a joy to find in a restaurant like this. Watch out for weddings and communions on Sundays, when service may suffer a bit.

GAIOLE IN CHIANTI

HOTEL

Relais Fattoria Vignale
Via Panigiani 15
Radda in Chianti (close by)
Tel. 0577/738300
Credit card: American Express
Price: moderate

RESTAURANT

Badia a Coltibuono
Coltibuono
Gaiole in Chianti
Tel. 0577/749424
Closed Monday and November
Credit cards: all

This typical Tuscan *trattoria* is on the Badia a Coltibuono estate, famous for its wine, extra virgin olive oil, and Lorenza de' Medici's cooking school (see page 41). The *cucina* is simple and never changes. *Salumi*, chicken liver *crostini*, homemade pasta with flavorful meaty sauces, and mushrooms in season are all tasty. Meat is stewed or roasted. Desserts are lackluster, but the chocolates, made by owner Giannetto Catinari's brother Roberto (see page 212), are a treat. The Badia a Coltibuono winery's products are featured, and the wines are well priced.

GREVE

SALUMI

Macelleria Falorni
Piazza Matteotti 69
Tel. 055/853029
Closed Monday, Wednesday, and
Thursday afternoons

After a drive on the via Chiantigiana, south of Firenze, with its breathtakingly beautiful countryside and vineyards that produce Chianti Classico wines, stop off in Greve for a stroll around piazza Matteotti. The shops are unexciting: the wine shop staff is surly and unhelpful, and the basket shop is half-filled with Oriental merchandise. The clear star of the piazza is the Macelleria Falorni. They butcher all the meat that goes into their fine *salumi*. Pork *salame*, fennel-laced *finocchiona*, crumbly *sbriciolona*, giant *soprassata*, and peppery *pancetta* are among their tasty homemade products. Another specialty is wild boar *(cinghiale)*, black-bristled with dark maroon meat, sold fresh, or cured as *salsiccie* (sausages), *salamino* ("little salami"), or *prosciutto*.

IMPRUNETA

POTTERY
Mario Mariani
Via di Capello 29
Tel. 055/2011950
Closed Sunday
No credit cards

Mario Mariani's artisanal production is wonderful. Each piece of pottery is handcrafted, then shifted to his kiln. Once the room-size kiln is filled, Mario kindles a hardwood fire that blazes for up to fifty hours. His terracotta production is small, traditional, and reasonably priced, although shipping makes these bulky pieces expensive. His cousin, also named Mariani, located next door, has a larger production of nontraditional decorative objects. Mario will take you over for a look if you don't find what you want at his place.

LARI

PASTA
Pastificio Martelli
Via S. Martino 3
Tel. 0587/684238

Pasta isn't a particular specialty of Toscana, and it is frequently overcooked in this region. In spite of this, Italy's best dry pasta comes from the tiny Tuscan village of Lari.

Home-style cooking simmering on an old-fashioned stove

What makes Martelli pasta so terrific? The factory is owned and run by the Martelli family, brothers Dino and Mario and their wives Lucia and Valeria. The secret of their pasta isn't in the water, or the 100-percent Canadian hard wheat (the best), ground into *semola,* the hard-grain equivalent of flour. Their pasta is extruded through bronze dyes, which produce a rougher surface that holds on to sauce better—but many pasta makers use bronze dyes. The secret of Martelli pasta is time. The pasta-making machines are never pushed to the maximum; the dough is kneaded gently and extruded with less pressure, leaving more air in the pasta. Most *spaghetti* are slowly dried for eight hours, but the Martelli pasta is dried for fifty hours, maintaining more of the grain flavor. The resultant golden rough-textured pasta, which looks as if it's been sanded, is produced in only four shapes. *Spaghetti* and thinner *spaghettini* are dried on rods, forming foot-long narrow U's. The barely ridged *maccheroni* are a tribute to Napoli, the birthplace of pasta, and the *penne* (quill-shaped pasta) are smooth, without the usual deep ridges necessary for most *penne* to hang on to the sauce. They all need to cook in more water than most pasta, Dino warned me, but the instructions are in Italian and English on the package. In the best Italian family tradition, twelve Martellis sit down to a bowl of pasta together every day. A visit to the factory is most fun on Wednesdays and Fridays, when extra-long spaghetti are made.

LUCCA

Surrounded by intact Renaissance ramparts, Lucca is a jewel of a city, with medieval monuments, Romanesque churches, and nearby villas in the green countryside. Garden fans shouldn't miss a visit to Villa Reale, Villa Torrigiani, and Villa Mansi.

HOTEL
Villa la Principessa
Strada Statale del Brennero
   1616
Tel. 0583/370037
Closed November 15 through
   February
Credit cards: all
Price: luxury

HOTEL
Villa Casanova
Via di Casanova
Balbano, west of Lucca (close by)
Tel. 0583/548429
Closed November through March
No credit cards
Price: moderate

PASTRY
Pasticceria Marino Taddeucci
Piazza San Michele 34
Tel. 0583/44933
Closed Thursday

Buccellato, a specialty of Lucca, is surely one of the world's most austere desserts: simple bread dough enriched, but not too much, with raisins, anise, and a bit of sugar. I haven't been able to work up too much enthusiasm for this ring-shaped cake, but the best version is produced by Marino Taddeucci. Look for Life Saver *buccellato* next to the bakery's sign.

CEREALS AND SEEDS
Cereali Sementi Marcucci
Via S. Lucia 13
Tel. 0583/9119
Closed Wednesday afternoon

Cereal, seeds, soap, and dog food is the unlikely combination of wares sold in this *simpatico* store. Large burlap sacks are filled with beans in different sizes, shapes, and colors, lentils from Castelluccio (see page 250), rice, polenta flour, and most important, emmer *(farro)* for the Lucca area's fantastic bean and emmer soup. The large sack of brownish pasta at the end of the row is made especially for dogs—it seems only logical that Italian canines would have a pasta all their own.

RESTAURANT
Giulio in Pelleria
Via San Tommaso 29
Tel. 0583/55948
Closed Sunday, Monday, August,
   and Christmas
No credit cards
Price: low moderate

Giulio in Pelleria is a classic *trattoria.* The *cucina* is regional, home-style, unpretentious, and fantastic. Emmer *(farro),* a wonderful wheaty grain, is cooked in bean soup. I find it hard to resist the *farinata,* a vegetable soup thickened with cornmeal. Meats, stewed for hours, are tasty. The horsemeat tartare will appeal to the intrepid, but isn't as bad as it sounds. Desserts are traditional, but the flan of candied fruit and Swiss chard is strange. Wines are from the Lucca area and not too exciting. The strictly local crowd of workers and families who pack this restaurant for lunch and dinner are onto a good thing.

MONTECATINI TERME

Montecatini, known to Americans for a line of beauty treatments, is famous in Italy for its waters, unpleasant tasting but remarkably laxative. The spa town, with its Belle Epoque architecture, is a pleasant place to recover from the rigors of gastronomic Italy, although it's not without its own temptations.

HOTEL
Grand Hotel & La Pace
Via delle Torretta 1
Tel. 0572/75801
Closed November to March
Credit cards: all
Price: luxury

When I think of spas, cures, and taking the waters, I think of the Grand Hotel & La Pace, with its century-old trees, park, swimming pool, tennis, fully equipped health center, greenhouse filled with orchids, and Belle Epoque ambience. Mud or ozone baths, seaweed treatments, massages, and sauna are all available at this luxury, truly "grand" hotel.

HOTEL
Park Hotel La Sorgente
Pieve a Nievole
Tel. 0572/83116
Credit cards: American Express,
   Visa
Price: low expensive

PASTRY
Ditta Stefano Desideri
Via Gorizia 5
Tel. 0572/71088
Closed Tuesday

Wafer cookies (cialde) are a specialty of Montecatini. A simple batter is poured, cooked, and pressed in a metal mold; two rounds of wafer thus produced are filled with a mixture of crushed almonds and sugar, and then re-cooked. Each of Montecatini's *pasticceria* has its own design stamped on these seven-inch disks. I love the pattern on Desideri's *cialde,* the best in Montecatini: a heron and spitting toad fountain. Brother and sister Stefano and Maria Grazia Desideri also make wonderful *brigidini*—eggshell-thin cookies delicately flavored with aniseed—without the usual dose of artificial coloring that most *brigidini* makers use.

RESTAURANT

Pier Angelo
Via IV Novembre 99
Tel. 0572/75871
Credit cards: American Express,
  MasterCard, Visa
Price: low expensive

Ristorante Pier Angelo is located in a recently restored Art Nouveau villa with stained glass windows, carpet, fine linens, crystal stemwear, and large cream-colored service plates. Although the inspiration behind many of the dishes is Tuscan, Pierangelo Borantini's *cucina* is innovative and professional, prepared with the finest freshest seasonal bounty. Meat and fish are beautifully cooked. The fried dishes are unbelievably light, greaseless, and crisp. Presentations are dramatic, with flaky pastry–topped soups and fanned-out vegetables—a bit formal, but somehow right in the villa setting. Leave room for dessert, skillfully prepared by Pierangelo's English wife, Roxana. Wines are first-rate—Italian, French, and Californian. Coffee is a special *arabica* blend that coffee-roaster Andrea Trinci (see page 212) has created for his friend Pierangelo. Spend the night in one of the two suites above the restaurant.

MONTEFOLLONICO

RESTAURANT-INN

La Chiusa
Via Madonnina 88
Tel. 0577/669668
Closed Tuesday except in August
  and September, and January
  through March
Credit cards: American Express,
  Diners Club
Price: expensive

Although it's difficult (impossible at night) to find La Chiusa, a farm-complex-turned-inn, it is worth the effort. The setting is breathtaking. Owner Dania Lucherini is beautiful and hospitable, and she can cook. The restaurant is small but spacious, beautifully restored in Dania's personal style. The *cucina* is revisited Tuscan, with vegetables from the La Chiusa's garden and local ingredients treated with the utmost respect. They make their own extra virgin olive oil, and Dania's husband, Umberto, searches out fine cheeses and wines. I have never ordered a meal here, but let Dania compose a series of *assaggi* ("tastes") and tell Umberto when I've had enough, a difficult decision. Flavors are intense, Tuscan, and combined with restraint. Mushrooms are the best I've ever had, firm and tasting of forest. Desserts are good but I always finish with the *pan di caffè*, a spongy coffee custard. Eight rooms for overnight guests are special, decorated with farmhouse furniture, equipped with the most fabulous bathrooms ever. Eating and staying overnight at La Chiusa is my idea of a treat!

MONTELUPO

POTTERY

Guido Dolfi
Via Tosco-Romagnola 8/B
Tel. 0571/519016
Closed Saturday afternoon and
  Sunday
No credit cards

Guido Dolfi makes wonderful majolica dinnerware and terracotta cookware. The patterns are traditional, the pottery is hand-made, and the charming yellow and blue Montelupo bird pattern, usually so poorly executed, is the best I've seen.

PANZANO

See pages 217–219 for suggestions of places to stay in and around Panzano.

SALUMI
Antica Macelleria Cecchini
Via XX Luglio 11
Tel. 055/852020
Closed Thursday and Sunday
afternoons, Monday, and
Wednesday

Dario Cecchini, following a 250-year-old family tradition, sells hard-to-find *Chianina* beef at his shop in Panzano, the heart of the Chianti area south of Firenze. His veterinary studies have made him a formidable judge of cattle, and he examines all beef on the hoof. Splendid full-flavored steaks, roasts, and cuts for boiled beef are Dario's specialties. The sausages and fennel salami are beautifully spiced.

PIENZA

Pienza, named for Pope Pio II, born there as Enea Silvio Piccolomini, is a jewel of a city. It was transformed (in only three years, from 1459 to 1462) by Florentine architect Bernardo Rossellino and the Pope, who turned the rustic hamlet of Corsignano into a graceful Renaissance town.

HOTEL
Posta-Marcucci
Bagno Vignone
Tel. 0577/887112
Credit cards: American Express,
Diners Club, MasterCard
Price: moderate

WINE AND
SPECIALTY FOODS
Club delle Fattorie
Piazza dei Martiri della
Libertà 2

Tel. 0578/748150
Closed Wednesday afternoon, and
Sunday from November to
Easter
Credit cards: all

The Club delle Fattorie, founded in 1969, offers a unique service. In a country known for its highly irregular postal service, Alberto del Buono has created a mail-order food and wine business that actually works. The catalogue features quality wines and special regional products not usually available outside their own areas, often packaged especially for the Club delle Fattorie. The selection of rare aged whiskys—twelve-year-old Lochnagar, sixteen-year-old Laphroaig, eighteen-year-old Tamnavulin, and a Macallan 1937 among others—is impressive. Dried *porcini* mushrooms, capers, balsamic vinegar, extra virgin olive oil, pasta, preserves, candied fruit, honey, cookies, chocolates, and natural cosmetics are all offered in the illustrated catalogue mailed to club members. The shop in Pienza sells all items listed in the catalogue. Prices are high. Mail and phone orders are accepted, and the Club will ship, although due to difficult Customs regulations they won't send alcoholic purchases to the U.S.

PIETRASANTA

HOTEL
Ariston
Viale Colombo 355
Lido di Camaiore (close by)
Tel. 0584/906633
Credit cards: American Express,
Visa
Price: expensive

HOTEL
Villa Iolanda
Viale Pistelli 127
Lido di Camaiore (close by)
Tel. 0584/64296
Credit cards: American Express,
Diners Club, Visa
Price: moderate

RESTAURANT
Sci
Vicolo di Porta a Lucca
No phone
Closed Sunday
No credit cards
Price: inexpensive

There are three tables in the dining room and two outside for lunch when the weather is nice. But the most important table is the one in the kitchen where the women work, preparing the home-style *cucina* that the local stoneworkers and sculptors adore. The food is unpretentious and gutsy, and the *fritto* of chicken and rabbit is fried in an iron frying pan. Vegetables, in true Tuscan style, are tasty but overcooked. When the food runs out, this *trattoria* closes, so be prepared to arrive early. Wines are not up to the rest of the delightful experience. Sci is open for lunch only.

PIEVE FOSCIANA

GRISTMILL
Ercolano Regoli
Pieve di Sotto
Pieve Fosciana
Tel. 0583/666095

Ercolano Regoli is a miller (*mugnaio*). His mill, where he stone-grinds corn, wheat, and smoked chestnuts, is powered by the swift-flowing Esarulo River. Ercolano's chestnut flour is intense, with a rich smoky flavor, ground as fine as baby powder. His wheat flour and cornmeal are also first-rate.

PIEVE SANTO STEFANO

HOTEL
Villa La Principessa
Strada Statale del Brennero 1616
Lucca (close by)
Tel. 0583/370037
Closed November 15 through February
Credit cards: all
Price: luxury

HOTEL
Villa Casanova
Via Casanova
Balbano, west of Lucca (close by)
Tel. 0583/548429
Closed November through March
No credit cards
Price: moderate

RESTAURANT
Vipore
No street address
Tel. 0583/59245
Closed all day Monday and Tuesday lunch
Credit cards: American Express, Diners Club
Price: moderate

Vipore is another one of those hard-to-find restaurants that is definitely worth the search. Cesare Casella is handsome, charming, and an outrageous dresser. He's wild about herbs and wine, and his parents' rustic *trattoria* has felt the influence of his obsessions. The *cucina* is pure Tuscan—seasonal, dressed with extra virgin olive oil, and flavored with some of the more than forty herbs growing outside the restaurant. *Salumi* are special, pasta is homemade, the grilled and roasted meats are cooked over aromatic wood, and mushrooms are splendid. The cheeses are carefully selected, and desserts are simple. A fantastic wine list is the result of Cesare's excursions, winery-hopping and tasting throughout Italy. It's a joy to behold and a pleasure to drink from. The country grocery shop annex sells local and Italian quality products.

PISA

Pisa, onetime powerful maritime republic on the shores of the Arno River, offers much more than the Leaning Tower. Architectural wonders stud the city, the botanical garden is fantastic, and the university has a world-class science department. Pisa also has a young group of noncompetitive wine-conscious restaurant owners who hang out together. They have made the city a haven for food lovers, and have earned praise for their dedication and passion.

HOTEL
Cavalieri
Piazza Stazione 2
Tel. 050/43290
Credit cards: all
Price: expensive

HOTEL
Villa di Corliano
Rigoli, outside San Giuliano Terme (close by)
Tel. 050/818193
Credit card: Visa
Price: moderate

RESTAURANT
Lo Schiaccianoci
Via Vespucci 104
Tel. 050/21024
Closed Sunday evening, Monday, and most of August
Credit card: MasterCard
Price: high moderate

Carlo Silvestrini inherited the name of his restaurant, Lo Schiaccianoci, "The Nutcracker," from the previous owner, but the *cucina* is original. Carlo sets out for the market each morning, ready to be inspired. And each day he returns to his restaurant, inspired, and composes a menu that takes advantage of the regional bounty that he's unearthed. Fish and seafood are nicely cooked, and flavors are balanced. The fish soup is intense and boneless; fried fish is lightly crisped and greaseless. The *cee* (young eels), raw and squirming in a plastic bin, won't appeal to the squeamish, but they are stellar—cooked in a tomato sauce, served with *parmigiano* cheese, a dish that breaks all the rules and succeeds. Seasonal desserts are creative and well prepared. Wines, reflecting the dedication of one of the young Pisan restaurateurs, are wonderful.

RESTAURANT
Al Ristoro dei Vecchi Macelli
Via Volturno 49
Tel. 050/20424

Closed Wednesday, Sunday lunch, and August
Credit cards: American Express, Diners Club, Visa
Price: expensive

The formula is a classic in Italy. Miranda Vanni presides in the kitchen, and her son, sommelier Stefano Vanni, in the dining room. Their restaurant serves light, fresh-tasting *cucina* based on quality fish and seafood from the coast, inland wild boar or pigeon, all perfumed with herbs or seasonal vegetables. Save room for the homemade desserts. Wines are wonderful.

RESTAURANT
Taverna Kostas
Via del Borghetto 39
Tel. 050/571467
Closed Monday and August
No credit cards
Price: inexpensive

Kostas Touloumtzis came to Pisa to study at the university, and became a convert to his contemporaries' passion about food and wine. His "taverna" is a simple, inexpensive student cafeteria at lunchtime, offering a fixed menu. In the evening the *cucina* is Greek, with some Tuscan influences creeping in occasionally. The wines, available anytime, are superb. Hooray for Kostas!

PONTE A MORIANO

HOTEL
Villa la Principessa
Strada Statale del Brennero
1616

Lucca (close by)
Tel. 0583/370037
Closed November 15 through February
Credit cards: all
Price: luxury

HOTEL
Villa Casanova
Via Casanova
Balbano, west of Lucca (close by)
Tel. 0583/548429
Closed November through March
No credit cards
Price: moderate

RESTAURANT
La Mora
Via Sesto di Moriano 104
Tel. 0583/57109
Closed Wednesday evening and Thursday
Credit cards: American Express, MasterCard
Price: high moderate

La Mora began over one hundred years ago, as a stopping-off point for mail, a resting place for horses, and a tavern serving local wine and fried fish from the Serchio River. Times have changed, but Sauro and Angela Brunicardi's restaurant is still firmly traditional. Sommelier and able host Sauro serves straightforward *cucina* based on the seasons, regional comfort food prepared by his wife, Angela, and chef Bruno Ercoli. *Salumi* are local, but I can never resist the *delizie del Serchio,* delicate, crispy, deep-fried whitebait that even fish-haters usually enjoy. The *minestra di farro,* emmer and bean soup, is a five-star dish, worth a gastronomic detour. Pasta is homemade, meats are

grilled or roasted with herbs, and cheese is local. Extra virgin olive oil is the house dressing, delicate yet full-flavored, olivey and green. Basic desserts are somewhat anticlimactic after La Mora's hearty *cucina,* and the *buccellato,* containing raisins with serious pits, is a bit austere but goes nicely with *vin santo.* Wines are splendid, and sommelier Sauro has one of my favorite selections of local, Tuscan, Italian, and foreign wines and spirits, all of impeccable quality. The *enoteca* in front of the restaurant sells wine and regional products of excellence. Whenever I asked other chefs or restaurateurs in Toscana where they liked to eat on their days off, the response was almost always La Mora. I agree.

PONTE ATTIGLIANO

BREAD
Forno Agnese
Via G. Braga 360
Tel. 0574/620081
Closed Sunday

One of my favorite breads comes from the Agnese family bakery in Ponte Attigliano, near Poggio a Caiano. Signora Agnese baked her bread, which has a kind of cult following in the area, until recently. Her daughter-in-law and grandson now run the bakery, everything is done the same way. The bread is made from Tuscan flour and starter. The oven is fired with wood, bread is placed on the oven's stone floor, the heavy iron door is plugged into the opening, and when it is time (something the Agneses know), the bread is done. On Saturdays bread is baked three or four times to satisfy the local demand. The Agnese bread is heavy—a one-kilo loaf looks half the size of a normal loaf of Tuscan bread. It's dense, wheaty, a bit sour, complex, and gummy when fresh. Agnese's bread is at its best one day old, barely toasted over a fire, rubbed with garlic, dipped in extra virgin olive oil, and sprinkled with salt and pepper.

Breadmaking tools are dusted with a patina of flour.

PRATO

Industrial Prato, considered an ugly duckling by the Florentines, is worth a visit, and has earned a place in the gastronomic hall of fame with their perfect *vin santo* cookie, unequaled elsewhere, and wonderful bread.

PASTRY
Mattei
Via Ricasoli 2
Tel. 0574/25756
Closed Monday

The quintessential *biscotti di Prato*, called *biscotti di mattonella* by the locals and *cantuccio* by those outside the city of Prato—an egg yolk–rich almond cookie far superior to all others—is produced by the Forno Mattei. They also bake a companion cookie, *brutti e buoni* ("ugly and good"), a squat, truncated cone of ground almond and egg white, clearly a move by the frugal Pratese to use the egg whites left over from making *biscotti di Prato*. The ladyfingers are

the best for making *tiramisù*, and their *torta con canditi*, a loaf studded with candied cherries and with a streusel topping, is a winner.

BREAD
Loggetti
Via Matteotti 13
Tel. 0574/25267
Closed every afternoon

Is it the water, the flour, the air, or the oven that makes Prato's bread so special? Saltless, made with a starter, flour, water, and yeast, it serves as a contrast to other foods, both in taste and texture. Most Pratese feel that the

best *pane* is produced by Loggetti, founded in 1921. The secret of the high quality, explained bakers Mario and Angelo, is in the mixture of local and imported flours, and the natural starter, used in combination with yeast. Each bread is signed, branded with the letters BL, for Logetti and his partner-cousin Bigalli, founders of this essential bakery.

BREAD
Barni
Via Ferrucci 24
Tel. 0574/20635
Closed Wednesday afternoon

A wood-burning oven in an old neighborhood bakery near Firenze

Some locals, and Florentines grateful for Giovanni Barni's delivery route in Firenze, prefer the bread from his bakery. Giovanni, his father, Luciano, and his grandfather, who was known as "Trentino," have always made their *pane* in a wood-burning oven with traditional methods, natural yeast, all-Italian flour, and some hand kneading on a wooden table. It's also my daily bread.

SPECIALTY FOODS
Giulebbe
Via dell'Arco 6
Tel. 0574/605370
Closed Wednesday afternoon

In Tuscan dialect *giulebbe* means "something sweet and special." All the wares that Osvaldo Baroncelli and Sauro Mazzoni have chosen to grace the shelves of Giulebbe aren't sweet, but they are special. Extra virgin olive oil, pasta, *sott'aceti* (preserved vegetables), and *marrons glacés* are first-rate. Imported and domestic products of excellence are just what I'd expect from Osvaldo, who also owns Prato's best restaurant.

RESTAURANT
Bruno
Via Verdi 12
Tel. 0574/23810

Closed Sunday, Thursday evening, and August
Credit card: American Express
Price: high moderate

Owner-sommelier Osvaldo Baroncelli seems to have made a wise choice when he hired youthful chef Franco Sacchetti, because the regional *cucina* they've produced is inspired. The appetizers are tasty, especially the *frittatine*—tiny pan-fried flans made with seasonal vegetables. First-course soups and homemade pasta are traditional; second-course meats are nicely done and flavored with herbs. Finish with seasonal *gelato.* Wines complement the *cucina,* and the local selections of Carmignano are a welcome sight.

SAN CASCIANO IN VAL DI PESA

RESTAURANT-HOTEL
L'Antica Posta
Piazza Zannoni 1
Tel. 055/820116
Closed Monday and August
Credit cards: American Express, Diners Club, MasterCard
Price: expensive

The Antica Posta is one of the Chianti area's best restaurants. Owner-sommelier Sandro Panzani has his own sense of style, and he knows what food should taste like. The *cucina* of youthful chef Stefano Chiesura is nontraditional, relying on first-rate seasonal ingredients. Sandro and Stefano, both with past experiences in other regions, have created an original, beautifully prepared menu, with homemade pasta, fresh fish and shellfish, and meat and poultry delicately napped with velvety sauces. The chickpea and clam soup is inspired, *risotto* is flawlessly executed, fish is moist and tasty, and meats are either grilled or sauced to perfection. The *Chianina* beef *carpaccio* and steak are both worth a detour. Desserts are tempting, especially the featherweight fruit aspic. Sandro's wine list is a winner, studded with local gems. The Antica Posta is just twenty minutes from Firenze, and at times it takes less time to drive out to San Casciano than to find a parking space near a restaurant in the city. The rooms are spare but convenient.

SAN GIORGIO A COLONICA

GELATO
Bar Pasticceria San Giorgio
Piazza San Giorgio 13
Tel. 0574/542491
Closed Monday

Realmo Cavalieri and his sister Maria Teresa make Toscana's finest *gelato,* always fresh, light, and creamy, worth a pilgrimage for true fans of this delectable frozen treat. All flavors are created with natural seasonal ingredients, and colors are pale, with no artificial colorings added. The summer selection of around twenty flavors does justice to ripe local fruit, especially berries and melon. Only ten flavors are available in the winter, when *gelato* is decidedly less popular with Italians and the

varieties of fruit are more limited. Heady chocolate, caffeine-rich coffee, smoky hazelnut, and tangy lemon, tasting of lemon and not peel, are all memorable, but many people come from far away to taste the splendid *Buontalenti,* a super-rich custard *gelato* flavored with secret ingredients and named after Francesco de' Medici's *gelato* maker.

SAN GIOVANNI VALDARNO

GLASSWARE
IVV
Lungarno Guido Reni 60
San Giovanni Valdarno
Tel. 055/944444
Closed Monday morning
No credit cards

The IVV glass factory in the Val d'Arno makes jars, dishes, vases, glassware, and pitchers—all mouthblown. The lines are simple and modern. A small IVV shop by the side of the road sells part of their attractive production for less than the normal retail prices. Some items are irresistibly inexpensive, although you'll have to ship them yourself.

SANSEPOLCRO

RESTAURANT-INN
Ristorante Paola e Marco
Via Palmiro Togliatti 66
Pieve Vecchia
Tel. 0575/734875
Closed Sunday evening and
**   Tuesday**
Credit cards: American Express,
**   Diners Club**
Price: moderate

The restaurant started off as an ambitious pizzeria in a hayloft, but Marco and Paola Mercati's enthusiasm has since transformed the adjacent farmhouse into one of Toscana's newest gastronomic luminaries. The dining rooms have been carefully restored and have terracotta floors, exposed brick and beamed ceilings, country-style furniture and handmade lace doilies. Marco and Paola have studied with stellar chefs, in both Italy and France, and their *cucina* is based on impeccable local ingredients, nicely cooked and formally presented. Two fixed-price menus—a five-course "territorial" of local ingredients and a seven-course "creative"—include aperitifs and first-rate after-dinner pastries. Mushrooms and truffles are served to advantage in season. Marco is seriously interested in wine, and his growing cellar of reasonably priced selections is a pleasure to drink from. He hosts special evenings, inviting fine winemakers to make a statement and show their wines. The combination of *cucina,* wines, and guests leads to a better understanding of a winery and its products, and is usually lots of fun. Spend the night in one of Paola and Marco's nine newly remodeled, inexpensive rooms, and check out the choice Piero della Francescas at the Pinoteca comunale, the local museum.

SAN VINCENZO

HOTEL
La Torre
Castagneto Carducci
Tel. 0565/775268ù

Credit cards: American Express, Diners Club, Visa
Price: moderate

RESTAURANT

Gambero Rosso
Piazza della Vittoria 13
Tel. 0565/701021
Closed Tuesday and November
Credit cards: all
Price: expensive

Fulvio Pierangelini is the owner, chef, and able purveyor of Gambero Rosso. The ambience, stemware, silver, and flowers are formal, and the creative *cucina* is carefully structured and personal. The raw materials are flawless—fresh fish that's known no ice, tender vegetables. Recently poultry, local lamb, and game dishes have been added to the menu, widening Fulvio's horizons beyond seafood and lightness. Desserts and *piccola pasticceria* are made by Fulvio's wife, Emanuela. Extra virgin olive oils and an exhaustive selection of wines are focused on areas of interest to Fulvio, and are nicely paired with the *cucina*.

RESTAURANT

Il Bucaniere
Viale Marconi 8
Tel. 0565/703387
No credit cards
Price: moderate

An effort like Fulvio Pierangelini's latest restaurant, Il Bucaniere, wins my undying respect. He has taken the local idea of a beach restaurant—really little more than a hut on the beach—and, armed with the same high-quality ingredients he's unearthed for the Gambero Rosso, he cooks simple, traditional seaside *cucina*. Classic pasta and *risotto* dishes are splendid, beautifully prepared; the *fritto* is light and crisp; grilled fish is dressed with extra virgin olive oil, and lemon for those who won't leave well enough alone. Dining here isn't a substitute for sampling Fulvio's creativity at Gambero Rosso, but it's a pleasure to see him devoting his skills to casual, reasonably priced, first-rate beach food.

SATURNIA

SPA HOTEL
Terme di Saturnia
Tel. 0564/601061
Credit cards: American Express, Diners Club, Visa
Price: luxury

If, after a few weeks of serious eating and drinking, you're having trouble fitting into your clothes, head for the Terme di Saturnia. Mud, massages, the health club, and the fitness program will get you back into shape. The spa's pool of sulfurous waters and their special line of cosmetic treatments will make your skin feel like a baby's.

RESTAURANT

Ai Due Ceppi
Piazza Vittorio Veneto
Tel. 0564/601074
Closed Tuesday and January
Credit card: American Express
Price: moderate

Another husband-and-wife team, Aniello and Bianca Michele prepare and serve Tuscan *cucina* but add a little something of themselves in each dish. *Acquacotta* (vegetable soup), homemade pasta, suckling pig, game, fresh mushrooms and truffles in season, are prepared by Bianca with respect for tradition. Finish with *ricotta* mousse or *vin santo* and cookies. Choose from the nice selection of mostly quality Tuscan wines.

SESTO FIORENTINO

TABLEWARE
Richard Ginori (factory)
Viale Giulio Cesare 50
Tel. 055/4210451

Richard Ginori is Italy's finest producer of porcelain. Located in Sesto Fiorentino, outside Firenze, the company was founded in 1735 on the Doccia estate of the Ginori marquises, and fused with the Richard company of Milano in 1896. The factory is large, modern, and manufactures over five million pieces of fine china annually. But in the midst of their mass production, small pockets of workers utilize traditional techniques, meticulously crafting and painting dishes by hand. These artisans, some wearing stereo headsets, deftly embellish plates with bands of color, golden borders, or intricate designs, repeating the same movements and patterns with an individual flourish that I found moving.

MUSEUM

Museo di Doccia
Via Pratese 31
Tel. 055/4210451
Closed Sunday, Monday,
Wednesday, Friday and
holidays

The Doccia Museum, next to the Ginori factory, is a gem, a must for porcelain collectors and lovers of the finely set table. It traces the history of Richard Ginori from its founding to the present day, with over 5,000 examples of their porcelain from all periods. Some of the museum's most exciting pieces—a swan's neck teapot, a pedestal candle holder, a wavy-edged glass chiller, an oval bowl with gold-leafed wild fruits, a water lily Art Nouveau candy dish, and Milanese architect Giò Ponti's bowl, tortoise paperweight, and cache-pot—have been reproduced recently, in limited numbers, for Richard Ginori's 250th anniversary.

TABLEWARE

La Botteguccia
Viale Giulio Cesare 19
Tel. 055/4210472
Closed Monday
Credit card: American Express

Across the street from the Doccia Museum, La Botteguccia sells Ginori seconds and close-outs, straight from the factory. Luck will determine the selection on any given day, but shipping costs will make your finds less of a bargain. Not all items can be charged.

THE SENESE SWEET TOOTH
•

Three candied-fruit-and-almond cakes, *panforte*, *panpepato*, and *torta margherita*, and two nut cookies, noble *ricciarelli* and rustic *cavallucci*, have satisfied all classes of Senesi from the thirteenth century to the present. *Panpepato*, first mentioned in a document dated 1205, is made of honey, almonds, candied fruit, lots of spices, pepper, cocoa, and a caramelized sugar syrup that gives this medieval dessert a more complex, less sugary flavor. *Panforte*, with spices but no pepper and a simple sugar syrup, is a more modern creation, and *torta margherita* is even more delicate—barely spiced, named in honor of Queen Margherita (of pizza fame, see page 35) but not taken too seriously by real *panpepato* fans. The lozenge-shaped almond-and-honey *ricciarelli* cookies are now made with honey and sugar. The *cavallucci*, made with ingredients that farmers had on hand—walnuts, honey, and aniseed—were originally jawbreakers to be dipped in *vin santo*, but have been softened up for modern tastes.

Nannini—Conca d'Oro
Via Banchi di Sopra 23
Tel. 0577/41591
Closed Tuesday

Nannini
Piazza Salimbeni
Tel. 0577/281094
Closed Sunday

Factory—Zona Industriale
Isole d'Arbia
Tel. 0577/395380

Nannini, with two shops in Siena and a factory on the outskirts of town, is the best commercial producer of the traditional Senese sweets. Their all-Italian almonds from Bari are tastier than the imported almonds most of the other producers use.

SIENA

The food in Siena's restaurants is miserable, and the locals are not to be found in any of them—Siena residents traditionally eat at neighborhood clubs *(contrade)*. Most tourists who come to Siena stay for only a few hours, and restaurants haven't gone out of the way to make this brief stay memorable. Visitors would be wise to snack on the traditional cakes and cookies, or to picnic in the spectacular countryside outside the town.

PALIO DINNERS

•

The *Palio*, Siena's medieval bareback horse race, complete with flag tossing and costumed pageantry in the *Campo*, the main square, occurs twice a year, on July 2 and August 16. The center field of the *Campo* and all the windows and balconies overlooking the course are packed with fans from the city's *contrade* (neighborhood associations), cheering for one of the ten horses, each representing a *contrada*.

The associations hold a number of dinners each year, with long tables set in the streets and flags with the symbol of their *contrada*, festooning the neighborhood. The food served may not be the finest in Toscana, but it's a rare experience. Dinners are also held the night before the race, in each of the ten *contrade* racing in the next day's *Palio*. The victory dinner, held for the victor two months after the race, and the *cena del piatto*, held in the spring, present more opportunities to attend these Senese street suppers.

Tickets may be purchased directly from the *contrade* for all celebratory dining with local revelers. For more information, contact the Siena Tourist Information to find out who won the *Palio* if you're interested in the victory dinner (Tel. 0577/280551), then contact the individual *contrada*—the following list is only partial—to get tickets.

Della Nobil Contrada del Bruco
Via Comune
Tel. 0577/286021

Società Civetta Cecco Angiolieri
Via Angiolieri
Tel. 0577/285505

Società della Giraffa
Via Verine 18
Tel. 0577/287091

Società del Nicchio
Via Pispini
Tel. 0577/286021

Società Trieste—Contrada dell'Oca
Circolo Ricreativo 55
Tel. 0577/280003

HOTEL
Certosa di Maggiano
Via Certosa 82
Tel. 0577/288180
Credit cards: American Express, Diners Club, Visa
Price: luxury

HOTEL
Palazzo Ravizza
Piano dei Mantellini 34
Tel. 0577/280462
Credit cards: all
Price: moderate

SPECIALTY FOODS
Morbidi
Via Banchi di Sopra 73/75
Tel. 0577/280268
Closed Wednesday afternoon

The best picnic possibility in Siena is Morbidi, with a selection of prepared dishes, cold salads, and typically overcooked vegetables to go, as well as bread, quality wine, first-rate *salumi*, and fine local *pecorino* cheese.

SINALUNGA

RESTAURANT-INN
Locanda dell'Amorosa
L'Amorosa
Tel. 0577/679497
Closed Monday, Tuesday lunch, and mid-January through February
Credit cards: American Express, Diners Club, MasterCard
Price: expensive

The Locanda dell'Amorosa is in a spectacular setting, two kilometers (about a mile and a quarter) from Sinalunga. The long cypress-lined drive is a passage that leads to another world, a stone-walled hamlet of the 1300s, with its graceful arches, frescoed church, and stone-and-brick restaurant. The *cucina* used to reflect the ambience—refined, rustic, and Tuscan—but recently it has strayed a bit too far from its traditional roots. Many dishes are puréed and insipid, but the homemade pasta, thrush pâté, grilled eel, and wonderful *Chianina* beef steak are full-flavored and well prepared, nicely accompanied by the much improved house wines. Desserts, especially the simple country *torte*, a kind of cross between a cake and a pie, are irresistible, and fruit *sorbetto* and *gelato* are nicely done. Stay overnight in one of the seven rooms or in the apartment, and bask in the most Tuscan of experiences. Go for a drive along the road to Siena in a landscape that's an emotional experience in all seasons.

TREQUANDA

CHEESE AND MEAT
Azienda Agricola Belsedere
Tel. 0577/662137
Closed during mass on Sunday

Belsedere, the working farm (almost impossible to find) of Countess de Gori Pannilini, makes superb *pecorino* from 100 percent sheep's milk. They also produce large and small salami, *prosciutto*, sausages, and *peposo*, a boneless cured ham rolled in pepper. If you visit the farm in the sweet countryside south of Siena, you can purchase fresh or aged *pecorino*, whole cold cuts, or freshly made *ricotta* directly from the spry, bright-eyed, octogenarian Countess.

VIAREGGIO

Viareggio, a turn-of-the-century seaside resort, is a favorite with vacationing Italians, especially in August, when the beach appears to be standing-room-only. Umbrella-covered beach chairs can be rented by the day, week, month, or season. Two wonderful wine bars, and a restaurant that knows what to do with fish, lure me to the Tuscan coast, but not at the height of the season.

HOTEL
Astor
Viale Carducci 54
Tel. 0584/50301
Credit cards: all
Price: luxury

HOTEL
Astoria Garden
Via Leonardo da Vinci 16
Forte dei Marmi (close by)
Tel. 0584/80754
Credit cards: all
Price: moderate

WINE BAR
La Taverna dell'Assassino
Viale Manin 1
Tel. 0584/45011
Closed Wednesday
Credit card: American Express
Price: low moderate

The Taverna dell'Assassino combines maritime decor with the paraphernalia of wine lovers—bottles, cases, crates. I need no excuse to skip dinner to snack on the fine *salumi*, or to stop in for a glass of wine before or after dinner. A lively crowd of vacationers and locals keep gentle Alberto Montalbano busy from 7 p.m. until he feels like closing, and many local restaurant owners finish the evening at his wonderful *enoteca*. The wine selection is astounding, a reasonably priced thrill for enophiles.

WINE BAR
Il Punto di Vino
Via Mazzini 229
Tel. 0584/43357
Closed Monday and November
Credit card: MasterCard
Price: moderate

Il Punto di Vino is a wine bar with a seasonal, mostly regional menu of three or four simple dishes that change daily. *Salumi* and cheese are tasty. The wine selection is formidable. Stop in for a glass of wine, a snack, or a full meal.

RESTAURANT
Romano
Via Mazzini 120
Tel. 0584/31382
Closed Monday, January, and the first week of July
Credit cards: American Express, Diners Club, MasterCard
Price: expensive

Romano and Franca Franceschini's modern, air-conditioned restaurant is one of the gastronomic peaks of the Tuscan coast. Franca's *cucina* is prepared with fresh, mostly local fish and shellfish, simply prepared, elegantly presented on large white plates. The flans of tiny pan-fried baby clams *(frittatine)*, perfectly cooked *spaghetti* sauced with seafood, and turbot baked with potatoes or mushrooms are all delicious. *Calamaretti*—thumbnail-size squid—are poached in a wonderful garlicky soup or lightly fried to a golden delicate crunch. The extra virgin olive oil and house wine come from nearby Montecarlo and are highly suited to the classic *cucina*.

The tasting menu offers a reasonably priced series of mostly creative seafood dishes. Romano ably pairs wines from his personal quality selection with Franca's tasty food. Desserts are generally anticlimactic. Service tends to be slow during the crowded summer season.

RESTAURANT
Calimero
Viale Europa
Torre del Lago Puccini (close by)
Tel. 0584/340264

Closed Monday
Credit card: American Express
Price: high moderate

Signora Dani is in the kitchen, and her husband Marco Pardini efficiently runs the dining rooms in this family restaurant, which specializes in fresh local fish and seafood. The *antipasto* is one of the best, and most ample, on the Tuscan coast. You'll be presented with a series of eight or nine simply prepared seafood dishes—delicate marinated raw fish, shrimp and beans, and mushrooms and fish combinations in season are just a few of the highlights. Pasta and second courses appear to be well made; each time I go I promise to pace myself, but I never make it past the appetizers. I've never even tried a dessert, but always have room for a *bocconcino Dai-Dai,* an ice-cube–sized chocolate-coated vanilla *gelato.* There's no wine list, and waiters aren't too well informed—you'll have to check out the glass-fronted refrigerators to see what's available.

UMBRIA

·

Coastless Umbria is in the center, the heart of Italy, a land of mountains, hills, valleys, lakes, and rivers, colonized by the ancient race, the Umbri. And after the Umbri came the Etruscans, Romans, Goths, Byzantines, Longobards, various noble families and republican regimes, and finally the Vatican, in a series of power struggles, bloodbaths, and disasters that taught the occupants of each village how to run for the fortress *(rocca)* that dominates each medieval hill town in the region.

The *cucina,* if not the politics or history, reflects the gentle simplicity of Saint Francis of Assisi. Umbrian dishes seem rarely to contain more than three or four ingredients, each one tasting like itself—plain, sauceless, minimalist cooking with the backdrop of an open fire for spit-roasting or grilling, and a wood-burning oven for baking the fragrant, wheaty bread. Tasty extra virgin olive oil is the regional condiment. Homemade hand-rolled pasta is dressed with the black winter truffle's evanescent earthy perfume. Grains play an important role, with ancestral flatbreads made from stone-ground flour and water cooked on the hearthstone. Emmer *(farro),* the wheaty-flavored grain that fed the Roman legions, is widely found in southern Umbria, cooked in soup, or ground and rolled into a substantial pasta known as *stringozzi, ceriole,* or *manfrigoli.* Spit-roasted suckling pig *(porchetta)* and game *salumi* made by artisan butchers are seasoned with herbs. Fish and eel from the lakes of Trasimeno and Piediluco and freshwater shrimp from the Tevere and Nera rivers grace the Umbrian table. Desserts are sweetened with honey, chestnuts, pine nuts, hazelnuts, and especially almonds. *Fave di morti* cookies and *serpentone* ("big snake"), a coiled cake with coffee bean eyes and a cherry tongue, are both based on the almond. All these foods seem to depend on the simple elements of Umbria for their flavors, and most are unavailable outside the region's borders.

It seems fitting that local artisans work with a material as basic as clay, making terracotta pottery in Deruta. The Museo del Vino in Torgiano has a fine collection of medieval, Renaissance, and baroque wine containers, from Deruta and other regions.

THE MENU

SALUMI

■

Prosciutto di Norcia ▪ prosciutto from Norcia

Salsiccia di cinghiale ▪ wild boar sausage

ANTIPASTO

■

Bruschetta ▪ garlic toast made with country bread and olive oil

Schiacciata ▪ flatbread, similar to pizza crust, baked with olive oil or enriched with onions or cooked greens

Torta al testo ▪ flat unleavened bread baked on a slab of stone

PRIMO

■

Manfrigoli, stringozzi, or *ceriole* ▪ homemade rustic pasta dressed with garlicky tomato sauce

Minestra di farro ▪ soup of tomatoes, vegetables, a *prosciutto* bone, and emmer

Spaghetti alla norcina ▪ spaghetti with an oil-based sauce of black truffles, garlic, and anchovies

SECONDO

■

Anguilla alla brace ▪ grilled eel

Anguilla in umido ▪ eel cooked with tomatoes, onions, garlic, and white wine

Frittata di tartufi ▪ black truffle omelette

Gobbi alla perugina ▪ deep-fried cardoons baked with meat sauce

Lepre alle olive ▪ wild hare cooked with herbs, white wine, and olives

Mazzafegati ▪ pork sausages with raisins and pine nuts

Palombe or *palombacci* ▪ wood pigeon, usually spit-roasted

Pollo in porchetta ▪ chicken cooked in same manner as suckling pig

Porchetta ▪ small suckling pig baked in a wood-burning oven with wild fennel, garlic, wild mint, and rosemary

Regina in porchetta ▪ carp from Lago di Trasimeno, cooked in same manner as suckling pig

Salsiccia all'uva ▪ fresh pork sausage cooked with grapes

Tegamaccio ▪ mixed lake-fish stew, with white wine and herbs

FORMAGGIO

■

Ricotta ▪ soft, fresh, mild, made from whey

Pecorino ▪ fresh or aged, sheep's milk, distinct

DOLCE

■

Cialde ▪ paper-thin sweet cookies, cooked on the embossed disks of a long-handled iron tool

Fave di morte ▪ almond cookies

Pinoccate ▪ pine nut cookies

Serpentone, torcolato, or *torcolo* ▪ almond and dried fruit dessert formed like a coiled snake

THE *W*INE LIST

Until fairly recently, Umbrian wines were pleasant, drinkable, and poor travelers. The only wine of note was golden semisweet Orvieto, a favorite of princes and popes. In the early 1960s the Lungarotti winery, under the leadership of Dr. Giorgio Lungarotti, concentrated its efforts on quality, and the resulting wines, especially Rubesco Riserva and San Giorgio, rich complex reds, and Torre di Giano Riserva, an elegant, smooth white, are among the best in Italy. New-style wines are crisp, the product of the latest technology. Most quality Umbrian wines are the result of the efforts of a few dedicated winemakers.

Cabernet Sauvignon di Miralduolo is an ample, dry red, almost purple, from Torgiano, made with Cabernet Sauvignon grapes. It is served with meat and poultry, and produced by Lungarotti.

Cervaro della Sala, made mostly from Chardonnay and aged in French oak, is produced by Castello della Sala.

Chardonnay di Miralduolo is a smooth, dry white, made with Chardonnay grapes from Torgiano, aged in wood. It is served with fish and poultry, and produced by Lungarotti.

Decugnano dei Barbi is a fresh, fruity red, made of Montepulciano and Sangiovese grapes grown near Lago di Corbara. It is served with meat and poultry, and produced by Decugnano dei Barbi.

There are two DOC *Montefalco* wines, both reds from the Todi area. The *Rosso* is a soft, dry red made from mostly Sangiovese grapes, and is served with meat and poultry. The *Sagrantino,* made with the Sagrantino grape, is a full-bodied, rich, dark purple wine, either dry *(secco),* sweet *(passito),* or lightly sweet *(abboccato).* Both wines are produced by Adanti.

Muffato della Sala, a semi-sweet white, is said to resemble Sauterne, and is produced by Castello della Sala.

Orvieto is probably Umbria's most famous DOC wine, a dry, light white, or a lightly sweet dessert wine *(abboccato).* Antinori, Barberani, and Decugnano dei Barbi produce the best dry Orvieto, served with fish and vegetable dishes, and Antinori and Barberani's lightly sweet wine is perfect with simple desserts. Decugnano dei Barbi's minute production of Orvieto Classico Pourriture Noble, made in the style of a Sauterne, is worth looking out for.

San Giorgio is a rich, full-bodied red, made in Torgiano of Sangiovese grapes enriched by Cabernet Sauvignon. It is served with meat and game, and produced by Lungarotti.

Solleone is amber, dry, and sherry-like, made from Grechetto and Trebbiano grapes. It is a perfect aperitif, and is produced by Lungarotti.

The *Torgiano* DOC, south of Perugia, includes both red and white wines. The white *Torre di Giano,* made from Trebbiano and Grechetto grapes, is fresh, fruity, and dry, served with first-course dishes, fish, and shellfish. The *Torre di Giano Riserva,* from the Il Pino vineyard, is aged in wood and gains elegance with aging. Red *Rubesco,* made from Sangiovese and Cannaiolo grapes, is balanced, full, and dry, served with meat, fowl, and game. The *Rubesco Riserva,* from the Monticchio vineyard, is one of Italy's finest red wines. All are produced by Lungarotti.

Spumante is mostly based on the Chardonnay grape and makes a lovely aperitif. It is well made by Decugnano dei Barbi and Lungarotti.

Vin Santo is a sweet or semisweet dessert wine made from partially dried Trebbiano, Malvasia, and Grechetto grapes, and aged in small barrels. It is served with simple desserts or cookies, or between meals. Top producers are Adanti and Lungarotti.

REGIONAL SPECIALTIES

BREAD

Umbria is one of the few regions where bread still tastes like wheat and natural yeast. Flatbreads are baked on an open hearth, in front of the embers of a wood fire where meat and poultry are cooked. Vaulted brick and stone ovens are fueled by wood, and the bread and cookies that exit from them have a crispness, a friability, that is unique. See page 257 for one such bakery.

EXTRA VIRGIN OLIVE OIL

Ancient olive trees (mostly Moraiolo, Leccino, and Frantoio olives) are an almost constant presence in the Umbrian landscape, and golden green and fruity olive oil is an important ingredient in the *cucina Umbra*. The delicate, clean, and decidedly olivey flavor will probably convert most holdouts to the world's finest condiment. See pages 258 and 259 for sources.

EMMER

Most people have never heard of emmer. In Italian it's *farro (Farrum triticum* in Latin), often erroneously translated in English as spelt. Emmer is an ancient form of wheat often found in the *cucina* of regions conquered by the Roman legions. It looks like dark barley and has a rich, nutty flavor and a nice *al dente* consistency. See page 252 for a source of whole emmer and emmer flour.

THE UMBRIAN LENTIL

Are the small lentils *(lenticchie)* from the area outside the city of Norcia tastier than all others? Yes, says the cooperative of sixty-five lentil farmers from the village of Castelluccio, and I tend to agree with them. Their high-altitude lentils, which are smaller and hold on to their skins during cooking, can be purchased directly from the cooperative in Norcia (see page 254, as well as in Perugia (see page 256).

TRUFFLES

Umbria is world-famous for its black truffles *(tartufi neri)*. Hunted by dogs in the forests, they flavor, but only slightly, many dishes in the fall and winter. For more information on truffles, see page 30–32.

PASTA

Pasta in Umbria isn't paper-thin, egg-yolky, rich, and elegant, as it is in Emilia-Romagna, but rather an essential Umbrian interpretation; stone-ground grain and water, rib-sticking, and a hearty first course. Spiga-doro (page 252) makes quality pasta industrially, an evolution of the Umbrian tradition.

PERUGINA CHOCOLATES

Perugina is an Umbrian success story. Founded in 1907 by the Buitoni and Spagnoli families with the intention of manufacturing sugar-coated almonds (*confetti),* it rapidly expanded. The company moved in 1913, added candies and chocolates to its products, and in 1922 introduced the *bacio* ("kiss"), invented and named by the offspring of Perugina's founders. They were an instant success. The center, made of ground hazelnuts and chocolate, is topped with a whole hazelnut looking decidedly nipple-like, and covered with chocolate. Perugina currently produces 200 million *baci* a year, making their own chocolate from beans. The hazelnuts are mostly Turkish, which cost less than the *tonda gentile della Langa* (see page 54). The traditional star-covered aluminum foil wrappers hold a piece of waxed paper, printed with a romantic quotation. Perugina also makes many other chocolate products, including a seasonal output of over three million gaudily wrapped and ribboned hollow chocolate Easter eggs ranging in size from three ounces to nine pounds. Each contains a surprise of dubious value. The factory is in Perugia (see page 256), and of course the candies are available worldwide.

DERUTA POTTERY

Glazed majolica pottery has been made in Deruta since the twelfth century. Early designs were simple, and grew more colorful and elaborate with the passage of time. The village of Deruta has a ceramics museum, located in the medieval Palazzo Comunale, and a state ceramics school, which ensures the future glory of the local artisanal tradition. The streets of Deruta are lined with factories and shops selling reproductions of this traditional glazed pottery (see page 252).

FLATBREAD GRIDDLE

The traditional flatbread of Umbria, *torta al testo,* is cooked on a flat griddle *(testo)* originally made of sand- stone, but now found in terracotta, cast iron, aluminum alloy, and even cement. They can be found in most housewares stores in Umbria, or on the steps of the Duomo in Perugia at the Tuesday and Saturday morning pottery market.

CITIES AND TOWNS

ARRONE

HOTEL
Fonte Gaia
Racognano, beyond Arrone from
   Terni
Tel. 0744/78241
Credit cards: American Express,
   Visa
Price: moderate

RESTAURANT
Trattoria Rossi
Località Casteldilago
Tel. 0744/78105
Closed Friday
No credit cards
Price: inexpensive

This is the essential Umbrian *trattoria,* located in the breathtaking valley of the Nera River known as the Valnerina. The *cucina* is composed of purely local ingredients, like lamb, game, trout, and fresh- water shrimp. Most dishes are dressed with herbs or truffles, pasta and desserts are homemade, and wines are local.

BASCHI

HOTEL
La Badia
Orvieto Scalo La Badia
Tel. 0763/90359
Credit cards: American Express,
   MasterCard, Visa
Price: expensive but worthy

HOTEL
Bramante
Via Orvietana
Todi
Tel. 075/8848382
Credit cards: American Express,
   Diners Club, MasterCard
Price: high moderate

RESTAURANT
Il Padrino
Civitella del Lago, strada statale
   448
Tel. 0744/95006
Closed Wednesday and July
Credit cards: American Express,
   Diners Club
Price: moderate to expensive

Gianfranco Vissani is the six-foot- five disheveled chef, visionary, and owner of both Il Padrino, a mostly seafood restaurant, and Vissani, a private room in the back with a unique gastronomic point of view.

The *cucina* of Il Padrino, the restaurant founded by Gianfran- co's father, is barely Umbrian, but it is based on first-rate, some- times expensive, fish (procured at Roma's dawn fish market) and meat, usually simply cooked. Dad grows the garden and makes the *prosciutto,* Mom bakes the bread daily (the tastiest I've eaten in years) in a wood-burning oven, Gianfranco and his wife cook, and his sister makes the pastry. Every- thing is well prepared, simply pre- sented, and flavors are nicely combined. The menu lists a lim- ited selection of fine Italian wines. The anonymous decor, ugly house plants, and music are worthy of a seedy motel. If you'd like a mod- erately priced meal, avoid *aragosta* (lobster), *spigola* (sea bass), *scampi* (prawns), and *tartufi* (truffles), and don't eat anything you didn't or- der or that's not on the menu.

RESTAURANT
Vissani
Civitella del Lago, strada statale
   448
Tel. 0744/950206
Closed Wednesday and July
Credit card: American Express
Price: expensive to outrageous

The perfectly executed dishes of Vissani, the restaurant behind the Formica doors in the rear of Il Padrino, are those of a genius, idiot savant, or idiot, depending on your point of view, and have little to do with Umbrian, Italian, or any other cuisine eaten on the face of this earth. The influence appears to be French, as are many of the ingredients and wines. If *porcini* mushrooms stuffed with blueberries, cooked in grape leaves, and served with a champagne sauce, or a foie gras scallop sauced with mussels and black truffles, or steamed salmon with strips of pork tripe in a lemon-marjoram sauce sounds interesting, this may be the place for you. A different bread, probably the best part of the meal, is served with each course. The *menu degustazione*, six or seven courses and five breads, is less expensive, the combinations more adventurous than the à la carte menu, but a selection or two from Vissani's beautifully chosen list of Italian and French wines will add more to your bill than you expected. There's also a cigar list, and a music list, although I don't know what happens if diners are of different musical inclinations. The decor is every bit as dreary as Il Padrino, but fancier—the plants are bigger, the drapes are heavier,

and china, silver, crystal, and orchids replace the simpler appointments in the restaurant up front. Evidently Gianfranco Vissani has been to France and has been greatly moved by the experience. Intrepid explorers may find his personal vision of cuisine of interest. It seems fitting that this restaurant is situated on the shores of an artificial lake.

BASTIA UMBRA

PASTA
Spigadoro (factory)
Via IV Novembre 2/4
Tel. 075/80091
Closed Saturday and Sunday

The Spigadoro factory in Bastia Umbra, with its all-Italian high-tech pasta machinery, spits out 2,000 quintals, or 441,000 pounds, of pasta a day. Their dried and packaged pasta is made from 100-percent durum wheat, usually Canadian or American, ground in the Spigadoro mill. This medium-size pasta factory also produces a small quantity of high-gluten pasta, extruded from bronze dyes, which create a rougher surface that holds on to the sauce better. Added gluten increases elasticity, and cooked gluten pasta remains *al dente* longer. It also contains more protein. Simonetta Crociani, who speaks perfect English (she grew up in Australia), will show you around the factory if you call or write in advance.

COLLI SUL VELINO

EMMER
Pietro Dohen
Casale San Nicola
Tel. 0746/646140

Pietro Dohen grows emmer *(farro)* in the area between southern Umbria and Lazio. His emmer is organically grown, and is full-flavored and holds up nicely under the tooth. It is sold whole or stone-ground. The flour *(farina di farro)* is used with whole wheat in breadmaking and for *manfrigoli*, a rustic pasta.

DERUTA

POTTERY
Ubaldo Grazia (factory)
Via Tibertina 181
Tel. 075/9710201
Closed Sunday

Ubaldo Grazia's family has been making majolica since the fifteenth century. He has the best selection of attractive, authentic-looking Deruta patterns, some dating from the sixteenth century, a particularly rich period for this pottery. Plates, bowls, espresso cups, crescent-shaped individual salad or vegetable dishes, pitchers, canisters, vases, egg cups, ashtrays, and mugs are stacked in piles in a jumble of rooms on the ground floor of this factory. Ubaldo works with some famous shops—the plate you pick up may have been made for Saks, Neiman Marcus, or Barney's. Artists also work with Ubaldo and his artisans, creating modern dinnerware with Umbrian materials. Paula Sweet's patterns are stylish, original, and can be ordered. Her crescent-shaped side dishes are a personal favorite. If you don't see anything you like, or if the colors are wrong for your dining room, Ubaldo will work with you to design something to suit your taste. Prices are reasonable, except for custom-designed work, but don't forget to add on shipping costs, which will make this hand-painted pottery less of a bargain. No credit cards are accepted, but they'll take checks, personal or travelers, and will ship.

FOLIGNO

Foligno, which is situated on the banks of the Topino River, is home of the first printed edition of Dante's *Divine Comedy,* and the Giostra della Quintana, a traditional tournament of costumed cavaliers from the ten neighborhoods of the city, held the second and third Sundays in September. Each neighborhood tavern *(osteria)* serves simple Umbrian dishes from the 1600s and local wines during the festival. For more information, contact the Foligno Tourist Information Center (Azienda di Turismo di Foligno, Porta Romana 126, Tel. 0742/60459).

RESTAURANT-INN
Villa Roncalli
Via Roma 5
Tel. 0742/670291
Closed Monday
Credit card: American Express
Price: moderate

Villa Roncalli is a small private villa on the outskirts of the city, a ten-room guest house with a restaurant that serves magnificent Umbrian family-style cooking. The restaurant is powered by three generations of the Scolastra family. Sandra, in the kitchen with her mother, prepares all the pasta and sauced dishes, and bakes bread in the wood-burning oven. Husband Angelo pampers meat, poultry, and game at the grill of a wood-burning fire, and sommelier–dessert creator daughter Luisa takes care of the two frescoed dining rooms. Vegetables receive special attention, and all dishes are dressed with tasty local extra virgin olive oil. Angelo Scolastra produces a pleasant Sagrantino, a rich red wine that suits the elemental Umbrian *cucina* of Villa Roncalli, and the wine list offers a lovely selection of quality regional and Italian wines.

ISOLA MAGGIORE

RESTAURANT-INN
Sauro
Lago di Trasimeno
Tel. 075/826168
Closed January and February
No credit cards
Price: low moderate

Sauro, a modestly priced, simple inn with eleven neat, basic rooms, is a perfectly peaceful getaway. It's located on the prettiest island in Lake Trasimeno, accessible by boat or ferry from Passignano sul Trasimeno. The restaurant's *cucina* is simple, home-style, composed of hand-rolled pasta sauced

with fish, grilled meats, local lake fish and eel, and rich desserts like *zuppa inglese,* all prepared by Signora Lina. Mostly local wines are offered, including some gems.

NARNI

RESTAURANT-HOTEL
La Loggia–Hotel dei Priori
Vicolo del Comune 4
Tel. 0744/726843 and 722744 (hotel)
Closed Monday and the second half of July
Credit cards: American Express, Diners Club
Price: moderate

Medieval Narni is perched on a hilltop dominating the plain of Terni. It has a fortress from the 1300s, and a Ghirlandaio fresco in the middle of the town council meeting room. La Loggia and the adjacent Hotel Priori are located on a tiny cobblestone side street. The *cucina* is mostly Umbrian, with some pasta like *bigoi* and the presence of *risotto,* both hints at the chef's Veneto origin. Emmer, a traditional Roman grain, is prepared like pasta, with a spicy *amatriciana* sauce, or ground into flour for the doughy homemade *manfrigoli,* or even made into *polpette* (grain cakes). Trout is served with a bowl of summer truffle sauce. Game—wild boar, deer, hare—is braised and served with polenta. A self-service buffet of *antipasti* could make a complete meal for many. The wine list is a major surprise, offering all the great local wines plus a few well-chosen se-

An amazing display of gelato cones

lections from other regions. In the summer, dine under large off-white umbrellas in a geranium-draped stone courtyard.

NORCIA

LENTILS
Consorzio Agrario
Via della Stazione 2
Tel. 0574/571765
Closed Sunday

The flavorful, organically grown lentils *(lenticchie)* of Castelluccio are available here, where you can buy them directly from the farmers cooperative that raises them.

ORVIETO

HOTEL
La Badia
Orvieto Scalo, La Badia
Tel. 0763/90359
Closed January and February
Credit cards: American Express, MasterCard, Visa
Price: low expensive

HOTEL
Virgilio
Piazza del Duomo 5/6
Tel. 0763/41882
No credit cards
Price: moderate

BAR-CAFFÈ
Montanucci
Corso Cavour 21/23
Tel. 0763/41261
Closed Wednesday

Locals stop in to chat with the sassy cashier-owner at the Bar Montanucci. The coffee is the best in Orvieto, but most people are attracted by the ambience. Wooden sculptures by the Michelangeli family and a vast variety of hard candies are displayed with almost equal zeal.

WINE, SANDWICHES
Cantina Foresi
Piazza del Duomo 2
Tel. 0763/41611
Closed Tuesday and January

Cantina Foresi is a perfect place to stop for a snack. Sandwiches *(panini)*, local wine, cheese—including Castello della Sala goat cheese—and soft drinks are sold from 8 a.m. to 8 p.m.

SALUMI
Dai Fratelli
Via Duomo 10
Tel. 0763/43965
Closed Wednesday afternoon, all day Sunday (winter), Sunday afternoon (summer)

Dai Fratelli makes some of the best *salumi* in the region, especially *prosciutto*, sausages, and salami made of wild boar *(cinghiale)*. The meat of the Umbrian wild boar is said to be tastier than boar of other regions because of its diet of truffles, plentiful in its natural forest habitat. Emilio and Filippo Patalocco hunt for boars in the area of Civitella del Lago, to supply their shop with meat cured according to methods learned from their father. The shop is filled with festoons of sausage, piles of salami, black-bristle-covered *prosciutto*, bottles of green Umbrian extra virgin olive oil, woodsy-scented dried *porcini* mushrooms, and an embalmed boar, just in case you haven't caught on to what most of the local specialties are made of.

GELATO
Gelateria del Duomo
Piazza del Duomo 14
Tel. 0763/41034
Closed mid-December to mid-February

The Gelateria del Duomo makes all the classic flavors of *gelato*. Chocolate and hazelnut are intense, and fruit flavors are all natural, made with seasonal fruit.

RESTAURANT
Antica Trattoria dell'Orso
Via della Misericordia 18–20
Tel. 0763/41642
Closed Tuesday, and mid-January to mid-February
Credit cards: all
Price: moderate

The restaurant's sign shows a bear holding a wine bottle and glass on a tray, and the interior is decorated with wooden and ceramic sculptures by local artists. So why are all the locals, and the chic Romans up for the weekend, eating in this unprepossessing *trattoria*, in the non-touristy part of Orvieto? Because Richard Annunziata and Gabriele di Giandomenico, an American and an Italian, serve

fresh-tasting country *cucina* spiked with fresh herbs. The summery vegetable-filled *frittate* and the local lamb are well prepared. Richard takes care of the wines, drinkable enough, but Gabriele's *cucina* deserves more. Finish your meal with coffee at Montanucci and a *gelato* near the Duomo.

RESTAURANT
Giglio d'Oro
Piazza del Duomo
Tel. 0763/419303
Closed Wednesday in winter
Credit cards: all
Price: moderate

Chef Enzo Cantoni and his wife, Silvia, until recently of the Villa Ciconia, have moved to the heart of Orvieto in piazza del Duomo. The *cucina* is the same, with good grill work and simple, nicely prepared food, but more attention is paid to quality local wines here. Drink an *aperitivo* downstairs while waiting for your table in the small upstairs dining room. The reasonably priced fixed-price tourist menu includes regional dishes and wine. Outdoor dining on piazza del Duomo, weather permitting.

TABLE LINENS
Maria Moretti
Via Maurizio 1
Tel. 0763/41714
No credit cards
Closed Sunday afternoon

Signora Moretti sells hand-embroidered linens and lace—including placemats, tablecloths, and centerpieces—in her tiny shop on the corner of piazza del Duomo.

CRAFTS
Michelangeli
Via Albani 1
Tel. 0763/35380
Closed Sunday afternoon
Credit cards: American Express, MasterCard, Visa

Simonetta, Donatella, and Raffaella Michelangeli have maintained the artisanal shop founded by their sculptor father, where wood is turned into fanciful sculptures, objects, and tables. Sit on the wooden benches outside the store, or on the horse if you're young enough, and enjoy the Michangeli pieces even if you don't buy one. The charming barnyard animals would make fun Christmas tree ornaments. The store is on the way to the Antica Trattoria dell'Orso.

PERUGIA

Perugia, with its Etruscan and medieval origins, imposing walls, and subterranean escalators that go under and through the walls at the Rocca Paolina, the fortress, is home to one of the major universities in Italy, with a substantial non-Italian student body. In fine weather it seems as if all of Perugia, not just the foreign students, strolls down Corso Vanucci and loiters in front of shop windows or in piazza IV Novembre with its cathedral, Palazzo dei Priori, and Maggiore fountain.

HOTEL
Brufani Palace
Piazza Italia 12
Tel. 075/62541
Credit cards: all
Price: luxury

HOTEL
La Rosetta
Piazza Italia 19
Tel. 075/20841
Credit cards: all
Price: moderate

BAR-CAFFÈ, PASTRY
Pasticceria Sandri
Corso Vanucci 32
Tel. 075/6101
Closed Monday

Sandri, with its frescoed ceilings and no-nonsense red-jacketed bartenders, is the best choice in town for traditional desserts, especially the *rocciata*, a powdered-sugar-covered swirl of a cake, and non-traditional chocolate *torta*. Skip the leaden rice pudding–candied fruit cake. A hot table *(tavola calda)* in the back of the shop offers prepared foods, which can be eaten off of tiny cramped tables or at the crowded bar.

LENTILS
Giuliano Finetti
Via Danzelli 1
Tel. 0756/29316

Giuliano Finetti's shop sells the special organic lentils from Castelluccio (see page 250) in 500-gram packages (just over one pound).

CHOCOLATES
Perugina
Via M. Angeloni 59
Tel. 075/7791

For a description of Perugina candies, see page 250.

Perugina is now part of Nestlé, the behemoth multinational corporation. Chocoholics interested in visiting the Perugina chocolate works should contact Dottor Saverio Ripa di Meana.

RESTAURANT
Cesarino
Via della Gabbìa 13
Closed Wednesday all year and
* Thursday lunch in the summer*
Credit cards: American Express,
* Visa*
Price: moderate

This typical Umbrian *trattoria* around the corner from charming piazza IV Novembre serves well-made traditional *cucina*. The open kitchen is the domain of two white-capped, rosy-cheeked women, who roll out the house pasta and prepare the tasty chicken livers in tomato sauce zapped with a bit of chili pepper, and who do all the stove cooking. The open hearth, with its spits and grills of roasting lamb, poultry, and sausage, is the province of a white-aproned man in careful attendance. *Torta al testo*—flat, unleavened bread baked on a slab of stone, split, and stuffed with arugula and a bit of cheese—is a splendid starter. Vanilla custard *gelato* is homemade, and the wine list is mostly local, with some pleasant surprises. Dine outside under an awning in the spring and summer, or downstairs in the winter.

RESTAURANT
Renato Somella
Via Baldeschi 5
Tel. 075/65819
Closed Sunday and Monday
Credit card: American Express
Price: high moderate to
* expensive*

Renato and his Irish wife, Joan, serve some of the freshest fish in Umbria. The classic marine *cucina* is well executed; fish and shellfish are grilled, fried, or steamed and served with sauce, homemade mayonnaise, bell pepper purée, or simply dressed with Umbrian extra virgin olive oil. Start off with oysters and a glass of Decugnano di Barbi's fine *Spumante*. Desserts and ices *(sorbetti)* are homemade, and the almost all-white wine list features regional and Italian wines of quality. A visit to Renato Somella is ideal when you can't eat another bite of traditional Umbrian *cucina*. Open for dinner only.

PIEDILUCO

On the road from Terni to Piediluco, the world's fifteenth-tallest waterfall, the *Cascata delle Marmore*, fuels an important hydroelectric plant. The dammed-up falls are unleashed for tourists on Sundays and holidays only.

RESTAURANT-HOTEL
Albergo Lido
Piazza Bonanni 2
Tel. 0744/68354
No credit cards
Price: moderate

The Albergo Lido, on the shores of Lago di Piediluco, has the kind of restaurant that Italians love to celebrate in. Weekend revelers of at least three generations, seated at tables laden with bottles of mineral water and wine, baskets

Norma Gelso

A wine and food scene in Perugia's medieval fountain

cialties include *schiacciata*, flat-bread similar to pizza crust (mornings only), *ciaramicola*, a liquor-soaked mountain of a cake, topped with meringue and colored sprinkles, and around twenty different kinds of cookies, traditional to Umbria and other regions as well. Luigi Faffa, great-grandson of the founder, presides behind the counter of this historic bakery.

SAN FELICIANO SUL TRASIMENO

OLIVE OIL
Alfredo Mancianti
Frantoio San Feliciano sul Trasimeno
Tel. 0575/67065

Faliero Mancianti bought the Frantoio San Feliciano in 1952 and produces fine extra virgin olive oil here. Son Alfredo has always felt strongly about the Umbrian land, the olive trees, and the stone mill where their olives are crushed, producing some of Umbria's finest olive oil. The Manciantis make two special oils from designated geographic areas, *San Feliciano* and *Monte del Lago*. They also make *Affiorato*, of the lightest oil that floats to the surface of the newly pressed oil. It's skimmed off the top, and is intensely olivey and costly. The Mancianti olive paste is also fine.

Mancianti can also be reached at via Poggibonsi 14, Milano, tel. 02/4078461.

of rolls and breadsticks, are served from long stainless-steel platters piled with predictable regional specialties. Your menu will probably include *carbonetti* (grilled lake fish), freshwater shrimp in herb sauce, homemade pasta, salmon trout and salmon-like *coregoni* fresh from the lake, and *tiramisù* for dessert. Owner Renzo Bartolucci's wines include some pleasant surprises, and more than a few disappointments. The experience on Saturday and Sunday, when huge banquets of up to 750 diners invade this otherwise peaceful lakeside restaurant, may not be your idea of fun.

PONTE VALLECEPPI

BREAD
Forno Faffa
Tel. 075/6920122
Closed Sunday

At Faffa, a family-owned and -run bakery established in 1851 outside Perugia, baking is done in an oven fueled by wood. All whole-wheat flour is stone-ground, and the resulting bread—made by hand with such special flour, with a starter to make it rise, baked in a traditional wood-burning oven—is fragrant, redolent of wheat. Spe-

SCHEGGINO

TRUFFLES
Urbino Tartufi (factory)
S. Anatolia di Narco
Tel. 0743/61133
Closed Sunday

The Urbino factory in Scheggino, truffle capital of Umbria, is the world's largest producer of truffle paste, *pasta di tartufo*. Black and white winter truffles and black summer truffles are collected around the world, cleaned, graded, and sold fresh, preserved whole in cans or jars, or puréed with oil or thrush pâté and packed in tiny tubes. For a visit to the factory, which is open year-round but works hardest in the early winter months, call or write for an appointment.

SPELLO

RESTAURANT-INN
Il Cacciatore
Via Giulia 42
Tel. 0742/651141
Closed Monday
No credit cards
Price: inexpensive to moderate

Assisi should be seen—but not experienced at great length unless hoards of pilgrims, their buses, and souvenir shops are your idea of fun. The hotels and restaurants, like those of many villages that live on tourists who visit once, never to return, aren't exactly motivated to serve the most inspirational food. When visiting Assisi I like to stay, and eat, at the Cacciatore, an archetypal Umbrian *trattoria* in nearby Spello. Everything is plain,

no frills, but the perfumes coming out of Signora Bruna's kitchen will make you overlook the lack of decor, and if you're lucky enough to show up on a calm evening in the spring or summer, you can sit on the terrace, with its quintessentially Umbrian view. All pasta is hand-rolled, truffles are fresh, meats and poultry are local—simply roasted, stewed, or grilled—and there's game in the winter and tasty local *pecorino* cheese from Monte Subasio. Golden, glossy fruit tarts (*crostata*) made with homemade preserves are hard to resist. Drink Lungarotti's Rubesco or Torre di Giano, or the simple house red, which is better than the white. Some of the hotel's eighteen rooms have the same breathtaking view as the terrace.

TERNI

HOTEL
Dei Priori
Vicolo del Comune 4
Narni (close by)
Tel. 0744/726843
Credit card: American Express
Price: moderate

WINE, OLIVE OIL
Vino Vino
Corso Vecchio 201
Tel. 0744/56683
Closed Monday morning
No credit cards

Vino Vino is one of the oldest stores in Terni, specializing in spices, nuts, paper cups, ruffled candy papers, and, as its name indicates, wine. Renzo and Gigliola Franceschini have assembled an

impressive selection of Italian, and especially Umbrian, wines. Renzo also produces his own stone-ground extra virgin olive oil, "Colle dell'Oro," from the northern hills outside Terni. Lucia makes original *bonboniere*—individual packets of tulle-wrapped candy-coated almonds given away at weddings, communions, and anniversaries. If you ask, they'll take you around the corner to a bakery that makes its breads and cookies in a wood-burning oven.

TORGIANO

RESTAURANT-INN
Le Tre Vaselle
Via Garibaldi 48
Tel. 075/982447
Credit cards: American Express,
*   Diners Club, MasterCard*
Price: expensive

Like Dallas, with its Ewings and its oil, Torgiano is home to the Lungarotti family, producers of fine wine, creators of Italy's best wine museum, and owners of Le Tre Vaselle, a beautifully restored forty-seven-room country inn, part of the Relais & Chateaux chain of luxury hotels. The restaurant serves some of the finest *cucina* in Umbria. Enjoy a glass of the Lungarotti sparkling *Spumante*, accompanied by bread rounds (*crostini*) spread with olive paste, in front of the fireplace in one of the comfortable sitting rooms. The *cucina* reflects the gracefully underrestored rustic simplicity of the hotel. Linen, silver, and crystal stemware seem natural rather than opulent, just as ingredients like mushrooms and truffles are presented as everyday fare rather than luxury items. Olive oil and balsamic sauce are the house dressings. Pasta is homemade, grill work is beautifully executed, vegetables are perfectly cooked, cheeses are tasty, hard to find, and local. Desserts are traditional. Don't skip the *cialde,* paper-thin wafers cooked on the medieval Umbrian version of the waffle iron, served with custard *gelato.* The Lungarotti-only wine list offers some amazing gems. What a joy to stay in one of the simply appointed rooms of this hotel, ably direct by Romano Sartore.

Wine samples are siphoned from a demijohn.

BALSAMIC SAUCE, OLIVE OIL
Lungarotti Osteria
Corso Vittorio Emanuele 33
Tel. 075/982143

Lungarotti's *salsa balsamica di mosto* is not a traditional Umbrian product. It's a dark brown sauce made from must, the unfermented juice of freshly pressed grapes, and undergoes the same production process as balsamic vinegar (see page 187). But since it's made outside the limited geographic area of production in Emilia, it can't be called *aceto balsamico.* The tasty, sherry-like Lungarotti sauce is made with a 100-year-old balsamic culture, aged in casks of seven different woods, packaged in a lovely glass cruet, and expensive.

The same interest in quality guarantees the fine Lungarotti extra virgin olive oil, produced with local olives.

Next door to the osteria is the Lungarotti wine museum. Both are open seven days a week, but closed at lunch.

MUSEUM
Museo del Viño
Corso Vittorio Emanuele 33
Tel. 075/982143

The *Museo del Vino* offers a global vision of wine. It traces the history of wine, from its Middle Eastern origins, through its evolution as a part of the meal, as a medicine, and in myth. An impressive collection of wine containers—Cycladic pitchers, Hittite jars, Attic wine containers, Etruscan bronzes, Roman glassware, and local winemaking utensils, beautifully displayed, make this the most attractive wine museum in Italy.

CRAFTS
La Spola
Via Garibaldi 66
No phone
Credit cards: American Express, Diners Club, MasterCard

La Spola's name, "The Shuttle," is a direct reference to its focus. The shop sells a variety of quality Umbrian handcrafts but specializes in hand-loomed traditional and contemporary fabrics. Embroidery, metalwork in copper and iron, baskets, terracotta majolica from Deruta and Gubbio, and other Umbrian pottery is also sold here. Ask the concierge at Le Tre Vaselle to open the store for you if it is closed.

LE MARCHE

■

Le Marche is divided from neighboring Romagna, Umbria, Toscana, Lazio, and Abruzzi by mountains and hills, crossed by parallel rivers that flow east to the Adriatic and the modern umbrella-paved seaside resorts. It's a region with a history of changing alliances, of separate states. The political cast of powers includes Gauls to the north and the Piceni to the south of the Esino River, Romans, Longobards, noble families, and the Vatican. It gets its name from the *Marca* of Ancona, Camerino, and Fermo, three border provinces, each governed by a marquis or margrave.

The *cucina* of Le Marche draws its inspiration and its ingredients from two main sources. Inland mountain dishes are based on freshwater fish, mushrooms, truffles, *marchigiana* beef, lamb, and *pecornno* cheese. Coastal shellfish and fish—prawns looking like mini-lobsters and delicate, almost opalescent, six-inch sole—are the bounty of the Adriatic, and are simply grilled with fresh bread crumbs. The jumbo olives of Ancona are pitted, stuffed with a rich filling, breaded, and deep-fried—surely a labor of love. Le Marche produces extra virgin olive oil, and Cartoceto's fruity olives are gently cold-pressed, producing a special extra virgin olive oil. A return to the use of grain, like barley and tasty emmer, found where the Roman legions marched, is underway, assisted by Massimo Schiavi's excellent products. Traditional desserts of cookies, served with a glass of dessert wine, aren't always easy to find in restaurants.

Most tourists come to Le Marche for the Adriatic seaside, lined for miles with row after row of chairs, beach umbrellas, and changing cabins. The beach isn't hard to find, because it's parallel to the road and the railroad tracks, backed by a solid mass of hotels. But Le Marche offers far more than a strip of sand to get tan on. Pesaro's wonderful Art Nouveau Villa Ruggieri and ceramics museum, Ancona's Roman triumphal arch, medieval Ascoli Piceno, Fabriano, Fermo, Jesi, and Gradara, fifth-century Osimo, Renaissance jewel Urbino, the religious shrine of Loreto, and Numana with its Greco-Roman past all present an alternative to the beach.

THE MENU

ANTIPASTO

Olive ripiene (or all'ascolana) · pitted giant green olives, stuffed with meat and Parmesan cheese, and deep-fried

Pizza al formaggio · yeast bread cooked with Parmesan and other cheeses

Pizza alla campagnola · flatbread enriched with lard and pork cracklings

PRIMO

Passatelli · strand-shaped cheese and egg dumplings

Vincisgrassi · rich lasagna with meat sauce, béchamel sauce, chicken livers, and black truffles

SECONDO

Brodetto · fish stew, made with a wide variety of Adriatic fish and shellfish

Coniglio in porchetta · roast rabbit with wild fennel, garlic, and bacon

Moscioli or *muscioli* · mussels, usually steamed, and baked or grilled with bread crumbs and herbs

Porchetta · suckling pig roasted with wild fennel, garlic, rosemary, and white wine

Potacchio · a stew of tomato, chili pepper, white wine, and herbs applied to either fish, lamb, poultry, or rabbit

Sarde alla marchigiana · fresh sardines, marinated in olive oil and herbs, then grilled, with bread crumbs

Stocco or *Stoccafisso all'anconetana* · salt cod, layered with olive oil and tomatoes, stewed with white wine

FORMAGGIO

Percorino · fresh or aged, made from sheep's milk

THE *W*INE LIST

The simple wines of Le Marche don't seem to have traveled well, although they are lovely with the regional *cucina* of seafood and sauced poultry. Few wineries aim at quality, but those that do are worth seeking out. Some wines, like those of Bucci, are easier to find outside their native region.

Rosso Cònero is a robust dry DOC red, made from Montepulciano and Sangiovese grapes grown south of Ancona, on the hills near Monte Cònero. It goes well with meat, fowl, and regional *cucina,* and is produced by Garofoli, MecVini, Moroder, and Umani Ronchi.

Rosso Piceno is a grapey dry DOC red, made from Montepulciano and Sangiovese grapes in the Ancona, Ascoli, and Macerata areas. It is served with sauced meat and fowl, and is produced by Cocci Grifoni and Villamagna.

Tristo di Montesecco is a soft, fruity, dry white made from an interesting blend of grapes, aged carefully in wood, and not too hard to find locally. It is served with a wide range of dishes, from seafood to sauced poultry, and is ably produced by Massimo Schiavi.

Verdicchio dei Castelli di Jesi is a fresh, dry white DOC wine, made from Verdicchio blended with Trebbiano and Malvasia grapes in the Castelli di Jesi area, west of Ancona. It is at its best with fish and seafood, in any course, and can be one of the region's best wines. Top producers are Brunori, Garofoli, Umani Ronchi, and Bucci, whose Villa Bucci Riserva is splendid, unusually elegant, and impossible to find regionally.

Vernaccia di Matelica is a delicate dry white DOC wine, made in the Matelica area, west of Ancona. It is served with fish and seafood, and is at its best produced by Fratelli Bisci and La Monacesca.

Vernaccia di Pergola is a rich dry red made of local Balsamina grapes in the inland hills of Pergola. It is served with roast and sauced fowl, and ably produced by Ligi-Montevecchio.

Vernaccia di Serrapetrona is a sparkling DOC red— dry *(secco),* semisweet *(amabile),* or sweet *(dolce)*—made from the Vernaccia di Serrapetrona grape. It can be served with practically any course of a meal, depending on its sweetness. Top producers are Attilio Fabrini and Raffaele Quacquarini.

Vino da tavola is made by most of Le Marche's leading wineries. Enzo Mecella makes white, oaky *Antico di Casa Fosca.* Bucci makes rich, elegant red *Pongelli.* Massimo Schiavi's wines frequently change names, but look for *Gallia Togata, Jubilè,* and *San Secondo,* all interesting whites by Fattoria di Montesecco.

REGIONAL SPECIALTIES

EXTRA VIRGIN OLIVE OIL

A small amount of dense, green extra virgin olive oil is produced in Le Marche, primarily from Raggiolo, Frantoio, and Leccino olives. See page 265 for one source.

Villa Bucci
Via Cona 30
Ostra Vetere
Tel. 071/96179 (or in Milano
  tel. 02/6554470)

Villamagna
Contrada Montanello 5
Macerata
Tel. 0733/429236

Olive trees often grow well in the same climate as grapes, and some of Le Marche's top olive oil producers—such as Villa Bucci and Villamagna—are also winemakers. The quality of their wines serves as a guarantee for their olive oil.

TRUFFLES

Three kinds of truffles are found in Le Marche. Summer *(Tuber aestivum)* and winter *(Tuber melanosporum)* are black truffles. The glorious *Tuber magnatum* are early winter white truffles. They are all found in oak forests of the Apennine mountains in the Acqualagna area. The black truffles are inexpensive, almost tasteless, and not in the same league as the white truffle, found from October through December. Truffles are hunted with dogs in Italy, not with pigs. For more information on truffles, see page 30–32.

CRAFTS

Pesaro has been an important center for the production of majolica since the sixteenth century. Majolica tiles, pharmaceutical jars, decorative pieces, and dinnerware with intricately hand-painted designs are a specialty of this city. The Ceramics Museum (see page 269) houses some lovely pieces, mostly from Umbria, Le Marche, and Romagna, and G. Molaroni produces fine reproductions (see page 268).

CITIES AND TOWNS

ACQUALAGNA

TRUFFLES
Truffa e C.
Via Rossino 5
Tel. 0722/79165
Closed Saturday and Sunday

Truffa e C. sells fresh and preserved *tartufi neri* and *bianchi*—black and white truffles. They also sell truffle paste, bottled sauces, cheese, boar sausage, chick-peas, and oil, all under the intoxicating effect of the truffle.

CALCINELLI

HOTEL
Principe
Viale Trieste 180
Pesaro (close by)
Tel. 0721/30096
Closed November
Credit cards: all
Price: moderate

HOTEL
Villa Serena
Via San Nicola 6/3
Pesaro (close by)
Tel. 0721/55211
Credit card: American Express
Price: moderate

RESTAURANT
La Posta Vecchia
Via Flaminia Vecchia
Tel. 0721/89249
Closed Monday and November
No credit cards
Price: inexpensive to moderate

Bread baked in a wood-burning oven is a special treat.

Pinetto ("little Pino") Pompili, his wife, Ivana, and their sons are responsible for the success of this totally anonymous *trattoria* with its decor of white stucco walls, circular neon tube lighting in mustard-colored fringed, domed shades, wine-filled refigerator, and brick pizza oven. The *cucina* is simple, home-style, based on Pinetto's scrupulous search for quality ingredients, especially fresh mushrooms, and on Ivana's traditional mentality. *Salumi* are local, pasta is homemade, poultry and meat are nicely cooked, but the specialty here is mushrooms—cooked with pasta, in salads with arugula and cheese, grilled, studded with chunks of garlic, or deep-fried. Pizza and *piadine* flatbreads are baked in the wood-burning oven in the evening. From September to January they serve local white truffles. Munch on a portion of *olive all'ascolana* (deep-fried stuffed olives) while waiting for your food to arrive, and drink a bottle of Jubilè, the best of the local wines. Ivana's anise cookies are lovely.

CARTOCETO

HOTEL
Principe
Viale Trieste 180
Pesaro (close by)
Tel. 0721/30096
Closed November
Credit cards: all
Price: moderate

HOTEL
Villa Serena
Via San Nicola 6/3
Pesaro (close by)
Tel. 0721/55211
Credit card: American Express
Price: moderate

RESTAURANT
Symposium
Via Cartoceto 38
Tel. 072/898320
Closed Sunday evening and Monday
Credit cards: American Express, Diners Club
Price: high moderate to expensive

Pinetto Pompili practically dragged me to Symposium to taste the *cucina* of his younger brother, Lucio. In the hills outside Cartoceto, in a former farmhouse surrounded by olive trees, Lucio prepares a professional, personal *cucina* based on the four seasons and his region's finest ingredients. He's close to both mountains and coast, and grows one of the most complete restaurant herb gardens in Italy. The decor is original, and tables are set with antique tablecloths and extra-large, hand-fagoted, handkerchief-quality linen napkins. Red-haired, freckled Lucio, continually dashing out the back door to pick some herbs, carefully contrasts and balances flavors with skill, and each dish makes sense. *Salumi* are homemade, pasta is hand-rolled, and barley is cooked like *risotto—al dente,* a revelation of a dish. Fresh fish, country meat, and just-picked produce are all beautifully prepared. Local *pecorino* is splendid, and desserts—traditional regional cookies, fruit ices, and especially custard *gelato* served with preserved wild cherries *(visciole)*—are tasty. After a *caffè* go native, rinsing out your coffee cup with anise liqueur. Local wines of quality help make the meal a memorable experience. Outdoor dining is under large canvas and wood umbrellas in the summer.

OLIVE OIL
Frantoio della Rocca di Vittorio Beltrami
Via Cardinal Pandolfi 1
Tel. 0721/898145
Closed Sunday afternoon

Vittorio Beltrami is a wine salesman with a passion for the olive tree, and for the process for turning its fruit into oil. Olives are washed, pitted, crushed with a pink Verona granite wheel, and pressed between mats to extract the oil in Vittorio's beautifully, respectfully restored olive oil mill, Frantoio della Rocca. He also makes *mono olivo* oil, using olives of one type only, and special olive oil from a particularly good area. Oil is stored in a grotto, in large traditional terracotta containers *(orci)*. His oil can be tasted in the area's best restaurants, but the only place to buy it is straight from Vittorio. A visit to the mill is a treat.

CESANO DI SENIGALLIA

HOTEL
Federico II
Jesi (close by)
Tel. 0731/543631
Credit cards: all
Price: expensive

HOTEL
Cantinella
Viale Matteotti 38
Ostra (close by)
Tel. 071/68081
No credit cards
Price: moderate

RESTAURANT
Da Pongetti
Statale Adriatica 96
Tel. 071/660094
Closed Sunday evening and
*   Monday*
No credit cards
Price: moderate

Four generations of the Pongetti family have worked in their restaurant, founded in 1888. Luigi Pongetti is at the helm of this Adriatic seafood restaurant, with his wife, Alda, and stepmother in the kitchen. What started out as an *osteria* for teamsters has evolved, but not too much. Every dish on the menu is a classic, and succeeds because of the absolute freshness of the Adriatic-only fish and shellfish: fish salad *antipasti,* homemade *tagliatelle* or *risotto* sauced with fish or clams, traditional *brodetto* (fish stew). Their fish tastes like the essence of the sea, sweet and squeaky. Practically everything is grilled, crunchy deep-fried, or simply poached, the latter served with a homemade mayonnaise yellow with egg yolks. The house wines are passable, but could stand some improvement.

FABRIANO

SMOKED TROUT
Aquarello
Via Campodiegoli 33/D
Tel. 0732/72003

Smoked trout isn't a traditional Marchigiano product. But there was a clear, cool mountain spring for raising trout and pike, and an abundance of the aromatic woods, herbs, and berries needed for the smoking process. The Cooperativa Agroittica Fabrianese had tasted smoked fish from other countries and decided they could do as well. They make smoked trout, eel, and pike, smoked over hardwoods, juniper, bay leaves, and coriander, all vacuum packed.

FALCONARA MARITTIMA

HOTEL
Monteconero
Monte Conero
Sirolo (close by)
Tel. 071/936122
Credit cards: American Express,
*   Diners Club, Visa*
Price: moderate

RESTAURANT-INN
Villa Amalia
Via degli Spagnoli 4
Tel. 071/912045
Closed Tuesday except in
*   summer, and January 5–20*
Credit cards: American Express,
*   Diners Club, MasterCard*
Price: high moderate

Amelia Ceccarelli knows what to do with local fish and seafood. Her villa in Falconara Marittima has been turned into an intimate three-room restaurant. Son-sommelier Lamberto pairs fine wines with his mother's cooking. The *cucina* is based on fine local ingredients, treated with a creative touch. Spend the night in one of the villa's seven rooms and taste some of Lamberto's fine selection of *grappa* and whiskey.

RESTAURANT
Da Ilario
Via Tito Speri 2
Tel. 071/9170678
Closed Sunday evening, Monday,
*   and June*
Credit card: MasterCard
Price: moderate

Ilario Berardi is the chef, sommelier, and animator of this restaurant. The *cucina* takes advantage of fresh seafood, local lamb and pork, and a wide selection of vegetables. Salads are dressed with extra virgin olive oil—local, Tuscan, or Ligurian. The cheese selection is wonderful, but desserts are less interesting. Ask Ilario to let you see his wine cellar, stocked with well-priced regional gems, and he'll jump for joy.

FANO

HOTEL
Principe
Viale Trieste 180
Pesaro (close by)
Tel. 0721/30096
Closed November
Credit cards: all
Price: moderate

HOTEL
Villa Serena
Via San Nicola 6/3
Pesaro (close by)
Tel. 0721/55211
Credit card: American Express
Price: moderate

RESTAURANT
Pesce Azzurro
Lungomare Sassonia
Tel. 0721/82027
Closed September through May
No credit cards
Price: least expensive meal in the book

I thought of Calvin Trillin when I stumbled upon Pesce Azzurro while looking for Trattoria Da Quinta (see following), and decided that a five-course fish dinner served with bread, water, and wine for less than 10,000 lire (under $10) couldn't be passed up. The fixed meal of this cafeteria, operated during the tourist season by the fishermen's cooperative, changes daily, and always includes two appetizers followed by a pasta course. You'll receive two kinds of fish for a second course, made from either local clams or *pesce azzurro*, literally "blue fish," the term used to indicate anchovies, sardines, mackerel, and a few other related fish. Pay for your meal, get a tray, and join the line. "Please hold plate of pasta with two hands," the sign on the wall commands with the voice of experience. Eat your meal outside under the pergola, or inside when it rains (a bit more claustrophobic), at the long, sticky, blue and white plastic-covered communal tables. The wine is miserable, but forgivable under the circumstances.

RESTAURANT
Trattoria Da Quinta
Viale Adriatico 42
Tel. 0721/808043
Closed Sunday and August
No credit cards
Price: low moderate

Quinta Darpetti cooks the best fish in Fano. Her *trattoria*, next door to Pesce Azzurro (see above), is across the street from the commercial, big-business industrial port, the antithesis of a fishing village scene. Da Quinta is always filled with fishermen and locals who enjoy her specialties: marinated anchovies, *risotto* or *tagliatelle* sauced with seafood, grilled and deep-fried fish. The waitresses are in a hurry, and not noted for their patience. Wines are unfortunate, and detract from Quinta's *cucina*.

FRATTE ROSA

POTTERY
Luigi Gaudenzi
Via delle Terrecotte 7
Tel. 0721/777138
No credit cards

Since 1730, the Gaudenzi family has been making glazed rustic pottery from the special clay of Fratte Rosa. The shiny black or brown traditionally shaped terracotta dinnerware, coffee and tea services, soup tureens, and umbrella stands are simple, elegant, contemporary looking, and reasonably priced—but don't forget that shipping will add to the cost.

MACERATA

HOTEL
Villa Quiete
Vallecascia
Montecassiano (close by)
Tel. 0733/599559
Credit cards: American Express, Diners Club
Price: moderate

RESTAURANT
Floriani
Borgo Compagnoni 9
Montanello (close by)
Tel. 0733/429267
Closed Monday
No credit cards
Price: low moderate

Carla and Andrea Cesanelli's Ristorante Floriani serves an enlightened version of *cucina marchigiana* with country elegance, in a setting of vineyards and olive trees. Some of their rustic traditional dishes are difficult to find elsewhere. The menu shows signs of careful research, and Carla and Andrea frequently experiment with recipes from the 1600s. Andrea is a sommelier and can offer splendid local wines, but the wines of Villamagna, their own production, are fine with the *cucina.* Extra virgin olive oil is also produced by Villamagna. Finish your meal with the fennel *grappa.*

PERGOLA

EMMER
Fattoria di Montesecco di Massimo Schiavi
Tel. 0721/778277
Always open

Winemaker Massimo Schiavi organically cultivates barley *(orzo mondo),* a tasty variety of hard wheat called *grano d'or,* and my favorite, emmer *(farro).* It's a rich nutty-tasting grain that the Roman legions planted to feed their troops, and that has become part of the gastronomic tradition of many regions. Massimo sells whole emmer, to be cooked in soups or like rice for a less starchy, more flavorful *risotto,* and stone-ground emmer, a whole-wheaty, bran-studded *farina* to be used in combination with other flours in baking and pasta making. Massimo also grows bean sprouts, and it's easy to tell which local restaurants are serious about what they're doing by the presence of these decidedly beany-tasting sprouts in their dishes.

PESARO

The summer beach scene in Pesaro is as umbrella-studded as its neighbors, but the city's wonderful Art Nouveau Villa Ruggeri, ceramics museum, the house where Rossini was born, and the gardens and fountains of Villa Caprile may tempt you to visit—but not in August, I hope.

HOTEL
Villa Serena
Via San Nicola 6/3
Tel. 0721/55211
Credit card: American Express
Price: moderate

RESTAURANT-HOTEL
Hotel Principe–Da Teresa
Viale Trieste 180
Tel. 0721/30096
Closed Monday and November
Credit cards: all
Price: moderate

The Hotel Principe is decidedly unattractive. But the vacationing families who book here year after year, and who eat twice a day in the dining room, know that an attractive edifice is pleasant but not necessary. The dining room has a one of the nicest views in Pesaro, of the unique Art Nouveau gem, Villa Ruggieri. After a look at the interesting menu and even better wine list, you probably won't mind the lack of architectural distinction or ambience. Sommelier Otello Renzi selects wines from his splendid collection (stop in for a late-night glass of wine in the *enoteca* downstairs even if you don't eat here) and pairs them with his mother's *cucina,* com-

posed of the best, freshest local ingredients Otello can get his hands on. Pasta is homemade and ethereal, sauced with fish; second courses are inventive, grilled or delicately floured and deep-fried. Finish with a refreshing fruit *sorbetto* or one of the rich but somewhat sweet desserts.

LEATHER ITEMS
Arte Cuoio
Via Saffi 12
Tel. 0721/25527
Closed Saturday and Sunday

Oscar Maschera and Claudia Serafini make attractive boxes out of leather. Their ice bucket, iceless wine chiller, laminate-lined trays, and circular, triangular, and rectangular-shaped storage boxes are all made of thick, sturdy, unblemished hide in black, brown, or natural. Cotton stitching is the only decoration on these elegant, spare classics.

POTTERY
G. Molaroni
Via Luca della Robbia 17/19
Tel. 0721/33181
Closed Monday morning
No credit cards

The best ceramics in Pesaro are produced by Molaroni. Since 1880, four generations of this family have been involved in the creation of hand-painted majolica tiles, vases, ornamental plates, pharmaceutical jars, soup tureens, platters, and dinnerware. Traditional designs are lovely and include the Pesaro rose pattern *(rosa di Pesaro),* a floral *(fiori Pe-*

saro), and my favorite, a striking black and white design of rampant lions and oak leaves known as *querciato*.

MUSEUM

Museo delle Ceramiche
Piazza Toschi Mosca 29
Tel. 0721/31213
**Closed Sunday afternoon and
   Monday**

The Museo delle Ceramiche houses a well-presented collection of Renaissance and Baroque ceramics, mostly from Umbria and Le Marche.

TABLEWARE

Firma
Via Mazzolari 12–14
Tel. 0721/34608
Closed Monday morning
**Credit cards: American Express,
   Diners Club, Visa**

If Pesaro's traditional ceramics aren't your style, check out Firma ("Signature"), a personal selection of beautiful objects of Italian and European design. Murano glass, Memphis ceramics, and the hospitality of Grazia Novelli are some of the highlights of this shop.

Molaroni has been producing Pesaro's most beautiful ceramics for over 100 years.

SENIGALLIA

HOTEL

Federico II
Jesi
Tel. 0731/543631
Credit cards: all
Price: expensive

HOTEL

Cantinella
Viale Matteotti 38
Ostra (close by)
Tel. 071/68081
No credit cards
Price: moderate

RESTAURANT

Riccardone's
Via Rieti 69
Tel. 071/64762
**Closed Monday except summer,
   and mid-November to mid-
   December**
**Credit cards: American Express,
   Diners Club, Visa**
Price: moderate

Riccardone ("Big Riccardo")— friendly, bearded, and *simpatico*— serves minimalist Adriatic seafood in his two-room restaurant. The emphasis on quality is evident in the entranceway display of extra virgin olive oils, local wines, aged balsamic vinegar, and chocolates from Roccati, all products that are up to Riccardone's high standards. Begin with the *antipasto misto* of fresh local fish, served with garlic bread *(bruschetta)* made with local extra virgin olive oil. Homemade pasta and *al dente* spaghetti are sauced with fish, and grilled shellfish and fish, including sweet six-inch sole *(sogliole)*, are given the traditional bread crumb and parsley treatment. Riccardone has his own ideas about what you should eat, and he probably won't let you order, but it shouldn't be a problem. The desserts and *sorbetti* are homemade, and the selection of local wines is impressive. The bathroom is one of the most attractive in the region.

URBINO

Urbino, with its spectacular art museum and botanical garden, is a little Renaissance jewel.

The hotel situation is difficult, however, and it's more interesting to stay outside town.

HOTEL
Bonconte
Via delle Mura 28
Tel. 0722/2463
Credit cards: American Express,
    Diners Club
Price: moderate

HOTEL
Oasi di San Benedetto
Via Abbazia
Lamoli (close by)
Tel. 0722/80133
No credit cards
Price: inexpensive

RESTAURANT
Vecchia Urbino
Via dei Vasari 3/5
Tel. 0722/4447
Closed Tuesday
Credit cards: American Express,
    Diners Club, MasterCard
Price: high moderate

Vecchia Urbino is trying hard, and with success. Son Gabriele in the dining room and mother Tina in the kitchen are hard workers, and the simple food they make and serve is quality. The brick and beam ceiling, terracotta floor, and rustic decor contrast with a more formal table setting, with long-stemmed roses and wine glasses. Some dishes have cute names with no hint of their content, like the "poet's trunk" or the "dessert of suavity," and can generally be avoided, but don't skip the special terracotta-pot-roasted meats, or anything on the grill. Vegetables are given respectful treatment, truffles are used to advantage from October through December. The wine selection is lackluster and could stand some improvement. Finish with *la moretta,* a coffee flavored with brandy, rum, anise, and lemon peel.

LA FESTA CONTINUA

And now that your vacation has slipped by too quickly, and you have fallen in love with Italy, pasta, *prosciutto,* and *parmigiano,* and with the plains of the Po or the hills of Toscana or the villas of Veneto or the truffles of Piemonte, and you're already thinking about when you can get back and where you'll go, how can you incorporate the Italian festival that you have experienced into everyday life at home? The following books capture the spirit of the Italian table.

Marcella Hazan's *The Classic Italian Cookbook, More Classic Italian Cooking*, and, best of all, *Marcella's Italian Kitchen* are written from a practical Italian traditionalist point of view, with general information on basic ingredients like rice, extra virgin olive oil, pasta, and balsamic vinegar and where to get them, and with recipes that range from simple everyday dishes to complicated holiday preparations.

Carol Field's award-winning *The Italian Baker* is one of the few cookbooks that I actually use. It is a personal favorite, not only for its useful hints and wonderful recipes for breads, pizza, cakes, and cookies, but for its scholarly research of regional Italian baking and modern approach to reproducing traditional food with everyday ingredients and equipment.

Burton Anderson's *Pocket Guide to Italian Wines* is compact, precise, perfect for liquor-store reference when shopping for wine. *Vino, The Wines and Winemakers of Italy* offers more in-depth coverage of the wines, and contains informative interviews with some of Italy's finest vintners, who discuss personal winemaking philosophy with the author, Burton Anderson, considered the leading Italian wine expert by Italians and Americans alike.

Leslie Forbes's *A Taste of Tuscany,* with its charming colored-pencil illustrations of the Tuscan table and authentic recipes from fine restaurants that prepare genuine food, is a visual treat that never fails to transport me to the countryside of Toscana.

I enjoy *Cucina Fresca* and *Pasta Fresca,* written by Viana La Place and Evan Kleiman, two Californians who fell in love with the fresh tastes of Italian food and adapted them to the *provincia* of California.

For a good drool, nothing is finer than Giuliano Bugialli's *Foods of Italy,* with its double-page color plates of *prosciutto* and luscious purple-skinned fresh figs, net-draped olive trees awaiting harvest, rows of golden traditional Mantovano desserts in the *Palazzo Ducale* in Mantova. The recipes seem overly complicated, calling for hard-to-find ingredients, but the photographs, too beautiful to risk the dangers of the kitchen, are guaranteed to stimulate your salivary glands.

So put a large pot of water on to boil, uncork a bottle of fine Italian wine, and get out your maps. *La festa continua.*

GLOSSARY

This glossary provides translations of Italian terms that appear frequently in *Eating in Italy* or on menus. It is not a complete "food dictionary." Dishes of specific areas are described under "Menu" and "Regional Specialties" for each region.

Don't be thrown by variations in endings. Italian nouns can end in *a, o,* or *e,* the plurals in *e* or *i,* according to their gender; and adjectives will have corresponding endings.

acciughe: anchovies

aceto: vinegar

aceto balsamico: balsamic vinegar

acqua del rubinetto: tap water

acqua minerale: mineral water; either *gassata* (fizzy) or *naturale* (still)

acqua non potabile: "water not fit for drinking"; sign may appear on fountains

affettato: sliced salami

affumicato: smoked

aglio: garlic

agnello: lamb

agnolotti: pasta stuffed with meat, egg, and cheese

agretti: a green that resembles chives and has a pleasant (not oniony) sour taste

agrodolce: sweet and sour

albicocca: apricot

al dente: just slightly chewy; applies to pasta and rice

alici: anchovies

alimentari: general grocery store

alla spina: on tap (beer)

allodole: larks

alloro: bay leaves; also called *lauro*

amabile: semisweet; used to describe wines

amaretti: sweet and bitter almond cookies

amaro: bitter

analcolico: nonalcoholic

ananas: pineapple

anatra: duck

anguilla: eel

anguria: watermelon

animali da cortile: "courtyard animals": chicken *(pollo),* squab or pigeon *(piccione),* quail *(quaglia),* guinea hen *(faraona)*

animelle: sweet breads

antipasto: appetizer

antipasto misto: assorted appetizers

aperitivo: aperitif, believed to stimulate the appetite

aperitivo della casa: house cocktail, usually made with white wine or *Spumante,* bitters, and a mystery ingredient

apribottiglia: bottle opener

aragosta: lobster

arancia: orange

aranciata: orange soda

arrosto: roast

arsella: wedge-shell clam; also called *tellina*

asiago: a hard, sharp, dry cow's-milk cheese

asparagi: asparagus

assaggi: "tastes"; a series of dishes, a tasting, of desserts *(di dolce),* of first courses *(di primi)*

astice: lobster

baccalà: dried salt cod

bacelli: fava beans (Tuscan)

baci di dama: chocolate-covered almond cookies

bagoss: a hard, aromatic, grainy cheese

bar: cafe serving alcoholic drinks, coffee, gelato, snacks, breakfast; also the place where you may find a public telephone, read the newspaper, listen to a sports match

barbabietola: beet

basilico: basil

beccaccia: woodcock

beccafico: fig pecker, warbler

Bellini: prosecco and peach juice cocktail

bel paese: a soft, mild cheese

besciamellá: bechaniel sauce

bianchetti: tiny anchovies; also called *gianchetti, schiuma di mare*

bianco: white

bicchiere: drinking glass

bietole: Swiss chard

bigoli: pasta made with a special press

birra: beer; may be *nazionale*

(from Italy) or *estera* (imported); *alla spina* means on tap

biscotti, biscottini: cookies

bistecca: beef steak

bitto: a soft, rich cheese

bollito misto: mixed boiled meats

borragine: borage

bottarga: pressed dried mullet roe

bottega: shop

boudin: potato-based blood pudding or sausage *(salume)*

branzino: sea bass

brasata: braised

bresaola: cured dried beef, sliced thin like *prosciutto* *(salume)*

brioche: croissants; also called *cornetti*

brodeto, brodetto: fish soup

brodo: broth

bruscandoli: wild hops

bruschetta: garlic bread

buridda: fish stew

burrata: a cheese, enclosing a butter center

burro: butter

cacciagione: game

cachi: persimmon

caffè: espresso coffee, served in a demitasse cup; also called *espresso; ristretto* means stronger, *lungo* means weaker; *corretto* means "corrected" with a shot of brandy or liquor; see also *Hag*

caffè d'orzo: coffee made from barley

caffè latte: *cappuccino* made with extra milk, served in a large cup

caffè macchiato: espresso "stained" with a little milk

caffettiera: espresso pot

calamaro or **calamaretto:** squid

caldo: hot

camomilla: camomile tea

camoscio: chamois

cannellini: white beans; see also *piattellini*

cannolicchio: tube-shaped razor-shell calm

cantina: cellar

capesante: scallops

capitone: large eel

caponata: eggplant salad

cappa santa: scallop

cappelletti: stuffed pasta

capperi: capers

cappone: capon

cappuccino: coffee topped with foamy steamed milk, the classic breakfast drink; also called *cappuccio;* see also *marocchino, caffè latte*

cappuccio: see *cappuccino*

capretto: kid

caprino: a cream cheese, sometimes made with goat's milk

capriolo: venison

carciofo: artichoke

cardi: cardoons, thistle-like vegetable

carpaccio: thinly sliced raw beef

carta da musica: "sheets of music": unleavened wafer-thin flat disk of cracker bread, from Sardinia

cartoccio: baked in parchment paper

casalinghi: combination hardware/housewares store

cassa: cashier

castagne: chestnuts; see also *marroni*

castelmagno: a rich-flavored mountain cheese, fresh or aged, rare

cavallo: horse

cavatappi: corkscrew

cavolo: cabbage

ceci: chick-peas

cee: elvers (young eels); also *cie, ciechi*

cena: dinner; see also *pranzo*

chiuso: closed

ciabatta: crusty flat "slipper" loaf of bread

cicchetti: "pick-me-ups"; little snacks served with a glass of wine (Veneto)

cie, cieche: eels; also *cee*

ciliegia: cherry

cinghiale: wild boar

cioccolata: chocolate

cioccolata calda: hot chocolate; at its best, hot, thick, almost black bitter chocolate; served *con panna* (with unsweetened whipped cream)

cipolla: onion

cocomero: watermelon

colazione: breakfast (also called *la prima colazione*); lunch; see also *pranzo*

colomba: wood pigeon

coltello: knife; *per parmigiano:* special knife for breaking off chunks of Parmesan cheese

congelato: frozen

coniglio: rabbit

conto: bill

contorno: third course, a side dish of vegetables or a green salad

coperto: cover charge, a fixed charge added to the bill in most restaurants

coppa: cup; also a salt-cured boneless ham *(salume)*, or a large rough-textured pork sausage

corbezzolo: fruit of the Mediterranean strawberry tree

coregoni: a salmon-like fish

cornetti: croissants; also called *brioche*

costoletta or **cotoletta:** chop or cutlet

cotechino: cooked pork sausage

cozze: mussels

crauti: sauerkraut

crema: custard

cren: horseradish

crescenza: a soft, creamy, mild cheese

crocchette: croquettes

crostata: open-faced fruit tart

crostini: chicken livers

crudo: raw

crumiri: polenta butter cookies

cucchiaio: spoon

cucina: cuisine, cooking, cookery, dishes

culatello: the heart of a *prosciutto crudo,* from the Parma area *(salume)*

cuore: heart

dattero di mare: date-shell clam

degustazione: a tasting

delizie: "delights"; specialty foods

distilleria: distillery

DOC: "Denominazione di Origine Controllata"; applies to wines controlled by laws determining geographic origin, grape variety, character, yield, and aging requirements

DOCG: "Denominazione di Origine Controllata e Garantita"; applies to wines controlled and guaranteed by laws determining geographic origin, grape variety, character, yield, and aging requirements

dolce: sweet

dragoncello: tarragon

droga: spice; also called *spezie*

edicola: newsstand

enoteca: wine shop

erbe: herbs

espresso: see *caffè*

estera: imported

fagioli: beans

faraona: guinea hen

farina: flour

farina di castagne: chestnut flour

farro: emmer, a grain with a wheaty taste

fave: fava beans

fegatelli: pork liver

fegatini: chicken livers

fegato: calf's liver

fetta: slice

fettunta: Tuscan garlic bread

fichi: figs

fichi d'India: prickly pears

fiera: festival, fair

filetto: fillet

finanziera: stew of chicken livers and sweetbreads

finocchio: fennel

finocchiona: fennel-laced sausage *(salume)*

fiocchetto: the part of the *prosciutto* other than the heart *(culatello);* also called *fiocco*

focaccia: a flatbread; naked pizza

fogolar: open hearth, traditional in Friuli–Venezia Giulia

fonduta: creamy melted *fontina* cheese, milk, and eggs, served with polenta or toast rounds

fontina: a delicate buttery-flavored cheese, compact and smooth

forchetta: fork

formaggella: a fresh cheese

formaggetta: small, soft tasty rounds of white cheese made from a mixture of cow's and ewe's milk

formaggio: cheese

formaggio di malga: a cheese made from the milk of cows grazing in Alpine pastures

fragoline: tiny wild strawberries

frantoio: olive oil mill

freddo: cold

friggitoria: fry shop

frittata: pan-fried egg flan; resembles an unfolded omelet

frittelle: fritters

fritto: fried

fritto misto: a variety of deep-fried foods, including meat, vegetables, fruit

frutta: fruit

frutta cotta: seasonal fruit cooked with wine and spices

funghi: mushrooms

fusilli: see *pasta corta*

fuso: melted

galletti: chanterelles

gallina: hen

gamberetti: shrimp

gassosa, gazosa: sweetened mineral water, sometimes with a slight lemon flavor

gastronomia: grocery store

gelateria: shop

gelato: frozen confection; not to be confused with the American product; see page 36 for flavors

germano: mallard duck

ghiaccio: ice

gianchetti: see *bianchetti*

gianduja, gianduia: combination of chocolate and hazelnut; specialty of Piedmont

ginepro: juniper berry

gnocchi, gnocchetti: potato dumplings

gorgonzola: a rich, blue-veined cheese

gorgonzola dolce: sweeter, creamier, and less aggressive than the classic blue cheese

grana: a grainy cheese with a nutty flavor, similar to *parmigiano*

granchio: crab

granita: water ices

grappa: alcoholic spirit distilled from pomace, the grape skins and pits left after the winemaking process

grappa monovitigno: grappa distilled from a single grape variety

gratella: rectangular cast-iron pan for stovetop grilling; also called *griglia*

grattata: grating; truffles are often sold by the *grattata*

grattugia: cheese grater

griglia: grill

grissini: breadsticks

groviera: Italian gruyere cheese

Hag: brand name of Italy's most popular decaf; used to mean decaffeinated coffee in general *insaccati:* "bagged meats"; sausages *(salume)*

insalata: salad

integrale: whole-wheat

lampone: raspberries

lardo: salt-cured lard streaked with pork *(salume)*

latte: milk

latte fritto: cinnamon-spiced deep-fried custard

latteria: store selling dairy products; also a cheese made from cow's milk, mild when fresh, more intense when aged

lattuga: lettuce

lauro: laurel; also called *alloro*

lenticchie: lentils

lepre: wild hare

lesso: boiled

limone: lemon

liscio: neat, as in a drink with no ice

locanda: inn

lombatine: veal chop

lumache: snails

maccheroni: macaroni; pasta

macchinetta da caffè: espresso maker

macedonia: fresh fruit salad, served for dessert

maggiorana: marjoram

maiale: pork

mais: corn

mandorle: almonds

manzo: beef

mare: sea

marinato: marinated

marocchino: strong, dark *cappuccino,* made with less milk than usual

marroni: chestnuts; richer and more flavorful than *castagne*

marzolino: freshly made *pecorino* cheese; also called *pecorino fresco*

mascarpone: a rich, sweet triple-cream cheese

mattarello: rolling pin

mela: apple

melanzana: eggplant

melacotogna: quince

melagrana: pomegranate

melone: cantaloupe

menta: mint

merenda: snack

merluzzo: cod

mezzaluna: crescent-shaped double-handled rocking knife

mezzo: half

midolla: the inside of a loaf of bread

miele: honey

milza: spleen

minestrone: vegetable soup

mocetta: *prosciutto* made from chamois; now more commonly made of beef *(salume)*

moleche: soft-shelled crabs

montasio: a mild, smooth cheese made from cow's milk

montone: mutton

mortadella: large smooth pork sausage studded with cubes of fat and whole peppercorns *(salume)*

moscardino: small, curled octopus

mostarda: chutney-style condiment

mozzarella: fresh, white, elastic cheese, made from buffalo's milk *(di bufala)* or cow's milk *(fior di latte)*

nazionale: domestic, made in Italy

nespolo: loquat, a small tart orange fruit

noce: walnut

nocciola: hazelnut

oca: goose

olio d'oliva: olive oil (see page 30)

oliva: olive

ombra: glass of wine enjoyed at midday along with some *cicchetti*—a Venetian term

orzo: barley

osei: small game birds

osteria: inn, restaurant

ostriche: oysters

ovoli: agaric mushrooms

padella per castagne: chestnut-roasting pan; looks like a long-handled frying pan with holes in the bottom

palombo: a tasty, medium-size sharky-looking fish

pancetta: salt-cured bacon *(salume)*

pane: bread (see page 28 for list of breads)

panettone: sweet yeast cake with raisins, candied citron, orange, and eggs, traditional at Christmastime

panino: sandwich

paninoteca: sandwich shop

panna: cream

panna cotta: rich cream dessert

papavero: poppy seed

parmigiano: Parmesan cheese; see *parmigiano-reggiano*

parmigiano-reggiano: a firm, straw-colored cheese with pale flecks, fragrant, delicate, and nutty, studded with crunchy granules

pasta: dough; pastry; pasta

pasta corta: short lengths of pasta, such as *penne, fusilli, rigatoni*

pasticceria: pastry shop

pecorino: distinctly flavored all or part sheep's-milk cheese, fresh or aged

pecorino fresco: freshly made *pecorino* cheese; also called *marzolino*

penne: quill-shaped pasta

pepe: pepper

peperoncini: chili pepper

peperoni: bell peppers

pernice: partridge

pesce: fish

pescespada: swordfish

pesche: peaches

pescheria: fish market

pesto: sauce made with crushed basil

petto: breast

piastra di terracotta refrattaria: terracotta pizza stone; simulates an Italian brick pizza oven in the home oven

piatto: plate

piatto unico: one-course meal

piccione: squab or pigeon

piccola pasticceria: "little pastries" or cookies, served after dessert in formal restaurants

piedini: feet

pignoli: pine nuts

pinzimonio: raw vegetables dipped in olive oil

pizza: pizza (see page 35 for toppings)

polenta: ground cornmeal (either white or yellow) cooked slowly with salt and water; served freshly made as a side dish, or cooled, sliced, and reheated with a sauce; frequently grilled in Veneto

polipo: octopus; also *polpo, moscardino*

pollastro: young chicken

pollo: chicken

polpettone: meat loaf

polpo: octopus; also called *polipo, moscardino*

pomodoro: tomato

porcini: a type of mushroom

porri: leeks

porzione: portion

posate: flatware

pranzo: dinner; lunch; see also *cena, colazione*

pranzo in piedi: quick stand-up lunch

prezzemolo: parsley

prezzo da vedere: "price to be seen," meaning you are charged according to the amount you eat

primizia: the earliest, and tiniest, produce of the season

primo: first course, usually pasta, rice, or soup

prodotto e imbottigliato: "produced and bottled"; guarantee of quality on a bottle of olive oil

prosciutto cotto: cooked ham *(salume)*

prosciutto crudo: salted air-cured ham *(salume)*

provolone: a smooth cheese, delicate to zesty, fresh or aged

prugna: plum; also called *susina*

pure: mashed potatoes

quaglia: quail

quartirolo: a mild, soft, smooth cheese

rabarbaro: rhubarb

radicchio: red chicory, served both raw and cooked

ragù: meat sauce

ramerino: rosemary; also called *rosmarino*

rape: turnip, turnip greens

raschera: a hearty, smooth cheese

ravanella: radish

raveggiolo: a soft, fresh cheese made from sheep's-milk whey, delicate and hard to find

reblec: a fresh curdled cream cheese

ribes: currants

ricotta: a soft, fresh, mild cheese made from whey

rigatoni: see *pasta corta*

ripiene: stuffed

riso: rice; *originario* is the shortest grain, followed by

semifino, fino, and *superfino,* the largest

risotto: rice barely toasted in butter, then cooked very slowly in broth, which is added gradually; served with butter and grated parmesan cheese

robiola: a soft, creamy, rich, delicate cheese made from cow's or sheep's milk

rombo: turbot

rosette: "little roses"; hollow, all-crust rolls

rosmarino: rosemary; also called *ramerino*

rospo: monkfish

rosso: red

rosticceria: rotisserie take-out store

sagra: festival

salamino: small-size salami

salame, salami: raw salt-cured pork sausage *(salume)*

sale: salt

salsiccia: sausage

salumeria: store selling cold cuts or cured meats *(salumi)*

salumi: general term for cured meats, such as *prosciutto,* salami

salvia: sage

san marzano: plum tomato

sarago: sea bream

sarde: sardines

sbriciolona: a crumbly sausage

scamorza: a firm, buttery, pear-shaped cheese

scampi: prawns

schiacciata: a flatbread

schiuma di mare: anchovies; also called *bianchetti, gianchetti*

secco: dry

secondo: second course, usually fish or meat

secondo quantità: "according to the quantity," meaning you are charged according to the amount you eat *sedano:* celery

selezionato e imbottigliato: "selected and bottled"; appears on bottles of olive oil where the makers do not raise and harvest the olives themselves

seltz: soda water

selvaggina: game

semi: seeds

semifreddo: gelato with whipped cream folded in

semola: flour made of hard grain

senape: mustard

seppia: cuttlefish

servizio: percentage for service automatically added to the bill in restaurants, in addition to the *coperto*

setaccio: sifter

sfoglia: sheet of egg-rich pasta which is made into noodles or filled with various stuffings

sfogliatelle: ricotta-filled flaky pastry

sogliola: sole

soprassata: cured raw ham, or large rough-texured pork sausage *(salume);* also called *soppressa, coppa*

soppressa: see *soprassata*

sorbetto: fruit sorbet

sottaceti: pickles

speck: ham marinated in brine with herbs and spices, then cold-smoked and aged *(salume)*

spezie: spices; also called *droghe*

spigola: sea bass

spremuta (di arancia): freshly squeezed orange juice

spremuta di pompelmo: grapefruit juice

spugnoli: morels

spumante: sparkling wine

squaquarone: a fresh, soft, sometimes liquid cheese

stracchino: a smooth, soft, full-flavored cheese

stracotto: braised beef

strutto: land

succo di frutta: fruit juice

sugo: sauce

surgelato: frozen

susina: plum; also called *prugna*

tabacchi: tobacco shop—the place where you can buy cigarettes, matches, salt, stamps, bus tickets; often also a *bar-caffè*

tacchino: turkey

tagliatelle: flat strips of egg pasta

tajarin: a type of egg pasta

taleggio: a smooth, soft, ripe cheese, similar to *stracchino* but more ample

tarocco: blood orange

tartufo: truffle; either black *(nero)* or white *(bianco)*

tartufo di mare: venus clam

taverna: inn, restaurant

tavola calda: hot table, take-out, or counter service for prepared dishes

tellina: wedge-shell clam; also called *arsella*

thè, tè: tea; served *al latte* (with milk) or *al limone* (with a slice of lemon)

tiramisù: a rich *mascarpone* dessert

tirata a mano: hand-stretched; used to describe hand-rolled pasta

tisana: herbal tea

toast: grilled ham and cheese on American-style bread

tome: a smooth, firm cheese, with some small holes

tomini: small rounds of goat or mixed-milk fresh cheese

tonno: tuna

topinambur: Jerusalem artichoke

tordo: thrush

torrone: nougat candy made of hazelnuts, honey or sugar, and egg whites

torta: cake

tortellini: fresh egg pasta rings filled with a stuffing

tostapane: bread toaster consisting of a hole-punctured stainless steel square topped with a wire grid screen, with a U-shaped metal handle

totano: flying squid

tovagliolo: napkin

tovagliolo di carta: paper napkins

tramezzino: sandwich

trattoria: restaurant

triglia: red mullet

trippa: tripe

trota: trout

tucco, tocco: sauce

tuorlo: egg yolks

un'etto: 100 grams, around 4 ounces

uova: egg

uova da bere: extra-fresh eggs

uva: grape, white *(bianca)* or purple *(nera)*

vassoio: tray

vendemmia: harvest of wine grapes

verdure: vegetables

verza: cabbage

vezzena: a smooth, fatty, bland cheese

vigneto: vineyard

vino: wine; white is *bianco,* red is *rosso* (see page 26 for special terms)

vino da tavola: table wine

vino della casa: house wine; also called *vino sfuso*

vin santo: aromatic dessert wine

visciola: wild cherry

vitello: veal

vongola verace: carpet-shell clam

zabaione: a dessert of egg yolks whipped with sugar and wine, served with cookies or as a dessert sauce

zafferano: saffron

zampone: cooked pork sausage packed in a pig's shin and foot

zenzero: ginger; chili pepper

zucca: squash

zuppa: soup

INDEX

■

NOTES

NOTES